THE DESIGN OF
BIBLIOGRAPHIES

. . . without good bibliographies, the world would resemble a library without catalogs: a hodge-podge of inaccessible ideas and knowledge.

Sharon Tabachnik

THE DESIGN OF
BIBLIOGRAPHIES

Observations, References and Examples

SIDNEY E. BERGER

BIBLIOGRAPHIES AND INDEXES
IN LIBRARY AND INFORMATION SCIENCE,
NUMBER 6

First published 1992 in the United States and Canada by
Greenwood Press, 88 Post Road West, Westport, CT 06881,
an Imprint of Greenwood Publishing Group, Inc.

English language edition, except the United States and Canada,
first published 1991 by Mansell Publishing Limited,
A Cassell imprint, Villiers House, 41/47 Strand, London WC2N 5JE,
England

Library of Congress Cataloging-in-Publication Data
Berger. Sidney E.
　The design of bibliographies: observations, references, and
examples / Sidney E. Berger.
　　　p.　　　cm. — (Bibliographies and indexes in library and
information science: no. 6)
　Includes index.
　ISBN 0–313–28425–3 (alk. paper)
　1. Bibliography—Methodology.　2. Desktop publishing.　3. Book
design.　I. Title.　II. Series.
Z1001.B4537　1991
010'.44—dc20

　　　　　　　　　　　　　　　　　　　　　　　　　　　91–34485
　　　　　　　　　　　　　　　　　　　　　　　　　　　CIP

Library of Congress Catalog Card Number: 91–34485

ISBN: 0–313–28425–3

Typeset by Fakenham Photosetting Limited, Fakenham, Norfolk
This book has been printed and bound in Great Britain
by Bookcraft (Bath) Ltd.

CONTENTS

For
Kim Merker and Harry Duncan, who got me started;
Don Krummel, who helped me along;
and Michèle V. Cloonan, who helped me finish off.

PREFACE

*We are slowly awakening to the fact that the flood
of Modern Bibliography has overtaken us, and we
are at length forced to confess that we are
unable to cope with it. Advancing with
stealthy line, it has found us
unprepared and unorganised,
and we have fled.* *

The 1965–6 edition of Theodore Besterman's *A World Bibliography of Bibliographies* lists 117,187 bibliographies, and it is estimated that more than 7,000 new ones are produced every year (Krummel, **128**†). This means that since Besterman died in 1976, another 100,000 full-volume bibliographies have been produced.

Campbell's words ring more true today than they did when they were first uttered nearly a century ago. And the statistics cited by Donald Krummel demonstrate this. So many books, articles, essays, talks, lectures, dissertations, and theses are being made public today that the spread of information seems to be getting beyond the powers of libraries to contain, organize, and make available even a small portion of it.

I remember having an epiphany as a child when I understood the notion that necessity is the mother of invention. If the necessity once was to spread knowledge beyond what manuscripts could enable, printing was born. We are at a point of need again. Today computers seem to be the hope to corral all this information – to give it shape and accessibility. But the computer presents other problems: Who will input all the information? How will it be encoded and made available? Is it all worth entering into a permanent – or even a

temporary – record? What form(s) will it take? Are these the best forms possible?

It is just these last two questions that are the concern of the present volume. One of the traditional ways of having access to information is through reference materials: etymologically, materials that *re-fer* us, i.e. carry us back, to what we seek. Reference tools take many forms, and, as Campbell and Krummel tell us, bibliographies are probably the most common form of such tools.

The present work started out as an attempt to discuss bibliographies from a particular perspective: their shape, both physical and intellectual. How was one to design a bibliography to offer the 'correct' information in the 'correct' order, and in the most usable physical form? The answers to this question – and there were many and contradictory ones – led me to a great range of topics, the subjects of this book.

I soon realized in doing my research that to present a thorough discussion of the design of bibliographies, I had to move outward to book design in general, and also outward to recognize the needs of different disciplines, different kinds of scholars, and, just as important, different methods of physical presentation. What machines were available to produce bibliographies? There are typewriters; printing presses of various kinds; computers with dot-matrix, ink-jet, and laser printers; and non-printed texts available on video display terminals; and the physical design problems that each of these entails present various kinds of challenges to the bibliographer, and

---

* Frank Campbell, *The Battle of Bibliography: Being an Extended Summary of part of a Paper read before the Library Association* (London: n.p., 1893), p. 3.

† References to entries in the bibliography of this volume are given as the author's name followed by a number in bold type.

present particular conditions that the user will encounter.

In discussing how he wrote *Pudd'nhead Wilson and Those Extraordinary Twins*, Mark Twain explains that he began with one idea for what he wanted and ended up with something completely different. He talks about how the unsuspecting writer is put upon by the story itself:

> . . . in the beginning he is only proposing to tell a little tale; a very little tale; a six-page tale. But as it is a tale which he is not acquainted with, and can only find out what it is by listening as it goes along telling itself, it is more than apt to go on and on and on till it spreads itself into a book.*

This is similar to what happened to me here. Originally, this volume was intended to be a long essay; but in the name of thoroughness, I felt it necessary to look at the elements of book design that affect the appearance of bibliographies. In fact, just about *every* element of book design pertains to bibliographies. So I have had to present a good deal about book design here. And since my subject was design, I realized that this implies things beyond the physical presentation of the page. How was the *information* to be designed? ordered? laid out in a logical intellectual way?

As I gathered information in a widening circle of pertinent areas, I realized that the kind of scholarship I was gathering would not be under the ordinary purview of scholars looking at bibliographies specifically or book design in general. For example, I found a whole world of information about legibility and another world of materials on computer applications (the two worlds often intersecting), neither of which would a scholar of bibliographies normally turn to, but both of which were germane to the design of bibliographies. For this reason, I have included an annotated bibliography of some of the works I read in the production of this book.

This listing of nearly 300 titles is obviously not definitive; nor are my annotations. This bibliography merely suggests the kinds and range of infor-

* Mark Twain, *Pudd'nhead Wilson and Those Extraordinary Twins*, edited by Sidney E. Berger (New York and London: W. W. Norton, 1980), p. 119.

mation available. And most of the annotations were necessarily brief and narrowly focused. Many of the books and articles represented have mountains of information that I did not feel it proper to offer, because of both space and the focus of the present study. I could have offered up more than ten times the number of entries and still not have felt that I was presenting the subject thoroughly. Many a reader may think that such and such a work should have been included; my only excuses are space limitations and human frailty.

Finally, I did not want to be like the art critic talking at length in florid prose about the beauties and defects of certain paintings but not showing the paintings. I felt that a sampling of pages of bibliographies would be useful. Some of the ones I chose were so ugly and base that they deserved reproduction, if only to receive the severe censure they have earned. Some have good and bad points, and, while not ugly, may be difficult to use because they are carelessly thought out, or, in an attempt to be too aesthetically pleasing, are illegible. Others were included because of their physical beauty and usefulness.

Bibliographies can be produced on a 1935 manual Underwood or Olympia typewriter and be eminently successful: clearly printed, well laid out, and *accessible*. Others can be done on the latest IBM computer, with varying fonts of the latest designs of computer typefaces, and printed with the most up-to-date laser technology, and yet be so poorly designed that they are repulsive and inaccessible.

The present study aims to help bibliographers and publishers produce reference books which a reader can open happily, not assailed by an obnoxious page, not having to squint to make out words set in particularly idiosyncratic typefaces, and not having to make a tortuous trek to the information she or he seeks.

There is no single right way. I hope to show that an elegant and eminently usable bibliography may take many forms, both physically and intellectually. Setting down rigid rules is illogical when one considers the scores of physical and intellectual variables that go into the design of a bibliography's pages.

Research for this book has been done in many

libraries (and a bookshop), to whom I would like to convey my appreciation. I have worked at Brown University, the American Antiquarian Society, Yale University, Harvard University, the British Library, St Bride's Printing Library in London, the University of Illinois at Urbana-Champaign, Clark University, the University of California at Riverside, the University of California at Los Angeles, and Maggs Bros. in London. Special thanks go to Kelly Kamborian of Brown University, who has retrieved scores of items for me, both from Brown and through Brown's inter-library loan department.

I am exceptionally indebted to Professor Don Krummel of the Graduate School of Library and Information Science at the University of Illinois (Urbana-Champaign), who encouraged me to expand the paper I wrote for him, and who offered many suggestions in the earlier drafts of this book. His wisdom and avuncular good humour helped me more than he can know.

A further indebtedness is to Laura Stalker of ESTC/NA, at the University of California, Riverside, for her exceptional assistance in proofreading these pages.

I would also like to thank Aaron and Rafe, my sons, for their understanding, forbearance, and support during the production of this book. Their contributions to it are subtle but significant.

But most of all I wish to thank Michèle Cloonan, my wife, for her good-natured prodding balanced by her infinite patience, her helping me to locate hundreds of sources, her careful and judicious proofreading, and her love in the face of my frustrations, lassitude, and mobile tempers.

LIST OF ABBREVIATIONS

AACR2	*Anglo-American Cataloguing Rules*, 2nd ed. Chicago: American Library Association; London: Library Association Publishing, 1988.
BIP	*Books in Print*. New York: R. R. Bowker (annual)
COM	computer output microform
CRT	cathode ray tube
comp.	compiler
ed.	editor, edited
esp.	especially
f., ff.	following page, following pages
MARC	machine-readable cataloguing
MLA	Modern Language Association
n.p., n.p.	no place, no publisher
p., pp.	page, pages
PC	personal computer
q.v.	which [work] see
rev. ed.	revised edition
rpt.	reprint
VDT	video display terminal
VDU	video display unit

INTRODUCTION

*... the newcomer to research, whatever his discipline, can
be forgiven dismay at the sheer bulk of the sources at his
disposal, sources which seem to multiply with
undisciplined rapidity. The threat to enlightenment lies
less in the insufficiency of information than in its
overwhelming flood.*
(Alston, **2**, p. 113)

Bibliographic material is quite inexhaustible.
(Ferguson, **69**, p. 27)

When the Preacher said, 'Of making many books there is no end' (Ecclesiastes 12.12), he anticipated the printing press and the tremendous boom in the computer age. Despite the misuse of the phrase 'paperless society' (people mistakenly interpreting this to mean that all texts will some day be presented on a video display screen rather than on paper, and that paper will become obsolete), more paper than ever is being produced, and more books are too.

And whether the texts in these books be fiction or non-fiction, pictorial or verbal, they all fall into some category of bookmaking, and they all have some subject matter. Even the subject heading 'Blank book' denotes a genre.

When anyone wishes to study the exemplars of any given subject or genre, possibly with the notion of writing about the history of those kinds of items, or even just to do research on them, she or he will turn to the 'bibliography' of the field. That is, the scholar will want to seek out lists of various kinds which will say where the objects of the research can be found. Primary and secondary texts may themselves contain lists of related items, either in the form of bibliographies or in notes. Perhaps a whole bibliography exists on the subject.

In fact, the first resort for many scholars or book selectors in libraries looking into the publications in a field is a bibliography. For, as Krummel says, 'The range of topics for bibliographies is unlimited' (**128**, p. 17). Since bibliographies are produced for the benefit and use of the reader, the compiler must present whatever data are relevant for the reader, and must organize the data in some logical and useful fashion. Also, the work should be presented in a physical format which yields the greatest, most 'comfortable', most aesthetic access to the data.

According to Carl Purington Rollins, it is essential not only that a bibliography contain useful and carefully organized information, but also 'that it be attractive as a piece of printing' (**199**, p. 108); the aim of the author and printer should be 'the production of a thoroughly useful and usable handbook' (p. 107). Krummel adds, 'A list that is handsome and well designed is a credit to the compiler; it reflects on the respect of the publisher, as it will also promote the respect of the readers who use it' (**128**, p. 148). While the author must be concerned with the intellectual content and its organization and 'design', the book designer must be concerned about the physical elements of which bibliographies are composed: the type style and size; the size of the book; the arrangement of type and blank space on the page; ink colour; the weight, colour, and gloss of the paper; and so on.

The optimum design of a bibliography is essentially the optimum use of typographic elements. For this reason, it is useful to begin with a discussion of the basics of book typography. But the discussion here will often take a bibliographical bent, since the focus will always be directly or peripherally on bibliographies. After treating typography, we will turn more directly to bibliographies themselves, their content, and the arrangement of the elements in them.

So much has been written about book design that little of what will be presented below will be original. In fact, every aspect of book design imaginable has been practically written to death. What I shall be doing is presenting brief discussions of the elements of design that one ought to consider in the production of a bibliography, drawing from many sources – listed in the bibliography to this volume – which can be consulted at length. As I have suggested above, it is impossible (and unnecessary) to be exhaustive about subjects treated at length in published sources; my aim is to show where further study can be done and, equally important, to mention the many things designers need to know about the design of bibliographies.

This is especially important in an era in which computers are making it possible for authors to be publishers – or at least designers, since many publishers are now asking authors to submit camera-ready copy. Authors with little or no training in book design suddenly find themselves trying to figure out what margins should look like, which typeface(s) to select, where and on which pages to place page numbers, how much and when to indent, and so on.

As a few of the scholars represented in the bibliography have said, all the research on legibility and readability which concludes that such a typeface in such a size should be used on a particular paper with so much leading – all this is silly effort, since a good typographer already knows what makes for a legible page. And, in fact, so does a reader, who knows in a few moments after picking up a text whether the page is congenial or not (irrespective of its content). Thirteen years ago I bought a book set in such a strange type that it was quite difficult to read, despite the fact that it was a book on *Illustrated Manuscripts and Printed Books in the First Century of Printing* (this was the subtitle of *Pen to Press*, Baltimore, MD: Art Department, University of Maryland; Depart-

ment of the History of Art, The Johns Hopkins University, 1977). It is set in Bernhard Modern, an elegant typeface for short poems, perhaps, but not for 32 lines of prose on page after page of text. Because of the type's high ascenders, there needs to be a good deal of space between lines. The page looks too white, and the letters themselves look a little squat beside the tall ascenders. The typeface calls attention to itself and away from the text. I would like to add, however, that this is a marvellous book, full of fine information, well written, on good paper, in a sturdy and attractive binding. It is a shame that the text looks so awkward because of the typeface.

(I ought to mention, parenthetically, that the publishers of *Pen to Press* did not include a colophon in the book, though the authors do mention the typeface at the end of the acknowledgements on page [viii]. Perhaps the fact that this typeface was designed [or, as the authors say, 'invented'] in Baltimore justifies its use for them. I believe the reader's comfort should have guided them more.

Also parenthetically, I have always wished that publishers would make it a practice to have a colophon. Then they would be thinking about such matters as typefaces and paper; maybe also the designer would be named and held accountable. The use of colophons at least shows that some care went into the design of the book.)

But not all books are designed by trained designers, some of whom, themselves, may need to brush up on basic design principles. The present volume should be useful as well to the new generation of desktop publishers, and to authors asked to produce camera-ready copy – people who have probably never had formal training in book production. And from what I have seen in commercially produced books in the last 20 years, there are many designers working at big publishing houses who might profit from a perusal of these pages.

This book is a gathering of sound (and some questionable) ideas about book design into a convenient volume, with a focus on the particular problems that bibliographies present with respect to their content and layout on a page.

Very little has been written on the design of bibliographies. An early essay and a very small book by Carl Purington Rollins (entries **199** and **200** in the bibliography) were useful, as my citing of them in the text below indicates; but they were brief and fairly narrowly focused. The book *Some Trifles which Make for Perfection* – with only 14 pages of text – offers only four models, none of which I would call 'perfect'. A cluster of works by Linda Reynolds (**188–90**), and by Herbert Spencer, Reynolds, and Brian Coe (**218–20, 222–3**) are the best modern treatments of the subject. But these were produced in very limited numbers for a small British audience; few copies are available in the United States. And these works are not so comprehensive as to cover many of the elements of book design that I discuss here. Furthermore, most of their studies look primarily at the production of bibliographies on a typewriter, and an old one at that. The models they offer allow for one typeface without italics (the only boldface type being an overstriking of previously typed text – a very slow and laborious method of producing a text). These authors are circumspect and keen about the things they present, but their works are more narrowly focused than the present study.

Kim Merker of the University of Iowa's Windhover Press taught me typography exactly 25 years ago. Since then I have taught The History of the Book, Printing on a Handpress, Book Design, and many other book-arts-related courses. I have had my own press for all these years, and have struggled with margins, typeface selection, binding problems, and the like far into many nights. And I have also done research toward the production of books and articles in the other half of my life as a scholar of bibliography, textual criticism, and medieval English literature. In a number of ways, then, I have concentrated on bibliographies and book design. (My last book was a large annotated bibliography, for which I produced camera-ready copy.)

Thus, the present study emanates from a quarter of a century of looking at bibliographies, printing books and pamphlets, designing pages, and rubbing my weary eyes. I have gloried in the beauty of many books, been repulsed by the ugliness of others, and cursed many a reference book for its lack of organization, its careless layout, and the inaccessibility of its information. There is nothing more frustrating than opening a bibliography, looking at one of its pages, and discovering that you are lost in a labyrinth; and then turning to the introduction only to find that the information you need is either lacking or dispersed through 15 pages of impenetrable prose. I hope the present study will prevent such books from being produced in the future.

Since two of my passions are research and typography, this book has been a delight to work on. I hope the myriad of minutiae that I present below do not prevent the reader from feeling the same delight in the topic.

In *The Making of Books*, Seán Jennett says:

> Bibliographies are boring things to compile, and the results of the boredom are all too often evident in the bibliography itself, expressed in uncertainties, hesitations, incompetencies, and inconsistencies. The compiler is frequently the author himself; it is a kind of work that he abhors and it is undertaken in the spirit of grim duty, whatever may have been the spirit in which the body of the book was written. Faced with a collection of minute bits of information, he is apt to become confused because he does not know how bibliographies are made. (**115**, p. 324)

The present text, I hope, will reduce the boredom; yield fewer uncertainties, hesitations, and inconsistencies; abate some of the abhorrence; and dispel the confusion. While I cannot do anything about the competence of anyone who compiles, organizes, and designs a bibliography, I can hope to open a few eyes, and to show how the beauty and usefulness of the product can produce a good deal of pleasure. If an author enjoys a subject enough to do research on it, she or he should learn to enjoy compiling the bibliography on that subject as well.

The compiler and designer should keep in mind Rollins's words:

> In summing up I would suggest that you remember that a bibliography is to be used; it must be readable; and as a 'book about books' it should reflect the most discriminating taste in printing and binding. More than a faint flavor of good breeding should linger about it. (**199**, p. 117)

2
BOOK DESIGN

... from the recent flood of annotated bibliographies it is clear that bibliographers themselves seldom agree on what their works should accomplish or on how they should be designed.
(Colianne, 47, p. 323)

BASIC PRINCIPLES

This chapter deals with the physical design of books. As I have noted, few authors have written on the physical design of bibliographies, but hundreds have written about *typography* – the generic term I shall use here for all aspects of book design. While the word implies the use of type, I include also use of blank space, paper, ink, binding, and, eventually, the 'typography' of the computer screen.

Most sensible scholars of literature would think it improper, not to say embarrassing, to write a book or an article on a subject that had already been covered well in print. But some scholars of typography have no such sense of shame. Perhaps the urge to get into print, to get promotions or tenure, or simply to see their names in the public eye makes some writers utterly unabashed about publishing ideas that have been before the public many times before. Sometimes it is because the writer has done inadequate research and does not know about the work of others. Sometimes writers use the research of others in their own writings, intentionally or unintentionally neglecting to cite their sources; in either case, plagiarism is in the wind.

A note of caution about using the work of others is appropriate here, drawn from experience. In compiling my *Bibliography of Medieval Drama*, I used the annotated bibliographies of others to gather sources. Many times I was unable to find items that other scholars had listed, mainly because of their inadequate citations. Sometimes I was able to find elusive pieces, only to realize that my sources had cited them incorrectly: a wrong volume number or year, an incorrectly spelled title or author's name, wrong page numbers, or the like. But it is in the area of annotation that one must be especially cautious. If my own annotations had been drawn from those of other bibliographers, I might have been quite embarrassed. My practice was to read carefully every book or article that I wrote annotations for. When I did, and then compared my annotations with those of other scholars, I was often surprised to see no similarity at all in content. Sometimes it was because the bibliographer in question seems not to have read beyond the title or the first paragraph; other times, it was because my focus in my annotated bibliography was different from the focus of the other bibliographer. For example, I was trying to give an overview of the subject matter in each work while other annotaters were looking for specific things, such as the role of women in the plays. When their own bibliographies were circumscribed by different criteria, their annotations often contained data radically different from mine. Thus, being caught at plagiarism may be one source of embarrassment; relying solely on inadequate or differently focused sources may be another.

Many of the data which follow in this chapter could have been drawn from many sources. And, in fact, many were drawn from multiple sources. It is amazing how many scholars, working independently, have done and redone the work of their predecessors, reaching the same conclusions. A modicum of research might have prevented a good deal of duplicated labour.

The great number of statements about book design is in proportion to the great number of books extant. Before looking at the individual aspects of book design, a few classic studies about the subject must be considered.

In a frequently cited statement, worth quoting in full, T. J. Cobden-Sanderson (46) said:

> The ideal book or book beautiful is a composite thing made up of many parts and may be made beautiful by the beauty of each of its parts – its literary content, its material or materials, its writing or printing, its illumination or illustration, its binding and decoration – of each of its parts in subordination to the whole which collectively they constitute: or it may be made beautiful by the supreme beauty of one or more of its parts, all the other parts subordinating or even effacing themselves for the sake of this one or more, and each in turn being capable of playing this supreme part and each in its own peculiar and characteristic way. *On the other hand each contributory craft may usurp the functions of the rest and of the whole and growing beautiful beyond all bounds ruin for its own the common cause.* (p. 1; my italics)

Stanley Morison's *First Principles of Typography* (156) is equally important:

> Typography is the efficient means to an essentially utilitarian and only accidentally aesthetic end, for enjoyment of patterns is rarely the reader's chief aim. Therefore, *any disposition of printing material which, whatever the intention, has the effect of coming between author and reader is wrong.* It follows that in the printing of books meant to be read there is little room for 'bright' typography. Even dullness and monotony in the typesetting are far less vicious to a reader than typographical eccentricity or pleasantry. . . . the typography of books . . . requires an obedience to convention which is almost absolute – and with reason. (p. 5; my italics)

Finally, Beatrice Warde (258a) wrote an essay the title of which suggests her thesis: 'The Crystal Goblet, or Printing Should Be Invisible'. Just as a crystal goblet should be invisible and let the beauty and purity of the liquid it contains show through, printing should not call attention to itself, but should let the text it contains show through: 'no cloud must come between your eyes and the fiery heart of the liquid' (p. 11). She says that printing is not, first and foremost, a work of art, but that 'the most important thing about printing is that it conveys thought, ideas, images, from one mind to others' (p. 13).

> Printing demands a humility of mind, for the lack of which many of the fine arts are even now floundering in self-conscious and maudlin experiments. There is nothing simple or dull in achieving the transparent page. (p. 17)

The idea that runs through these three writers' works is that the text comes first; anything that obscures it in any way should be avoided. Any element of the text's medium that calls attention to itself and away from the text itself is an intrusion, a diversion of the mind; it is wrong. To achieve this primacy of text, one need not give up elegance. This is an idea I will return to throughout the discussion below.

From these general notions about book design we may now turn to the specifics of typography – the things a designer must consider in planning a book.

THE PAGE

As any good typographer knows, a book designer does not look at one page at a time; the two-page spread is the basic unit of a printed book. But on each page itself there are many typographical elements which must be attended to. The first is TYPE.

Type

Hundreds of people have written about type, covering several issues. The first is its SIZE. Writers have advocated, for bibliographies, anything from 6-point type to type the same size as that of the text, which is usually between 8- and 12-point. But of course comments like this must be weighed against the typeface chosen and other elements. Hovde (110) says that readers tend to prefer larger types, but that preference varies from one reader to the next. So anything one can say about type size (or, for that matter, about any feature of typography) must be taken cautiously since no two readers will necessarily have identical preferences.

Another issue relating to type size concerns whether we are looking at a book-length bibliography, or a bibliography of a few pages at the end of a book. If the latter, it will not be consulted with the same intensity as will a book-length bibliography. The type for a short list at the end of a book 'may be one or two points smaller than the body copy size' (Labuz, **130**).

Some of the more thorough studies of type size were done by Paterson and Tinker. Their 'Studies in Typographical Factors Influencing Speed of Reading. II. Size of Type' (see **171**) argues that '6, 8, 12, and 14 point type are all read slower than any other size of type' (p. 128). But they point out that this is for a line of 80 mm (3⅛ inches). Here we have one of the sources of confusion, for all kinds of statements about the 'optimum' type size must be made with respect to the length of the line (see below). Hence, Paterson and Tinker's conclusion must be weighed carefully: '10 point type yields the fastest reading [with no loss of comprehension] and is thus the optimum size of type (in comparison with other sizes used) for efficient reading' (p. 130). In their book, *How to Make Type Readable* (**167**), which summarizes many of their findings, they conclude that 10-point type is not necessarily the best for speed reading; 11-point is better, and so is 9-point (see Appendix II). It is just such confusion that makes such definitive statements as '10-point type is the best' suspect.

Ernst Reichl says that what is considered legible in the United States is different from that in Europe. 'A large-faced 10 point type – such as Baskerville or Janson – is the smallest that can be used for straight reading matter in the U.S.A.' (**184**, p. 10). And Frank Romano points out the relationship between type size and line length by giving a table showing the minimum, optimum, and maximum line lengths for most text types (see his table at entry **201**). In ignoring the actual choice of typeface and leading, this chart, while useful, nonetheless presents only part of the picture.

The final word is that the designer must select a legible typeface that reads well, and consider the other factors that I shall now attend to. Depending on the typeface and the other factors, anything from 8- to 12-point type will be suitable for setting bibliographies.

Other aspects of type are its WEIGHT, WIDTH, and X-HEIGHT. Buckler discusses the stroke-width-to-height ratio of type (**30**), and Lawson (**130a**) speaks of the weight of type in terms of 'A letter's relative amount of blackness' (p. 29). He says, 'In types used for continuous reading, two weights are generally used – the original design, called either regular or light, and a boldface' (p. 29). He points out that some typefaces have 'as many as eight or nine different weights' (p. 29). One rule of thumb is that the heavier the weight of the type (i.e. the thicker the strokes), the less white space exists around each stroke and the less clear each letter is. But of course this varies for every typeface. Similarly inconclusive things could be said about the width and x-height of faces. Clarity of a face is dependent on the basic shape of the letters as well as on these other factors.

Additional features of type that must be considered for the printing of a bibliography are whether the types will be ROMAN or ITALIC, REGULAR or BOLDFACE. (We can assume that no idiosyncratic, decorative types would be used in the printing of a bibliography.) This is an important issue, as we shall see later, because part of what has been called the typographic coding of a bibliographical entry concerns the typographical variations that help to draw the reader's attention to particular elements in an entry, and help to distinguish these elements from one another. For example, if the reader knows that the authors' names are always in boldface, that is what will be searched for when she or he looks for names. Likewise, if titles are always in italic type, the eye will scan for italics when looking for a title.

Studies seem to indicate that roman type is more legible than italic, and regular is more legible than boldface. But again it depends on many other factors, not the least of which is the typeface chosen. The same goes for UPPER- and LOWER-CASE TYPES. There seems to be a split decision on whether the entries should contain some element (names, titles) in full caps or a mixture of caps and lower-case type. Dearborn, Johnson, and Carmichael say that full caps focus the reader's attention on that which needs to be stressed (**58**). And

Turabian (**253**) says, 'If desired, the authors' names may be typed in capitals throughout' (p. 199). Paterson and Tinker (**167**) say that upper- and lower-case types are more legible than full caps (p. 23); Linda Reynolds (**186**) says, 'Research has shown that words in capitals are less easily recognized than words in lower case because they lack the distinctive outline created by the ascenders and descenders of lowercase letters' (p. 86). (Herbert Spencer says the same, **214**, p. 55; so does Zachrisson, **273**, p. 43.) Rather indecisively, Rollins says, 'In bibliographical listings the use of capitals for titles sometimes makes the words in capitals stand out with too much emphasis. An interesting variant is to use a large size of small caps. Sometimes capitals of a smaller point size can . . . be successfully employed' (**200**, p. [12]). Spencer, Reynolds, and Coe (**223**) say that the use of capitals was 'not especially helpful' (p. 141) in allowing the user to locate particular elements in the entries. Tinker and Paterson (**240**) even use scientific analysis to conclude that text set all 'in lower case letters was read 13.4 per cent faster than that in all capitals' (p. 240). And Williamson (**269**) says that 'Small capitals, with or without initial capitals, are often used for authors' names, but this can look clumsy; a combination of capitals and small capitals is out of fashion, and if small capitals are letterspaced as they should be, the names appear to be over-emphasized at the expense of the titles. Roman upper- and lower-case will prove clear enough for names' (p. 182).

All of this tends toward the use of upper- and lower-case letters. But some texts are still produced on typewriters or old personal computers and printers, which are capable of few typographical variations – unlike most PCs today. So the use of full caps may be the best option for typewriters or older computers and printers. (But see the discussion under typographic coding in Chapter 3.)

A related issue pertains to the use of capital letters in the titles of books and articles in bibliographies. One method is to capitalize all 'key words' (everything but prepositions and conjunctions), but to capitalize prepositions and conjunctions if they are the first words in the title or subtitle:

'Damn Your Eyes: An Examination of *Oedipus Rex*'

Some publishers capitalize only the first word and all proper nouns in titles:

Finally, breakfast in Capistrano: when the swallows came back

My own preference has been shaped by my indoctrination in the humanities: I like the former method, capitalizing all key words. But, as I shall say again, the discipline in which the work appears should influence the decision of the bibliographer, since different disciplines do it their own way. Give the readers what they are familiar with.

A similar discussion has been going on for decades about SERIFFED and SANS SERIF TYPES. Crosland and Johnson (**56**) say that serifs increase legibility. Dreyfus (**62**) points out that 'there is often no statistically significant difference between our ability to read type faces seriffed or sans serif' (p. 9). But McLean (**148**) says, 'Sans-serif type is intrinsically less legible than seriffed type' (p. 944). And David Robinson (**195**) gives us a scientific reason for preferring serifs: 'the neurological structure of the human visual system benefits from serifs in the preservation of the main features of letters during neural processing' (p. 353). However, Spencer (**216**) says that 'sans serif or square serif faces are preferable . . . [and] sans serif numerals are preferable for tables' (p. 14). Tinker (**238**), perhaps the most scientific researcher of all whose work I read, says, 'A serifless type . . . is read as rapidly as ordinary type, but readers do not prefer it' (p. 64).

Preferences for types with serifs should prevail if their actual legibility is no greater than sans serif faces. And there is an abundance of excellent faces available, on typewriters, computers, and printers, as well as in print shops.

Another issue concerning type is whether (or when) to use ITALIC and when to use ROMAN TYPES. Since it is advisable to use some kind of typographic coding to separate elements within a bibliographic entry from other elements, one convenient way is to use italics. Without reviewing all the scholarship on the subject, I can summarize by saying that while roman type is consistently called more legible than italic, it is still useful to use the latter. As I will explain later, if you give up a small amount of legibility in favour of a typographic form that helps a reader to locate the part of the entry she or he needs, the slight loss of legibility is well spent.

Other issues concerning type deal with the use of KERNS and LIGATURES – though not terribly significant, still worth mentioning briefly below – and the large issue of just which typeface to select. There are thousands of them. Randall Rothenburg (**201a**) says, 'Some 44,000 type families have been created since Johann Gutenberg invented movable type around 1450. These families, or collections of similar typefaces in different weights and styles, consist of around 176,000 separate typefaces in forms like bold, italic and condensed' (p. D6). He adds that about 3,000 type families are in use today. The tendency of some designers is sometimes to select the newest, most startling type which calls attention to itself. Some, however, rely on the classical faces which are subtle, unobtrusive, clear, and effective – faces like Bembo, Cheltenham, Bodoni, Centaur, and numerous others. For a bibliography (as for most book typography), the less the face calls attention to itself, the more the reader can concentrate on the text.

We can now move on to the spaces around the type. A good deal has been written about LETTERSPACING. This is the addition of spaces between letters to give them an even look in a line. That is, all letters, theoretically, should be the same distance from one another for the most uniform look on the page. This, of course, is not possible on a typewriter, since letters of varying widths must fill a space of a uniform size. (Monospacing, as this is called, can now be replaced on computers and the new electronic typewriters by proportional spacing.) This is also the case for some of the earlier computer printers. But most lower-case fonts are designed to fit properly – that is, in most well-designed typefaces, the lower-case letters do indeed seem to be exactly the same distance apart. In the days of hot-metal type (which are stubbornly still with us, I am happy to say), an inexperienced compositor might have tried to justify a line by putting spacing between the letters. This throws off the balance in the line and makes for an unsightly and annoying page. (Getting perfect letterspacing in the original design of the type is called 'fitting'. The best treatment of the fitting of type is by Blumenthal [**22a**].)

In some typefaces, some letter strokes are so long that they exceed the body of the sort. (The sort is the individual piece of type and it has been frequently noted that when a printer ran out of pieces of type, he was *out of sorts*. This is the origin of that idiom.) This is especially the case with many italic faces. The part which 'sticks out' is called a kern. So, for example, the top stroke of the *f* might be long enough to conflict with the central stroke of other letters such as *b* (as in *halfback*), another *f* (*stiff*), an *h* (*halfhearted*), an *i* (*unfit*), an *l* (*fly*), and possibly other letters, depending on the typeface. If there is a conflict, the type designer must do something about it, lest either the two (or possibly three) letters (*stiffly*) sit crooked on the line, or the kern breaks off. Of course, this is a problem with computer typefaces as well, for it would not do to have parts of two different letters sitting on the same spot on the page. What the designer does is to create ligatures, that is, places where the two conflicting letters are no longer in conflict, but join up. Fonts of type would thus have ligatures such as *fi, ff, fl, ffi, ffl*, and even *ft*. Ligatures such as those I mention above (*fb* and *fh*) would not normally be created. So, if a typesetter is following the copy of an author who has the word *halfback*, some form of letterspacing must be put in between the *f* and the *b*. There is practically no way around it. The result might be a word which looks as if it is trying to be two words. With computer-generated typefaces, perhaps *fb* and *fh* ligatures could be created *ad hoc*. But this was not the case in old print shops, and some books today are still printed from hot metal.

One problem related to letterspacing is the appearance of RIVERS on the page. Reichl (**184**) mentions this occurrence of blank lines that run down a page where spaces in succeeding lines happen to line up. He says, 'To avoid holes between words on a page of this kind, compositors not familiar with book composition will sometimes letterspace bad lines. This must not be tolerated; holes are still the lesser evil' (p. 18).

But since, as I have said, most lower-case alphabets are designed to give the appearance of perfect letterspacing, the real problem is generally to be found with the upper-case letters. The rule of thumb here is to have the upper-case letters appear to be a uniform distance apart from one another.

This will require adding space between some letters and none at all between others. The not uncommon pair *VA* look quite far apart in many typefaces; while, of course, the pair *MM* will almost always look quite close. I once heard of a man who, in handsetting a long text in full caps, was either adding thin spaces between letters where necessary, or laboriously shaving down sorts in combinations such as *VA*. It was taking him forever. Perhaps such niceties can be adjusted instantly on the computer, if the designer of the programs is also familiar with type. (See Kindersley, **117**; and Knight, **120**.)

All of this discussion about letterspacing – and its importance in the setting of upper-case letters – is pertinent to bibliographies because many writers and designers have thought it appropriate to print last names, full names, or titles in full caps. Carelessly set caps can look quite bad on a page, and can be distracting. In such instances, good letterspacing is essential.

Interestingly, Crosland and Johnson (**56**) have studied reader preferences with respect to letterspacing for lower-case letters, and they find that legibility increases with interletter spacing for 'letters [e.g. *p, b, g, d*] whose shapes do not contrast greatly' (p. 121).

A related subject, WORD SPACING, can be dealt with more succinctly. Generally, there should be a uniform space between words. An old printer's rule is that 'Words should be close to each other (about as far apart as the width of the letter "i")' (McLean, **148**, p. 45). As I will discuss below, justified setting (that is, lines which are flush left and right) may present a problem, for adding or subtracting spaces between words is the printer's standard method of justifying a line. This is particularly a problem for lines set to a short measure, because there are few words in each line; this sometimes necessitates adding a good deal of space between words to justify the line. The best suggestion is to try to keep uniform word spacing. Not only does it look best and promote the most legible text, but it also helps to prevent rivers from flowing on the page. (See more below under justified and unjustified text.)

LEADING (also called INTERLINEAR SPACING) is one of those features of a page which can be seriously abused. Some typographers apparently think that adding spacing between lines adds elegance to the page. It certainly can be used to lengthen an essay into a short book. Vladimir Nabokov resurrected a short piece (*The Enchanter* [New York: G.P. Putnam's Sons, 1986]) – what he describes as a novella – of 55 typewritten pages. With the help of numbering all the preliminary pages (20 of them) and all the pages of the postscript (28 of them), and especially with leading twice the x-height of the type used, the entire volume stretches to 127 pages – enough to bind in hard cover, put a dust jacket on, and sell for the price of a full-length novel (the book came out in 1986 for $16.95). The page has so much white on it that one feels subtly cheated. Too much leading destroys a page's sense of unity and 'distorts the typeface nearly as much as too little leading would' (Reichl, **184**, p. 14). However, too little leading may make it difficult for the eye to move from the end of one line to the beginning of the next, especially for long lines and a small typeface.

Becker *et al.* found that 'different typefaces required different amounts of leading to allow most appealing composition' (**14**, pp. 61, 66). They also claim that sans serif and italic types 'may need one point more leading than roman types' (p. 66). Bentley (**16**) claims that unleaded text is slower and less comprehensible to read than leaded text; also, text leaded up to 7 points ($\frac{1}{10}$ inch; 2.5 mm) increased legibility. But this, of course, ignores type size and line length, among other things. Greene (**90**) claims that leaded texts, in the experiments he ran, were read 3.3 per cent faster than texts set solid. And Hovde (**110**) adds that while readers prefer more leading, other variables should be considered, such as the amount of reading they do and their reading rate. Labuz (**130**) says that 'leading should be about 20 per cent of the type size' (p. 62). And Luckiesh (**141**), who is usually more articulate and consistent, says that all speed-of-reading criteria failed to show any significant difference with variations in leading, and that the practical optimum in readability was with 3-point leading. But he neglects to take into account the type size and line length.

Paterson and Tinker, who have plenty to say about nearly every aspect of typography, show that leading must be considered in conjunction with LINE LENGTH and type size. They assert that

10-point type can be set to a measure of from 17 to 28 picas (with an optimum of 19 picas) without loss of legibility, and that 10-point type with 2-point leading yields the greatest legibility. Also, 8-point type needs 2-point leading (Paterson and Tinker, **167**, **172**). They conclude that 'it is probable that optimal leading will vary somewhat with type size, being smaller for small type and larger for large type' (**172**, p. 397). This skipping from 'definitive' statements about line length and its relation to leading, to statements about leading which ignore line length is typical of much of the scholarship on the subject. Also typical are vague statements such as the observation that leading allows 'line length to be extended without loss of legibility' (Spencer, **214**, p. 55). This vagueness is balanced by sometimes overbearing specificity, as in Tinker's recommendations (**235**): a 6-point type set 14 picas should be leaded 2 to 4 points; 6-point type set 21 picas should be leaded 1 to 4 points (note the lapse in logic here), and so on for types of 8, 9, 10, 11, and 12 points. (See also Appendix II.) Or see Romano's table (**201**), which shows leading variations for ten different type sizes.

And there are many statements about the 'proper' line length which mention optimum number of characters or words, inches or millimetres. Krummel says, 'Because of the density of information [in a bibliography], it is more important for the lines to be short, between 65 and 100 mm (approximately 2.4–4 inches) wide; in a normal book typeface, 65 mm would provide about 40 characters in 11-point or 43 in 10-point, whereas 100 mm would allow some 60 characters in 11-point or 65 in 10-point' (p. 130). McLean (**148**) says that 'the normal principles of book readability' call for 'about 10–12 words a line and with some interlinear spacing' (p. 48). Romano (**201**) advocates 55 to 60 characters. Legros and Grant (**134**) say, 'It is recommended that the length of the line should not usually exceed 4 inches in books of 10-point type and upwards, and that this maximum should be reduced in proportion to the body if smaller sizes are used' (p. 157). Reichl (**184**) mentions 'The old printer's rule that type should be set to a line 1½ times the length of its lower case alphabet' (p. 16), while Labuz (**130**) says that the measure should be set from 1½ to 2½ alphabets long.

The overlapping of recommendations usually occurs because these writers are drawing from common sources; the lack of agreement appears because one cannot be definitive about any of these variables (line length, type size, and leading), or because of the many variables in other things: typeface, readers, paper, and so on. In the end, the typographer must use her or his own aesthetic sensibility. Just by looking at the page and trying to read it, one can tell if it is 'right' or not. Krummel is at least on the right track for bibliographies when he says that the density of the information they present suggests that a well-leaded bibliography page is more congenial than a page set solid.

One consideration obliquely related to line length is the appearance of WIDOWS and ORPHANS on the page. A widow is an incomplete first line of type at the top of a page, at the end of the paragraph which began on the previous page. An orphan is the first line of a paragraph which appears as the last line of a page. These two typographic structures look as if they are stranded alone, and typographers try to avoid them. One way is to add a line into the text on the page which precedes either of these waifs; another way is simply to leave the last line of the page blank. The orphan is moved, to be the first line on the following page; the widow is joined by what was formerly the last line of the previous page and becomes the second line on the new page. Most computer typesetting programs have measures against these phenomena; my own, called 'widow and orphan control' (it sounds like a brutal military unit), automatically cuts a page short if there is going to be a widow or an orphan. It is better — and perfectly sound typographically — to have a page short one line than to have one of these unsightly structures. But using an automatic control is a danger in a bibliography. Almost as bad as a widow or an orphan is a bibliographical entry of four lines that gets split up onto two pages. Better to have a page two lines short than to split an entry in half. In composing a bibliography, one should set the 'widow and orphan control', and then monitor and override it when the final printout is to be made if a four-line entry is broken up into two lines on each page.

I once watched an inexperienced typesetter who needed to add a line to a page so that the type block would come out the same length as on the facing page. What he did was put enough leading between the lines to add up to an extra line. This did make the last line on the page line up with the last line on the facing page, but it distorted the REGISTRATION – the alignment of lines on facing pages and on the recto and verso of the same leaf. Registration is merely an optical effect. Theoretically, it makes no difference whether lines align. But, in practice, it looks bad if they do not. Since the gutter – the inner margin – is supposed to be the smallest on the page, the two facing pages hang together close enough to one another to show whether the registration is good or not. Misaligned pages upset the optical balance and symmetry of the spread, and, for many readers, are annoying. Also, registration on the two sides of a single leaf aims to prevent show-through. Even opaque papers often have a hint of show-through. Poor registration in which the lines on one side of the sheet appear between the lines on the opposite side of that sheet is quite distracting. Though this is really the responsibility of a printer, authors can help by specifying the number of lines per page, if this is possible (as when producing camera-ready copy), and by asking the typesetter not to break up the entries in such a way that only one or two lines of an entry appear alone on a page. (More on registration below.)

Considerations of leading, line length, widow and orphan control, and so on cannot be seen outside the context of the COST of the book. This is not as base a consideration as it seems, because there are economic factors in book production. Greater leading means more blank space, which in turn means a longer book. More pages means more paper and even more binding materials, which means more money. What I am presenting for the most part here is the ideal page in the ideal book. That ideal, from the point of view of the person or company financing the book, might differ from that of the designer or author. In the middle of a section on the physical design of books, it may seem discordant to bring in economic factors. But the physical elements are what will ultimately cost money. And, in fact, cost is an underlying factor throughout the production of a book, for the author as well as the publisher (if they are different).

Layout

There are many other physical features of a book that need to be discussed. LAYOUT is a general term for the shape and placement of the printed part of the page. One feature of layout is whether the book is in a PORTRAIT, a LANDSCAPE, or a SQUARE shape. Portrait layout is the standard, with the height greater than the length; landscape is the opposite. Since, by custom, books are usually in a portrait layout, that is the recommended shape. Some art books and books which strive to be arty may be printed in the landscape or square format. But such shapes call attention to themselves from their awkwardness – their uncommonness – and thus draw the reader's attention away from the text, however subtly. Bibliographies are not meant to be works of art (except in the intellectual sense), and should probably not be printed in sizes or shapes other than what readers expect from their reference books.

Related to page shape is the SIZE of the page, which, of course, is related to the size of the book. Many years ago I went to a lecture at the Roxburghe Club (a book collectors' club in San Francisco); the guest speaker was Ansel Adams, who was talking about books and their design. One of his opening remarks was, 'No book should be so big that it cannot be taken comfortably to bed.' My own corollary to this is that no page should have so much text on it that when readers turn to it they know they will be there for ten minutes or more. Wroth (272a) shows how the sizes of books traditionally were linked to the sizes of paper available to the printers. As usual, Paterson and Tinker have something to say about this: the 'size of the page is a matter of whim' (167, p. 84) – not very helpful. But they do emphasize that this is one of the variables in book design that, within limits, makes little difference to the legibility or usefulness of a book. Rollins (199) makes one sensible statement about bibliographies specifically: the book should be 'a workable size' (p. 111) – e.g. octavo, c. 6½ × 9½ inches (165 mm × 242 mm), or as small as 5½ × 8½ inches (140 mm × 216 mm). But Spencer and Reynolds (216) say that 'an 8½ × 11″ [inches; 216 mm × 280 mm] page is suitable for most readers; avoid oversize formats' (p. 18). And Trevitt (248) even says that the designer, when deciding on a page size, should consider the size of the press and paper available, whether a reprint in a small run is contemplated, whether there will be illustrations in the text (and of what size), and the length of the text. A long text printed on a small page will yield quite a fat little volume. For bibliographies, one might also consider the shape that each entry will take. If a presentation of the bibliographical data is to appear with each piece of information on a new line (see below in the section on the arrangement of data in bibliographical entries), then there will be many short lines; this suggests that either there should be a TWO-COLUMN FORMAT or there should be a fairly short line setting – hence a smaller format book. Van Hoesen and Walter (257) say, 'The publisher will, of course, know the fashions in books, the trade conditions, etc., and, accordingly, suggest the proper format' (p. 39). Whether we can rely on all publishers to suggest proper formats is debatable. My own view, as I have suggested, is that the page should have a congenial appearance – about as vague a recommendation as one can expect for a feature that can have such great variation with no loss of legibility or beauty.

The wider the page, the more room there is for a two-column format. Several writers suggest that this format is eminently usable for readable books, and a few even recommend it for bibliographies. Foster (75) argues that the single-column format of 5⁵/₁₆ inches (135 mm) was read more slowly than two columns of 2³/₁₆ inches (55 mm). Once again, Paterson and Tinker have their say: they assert that readers prefer double-column to single-column formats (167, pp. 100–2), and that if two columns are used, intercolumnar rule is preferred to blank space between the columns, with a ½-pica space on each side of the rule. The second preferred arrangement is to have a 2-pica space with no rule between columns (pp. 105–6). A. M. L. Robinson (194) says simply, 'Double column is not recommended' (p. 67).

One warning about multiple-column printing is that with the shorter measure that results, getting good word spacing might pose a problem. And setting ragged-right (i.e. unjustified) lines might look awkward in narrow columns. On the other hand, one of the suggested methods of laying out the data in a bibliographical entry is to have different data fields on separate lines. This could result in many short lines. For example:

Francis, Dick.
The Edge.
New York: Putnam, 1989.

(This is not necessarily how I would lay out these lines; but it is a possibility, and it does produce quite a short column of information.) My own recommendation about columns and line length is based on intuition and experience: use a one-column format and a type size, line length, and leading sufficient that the reader's eyes will move easily from one line to the next. This is undogmatic, flexible, and open to the designer's choice of typeface, type size, line length, and other typographical elements.

Another of the complex considerations of layout is the MARGINS. There has been a good deal written about these, and a good place to begin is with the words of Philip Stern (225a): 'The subject of book margins is obscured by mathematical mysticism, vague references to the Greek law of the golden mean, and other well-meaning but often impracticable terms. . . . margins should be wide enough to be pleasant and proportioned so that the inside margins are smallest, the top margins large, the outside still larger, and the bottom margins largest of all' (p. 246). He offers a diagram showing the 'classical' 2:3:4:5 margins, with the following caption: ' "The law of ideal margins" is simple in theory and diagram but difficult to follow in practice, since no two type pages are alike' (p. 147). Of the diagram he says, 'Don't pay much attention to it. The law of the ideal margin is broken in almost every book on your shelf' (p. 246).

Perhaps the best-known statement about margins is that of Alfred W. Pollard (176a), who reiterates the old notion that the inner margins should be the smallest, and so on, and questions whether this is 'artistic rather than utilitarian' (p. 67). He then talks of 'the appeal of tradition' (p. 68) espoused by William Morris and others who opted for this pattern. He offers some historical and practical reasons for the margins to be like this. For example, when people read books, they usually hold them by their lower or outer margins;

if these are wide, the fingers will not obscure the text. Similarly, with manuscripts (which were the early models for printed books), the scribes could more easily write on the uppermost and leftmost portion of the page than at the right margin and the bottom; hence space was left because of this inconvenience. (I do not accept this argument, since scribes had to write on both versos and rectos; but more important is the fact that they were probably writing on a single leaf or a few leaves – before the book was bound.) Another reason for this tradition, Pollard suggests, is that in manuscripts there was a need for room for annotations and scholia. The tradition which allowed for marginal notes led to the wide margin in the early printed books, and readers got accustomed to this. Another notion which supplements Pollard's is that the scribes and early printers knew that the codex would be composed of sheets folded at the top and inner margins, the two fairly fixed dimensions; a binder would scarcely trim to fit the book into boards from the top, and could not trim from the inner margin or the pages could not be sewn through. Since the practice was generally to trim from the outer and lower margins, printers would leave these the largest.

At any rate, there have been many diagrams drawn and methods devised or 'discovered' to indicate the 'ideal' or 'perfect' margins. Pollard mentions also a 1:2:3:4 arrangement, among others, and Paterson and Tinker (**167**, **168**) say that margins should compose about 50 per cent of the printed page. They provide a model for determining the size and shape of the type area (hence of the margins; see **167**). But there is a good deal of variation possible, and Reichl (**184**) says that 'a large variety of margin treatments is acceptable to our eyes' (p. 22). He says that generally a small margin 'detracts from reading ease', while 'A standard page will be found to contain about 10% more unprinted than printed area' (p. 22). And despite the vogue for large-paper copies in the nineteenth century, margins too wide detract as much as margins too narrow.

'Margins too narrow' deserves a whole paragraph. There is no clearer sign of parsimoniousness in a publisher than pencil-width margins. The effect on some readers (especially on me) is that thin margins suggest a cheapness in the entire pro-duction. I think that the paper and binding must also be cheap; that the ink is cheap and will eventually burn its way through the acidic paper; that the boards will eventually warp and the low-quality cloth buckle off; and that the poor author, whose years of toil produced the text, will never see enough royalties out of his labour to cover the costs of his research and buy a loaf of bread for his hungry children. This bathos is engendered by narrow margins. And in a bibliography – a reference book likely to be in the possession of a scholar who makes marginal notes – thin margins are an abomination. I am sure that a buyer would be willing to pay the few extra cents or pence it would cost the publisher to be a little more generous with the paper in the book. Narrow margins are the publisher's way of saying: 'We have saved you some money, but you will not be able to write in the margins and your fingers will cover up a part of the text when you hold this book. We knew what we were doing, and we thought the money you saved would really be appreciated. Like it or not, here's the book.' This does not even consider how ugly a page narrow margins make. Publishers (and binders who have been some of the world's worst enemies of margins) should respect the author, the text, and the reader, and offer generous margins all around.

Biggs (**22**) shows a few different methods for determining perfectly reasonable margins, and Tschichold (**251**) claims to have discovered the classical means of designing a manuscript page. The method he delineates works for any size or shape rectangle (the larger rectangle, that is, which is formed by a two-page spread).

For our purposes here, bibliographies at the end of longer books (as opposed to whole volumes which are bibliographies) may well be set in a typeface smaller than that of the rest of the book – a fairly common practice. The notion is, apparently, that the text of the book is to be *read*, while the bibliography is merely to be consulted. Hence, the eyes can stand taking in smaller type since they will not be on it as long as they will be on the text. But the problems of impaired readability and legibility for smaller typefaces militate against using a face so small that it is difficult or uncomfortable to read for any length of time. If the margins are so small that the page has a long line length, then I

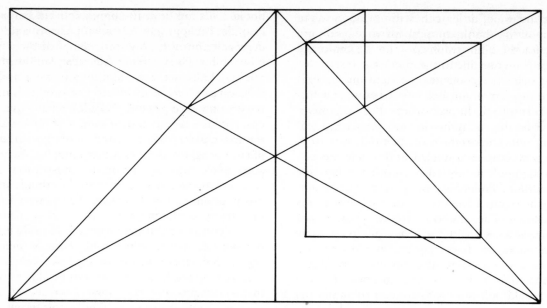

Figure 1

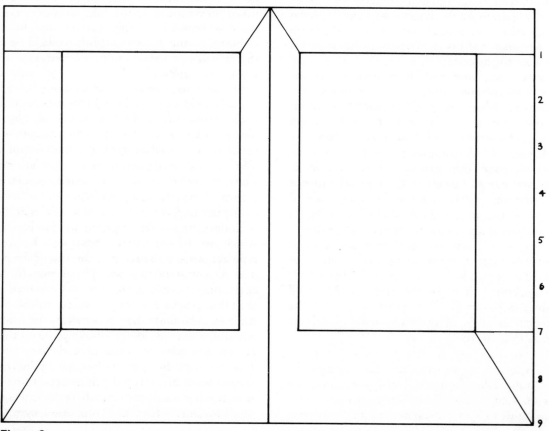

1

2

3

4

5

6

7

8

9

Figure 2

suggest the use of at least the same size type as in the rest of the book, or perhaps a two-column format for the bibliography, so the eye can make the shift from one line to the next accurately.

I have spent a good deal of time on margins because they are about half of what we see when we look at a page. Ill-proportioned or excessively wide or narrow margins can be distracting; and anything which takes the reader's mind away from the text, no matter how subtly, is a defect in the book's design. (In my own printing I like the margins that Tschichold's plan yields, but I never stick to it rigidly. The eye is the final arbiter for me. I also know for my own printing what kind of binding my books will have. If I know the spine will be pliant or that a pamphlet will open up fully, then I can adjust the inner margin down somewhat; but if I know the book will have a stiff spine, I might allow a small amount of additional space on the inner margin, which may necessitate adjustments in the other dimensions.)

Also part of the layout of the page is the use of GRIDS, mentioned by some of the scholars who take an architectural approach to the design of a page. McLean (**148**) says, 'The grid is the invisible framework within which all books, magazines and newspapers are designed. It is a boon to the designer and printer; it also helps the appearance of the printed page' (p. 132). A whole book has even been written on the subject (see Hurlburt, **110a**). Grids can be as simple as the rectangle of space in which, for example, the text of a novel is set – a one-unit grid; that is, a single rectangular (or square) block of type on the page. But in some

Figure 1. One method for determining ideal margins on a two-page spread, regardless of the original shape of the page. This method is explained in detail in Tschichold (entry **251** in bibliography).

Figure 2. Biggs (see entry **22** in bibliography) shows a few ways to determine margins. He says, 'This is a pair of pages, each of which is in the proportion of the Golden Section. The type area is arrived at by first drawing diagonals. . . . The height of the page is divided into nine equal parts. A horizontal line is drawn across both pages at the first and seventh of the nine divisions. From where the first line cuts the diagonal a vertical is dropped to the seventh division. This horizontal cuts the diagonal to give the fore-edge margins' (p. 59).

books grids can be quite complex. In the Benjamin Franklin bibliography (*Benjamin Franklin's Philadelphia Printing 1728–1766*, compiled by C. William Miller; Philadelphia: American Philosophical Society, 1974; see Appendix I, Example 12), since the compiler chose to offer a photofacsimile of most of the title pages of Franklin's books, nearly every page is designed with some grid in mind. For the most part, grids are used in texts with many illustrations, since the designer must break up the page in some way, separating illustration from text (unless the illustrations are all full-page facing full pages of text – in which case the simple one-unit grid is all there is).

The grid serves as a sort of designer's shorthand, a blueprint which tells the designer, in general, where different elements of the text, visual and verbal, may go. McLean points out that it is possible to design every page anew, but this is expensive and time-consuming. And what is more, it surprises the readers on every new turning of a page, for they will not know where to fix their eyes when they turn the page. The moment of adjustment to orientate themselves is quite brief, but nonetheless the act of adjustment could be subtly disorientating. This is how I feel whenever I use the Franklin bibliography.

The designer must often know something about the subject matter of the book, because an arbitrary use of grids may tend to obscure or de-emphasize certain parts of the text that the author wanted stressed. Like most other areas of typographic design, the various portions of the grids must not be idiosyncratically placed, and must not call attention to themselves beyond what the contents of each grid ought to do by its own subject matter.

In designing bibliographies, the grid can be useful as part of the spatial coding that I will cover later. In short, however, each bibliographical entry will have a particular shape, one which may be predetermined by how the entry is to be laid out in the first place. For example, in a one-column format, each entry will run margin to margin in the shape that the designer has given to it. Some entries may run one or two lines, others may run a page or more; but they will all have similarities in shape, especially at the beginning of the entry, which will indicate to the readers the key elements in each entry. They will also end with similar shapes, identifying the conclusion of the entry to the reader. In other words, the left-right dimensions of every grid in a bibliographical entry will be fairly uniform from one entry to the next, while the vertical dimension may vary.

There is one further observation about grids, pertinent to the setting of poetry, but also applicable to some bibliographies. Verse naturally has lines of uneven length. And some bibliographies which place different fields of bibliographic data onto different lines will have the same 'problem'. I call it a problem because a designer tries to create a grid – that is, to determine a line length – based on the longest line of text. If the poet did not break a line (and line breaks in verse often carry meaning), then the printer should also try not to break any. And if the bibliography is set up in such a way that certain fields of data appear on individual lines, it may be desirable to maintain the coherence of those fields by keeping all the data they carry on one line. So the grid should be designed wide enough to carry all the data (or the full text of the longest poetic line) on a single line of type. The problem arises when the grid is designed for the longest line, but then the text itself contains a group of very short lines all in a row – possibly even taking up most of a page vertically. Then the page could look lopsided, as if all the text were floating into the inner margin, and the rest of the page were an open sea of space.

One printer of verse faced just this situation: having a wide measure for nearly all the lines in the book, but running into several pages of very short blocks of text (i.e. with a short horizontal measure). He solved this problem by printing a box on the page – in an unobtrusive, very light-yellow ink (which matched the paper of the binding) – a box which clearly delineated the page grid. What he did was to confine the text; rather than floating on a wide blank page, the lines of verse were contained in the delimiting grid. They no longer seemed to be at sea. It is conceivable that a bibliography would have a similar problem, if the designer chose the method of presenting different pieces of the bibliographical data on separate lines. The use of a visible grid may be a solution.

Several writers mention the use of RULE in the layout of a page. As I have just said, rule can be used to delineate the grid(s) on a page. But it has other uses. It can be used between columns or for decoration. There are several kinds of decorative rule, but generally in the setting of a bibliography – or, for that matter, any serious text – the niceties of decoration tend more to distract from than to emphasize the text. A subtle tapered rule (also called a bulged rule – it depends on whether you are describing the middle or ends of the line) may be used occasionally to set one portion of a text off from another. (It is also called a 'swelled rule', a term that has always suggested to me the need for a doctor or an ice pack.) For example, a bibliography arranged chronologically may have a tapered rule denoting the end of one year and the beginning of the next.

One problem frequently encountered in bibliographies is that one can hardly tell the end of one entry from the beginning of the next. This is shoddy design, often caused by a penurious publisher who wants to reduce the number of pages in the book. Jacob Blanck's *Bibliography of American Literature* (*BAL*) suffers from this ailment. (See Appendix I, Example 20a, b and c.) Though rule between every entry would soon become an eyesore, it would help the reader move from one entry to the next without having to go on an expedition.

Occasionally a bibliography must contain TABULAR MATTER. (My own entry for Romano, **201**, includes an example.) Sometimes it is useful, if not necessary, to use rule to segment the data. Either it separates bits of text that are otherwise too close to one another, or it aligns pieces of the text that are otherwise too far apart. Also, rule can separate the title of the chart from the data it contains and from its caption below. The only general rule to follow is to use rule of an appropriate weight for the text type. Very fine rule may be satisfactory (if it prints evenly and clearly); very heavy rule may overburden the page. Once the page is set, without rule, assess whether any part of the page needs to be separated from another part. If this needs to be done and can be done tastefully with space, use space. If not, perhaps rule is the answer. But, as Mark Twain said about the adjective: 'When in doubt, strike it out' (Samuel Langhorne Clemens, *Pudd'nhead Wilson and Those Extraordinary Twins*, p. 47; for full citation, see note, p. viii).

Though I have already mentioned this, the use of ILLUSTRATIONS needs one more paragraph. Normally bibliographies do not have illustrations, or they may have facsimiles of title or text pages on a leaf facing the text. Though illustrations break up the monotony of a text, they must not be used gratuitously. They must have a specific reason for being there. If the bibliography aims to show typographical variants in different copies of an edition, if the text of the item is noteworthy for its typography in some way that might be useful to the reader, or if an illustration will save the bibliographer many words in trying to describe some physical peculiarity of a book, and if the publishers say they can afford to add illustrations to the text, then it may be useful and practicable to have them. One desideratum, however, is that the illustration be properly captioned and tied clearly to the item in the bibliography that it illustrates.

A number of times now I have mentioned JUSTIFIED and UNJUSTIFIED setting (the latter sometimes called RAGGED-RIGHT setting). Once again there is more than a millennium of tradition (albeit somewhat inconsistent tradition, if such a concept is not self-contradictory) with respect to the justification of lines. In other words, if we have a constant left margin, should the line length be allowed to vary to create an uneven right margin? Both sides of this issue can be strongly defended.

One of the things which makes for an appealing page is its symmetry, which is naturally upset with unjustified lines. (But see below.) On the other hand, to justify lines often means increasing or reducing spaces between words or breaking many words between syllables to make all the words fit. This sometimes creates a line set very tight, with the words running into each other, possibly above a line set loosely, with lots of space between words. Forcing an increased amount of space into a page tends to increase the number of rivers. (See above in the discussion of word spacing.) The shorter the line, the fewer words (and characters) the typesetter has to play with, and the more uneven the word spacing will be in a justified text. The longer the line, the more the typesetter can spread out the extra spaces (or the space reduction). Theoretically, the longer the line, the more even one can make a justified page. But only with no justification can the words truly be evenly spaced.

Some scholars insist on consistency in typography, and thus stress the importance of uniform word spacing. But that is nearly impossible to achieve with justified lines. Burnhill (32) speaks of 'the irrational practice of horizontal justification'. And Carter, Day, and Meggs (41) say that the uneven right-hand margin serves as a code in the reader's periphery: 'If properly used, flush-left, ragged-right typography provides visual points of reference that guide the eye smoothly down the page from line to line. Because each line is either shorter or longer than the next, the eye is cued from one to another. In a justified setting, all lines are of equal length. Lacking are visual cues that promote easy reading' (p. 88). They also say that the even word spacing that unjustified lines allow will help control line breaks, which need not be forced, but which may enhance meaning. Eric Gill (80) encourages the use of ragged-right setting, mentioning 'the tyrannical insistence upon equal length of lines' (p. 92).

On the other hand, Evers (66) says that 'Exaggerated short lines [which are sometimes the product of ragged-right setting] . . . tend to emphasize the ragged end and irritate the reader' (p. 74). Several experiments showed that justification is equally legible as unjustified typography. Fabrizio, Kaplan, and Teal (67) say that 'Neither speed of reading nor level of comprehension . . . differed significantly' (p. 94) in their experiments. (See also Gregory and Poulton, 91; Hartley and Burnhill, 100; Miles, 154; Spencer, 214; Teal et al., 233; Trollip and Sales, 249, who call it 'fill-justified' text; and Zachrisson, 273. All these scholars say the same thing: there is no difference in readability or comprehension with the two modes of setting.)

The ragged-right setting could upset a reader who wants uniformity and balance. This is the argument presented above concerning the 'need' for symmetry on a page. But a well-set page of unjustified text has many lines reaching out to and touching the right margin. This does something optically to the page: it tells the reader where the right margin is, and the reader is able to supply an invisible line down the right margin. A designer once told me that he liked to set ragged-right prose, but that he tried his best to set the first and last line of the page to the full measure. That way, he said, the reader knows exactly where the margin is. Many times I have read a text through, not even realizing that it was set unjustified. In fact, someone once asked me after I had read through a long pamphlet what I thought of the typography; the text was so interesting and the typography so unobtrusive (as it should be), that I did not even notice the ragged-right margin. I even said that I thought the page had been set flush right. What many readers do, in such a situation, is to recognize — only half-consciously — where the grid is on the page. A well-used grid on a well-designed page will make it unnecessary for the designer to have to agonize over whether to justify the text.

There are a few other elements of page design to consider. *The items in a full-length bibliography should be* NUMBERED. And the bibliography should have an INDEX. No method of organiz-ation will automatically reveal to readers every-thing they want to know about the contents of the bibliography. If the organization is chronological, the index should offer access by author, title, sub-ject, or whatever else the user might search under. I will cover this in more detail later. But the point here is that the index can be compact, usable, and efficient if it refers readers to the proper entry by citing numbers, not full (or abbreviated) names, titles, or page numbers.

Bibliographies usually have some clear focus; therefore, users want to search through them. The search will be hindered if the entries are not num-bered, or if the numbers are buried somewhere on the page, as is the case with the most recent volumes of *A Checklist of American Imprints* — as in the 1839 volume (compiled by Carol Rinder-knecht; see Appendix I, Example 19a, b and c), in which each bibliographical entry is set like a small paragraph, looking like prose, and the number is run in at the very end of the 'prose'. The number is so well integrated into the lines of text that it is not made prominent in any way. It is quite difficult to search by the numbers in this bibliography. Since a good deal of the searching done in a bibliography is by the numbers, it is logical to put them in some prominent, immediately visible place. Extending to the left of the rest of the entry is useful. (I will say more about this, too, under the rubric of Spa-tial coding in Chapter 3.) The index should allow a reader access by any means not already created by the setup of the page. Thus, for example, if the bibliography is arranged alphabetically by author, the index need not list authors since they are already locatable. But subjects would not be, in an alphabetical listing of authors. The compilers should know what their readers might want to search for, and should give access to it all in an index.

Another topic pertaining to the design of a page is HEADLINES or RUNNING HEADS. These are use-ful, but they are expensive. They often cannot be put in until the book is set into type and divided into pages. Then the author must put the running heads in, unless she or he feels that the publisher/ editor/typesetter can be trusted to do it. (Would you trust a typesetter?) It takes time, and time is money.

Running heads are designed to tell the reader what is on the page; but the subject matter of a bibliography should be fairly well delineated and clearly focused. The reader should not need to be told what the subject of any given page is. An alphabetically arranged bibliography instantly shows readers where in the sequence they are. (Of course, there are bibliographies that cover a wide range of topics or are broken into many parts. For instance, Carl J. Stratman's *Bibliography of Medieval Drama* [2nd ed. New York: Frederick Ungar, 1972; 2 vols.] contains separate sections for collections of plays, individual plays, general studies, mystery and miracle plays, morality plays, and so on. Though the broad categories are expressed in headlines, the individual plays are not; this sometimes makes this bibliography some-thing of a headache to use, especially since it is in two volumes, and the index is at the end of volume 2. This requires the reader to go from volume to volume to find the items or subjects she or he needs. Rollins (**199**) recommends that bibliogra-phies be published in a single volume.) Also, the running head may contain a number, a name, or a subject which will help readers know where they are in the text. This is especially helpful if the work is alphabetical and there is a second or subsequent entry for a writer. The use of a long dash to indi-cate 'same author as in previous entry' would make it impossible to tell where one is in the alphabetical sequence. This is the case also if the page begins in the middle of a long annotation. In both situations, the running head tells readers where they are. In some bibliographies, therefore, headlines are quite useful. But in most they pose problems greater than the help they give. Most well-structured bibliographies with a clear focus and handy index should not need headlines.

PAGE NUMBERS are so much a part of a book's make-up that we all expect to see them easily when we look for them on a page, but we also expect them to recede from our view in our concentrated reading – they are the ubiquitous but unobtrusive guide to our place in a book. Since they traditionally appear somewhere in the margins (any placement within the main grid of the text block is inexcusable and – for a bibliography – sheer madness), there is a good deal of latitude (and longitude) for their location.

But two things are important to keep in mind with respect to page numbers. First, they are designed to be located easily; so the idiosyncratic placement of them on either or both the inner margins is contradictory to their function. They should be somewhere on the page that is exposed when one flips through the book. This means on one of the outer margins or on the bottom of the page. The publisher of my own bibliography on medieval English drama (Garland) insisted that the numbers be at the bottom centre of every page. Since I produced camera-ready copy, it was little trouble to program this placement into the computer.

The second thing to remember is that for a bibliography, which already is replete with numbers, other numbers on the page which do not have specifically to do with the bibliographical data in the entries may compete for the reader's attention with the numbers in the entries. My own recommendation is so classical that it is boring: place the numbers at the top outer margins (directly or diagonally above the last character in the first line of text on rectos and the first character in the first line on versos; at the bottoms of pages in the equivalent positions is good, too). This not only puts them in the most prominent place on the page for one flipping through the book, but it also moves these numbers as far away from the numbers in the bibliographic entries as they can possibly be. Besides, they are so commonly found there that they will not be a distraction. Finally, the page

numbers should probably be in the same typeface as the rest of the text, and probably no smaller or larger. Pages beginning new sections in the book, say between two main parts of the bibliography, may not need numbers. The alternative is to number these new-section pages in the centre bottom, the rest of the book in the upper, outer margins. McLean (**148**) says that the folios (the old word for page numbers) 'must be identical on every opening, merely because they have got to be somewhere, and it is an unnecessary nuisance, first to the printer and secondly to the reader, if the position varies' (p. 132). The main things to strive for in the placement of page numbers are consistency and visibility.

Two things related to one another must be mentioned: PAPER and REGISTRATION. Though not strictly the provenance of typography, paper is related to it since the type must appear somewhere. Paper is the medium for the vast majority of bibliographies. (Other media will be covered below.) As with other areas of typography, there is enough written about paper to wipe out a forest.

My first observation is based on the obvious: 'peculiar' colours are distracting. By 'peculiar' I mean colours that we are not accustomed to seeing in books. And that means most colours other than white or cream (or some shades between them). And, in fact, some cream-coloured papers are too creamy — more on the order of Bailey's Irish Cream than what we might call 'eggshell' or 'off-white'. Innovation and 'artistry' aside, traditional paper colours are the least obtrusive and should be used.

My own *a priori* observations are shared by many writers and are backed up by scientific investigation. Betts (**17**) says that white or slightly tinted papers produce excellent readability (though his study is tainted by his support of the paper made by the company which funded his experiments). Borko (**23**) says that 'gloss interferes with the visibility of the type' (p. 46); he suggests that paper should exhibit the optimum opacity and bulk (though he is not specific about what these optima are). Eric Gill (**80**) advocates a good smooth surface for the paper. Paterson and Tinker (**167**) say that either glossy or dull stock yields the same legibility, but, because of the 'opinions and prejudices of the overwhelming majority of readers who believe that they can read material printed on dull finished paper more rapidly than material on glazed paper', they recommend dull-finished paper (p. 136): 'It is good business to give the readers what they want' (p. 136). Spencer and Reynolds (**216**) say that 'paper should preferably be smooth blue-white, opaque, and gloss coated for maximum contrast; textured and tinted papers should be avoided' (p. [9]).

Other features of paper are its texture, the smoothness (or unevenness) of its edge, its crispness (a function mostly of the amount and kind of sizing it contains), and so on. For sumptuous bibliographies for which expense is not a consideration, a lovely Fabriano handmade, modern laid paper with its deckle edge and watermarks is exquisite. But seriously, commercially produced books will need to use a wood-pulp paper, simply because of its lower cost. Excellent, alkaline papers are available from many companies. Ellen McCrady's newsletter *The Alkaline Paper Advocate* lists many papers from commercial mills throughout the United States and United Kingdom which are permanent and durable and can be had in perfectly reasonable colours, with no show-through. In many cases, these papers cost no more than acidic papers; in fact, they actually cost less to produce, and their price is coming down or at least holding steady relative to the economy. I stress the permanence aspect because acidic papers eventually self-destruct; no author or publisher wants to see the product of years of toil eating itself to death. 'Dust to dust' was not meant of books, but books on acidic papers are as mortal as mutton or a tree. Deacidification – mass deacidification or individual treatment – is expensive, and is usually done only after some damage has taken place. One of the bibliographies I frequently use in my work (James Kelly, *The American Catalogue of Books*, 2 vols.; New York: John Wiley & Son, 1866, 1871) has been crumbling for decades. I am afraid to use it, for I never know which page will be the next to detach itself. Even picking up the fragments is frightening, for they sometimes decompose right before my eyes. No amount of deacidification will resurrect these volumes.

A note on deckle (sometimes called 'deckled') edges is in order. Originally, deckle edges were a defect in the hand papermaking process. They were formed where fibres from the vat stuck onto the deckle when the vatman was forming a sheet on the mould. The deckle is a rectangular frame which fits over the top of the hand mould and holds the fibres onto the screen (rather than letting them run off the edge) just after the mould has been lifted out of the water and when the water is draining through the screen. Without the deckle, fibres and water run off the edges of the mould, and the paper will be quite thin along the edges. Also, the deckle helps guarantee the uniformity of the size of the sheet from one to the next (though when the paper dries it shrinks; therefore, the sheet is generally a fraction smaller than the inner dimensions of the deckle).

Deckles were a nuisance to printers, who wanted a straight edge for aligning the sheet in the press; so the deckle edges were generally cut off before the paper was printed on. When machine-made papers began to replace handmade, the deckle – a sign of the more expensive handmade sheets – was thus a sign of quality paper (the theory being that handmade paper was superior in quality to machine-made; in fact, while it was usually more expensive, it was not necessarily of higher quality). There has thus been a vogue for handmade papers as a sign of richness and high quality. And since the deckle was one 'proof' of a handmade sheet, it was sought after by 'fine' printers. However, soon papermakers could adapt their machines to create machine-made deckles. So much for the myth that deckles indicated handmade papers.

But the myth survives, and so do the machine-made deckles. Some publishers still print on deckle-edged papers (and can then charge a few dollars or pounds more for the books). Aesthetically, I appreciate the deckles; to get a good deckle the paper must have good bulk, and it usually has a pleasant, almost three-dimensional surface. But bibliographies are reference books. They are usually flipped through by pressing the thumb against the curled-up edge of the text block. Deckle edges make it nearly impossible to get a smooth riff through the pages. And even turning deckle-edged pages one at a time can be a nuisance. I strongly recommend the use of deckles on volumes of new poetry; I also recommend smooth-edged, sharply cut paper for the edges of the pages in a bibliography.

Registration, which I have already mentioned above (under widows and orphans), is more a function of good printing than of good typographic design, but both printing and design contribute to good 'backing-up'. The idea is to superimpose lines of type on opposite sides of a leaf to reduce show-through. Poor registration can be disastrous, because if the paper is translucent enough (and surprisingly many papers are), the lines printed on the opposite side of a leaf will appear between the lines of the observed page. It is so obviously a problem that printers and typographers – and readers – are aware of it. I am embarrassed to bring it up. But if Spencer and Reynolds do, so should I. They say, 'Show-through effectively reduces the contrast between the type images and the paper and is therefore likely to impair legibility' (**215**, p. 2). They conclude 'that legibility is not greatly affected either by printing condition or by paper opacity until paper opacity falls below about 2.0. At opacities below this figure, double-sided printing is significantly less legible than single-sided, and interlinear show-through causes significantly more impairment than show-through which is aligned with the type image being read' (p. 2). It is good to know that such formal experiments have been done to verify what readers and book designers have known for centuries. Now we have a scientific figure of opacity (2.0) which we can use when we order paper for the printing of our bibliographies. I do not mean to be flippant about this, because it was a serious problem that led to this experiment in the first place. If there were no books exhibiting show-through, especially with improper registration, Spencer and Reynolds would not have had to study it, and I would not be writing this.

As for INK, use black. Black on white (or cream) gives the best contrast, and is thus more legible than any other colour; the eye is most accustomed to texts in black ink; readers expect to see black. Anything else is idiosyncratic and distracting. Occasionally, a designer might try a second colour for a bibliography to code particular elements. For example, all personal names (filing elements) could be printed in red. This would help the reader spot the filing element instantly for any given entry. But a page with good spatial and typo-graphic coding does the same, with no loss of efficiency, and with no distracting patch of colour on the page. The simplest advice is to use black ink.

Though somewhat peripheral to typography, the BINDING of the book does play a role in its use. As I mentioned above under the rubric of 'page size', Ansel Adams's dictum that a book should be small enough to be taken comfortably to bed obtains here. The binding is one of the more expensive aspects of book production, and many a publisher has chosen to cut costs in this department. In the simplest terms, there are hard covers and paperback bindings (not to mention pamphlets, stapled typescripts and xeroxes, spiral bindings and ring binders). Without giving a dissertation on bindings, I will say that some bibliographies get a lot of use. A good hard cover, made of boards that are 'not too heavy' for the text block, will extend the life of the book. I also advocate the use of a quiet, subtle colour for the book's cover. Any bright colour on the protruding outer edges of the boards could catch the reader's eye and be distracting. But this is really being oversensitive. A binding that will hold together for a long time, and will open easily and lie flat – whether paper or boards – is all we should hope for. Any more than this is a bonus.

One relatively neglected area of typographic study is the use of PUNCTUATION. A few authors pass over it lightly, but none speaks extensively about it, probably because fonts of type automatically come with their own pointing, and people who think about other areas of type probably do not give a moment's thought to the accompanying punctuation. Dreyfus (**62**) says that it is important to give accent marks and punctuation an appropriate weight for visibility. And Van Hoesen (**257**) talks of the proper use in bibliographies of ellipses, square brackets, semicolons to separate the main from the explanatory title, colons between independent titles, and so on. I will say more about punctuation below under the heading of 'Order of Elements' in a bibliographic entry. (Related is the use of underlining, which will be treated below under Typographic Coding.)

The tendency in the past few years has been to avoid ROMAN NUMERALS in favour of ARABIC, even if the original text uses the former. Compilers of bibliographies will surely encounter such things as 'vol. III', or '*PMLA* XCIII', or, for their annotations, 'Chapter IV'. It is not that we cannot trust our readers to know how to decipher these numbers (though some probably cannot); it is more that these numerals are old-fashioned, serving little purpose except to perpetuate what is now an archaism; they take up more space than do arabic numbers; and they could lead to confusion, depending on the typeface selected. If the work is set in sans serif type, there could be confusion between roman numeral 'two' (II) and arabic 'eleven' (11). I have had this very problem a number of times. Gibaldi and Achtert (**78**) speak specifically for the humanities in their *MLA Handbook*, but they voice a general opinion when they say: 'Although there are still a few well-established uses for roman numerals, . . . common practice today is to use arabic numerals to represent virtually all numbers' (p. 40, sect. 2.4.1). The only uses the MLA still allows for roman numerals are in names (Henry VIII, John Paul II, Elizabeth I) and in citing act and scene numbers for plays (Act IV, sc. iii). (The authors also mention that some older typewriters do not have the arabic numeral *1*, so the typist may use the lower-case letter *l*.) The even more widely used *Chicago Manual of Style* (**44**) says that 'for clarity and economy . . . arabic numerals are used throughout [the bibliography] for volume numbers of printed material' (p. 440, sect. 16.10); also, 'Volume numbers for books, as for journals, . . . are always given in arabic figures even when they appear as roman numerals in the book itself' (p. 450, sect. 16.43); similarly, 'The volume number follows the journal title with no punctuation separating them. Arabic figures are used for volume numbers even when a journal itself uses roman numerals' (p. 462, sect. 16.103); and, finally, for chapter headings, 'The University of Chicago Press prefers arabic figures to roman numerals for chapter numbers' (p. 574, sect. 19.53). While there may sometimes be an appropriate place for the now almost quaint roman numerals, the world of the computer should put them comfortably to rest with the ancient Romans.

Legibility

Topics that have come up time after time thus far are LEGIBILITY and READABILITY. There seems to be an endless stream of literature on these, mostly on the former, and mostly reiterating the work done in the 1930s and 1940s by Luckiesh and Moss (**138–45**) and Paterson and Tinker (**167–73, 235–46**). The bibliography of the writings of Tinker alone runs to over 100 items (see note at entry **235**); as Spencer says, Tinker is 'the most prolific writer on legibility research' (*The Visible Word*, **214**, p. 118). A glance at the index entry for the topic 'Legibility' will indicate just how many have written on it.

Some writers make a distinction between legibility and readability (and even visibility); many use the words interchangeably. These qualities are of course affected by all the features of typography that I have been speaking of, and are complicated by many human and environmental factors such as luminosity (i.e. illumination – the power of the light source, either in the room where the reading is being done, or on the screen from which the text is being read); the length of reading time; the angle of viewing the text; the distance from the text; the reader's blinking rate; the kind of screen being read from; whether the letters are made up of continuous lines, segmented lines (as on a digital watch), or a dot matrix; the amount of eye strain the reader is experiencing; eye movements; the features of the work station; and so on. The inventiveness of researchers in coming up with topics to research is truly bewildering.

I will leave it to the reader to go through the present index to select a pleasant evening's reading on the subject of legibility. But I think it worth mentioning here that a good deal of what has been committed to paper about this subject is repetitious beyond measure and not always germane to any aspect of human endeavour I can conceive of. Rollins's (**198**) ideas on this are worth quoting in full:

There has been a deal of nonsense written about the legibility of type, the proper length of line and the 'ideal' size. I once heard a psychological adept dogmatize on the subject of the proper type for children's books, asserting that ten point type and 88 mm. were the correct size and line. The poor woman did not know that the difference between a ten point Caslon Old Face and a ten point Antique Old

Style with short descenders is like the difference between Ichabod Crane and the Dutch farm wife. And as for 88 mm.! Heaven help the average printer who is confronted with that unit of measurement. The trouble with the attempt to decide upon the most legible or the most readable type face is that there are too many factors involved to be controlled by any system of valuation so far devised. The trained eye of the skilled printer is more to be depended upon than all the investigations so far conducted. The trained printer knows that Caslon, for instance, if printed carefully on dampened paper, is quite different in effect – in readability and legibility – from its appearance on hard, smooth paper, that short descenders plus leading are a contradiction in terms, and that the right length of a line has to be controlled by the size and leading of the type – or vice versa. (pp. 28–9)

Dreyfus, more succinctly, says, 'research into the legibility of type has proved very little of value that printers have not already discovered by experience' (**62**, p. 8).

Most of the studies on legibility were conducted by 'scientists', in laboratories, with 'subjects', some hooked up to electric wires, some in peculiar, box-like cubicles, and all of the subjects knew they were in an unnatural setting and were being observed. The descriptions 'legible' and 'readable' were purely subjective. How is one to measure such things? The criteria for determining these qualities were speed of reading and retention; the theory was that the more legible a text was, the more quickly it could be read and the more it could be retained. Whether these were valid criteria or not remains to be seen. No one reads two texts – no matter how similar they are – in exactly the same way at two different times. It depends on too many human variables, including such things as what is on the reader's mind while she or he is reading, what the temperature in the laboratory is, whether the reader is self-conscious about being in a laboratory setting, and so on. In fact, no report that I read mentioned whether the subjects were fully 'acclimatized' to the laboratory setting and made fully comfortable with the experimental process (if that is possible) by the time the data which were used for the experiments' conclusions were recorded.

I suppose someone had to do these legibility studies. But, as Rollins and Dreyfus and a number of others say, the eye, intuition, knowledge, and good taste of an experienced designer – one completely ignorant of all the legibility studies – will yield an eminently legible, readable page. (Unfortunately, not enough designers have all these attributes. I have seen, and shall present below, a sampling of many abominably designed bibliographies.)

Concerning type and the other typographic elements I have discussed so far, it is ultimately impossible to say anything definitive with respect to 'optimum presentation', 'best use', and so on. The problem is that these issues are extremely complex – with the thousands of typefaces available, the many kinds of texts (even varieties of bibliographical texts) possible, the many kinds of papers and inks available, and the millions of variations in the readers, both in taste and in visual perception. In general, it seems as though the centuries-old tradition of having seriffed roman type, which readers are quite accustomed to, in a medium weight, with a clear, simple, traditional design, in a size between 8 and 12 points and with appropriate leading between lines in a line containing approximately 10 to 12 words, printed in black ink on white or light-cream-coloured paper, will yield the best reading page. The sensitivity and experience of the designer, the flexibility of the publisher, and the care the author has taken in putting the text together in the first place will guide the work to its 'optimum' presentation in the terms we have now examined.

The many individual units of typography that I have discussed thus far can be worked into a larger picture of the typography of the sentence, the paragraph, and the page, to which I will now turn.

When we read prose we expect a particular look to the text. Even from a distance, beyond our range of reading, we can see a justified-left page, with either ragged-right or justified-right margin, lines running parallel to one another across the page, some indication of paragraph changes (either indentation, paragraph spacing, or some other typographic device), and the like.

Earlier in this century, when FUNCTIONALISM was a force in art, its tenets were adapted to typography; Tschichold and others explored the relationship between function and form on the printed page. Typefaces were secondary to the way type was used. Tschichold, in his classic text *Asymmetric Typography*, said, 'We aim for simplicity' (**250**, p. 28), and the simplest, clearest type designs were the sans serif faces. He said, 'Sans serif, although it is no longer new, is so simple and clear that it is by far the best all-purpose type for today and will remain so for a long time to come' (p. 28). The footnote to this statement says, 'This being the author's opinion in 1935' (p. 28; Tschichold later reversed many of the views he expressed in this book).

This movement, along with the experiments on legibility that began in earnest in the 1920s, spurred a great number of typographers to rethink the classical patterns of layout. They looked at new, different, and truly experimental ways of conceiving a page, asking the question, 'What changes can we make to the traditional forms that will improve our speed of reading and comprehension of the text?' A few proposals are worth looking at here since they touch upon the shape of the text; and as we shall see, shape plays an important part in our design of a bibliographic page.

Tschichold, to begin with, challenged the notion that symmetry in the presentation of a text was essential. Though his typography used many of the features of classical page presentation (such as the precise use of leading, indentation, proper type sizes and type mixtures, and even appropriate paper), it allowed for a freer use of space than had been permitted up to then. This 'New Typography' (new when it was created in Germany in the 1920s) was a reaction to conformity to old methods of design that had been adopted for centuries; after centuries, the adopters used it merely without thinking until they produced some of the crassly designed books of the nineteenth century. Lines of text, text blocks, page numbers, and anything else that was to appear on the page could be placed off centre or centred — whichever looked best. Asymmetric and symmetric typography, then, were not in opposition, but worked in harmony to produce pages that had a function in the typography, not just in the text.

The New Typographers did not aim to be radical merely for the sake of radicalness, but because sensitivity to the text made it practical to put certain things into certain places on the page. Form carried meaning. Even if we do not honour or use the New Typography much these days, the important thing is that it showed a strong concentration on what was actually happening on a printed page, rather than a mindless reiteration of old designs.

I do not mean to go off on a tangent about ASYMMETRIC TYPOGRAPHY. It is an appropriate subject here because it helped to spawn a number of typographic experiments, either directly or indirectly in that researchers were willing to challenge traditional typography and try to find a new and better way to get their messages across.

North and Jenkins (**160**) presented the so-called 'SQUARE-SPAN' TYPOGRAPHY and the 'SPACED-UNIT' TYPOGRAPHY as means of improving legibility and reading speed. (See entry **160** in the bibliography for samples of these layouts.) The theory behind these styles is that the eye does not read continuously across a line of type, but takes in clusters of words at a time. Spaced-unit presentation offers a few words at a time, on a single line — just enough for a reader to master at a glance. These units are separated by spaces, and the eye leaps from one unit to the next. North and Jenkins claimed that this was the fastest and best method of typographic arrangement, and they 'proved' this with experiments showing that subjects read faster and understood more of their texts when they read text set in this way.

They also showed their square-span typography. Theoretically, the eye can efficiently perceive not just horizontally, but vertically as well. It can take in two lines at a time. In the square-span setup, two short lines composed each unit of the text. This was followed by a space, and then the next pair of lines. Though they admitted that this method was not as efficient as spaced-unit layout, they claimed it was an eminently practical means of presenting a text.

What they did not consider were the audience's unfamiliarity with these layouts and the increased cost, occasioned by the additional amount of space (i.e. paper), printing in this method would incur. It is difficult to buck the traditions of millennia, traditions that have ingrained patterns of reading that are almost primeval. We automatically look to the top left side of a page when we turn to a new spread (even readers of boustrophedon texts began at the upper left) and work sequentially. These methods – square-span and spaced-unit presentation – have their own logical sequence, but with areas of space on the page; the authors writing about these methods of printing claim that the unfamiliarity with the layout is soon overcome and forgotten by a reader. I believe that no amount of familiarity would make readers forget completely that they are looking at an experimental page. The potential for distraction is constant and ubiquitous.

To complicate matters, Nahinsky (**159**) claims that North and Jenkins were incorrect in their findings. He says, 'The square-span style yielded comprehension spans significantly superior to both the other styles investigated' (p. 39).

To add even more to the complications, Coleman and Hahn (**48**) and Coleman and Kim (**49**) add different styles to these experiments. Along with the square-span and spaced-unit styles, they also tried 'THOUGHT-UNIT' and 'VERTICAL' styles of printing. In the former (called by Carver [**42**] and by Carver and Darby [**43**] 'chunked typography'), we are presented with not merely little phrases, but thought-unit phrases, each phrase carrying some logical, full or partial thought (e.g. prepositional phrases, or whole independent or dependent clauses). The vertical style presents thought units in a vertical arrangement. This necessitates a page with three or four columns. Coleman and Kim (**49**) argue that established reading habits were difficult or impossible to suppress, even though 'vertical, spaced, and square span [styles] were all significantly superior, vertical being the most superior' (p. 266) in terms of speed. The key idea here, it seems to me, is that it is difficult or impossible to suppress old habits. W. S. Brown (**28**), as recently as 1970, was advocating vertical typography (five columns per page, with one or two words per line) to try to increase reading speed. In 1955, Tinker (**239**) had already claimed that 'the vertical reading required fewer fixations, fewer regressions, a longer pause

duration, and more words read per fixation' (p. 447). He cites as a reason for this the 'increased efficiency in perceiving larger groups of words per fixation due to the shape of the area of clear vision' (p. 448). But he concludes that habit will continue to play the major role in the readers' abilities to read more efficiently horizontally, and that 'the efficiency of vertically arranged printing is apt to remain largely a matter of theoretical interest' (p. 449).

These experiments were partly made possible by the new kinds of thinking about the layout of a text block that asymmetric typography permitted. All of this is germane to bibliographies because they are composed of relatively short pieces of information; or, to use the phrase of these New Typographers, bibliographies are composed of many thought units. They can be arranged on a page in the form of a paragraph of prose (a particularly irksome and eminently uncongenial style of presentation of bibliographic data), or they can be presented (as I have indicated above under 'columns' – p. 19) with new data fields on separate lines:

Doctorow, E. L.	Doctorow, E. L.
World's Fair	*Billy Bathgate*
New York	New York
Random House	Random House
1985	1989
Francis, Dick	Francis, Dick
Twice Shy	*The Edge*
New York	New York
G. P. Putnam's Sons	G. P. Putnam's Sons
1982	1989
Paretsky, Sara	Sayers, Dorothy
Blood Shot	*The Five Red Herrings*
New York	New York
Dell	Harper & Row
1988	1959

While this is not my choice of an ideal layout, it would work quite well in two or three columns, perhaps with the lines following the first in each entry indented a space or two, as in the second column. This combines the vertical and the thought-unit typography, with some influence from the square-span style.

There is precedent for this notion of vertical

alignment in bibliographies. Hartley (99) talks of the run-on and the vertically grouped styles of bibliography entries, the latter with new elements on successive lines.

To reiterate an important point: there is no single 'right way' to design a book. The features of book design that I have discussed thus far do not exist in unique manifestations; and where there are many choices, no single choice is always best. Some may be better than others for particular audiences and for certain texts. And the final judgement on the success of one series of choices over another will ultimately be subjective. People's tastes vary – and any given person's taste may vary from one year, or even one hour, to the next. Finally – and I know this from personal experience and years of observing people's reactions – sometimes I will look at two different presentations of the same text and cannot choose between them. My aim here is more descriptive than prescriptive.

Until now we have been considering general elements of typography – mostly pertaining to the physical layout of a page, but with glances at bibliographies throughout. We now turn more directly to bibliographies, and will consider the more 'intellectual' elements of their content and shape.

3
BIBLIOGRAPHIES:
their content and shape

There is a certain puckish pixie – a veritable elf on the bookshelf who dwells in the land of the questing biblio-grapher. He it is who beckons the toiling student onward, from dusty attic to musty cellar in the never-ending search for elusive tomes and unrecorded titles. But always – in-variably it is just after one's opus is irretrievably in print – one discovers a secret cache that our wily sprite had con-cealed. Now he conjures it forth with impish glee, to con-found and bedevil us, and to prove, if proof were needed, that bibliography is never definitive.
(Charles Eberstadt, quoted by Robert B. Harmon, *Elements of Bibliography*; see 97)

Some of the remarks in this chapter may not seem to be directly about the design of bibliographies – but they all are. The design of such reference works depends on a wide range of factors: the types of bibliographies possible, the expertise and personality of the compiler, the subject matter of the list, and many more things.

Before entering into the central material of this chapter, I would like to say something about the compiler.

The compiler

Many sources say that the compiler of a biblio-graphy should have some expertise in the subject of the list. Madan (**149**) says, 'The bibliographer must be a master of the subject which he treats before he can really estimate the place and import-ance of each book which comes before him' (pp. 91–2). Stokes (**227**) says, 'The compiler of a bib-liography needs foremost to be a specialist in that subject field rather than primarily a bibliographer' (p. 128). The more knowledgeable the compiler is, the more accurate, well focused, and meaningful the bibliography will be. Also, the more complete it is likely to be, since an expert in the field will know not only the literature but also the other scholars working in that field. (For my biblio-

graphy on *Medieval English Drama*, I contacted people all over the United States, in Canada, and in Britain whom I knew from their publications and from having met them at medieval studies conferences. Through my contacts I was able to get a table of contents for a forthcoming book, and the complete page proofs for another. One of my contacts made it possible for me to get some very obscure articles published by a small women's college in Japan. Another offered me free access to his card file of scholarship on the field.) Sometimes it is not only *what* you know that counts, but also *whom* you know. Also, a good list could emanate from a strong personality: a serious and thorough bibliographer can be quite aggress-ive at times. One must assert oneself with other scholars, librarians, interlibrary loan personnel, booksellers, and anyone else who might be able to be a guide to sources.

An expert in the field who is not a bibliographer will not necessarily produce a good bibliography. One needs to know the finer and grosser points of bibliography – how and where to look for sources; which reference books are available and where, and what to do with them; what people to 'use'; which libraries to contact; and so on. One must be willing to stand in front of a range of books at a large library and paw through hundreds of dirty old volumes looking at indexes, tables of contents, running heads, titles, chapter headings and sub-headings, and dust-jacket blurbs to find pertinent entries for the bibliography being compiled. And one must be able to say 'Enough!' and quit before the bibliography outgrows and outlives the compiler.

Compiling a bibliography requires tremendous stamina, and only the strong should attempt it. It requires powerful perseverance, an attention to fine detail (a misplaced full stop or an inaccurately transcribed number can lead a reader up a cul-de-sac), and a great resilience in the face of what may seem to be great odds, other people's utter incompetence, and the malice of the gods. One of the items that I needed at the University of Illinois (where I did some of the research on my bibliography of medieval drama) was a journal, which that university had a full run of, even though it was an uncommon serial in the United States. About 75 volumes were on the shelf, but not the one I wanted. After searches, nearly combative encounters with librarians and others, and the virtually fruitless and endless conversations with the interlibrary loan staff (who refused to try to order something for me when their own library had a 'full' run of the damn thing), I convinced the interlibrary loan office to get me the only circulating copy available from another university. In a few weeks the volume arrived: however, the issue itself had been misbound, and lacked the entire article that I needed, containing instead a duplicate signature of an article on something completely unrelated to my subject or my anger. At another time, working on the same book, I found a citation for an article which was in a periodical housed only at Harvard. When I got there, I surveyed the entire run and could not find the article. Someone had made an error in transcription, and I was left in the dark with only my cursing to keep me company.

A compiler must be nearly a perfectionist, because imperfections can only lead others to go astray and will incur their wrath. But I say 'nearly' because no one is perfect; and no bibliography is perfect. The 'nearly' allows us to survive the imperfections of the bibliographical (and human) world around us. Often *we* know what we want

and need for our bibliographies; *we* know where these things are; *we* know how to get them and what to do with them; but we are dependent on librarians, other scholars, on-line catalogues, telephone lines, and other intermediary agents which conspire to thwart our excellent work and threaten to expose it to the invective of unsympathetic critics who have never compiled a bibliography themselves. A good compiler of bibliographies is patient, assertive, punctilious, persevering, long-suffering, strong-willed, and a bit mad. Who, after all, but a madman would undertake one of these things in the first place? (Actually, one answer to that question is that a naive person would. I never knew how innocent I was when I signed that contract to produce the drama bibliography. It'll be a snap, I thought. I never anticipated encountering the avenging agents that I listed above.)

The audience

A good bibliography has a specific and well-defined audience in mind. When the readership is clearly defined, the bibliography should not contain superfluous, inappropriate entries. As a professor of writing for many years, I always stressed to my students that writers must undertake thorough audience analyses to avoid insulting or befuddling their readers. Keeping the audience in mind will help the compiler to select pertinent items, and will also help to focus the content and level of the annotations. In my bibliography on medieval drama I listed a couple of children's books, even though mine was for an adult, scholarly audience. The children's items had titles that might seem appropriate for scholarly enquiry, and I wanted to tell my readers not to bother with them. An annotated bibliography is a guide to what to – and what not to – consult. Including the children's items was to save my readers the time I had to take to find the works in the first place.

Hill (**104**) points out that different audiences will even be familiar with particular typefaces and layouts; students in art and engineering showed different attitudes toward the different typefaces Hill used in experiments on readability. And, as I note elsewhere, since different disciplines have their own styles for the presentation of data in bibliographical entries, analysing the audience will help the compilers determine which styles are most appropriate for their particular readers. Rollins (**199**) adds, 'A decent respect for the uses to which such books are put should govern the printer in determining the shape of his volume' (p. 111). (See also Stokes, **227**.) Trevitt (**248**) goes so far as to observe: 'The reading public seems to be wary of very long books and is said to be positively antipathetic to short ones, and a lot can be done typographically to fit long and short books into moderate extents' (p. 8). In other words, not only in the specific content and its particular arrangement, but also in terms of subtler things like the bulk and size of the volume, the compiler and typographer should design with the reader/buyer in mind.

Types of bibliographies

Until now I have used the word *bibliography* without discriminating between a whole volume devoted to a particular topic and a list of works at the end (or beginning) of a book which supplements and gives sources for the larger topic of this book. In our relatively general discussion of page design and book design, the distinction between volume-length bibliographies and those at the ends of books was immaterial. But it may be useful here to discuss these two different species of the same family.

When a scholar wants to show his audience where his thoughts come from or what they were inspired by (and also, possibly, to escape the charge of plagiarism), she or he may include a bibliography, often at the end of the volume. It may be a complete list of all items consulted for the book, whether these were used in the book or not; or it may list only the ones actually used (in which case some stylebooks recommend the term 'works cited'); it may be a 'comprehensive' (usually a misnomer) bibliography; or it may be what is usually called a 'selected bibliography'. This last term has always amused me: naturally no bibliography is exhaustive, as Eberstadt says; and it cannot be otherwise than that the listing was of works 'selected' by the author (or someone else). What is implied, of course, is that the works listed there have been chosen from a much wider field, and that these are the 'quality' works, the rest being unworthy to be among the select. (Joseph Blumenthal [*The Printed Book in America*, Boston, MA:

Godine, 1977] uses the peculiar term 'Selective Bibliography' [p. 233]. See Appendix I, Example 1.)

Bibliographies in larger books can give works a sense of scholarliness that they do not really deserve. They imply that all these works have been read, understood, and digested by the present author, when, in fact, the items listed there may never have all been seen by the author. It is incumbent upon the compiler of the bibliography to state in the introduction to the volume (or in a separate introduction to the bibliography itself) what the relationship is between the works cited and the volume as a whole.

Where should these bibliographies-in-books appear? Many books have them at the end of each chapter; some have them at the beginning, before the text begins; others have them at the end, before the index. Tradition dictates that they be put at the end of the volume. Having them at the end of each chapter does link pertinent, focused bibliography entries with the subject matter in the chapter. But then the overall picture of the writer's scholarship is lost, and access to each little list is difficult: one must search for each chapter ending.

Entire books are bibliographies. (In fact, this is what Besterman lists; none of the more than 117,000 bibliographies which he documents is a list in a book.) They, too, can be either 'comprehensive' or selected, but most often they are (or strive to be) the former. It looks like better scholarship. It could be embarrassing to present a selected bibliography which lacks serious and important titles; but it would be even more embarrassing to offer up a comprehensive listing which lacks *anything*, least of all the important titles in the field. As I have indicated, Madan (**149**) states it quite clearly: 'The bibliographer must be a master of the subject of which he treats before he can really estimate the place and importance of each book which comes before him' (pp. 91–2).

Now, the phrase 'types of bibliographies' can be interpreted in other ways. There could be author, subject, or title bibliographies. Barzun and Graff (**12**) mention national, topical (i.e. subject), and current bibliographies. But, as Breslauer (**26**) points out, any list of books, even if it is not focused at all, can be considered a bibliography; he mentions dealers' catalogues, book-fair catalogues, and publishers' and printers' lists. A dealer's catalogue may be a completely random sampling of books available in the dealer's stock. I have read thousands of these over the decades, and some defy classification. I have seen mimeographed lists in no order whatsoever; the dealer just listed books as he pulled them from the chaotic shelves or boxes he found them in. If there is any unity at all in such a 'bibliography', it is that these are all books being sold by a single firm.

Colaianne (**47**) points out that an 'author' bibliography may actually be an 'authors' list (e.g., Renaissance sonneteers); a title list can relate to a single title (e.g., a bibliography on *Beowulf*); a genre list can be on one or a number of genres (science fiction; or science fiction, fantasy, futurism, and the occult); there could be a list on a literary or artistic movement (Neoclassicism, Expressionism, Bauhaus); or one on a literary theme (racism, feminism). These are just a few kinds within the humanities. In the sciences there could be a bibliography on any of scores of branches of science, or a list on their research methodologies. Other authors mention regional or trade bibliographies. Stokes (**226**) sums up the types (as he breaks them up into categories) as general, special, particular, personal, and local.

Another way of breaking up the subject is to say that the work is alphabetical or chronological (the two most common arrangements). Other breakdowns (say, by genre or locality) may work in coordination with alphabetical or chronological classification. In fact, there is often a double or even a triple scheme. There could be a list arranged first by cities (New York, Chicago, Los Angeles, Podunk Center), then by century (seventeenth century, eighteenth century, nineteenth century), then by topic (immigration, emigration, population), and, finally, alphabetically by author (or chronologically with respect to the date of the sources themselves and then, within a single year, by author).

Subject matter

There can be a bibliography about anything collected – and that is everything. The subjects are endless. As I have said a number of times, compilers can strive for comprehensiveness, but cannot expect to achieve it except in certain instances. For example, one could do a bibliography on the books of a famous collector (who is deceased); this would entail a listing of all the books known to have been in the possession of that person; or of some author, though unpublished or unknown things could always appear, as Eberstadt says. But this could be a finite list. Also, one could catalogue all the items in one room of a library; this, too, would normally be finite if it were impossible to add to or subtract items from this collection. Or there could be a list of all publications by a given press (but that implies all variants, ephemeral items, and even half-done and discarded projects). Where does one draw the line? The answer is, in the compiler's introduction, which should spell out precisely what the scope of the bibliography is. (See below under Introduction.)

Facsimiles

What information does the reader need in a bibliography? I will cover this in more detail in sections below, but for now I would like to look at the title page, one of the prime sources of information for the bibliographer. Gaskell (**77**) has a section on the transcription of title pages. Admittedly, his focus is for students of historical and textual bibliography, not bibliography compiling and designing, which is the subject of the present study. But the question that this paragraph begins with touches on the transcription of title pages.

For most books, titles are short enough to be given in full. And, in fact, the information that most bibliography compilers need to give is sufficiently short that what appears on the title page can generally be given in full. However, some title pages, especially of seventeenth-, eighteenth-, and nineteenth-century books (and even of some modern volumes), contain lengthy texts.

How much information from the title page compilers give depends on the nature of the bibliographies they are compiling. For scholarly lists aimed at students of the history of the book, at textual critics, or even at book dealers who need to distinguish one copy from another, the more complete the title page transcription is, the better. Gaskell says,

> Bibliographers commonly transcribe a book's title-page in full by the method called quasi-facsimile, and this for two reasons: first

because it normally brings together in their original form all the necessary details of author, title, printer, publisher, and place and date of publication; and secondly because it provides a wealth of arbitrary but characteristic typographical detail which will usually serve to distinguish one setting of a title-page from another. (p. 322)

Gaskell then talks about the drawbacks of this method, which are that details of the typefaces used and other factors such as the appearance of the decorations and the actual placement of any typographic feature are not explicit in quasi-facsimiles. As I have said, the vast majority of bibliographies do not need such breadth of transcription. But since this is a book on bibliography design, and some bibliographies *will* need such inclusiveness, this issue must be dealt with here. Gaskell's discussion is thorough and sensible, and should be consulted by anyone listing such precise and extensive data as full-page title transcriptions. (See Gaskell, pp. 322–8.) But another type of transcription is possible, especially today with inexpensive and readily available technology. Actual facsimiles can be produced which will save time and prevent errors in transcription. The Benjamin Franklin bibliography that I have mentioned offers many reproductions of title pages. But since these add to the book's cost, they should be used only when they are necessary, not just to spruce up the production. Will a reader need to see the actual page layout of the original? Will showing the original present any information that a transcription would not present? Will readers be adequately informed without a facsimile? Compilers must analyse their audiences and know to what use their bibliographies will be put.

Organization

When we speak of the organization of a bibliography, we could mean two things: how all the entries are organized (e.g. alphabetically, chronologically) or how each entry is laid out (what comes first, second, third, and later in each entry). First we shall consider the overall layout in the work.

Organizing the whole. Bibliographies have traditionally been organized in a few fairly logical ways. The most popular is probably alphabeti-

cally. Barzun and Graff (**11**) call all bibliographies 'lists', and they say that 'All but a few lists follow the alphabetical order' (p. 75). I have already mentioned other methods of organizing the entries. One of my recommendations is that *the organization of a bibliography should be recognizable from a perusal of a single two-page spread*. This is not always possible, since some annotations will be fairly long and may take more than a page or two. The point I am making here is that the organization should be immediately visible to a reader on a scan of some representative pages. Pollard (**176**) says:

> Whatever arrangement be adopted it must be easily Intelligible [*sic*] to those for whose use the bibliography is intended. An arrangement which no one is likely to understand, save its author, stands self-condemned. The idea to be aimed at is a system which explains itself. (p. 32)

If the work is broken into several categories, then a running head should give the name of the category and also possibly the number (or letter and number) of the category. Thus, readers will know immediately which subhead is represented by the entries on the page, and maybe also where in that subcategory they are.

The simplest case, of course, is with a bibliography which is one large alphabetical sequence (or one chronological sequence). Readers can see exactly where in that sequence they are at any moment. (Such an arrangement does not require even running heads.) Bibliographies which cover several topics under the main one of the volume should delineate each clearly; and doing so in some way on each page makes the work much more usable and convenient than would not doing so.

I have seen some bibliographies so convoluted and complex, so confusing on any given page, that they are impenetrable. Only a careful reading of the introduction unravels all (or some) of the mysteries. But some bibliographies will remain barriers to comfortable scholarship and monuments to frustration because their organization seems to have been modelled after Chaos or a cattle stampede. The stupendous project of listing all the Tauchnitz editions and their variants, undertaken by William B. Todd and Ann Bowden, is a case in point. It is truly a magnificent gathering of information, but its pages are so formidable that it seems as if the reader would have to work as many years as the compilers did just to understand what is going on. (See my comments on this work in Appendix I, Examples 23a–e.)

In a word: make the organization clear, simple, and understandable at a glance. Your readers will love you for it.

Organizing each entry. As I have said, many disciplines have their own bibliographical style sheets. Some disciplines are dogmatic; some recognize that there are other methods than their own and are more flexible. Bibliographers must first know who the audience is; that is, what discipline is the work most likely aimed at? Then they must study the bibliography of the field, both the style sheets (of which there are likely to be some) and the lists in works published in the field. It does not make sense to choose a style which is eminently logical and understandable if the audience is likely to be unfamiliar (and hence possibly uncomfortable) with it, when a usable and familiar style is readily available.

Gibaldi and Achtert's *MLA Handbook* lists the style manuals for Biology, Chemistry, Geology, Linguistics, Mathematics, Medicine, Physics, Psychology, and the United States Government Printing Office, though there are many others, some drawing from one or more of these sources, some idiosyncratic. In fact, many publishers and periodicals have their own style manuals which they ask authors to follow. It is economical for them to have their typesetters familiar with only one style rather than taking the time to learn others.

The following discussion is complicated by the many possible ways scholars have of citing sources in the text. The old method of using footnotes for every in-text use of a source is still used by some journals. Though it takes space, and though it results in some overlap with the work's bibliography, it is none the less still being used. About a decade ago the Modern Language Association (MLA) devised a new and very practical solution to the overlap in data. Rather than give full citations in the first footnote reference for a source and abbreviated notes for subsequent citations of that source, the MLA prescribed brief parenthetical citations that succinctly identify the work and give the page number; the full citation is located in the section called 'Works Cited'. It looks like this:

> Medieval England, for example, produced many sermons, poems, and plays in her honor (Garth 12–14). In seventeenth-century lyric poetry, the Magdalene was, according to Mario Praz, 'the supreme star' in the constellation of saints . . . (205). (Gibaldi and Achtert, 78, p. 204)

In the first sentence in this example, the source of the information is not mentioned in the sentence itself, so it is given in abbreviated form in the parentheses. In the second sentence, the author is mentioned, and therefore the only reference needed is the page number. The full citations will be found in 'Works Cited' or the bibliography of the essay or book. (My own method here is complicated because I have keyed my citations to items in a numbered bibliography. When I have a number it refers to the item in the works cited; therefore, to distinguish these numbers from page numbers, I have used *p.* or *pp.*) However, if full citations are given in notes or by some other method, then the bibliography becomes a pleonastic redundancy. For example:

> As Jonathan MacIntosh notes, the apple has been around since Adam and Eve (*Pomology and Its Discontents*, Appleton, WI: Winesap and Mott Printers, 1977: 22).

While this method takes up a good deal of space in the text, it does prevent the setting of footnotes and a full bibliography. Yet another method I have seen is the use of bracketed numbers in the text, the numbers referring to numbered items in the bibliography:

> James Goodbar was a crackerjack confectioner in Ohio before the war [5].

The bracketed number refers the reader to the fifth item in the bibliography.

In other words, various methods of in-text citation and footnoting may affect the comprehensiveness of the entries in the bibliography.

Before turning directly to standard bibliography styles, I would like to dispense with one type of arrangement right now: the classified. Such a styling is like the Dewey Decimal System or the Library of Congress Classification – it uses an artificial group of codes (letters or numbers or both, or perhaps punctuation or some symbols) as the basis of arrangement. Since the codes *are* artificial, they are not logical. Therefore, readers cannot look things up in a logical way; they must know the codes. Or there must be a thorough index, a thesaurus, or a concordance. While this is a perfectly usable method of arranging entries in a bibliography, it unnecessarily burdens the reader, especially when there are more usable methods of arrangement available. Such a method is useful more for large collections of books than for a single, focused bibliography.

Since we are discussing individual entries, not the entire list, we must look at a few possible types and consider what they *must* contain as well as what else they *might* contain.

If the work is an author bibliography, then there will naturally be no alphabetical listing by author since every work in the list will be by the same person. The author's writings may, however, be listed either chronologically or alphabetically, or perhaps by genre (and then alphabetically or chronologically). If the author bibliography also contains a section of criticism, that part may be arranged alphabetically or chronologically. If the aim of the compiler is to show the history of the criticism, a chronological arrangement is logical.

For other bibliographies, any method will work, but the alphabetical is the most popular because it is familiar, easy to arrange, and especially easy to locate authors' works in. If the alphabetical style is used, a typical entry will begin with the last name of the author (or the first key word in a title if there is no author).

Autry, Gene. *We're No Angels.* Los Angeles: Diamond Press, 1990.

The Baseball Hall of Fame Book of Losers. Cooperstown: Hall of Infamy Press, 1985.

Howard, Frank. *Uh, What Was the Question, Please?: My Best Post-Game Interviews.* Hollywood: Home Run Publishers, 1983.

These examples are typical of entries in the humanities. The last name comes first, followed by a comma, then the first name, a full stop, an italicized title, a full stop, and the publication data, which offer the city followed by a colon, the publisher, a comma, and the date (as in the examples above). There are different means of alphabetizing names (especially problematical are *Mc, Mac, O', van, Van, vander, Vander,* and other patronymic prefixes, along with hyphenated names; Stokes [227] mentions the 'letter-by-letter' and the 'all-through' methods). The compiler should describe her or his alphabetization scheme at the beginning of the text.

Some style manuals require only initials for all names beyond the last name:

Smith, R. F.

I have seen other methods, for example giving first name first. The belief is that an alphabetical arrangement is all that is needed, and that the readers will be able to find the names they need by looking into each line. The method of using last name first was developed to aid the user, since the filing element will be out on the left-hand side of the line in the easiest spot to locate in the line. Using first name first defeats this, and makes the search more complicated for the reader.

The practical last-name-first method has been adopted by most modern publishers. But one of the amusing by-products of this method is that many publishers use last name first in footnotes, where it makes no sense. The filing element that the reader is searching for is the note number, not the last name of a writer. A concomitant silliness is the use of last name first for the *second* name in an entry:

Flaggs, Seymour, and Wright, Sybil.

Since the researcher is seeking the *F* in Flaggs, there is no reason at all to reverse the other names.

Names are key elements in the scholar's search, and they should stand out in some way. As I will explain later (under typographic coding), there are different ways of styling names to make them more visible. But for now, *The Chicago Manual of Style* (44) will have the last word on alphabetical arrangement: 'The bibliography arranged in a single alphabetical list is the most common and usually the best form for a work with, or without, notes to the text' (p. 423).

One last point about names: if a name is repeated in the bibliography (i.e., if there are two or more works by the same author), it is quite useful to designate second and subsequent appearances of the names with a long dash (in type, a 3-em rule). A manual I once read advocated a dash (made up of hyphens) the same length as the author's name. Just as effective is the use of three (or four) hyphens (see Appendix I, Example 19). The only problem with this method is that if there are many items by one person, that person's name appears once, followed by page after page of entries beginning with dashes. If readers want to find out whom the dashes represent, they may have to turn back several pages. To prevent this, the name could be repeated as the first entry on every two-page spread. This too could lead to confusion, for a reader might think that since the name was spelled out, it was that of a new author. This would probably take less time to figure out than the other method of pages and pages of dashes. (More under typographic coding.)

The next essential element in a bibliographical entry is the title of the work. And it is generally present as the second element. It must be distinguished as a title by some typographic means. The old typing practice was to underline titles of books (and all words which were to be italicized), and to put article titles into quotation marks. Underlining was thus a substitute for italics, which typewriters formerly could not produce. The standard practice these days is to italicize titles. Some bibliographies use boldface type, and some, produced by printers with more fonts available, put the titles into large and small caps. (More under typographic coding, below.) Some even use quotation marks for all titles, whether they are those of books or of articles. My own preference is italics for book and journal titles, and quotation marks for articles or chapters in books. These are the most common and recognizable styles, and are also easiest to produce.

Another issue concerning titles is how much of them to give. Some publishers, especially in the natural and social sciences, are content with abbreviated titles. My own pack-rat instinct is to ask for the complete title (or, if it is one of those

nineteenth-century, page-length titles, I would like to see a good portion of it). But I know this is the bias of having been indoctrinated in the humanities. Short titles are sufficient, as long as they are long enough to distinguish them from all other titles by the same author(s). A good case in point is the series of articles by Paterson and Tinker (169–73), which all begin with the same eight words. There is no effective way to abbreviate these titles and to guarantee that the readers will understand the meaning of the abbreviations.

Also essential are the publication data of the work, to help the researcher get to the original. There is a good deal of variation in this data field. Some publishers offer the city and date; some give the publisher as well. Some give publisher, city, date. Some give city, publisher, date. Perhaps the saving of space and compositor time is an economic factor; but my own feeling is that the more information the readers have, the more likely they will be to find the item in question. Many times I have wished an author had given the publisher's name. Publishers' names can be given in full (W. W. Norton and Company) or can be given in short form (Norton). Either way is acceptable, as long as the short form does not leave the reader in doubt. (For example, the 1989–90 volume of *Books in Print* [*BIP*] lists no fewer than eight publishers named Paradigm, one each from Maryland, Colorado, Idaho, Massachusetts, Rhode Island, and Vermont, and two from California. *BIP* even says at the Rhode Island entry: 'Do not confuse with other companies with same name in Greenbrae, CA, Sarasota, FL, Burlington, VT' [when there is no Sarasota company listed], and it says at the entry for the Vermont Paradigm, 'Do not confuse with other companies with the same name in Greenbrae, CA & Osprey, FL' [when there is no Osprey company listed]. It is best to stick to full names when necessary; the compiler should check *BIP* for each company named.) I prefer the MLA style:

New York: Norton, 1991.

to the shorter versions:

NY: 1991.

But compilers should probably follow the styling

in their own disciplines to produce a work least distracting to their readers.

Bibliographies should contain such information as the edition and the number of volumes, and may also give the series title if there is one, the publisher's address, the pagination, and even the size of the book, the number of copies printed (if this is available), the prices or other data on the availability of the works (if they are still in print), and a list of locations of copies. This last feature can be most useful for scholars working in an area replete with antiquarian, rare, or out-of-print books. I recognize that some of this information might be superfluous to many bibliographies, and some of it might also be difficult to come by. The compiler experienced in the field should have a sense of how much information is in order. I do not say this casually. When I was putting together my bibliography on medieval English drama, I understood that the book would be used by beginners and experts alike. For this reason I offered not only the bibliography itself, but also lists of the plays in each of the play cycles. Even experts might find it useful to have those lists at hand. For another bibliography that I am compiling – which focuses on limited-edition, fine-press books – my readers will want information about paper, types, numbers of copies printed, binding information, and even variations within an imprint. Readers of this bibliography, mostly collectors or the dealers who sell to them, will want to know if an item was produced in both a signed and an unsigned version, or if some of the copies have coloured illustrations while others were in black and white; they will also want to know if there is a dust jacket, and maybe even the colour of the inks. The audience of the work will help to determine what is included in each entry.

Punctuation

I have already discussed the punctuation one might use in bibliographic entries. But a few comments are in order here. From the perspective of overall content, the central part of the entry should contain three distinct fields of information: author, title, publication data. These may be presented as the equivalent of three distinct sentences; in which case, each should conclude with a full stop. The parts of the entry which follow – the

annotations and perhaps other comments, lists of criticism, and anything else the compiler includes – may be punctuated in ways appropriate for whatever they are. Annotations will probably be in the form of sentences (either whole or fragmentary). Notes will be in sentences. A list of criticism will be in the form of a smaller bibliography. (See the sample from my *Medieval English Drama* bibliography: Figure 3, on page 42.)

The first listed name is generally given in reverse order (i.e., last name first). Therefore the last name should be separated from the rest of the name in some way. I have seen 'Johnson [F.P.]', which, I suppose, is clear enough; but the use of brackets is unnecessary and potentially confusing. The simpler 'Johnson, F.P.' is clear and unambiguous. Note that there is no space between the initials; the full stop is sufficient to distinguish the *F* from the *P*.

As for titles, the main title is usually separated from the subtitle by a colon, followed by a single space. Some titles, however, have their own distinct punctuation, which should be followed.

For publication data, one common sequence is the city, a colon, the publisher, a comma, and then the date, followed by a full stop. But many style manuals do not give the publisher, and some use commas or parentheses rather than a colon; the variations are great in this field. But I do not mean to prescribe when there are so many acceptable variants. The only thing I advocate is that the compiler choose a system of punctuation which is appropriate for the field of study of the bibliography, and apply it consistently.

Annotations

Bibliographies may or may not be annotated. The unannotated kind can be a temptation to compilers, for all they have to do is list the citations they find in other sources. This leads to error – not only because straight transcription is likely to produce errors, but also because sources are not infallible. Many times I have seen errors in citations, and then I have seen the identical errors in the sources of the compiler. It is clear that someone (and more than one person) did not check sources. (I could write a book on transcription and proofreading. One exercise I gave my students was to copy verbatim a five- or eight-line passage from a bibliography. Not one student in the class did it perfectly.)

My message here is that bibliographers should check their sources at first hand. This can be an irksome exercise, and one which will make librarians curse you and the interlibrary loan department hate you forever. Unannotated bibliographies should be just as rigorously researched as annotated ones.

Annotated lists normally require first-hand work with sources. (On a rare occasion one might find an already annotated bibliography; but can we rely on the insights and experience of someone else?) I worked with a number of annotated bibliographies and found that while scholar A said one thing about a work, scholar B said something completely different about the same work; there was often practically no overlap. I tried to be circumspect in my own annotation of the same item, but the 'comprehensiveness' of a précis is determined by how much information the original has, how much space one has for the summary, and what slant the bibliographer takes. In the annotations in the present volume, for instance, for many of the entries I have narrowed the focus to anything pertinent to bibliographies, and I have had to ignore many other data the books and articles contained. The introduction to the bibliography should clearly state what the focus of the work is in order that readers will know how 'comprehensive' the annotations are intended to be.

One of the more thorough treatments of annotation is Colaianne's essay, 'The Aims and Methods of Annotated Bibliography' (47). This essay counsels us not to express value judgements in annotations; the aim of the précis is an unbiased recounting of *what is there*, not how good or bad it is. Another thing to watch for is the tendency in annotation to look for the thesis of an article in the opening paragraphs and the conclusion in the closing paragraph. I have read too many ill-constructed articles to trust that method. Often the body of an article has little to do with its introduction and conclusion. And, in fact, some conclusions seem to have been written by someone who has not even read the article, let alone written it. My own device for criticism without criticizing is to quote extensively, if necessary, from particu-larly impenetrable and obtuse essays; this lets the author hoist himself.

Annotations should be as long as the publisher will allow (since publishing is, after all, a profit-making activity), and as short as you can get away with without omitting something important. My own prejudice is to give more rather than less. Madan (**149**) warns against both *'inaccuracy and scantiness of information'* (p. 93) and *'superfluity of information'* (p. 94; his italics). Sometimes reaching a fine balance is difficult.

The annotations can be full or partial sentences (e.g., 'Looks at a wide variety of subjects pertaining to bibliographies'); but once one form is adopted it should usually be continued throughout the annotations (though it is possible to use mostly partial sentences with occasional full statements included, as I have done). The annotations should not repeat anything that is explicit in the title (e.g., Title: 'Ocular Imagery in *Oedipus Rex*'; Annotation: 'Looks at eyes in the play.').

A last comment about annotations concerns the so-called 'disclaimer' that they should probably have — as one bibliographer put it:

> The annotations do not purport to be comprehensive summaries of the items' scholarship. In some instances, especially for some monographs, I have had to reduce the annotation to little more than a slightly expanded table of contents. No scholar should rely solely on a bibliography for her or his own work, and the annotations are intended to lead readers to appropriate sources, not to be substitutes for these sources. Hence the rather sketchy treatment of some books, which a serious scholar will read in full.*

Introductions

I cannot stress enough the importance of introductions to bibliographies. The compiler owes the reader some vital information. For example, an introduction should spell out the scope of the work: what is included and what has been excluded. Explaining the exclusions may obviate a good deal of criticism. This, the first of his five

* Sidney E. Berger, *Medieval English Drama: An Annotated Bibliography of Recent Criticism* (New York and London: Garland, 1990), p. 119.

requirements for a bibliography's introduction, Patrick Wilson calls the domain. He (**271**) says also that the introduction should explain the principles of selection, comment on the bibliographical units that will be listed and described ('The size of the listable unit has a profound effect on the value of a [bibliography]' [p. 61]), discuss the information fields ('We must . . . know what information we can expect to find about an item, [and] what conclusions we can draw from the absence of a piece of information' [pp. 61–2]), and explain the organization of the bibliography.

This last requirement complements my own dictum above that the organization of the bibliography should be apparent from a perusal of a typical two-page spread. Even if this is the case (and, sadly, quite often it is not), the author owes her or his readers a clear explanation of how the bibliography is organized. Such an explanation will allow 'immediate and direct identification of items that fit some description without the necessity of scanning all the descriptions of the items listed' (Wilson, **271**, p. 62). The National Library of Canada has issued an excellent little pamphlet, *Guidelines for the Compilation of a Bibliography* (**92**), which explains what the introduction should contain. The front matter should define the subject, state the purpose, identify the audience, specify the scope, explain the procedures followed in the compilation of entries, cite sources consulted (and libraries used), identify the 'bibliographic form or style manual used, with sample citations' (p. 11), explain the organization, give a key to abbreviations used, and mention any additional features. Once the readers have finished the introduction, they should be able to make their way comfortably and knowledgeably through the bibliography with only minimal consultation of the front matter – perhaps to look up a symbol or an abbreviation.

Abbreviations and symbols

Some writers assert that every entry should contain full documentation, fully spelled out. However, abbreviations of two types may be used. The first are what are called editorial abbreviations, including the common ones we see often, such as *etc.*, *p.* or *pp.* ('page[s]'), *l.* or *ll.* ('line[s]'), *e.g.*, *ed.* ('editor' or 'edited'), *rev. ed.* ('revised edition'), *c.* or *ca.* (*circa*, 'about'), *comp.* ('compiled' or 'com-

piler'), *vol.*, *n.p.* ('no place' or 'no publisher'), and so on. The second type are abbreviations designed for the specific text, such as shortened forms of journal titles. Hill and Cochran (**105**) say that no abbreviations should be used: 'Abbreviations save some space but they sacrifice much time spent in checking and translating' (p. 102). Madan (**149**) warns against the overuse of symbols and abbreviations, which inhibit the smooth use of bibliographies. Reynolds (**186**) takes a slightly more flexible and imprecise stand when she asserts that the volume should not contain unnecessary abbreviations, and Tufte (**152**) is equally evasive when he says that abbreviations should be avoided where possible. Tabachnick (**230**) says only that abbreviations should be adequately and conveniently explained. Borko and Bernier (**23**) say that only those abbreviations which are immediately recognizable to a reader should be used. But if abbreviations are well designed and not arbitrary, and if they are used often enough, readers will become familiar with common ones, though they will have to turn to a chart for the less common ones.

In the humanities, shortened versions of some journals are immediately recognizable to scholars in the appropriate field: *PMLA*, *PQ*, *MLQ*, *MLN*, *PBSA*, *JEGP*, *N&Q* (respectively, *Publications of the Modern Language Association*, *Philological Quarterly*, *Modern Language Quarterly*, *Modern Language Notes*, *Papers of the Bibliographical Society of America*, *Journal of English and Germanic Philology*, *Notes & Queries*). Some abbreviations can be slightly longer and instantly recognizable: e.g., *EngStud* (*English Studies*), *SewRev* (*Sewanee Review*), *DramRev* (*Drama Review*). For journals with single-name titles, it may be best to spell out the entire title: e.g., *Gamut*, *History*, *Mosaic*, *Spectator*. There are common titles in other fields, such as *JAMA* (*Journal of the American Medical Association*), *HLR* (*Harvard Law Review*), *JAP* (*Journal of Applied Psychology*), and others. The compiler of the bibliography should be familiar with the periodicals in the field, and should know which her or his readers will recognize from common abbreviations.

Abbreviations save time, space, and money for the publisher. They may slow down a reader occasionally, but even readers do not always want to have to read through the full titles of periodicals.

Two leap to mind for me: frequently cited serials in my drama bibliography were *REEDN* (*Records of Early English Drama Newsletter*) and *EDAMN* (*Early Drama, Art, and Music Newsletter*). And why always spell out *Proceedings of the International Beast Epic Colloquium*? or *Journal of the Australasian Universities Language & Literature Association*? *PIBEC* and *AULLA* are much more compact and less irritating.

Symbols are another matter, for, while abbreviations often contain some hint of their meaning, symbols are arbitrary substitutions. The symbols can be combinations of letters and numbers, or they can be asterisks (*), daggers (†) or double daggers (‡), crosshatches (#), section marks (§), or other exotic shapes. Todd and Bowden use a bewildering array of letters and symbols: H:6, Td, –, C3, Hr:, Ta, s, @, o, w, x, y, z, <, and several others (see the sample pages from the Tauchnitz bibliography in Appendix I). Beyond these there are also abbreviations for libraries and archives and a separate list for 'References' (i.e. bibliographic sources). Mastering this bibliography is a herculean task. One of its pages looks like a text in higher mathematics or advanced logic.

My own advice is, try to avoid symbols or, at worst, keep them to a bare minimum; if possible, run a key at the bottom of the page, as some dictionaries do for pronunciation guides (see Appendix I, Example 23). Try to give abbreviations an intellectual coding that enables the reader to guess their meaning without consulting a chart. If there are only a few, a foldout chart somewhere in the book will allow constant access to a key to the abbreviations (though that could add significantly to the price of the book). The compiler's and designer's aim should always be the ease of use and immediacy of accessibility of the reader.

Numbering of entries

Many bibliographies contain no numbers for the entries. This, I think, is often a mistake, especially for long bibliographies. For quick reference, numbers are very useful. (Lettering the entries for bibliographies that contain more than 26 entries is a form of madness.) Numbers for entries serve many functions. To begin with, they shorten the reader's search if an index cites entries by number rather than by page number. Also, they can be used in scholarly references to the bibliography, avoiding repetition of other data from the entries. Standard bibliographies in many fields are cited by compiler and entry number only. For example, for early American imprints, Charles Evans's *American Bibliography* is indispensable; items in it are usually cited as follows: Evans, 17580 (or sometimes even E 17580). Evans's work stops in 1800; the follow-up volumes by Ralph Shaw, Richard Shoemaker, and others are often cited as *AI* (i.e. *American Imprints*), followed by the appropriate entry number. Many book dealers similarly cite their sources for the scholarship they exhibit in their catalogues. These few examples could be multiplied a thousandfold. I need say no more to justify the numbering of entries.

The one additional thing to add is that the numbering system should be as simple as possible. Even in a bibliography divided into many sections for the many subheadings that there are for the subject of the work, there is usually no need to begin a new numbering system. However, it might be useful to code the numbers to show the readers where they are in the bibliography. For example, for a list on a literary subject, it might be useful to have the letter *T* to indicate texts, *A* or *Co* to show anthologies or collections which contain the texts, and *Cr* to indicate criticism of the texts. Thus, one section will have entries numbered 'T1, T2, T3', and so on; the next section might have 'A93, A94, A95'; and the last section would have 'Cr203, Cr 204'. But with accurate headlines, this complication in the numbering system is unnecessary. Another bit of advice is, avoid complicated decimal systems. I have seen such things as 'II.5,iii.ddd.' in some bibliographies. In Wilfred J. Ritz's bibliography on *American Judicial Proceedings* (see his appendix), there are numbers such as '5.02(34) (b)' (p. 208). This is a forbidding system. I reiterate: the simplest system is the best. (More about numbering under the heading Spatial Coding.)

Index

A number of times throughout this discussion I have mentioned indexes. The entries in a bibliography must be arranged in some order – an arrangement which is itself intended to aid the reader in finding entries. An alphabetical arrangement allows the reader to thumb through easily to find an author. An arrangement by subject matter or date also lets the reader progress logically and sequentially through the pages to a particular point. But the fact that there are at least these three arrangements (in reality there are many more) shows that the thumbing-through will yield something sought for only one of the arrangements. (Let me eliminate the possibility that the data could be presented in full in two or three sequences; this is wasteful of paper and money, and few publishers would be willing to pay for it.)

Since the information in the bibliography is accessible through only one arrangement of entries, access that would be possible through other arrangements should be made available by some other means. The traditional and logical means is an index. Whole books have been written about indexing, and I shall not expatiate here on the types of indexes, the use of natural or inverted order of their entries, how thorough or abbreviated they should be, whether they should cite item or page numbers, and so on. That is truly the subject of a large volume. But a few observations about indexes in bibliographies may be useful.

Generally, the compiler knows the topic as well as anyone involved with the production of the book. Though there are professional indexers, probably the compiler of the bibliography is the best person to compile the index.

The compiler of the index should know what kinds of information his or her readers would look for. Hence, the most effective arrangement, whether by author, date, subject, etc., will yield the greatest amount of information to the reader. The compiler should also know what the readers would look for in each of the different searches based on the different arrangements. Whatever is desirable to be located (in arrangements other than the one chosen for the bibliography) should be made available in an index.

The index should contain as many cross-references as are necessary to guide the reader to the proper heading.

Uniformity in entry

Though one would think that this need not be said, there should be uniformity in the layout of each entry, both physically and intellectually. I have seen some bibliographies that seem to have been put together by different people at different times, resulting in a lack of uniformity in the placement and order of things on the page. All entries must be constructed alike. (One possible exception occurs when an entry in an annotated bibliography, for whatever reason, is accompanied by no note.) The reader will become accustomed to the list's style and will automatically look in identical places in each entry for particular pieces of information. Any variation in styling will be jarring and will slow down the reader.

Coding

This is the term for some of the more complex elements in bibliographic design. As Spencer, Reynolds, and Coe (**218–20, 222–3**) explain, bibliographies are made up of a group of logical units. 'In materials which have a clearly defined logical structure, such as bibliographies, it is especially important that the elements within each logical unit should be clearly distinguishable from one another' (**218**, p. 2). They point out what typographers and book designers have known for a long time: that there are ways to highlight particular parts of a page – particular elements in entries – to make them stand out and easy to spot. The two ways of achieving this distinction on the page are typographic and spatial.

Typographic coding means treating the type in particular ways to make things appear more prominent or distinct on the page. As I have mentioned, with an ordinary typewriter there are few options. Some parts of bibliographic entries can be typed in full caps or underlined. Some modern electronic typewriters can do boldface types, and, with removable print balls or wheels, can even do italics, and these typewriters may have fonts containing special characters.

Generally, with the typewriter, the typographic options are so few that there is not much one can do except use full caps for names and underlining for titles. But the computer opens up new typographic possibilities. My own modest PC can do regular type, SMALL CAPS, FULL CAPS, **boldface**, and all four of these in *italics*. Small caps, italic, boldface is ugly, but it is a possibility. And, in fact, I can do all of these underlined or even with a double underline. The combinations and permutations are many.

Were the typographic possibilities on the typewriter sufficient? and what, typographically speaking, have we gained with the computer? Typewriters were an intermediate stage between the composition and the printing. And the printing was done with types, which offered whatever variations were necessary. When we had nothing but typewriters, we managed. They were sufficient; but the added options offered by computers allow more flexibility and improvement. As I will discuss later, computers have made authors into typesetters and designers.

Assuming, however, that we have the full range of typographical variants of a well-stocked printing house available to us, what can we do typographically to maximize the readability and accessibility of the bibliography? My own experience suggests that very few typographic codes are needed to produce an eminently usable work. Other than regular upper- and lower-case types, all we really need is italics. On occasion, small caps might improve the appearance of the page, but I believe they are not necessary. If we see the main bibliographic entry as being composed of three content areas or fields (author, title, publication data), then having the name in regular type, the title in italics (or in quotation marks for journal titles), and the publication data in regular type will suffice. The words in italics or in quotation marks are perfectly distinguishable from the other parts of the entry. At a glance one can see where the author field ends, where the title field begins and ends, and where the publication data field begins. And the publication data field will have numbers to distinguish it further from the title.

Underlining should probably not be used, since more elegant, sophisticated, and 'traditional' methods of coding are available. Underlining was used originally to replace italics, which was not available on a typewriter. Titles in many bibliographies are printed in boldface roman type; but this is more an affectation than a necessity. Italics or quotation marks are all one needs for titles.

One frequent typographic feature usually used for authors' names is full capital letters or, sometimes, a combination of caps and small caps. (See the McCorison Vermont bibliography in Appendix I, Example 10.) There is really no need for these if the spatial coding is sufficient (see next section). My primary complaint is that the use of full caps makes it impossible to distinguish between *MacDonald* and *Macdonald*, *van Dyke* and *Van Dyke*, and similar names. To clarify, one may have to break up the full-caps pattern with the use of small caps or lower-case letters.

When Spencer, Reynolds, and Coe did their experiments on typographic coding in the early 1970s, they were more concerned about typewritten texts than about typeset ones. The ten examples they give of variants in spatial and typographic coding could be produced on a typewriter (see Appendix I, Example 3). With the exception of System 4, which uses boldface type (which most typewriters in 1974 could produce with only marginal success with overtyping), all the entries were typewriter produced. Linked with spatial coding, the two entries that scored highest in legibility experiments were Systems 7 and 9 – those which used upper- and lower-case letters (see entry **223**). They say, 'Capitals were not especially helpful' (p. 141). My own feeling is that the distinguishing features of italic and roman type (or the use of quotation marks) are all the designer needs to help readers identify the three content units in bibliographical entries. The more '*TYPOGRAPHY*' there is on the page, the more it calls attention to itself and distracts the reader from the text (this sentence is a case in point).

Spatial coding

In addition to using typographic elements to distinguish fields in bibliography entries, one may also manipulate the printed area – the space – on the page. In normal typography for prose, new paragraphs are generally marked in one of two ways: either an indentation of the first line, or a line break between paragraphs. These are both examples of spatial coding. In the first, a blank space is created at the left margin where the indentation is, indicating the new paragraph. In the second, the space is the length of the line. Both inform the reader that a new paragraph is beginning.

Many designers recognize the indentation as a relatively recent and artificial means of distinguishing paragraphs. Medieval scribes barely recognized the notion of 'paragraph', and if a significant change in content were to be signalled in a text, there were 'typographic' (i.e. scribal) ways of showing it, usually with some symbol like the paragraph sign. When printing came in, indenting new paragraphs developed partially as a means of breaking up the monotony of the printed page. In the earliest printed books, however, there was usually no paragraphing as we know it, but rather something akin to the scribal practice of marking new sections of thought in a typographic way. Sometimes something like the paragraph sign was used; sometimes (as in manuscripts) space was left for a rubricator to draw in a majuscule marking the beginning of the new section (not all these spaces were filled in – many were never got to); eventually this gave way to the actual printing of majuscules. Only later was indentation used. Since the indentation which marked a new paragraph was designed to indicate a new section of thought, it was never necessary to indent the first paragraph. of a text or of a section which was itself marked off by some other means. Many typographers do not know this, and use a superfluous indentation at the beginning of a text or of a portion of a text already marked off as a new section.

There are other kinds of spatial coding besides indenting and interlinear spacing, especially for bibliographical entries. For instance, each new content field can begin on a new line, as in the example I gave above. Lines can be 'outdented' (to use the particularly irritating neologism of an American printer/designer); that is, the first line of an entry can extend 1 em or 1 en into the left margin. What this really is, however, is what is known as the 'hanging indent' – just a variant form of indentation – in which the first line of an entry is flush left, and all other lines are indented some uniform measure. My own bibliography uses this and I believe it is quite effective for my purposes (see Figure 3). For my audience, which would rely heavily on my index for subject access to the entries, it was essential that I make the entry numbers prominent. I also wanted the alphabetical sequence of names to stand out. So I had a hanging indent of ten spaces, which guaranteed that the numbers and names would stand apart from the rest of the bibliographical data and the annotations. I also used a space between entries and a space between the bibliographical data and

the annotation. Each part of each full entry, therefore, is clearly distinguishable. My list also included references to reviews of books, which were presented as a third content area of the full bibliographical entry (the first being the main part of the entry, and the second the annotation). The reviews which ran over a single line needed yet another hanging indent to help distinguish them from one another.

Some bibliographies which are not constrained for space (i.e. those which the publishers are willing to spend some money on) have generous margins, plenty of space between entries and parts of entries, and even facsimiles of title pages. The Benjamin Franklin bibliography (which I mentioned under the heading of grids, above) tries to offer a facsimile for most entries. And David Farrell's bibliography *The Stinehour Press* uses space generously (see Appendix I, Example 11).

Spatial coding can be used, therefore, to distinguish one entry from another, or parts of entries from each other. And combining the possible variations in spatial and typographic coding can eliminate the need for such expensive or unnecessary complexities as the use of full caps, small caps, boldface type, or any one of a number of printers' ornaments which are sometimes used as visual cues.

Spencer, Reynolds, and Coe published in a few periodicals the results of their experiment on the combination of spatial and typographic coding. Their results indicate a number of things. For example, for alphabetical listings, spatial coding is more effective than typographic when someone scans for names, but typographic coding surpasses spatial coding for second elements in the alphabetically arranged entries. They say, 'The design must not only reflect the logical structure of information, it must also facilitate its retrieval' (**219**, p. 19). They add,

> Retrieval from an index is a process of using what is known to find what is unknown; usually the alphabetically ordered first elements of the entries are used to gain access to other information within the entries, but in some situations access via some element other than the first may also be required. The choice of spatial and/or typographic coding systems

Figure 3

Chap. 5 is on "Antichrist in Medieval Literature" (146-203). Covers the drama (163-87), with references to English plays in the Chester cycle (180-87). With notes, bibliography, and index.

Rev. B.D. Hill, *LJ* 106 (Sept. 15, 1981): 1730.
D.P. Walker, *THES* 465 (Oct. 2, 1981): 18.
Choice 19 (Dec. 1981): 517.
ChrCnt 98 (Dec. 23, 1981): 1348.
D.J. Osheim, *HRNB* 10 (Mar. 1982): 118.
C.T. Davis, *AHR* 87 (June 1982): 760.
RSR 8 (July 1982): 275.
Specu 57 (July 1982): 601.
Peter W. Travis, *EDAMN* 5.1 (Fall 1982): 12-14.
E.D. Craun, *History* 67 (Oct. 1982): 461.
TheolT 39 (Oct. 1982): 357.
Ronald B. Herzman, *StudAC* 5 (1983): 164-66.
ChHist 52 (Sept. 1983): 355.
CHR (Jan. 1984): 123.
JRel 64 (Jan. 1984): 119.

539. ---. "'Nowe Ys Common This Daye': Enoch and Elias, Antichrist, and the Structure of the Chester Cycle." In Homo, Memento Finis: *The Iconography of Just Judgment in Medieval Art and Drama*, 89-120. Ed. by David Bevington. Kalamazoo: Medieval Institute Publications, Western Michigan University, 1985. Early Drama, Art and Music Monograph Series 6. (See # 186 above.)

Looks at human and supernatural characters and the play's moment of decision in which Antichrist is taken to hell and Enoch and Elias are taken to heaven. Also deals with the Antichrist tradition --its iconographic and exegetical features and the prominence of Enoch and Elias.

540. Epp, Garrett. "The Semiotics of Flatness: Characterization in Medieval Cycle Drama." *Scintilla* 2-3 (1985-86): 132-40.

Treats "round" and "flat" characters, the latter being the rule in the cycle plays. Combines this notion with that of medieval realism, which states that "Ideas constitute the eternal, immutable reality of things" (133). Examines characters in these terms, concluding that "these characters are signes, or *semes* . . . suited to the popular didactic purpose of the cycle" (139). (See review of this article by Reynolds, entry # 1381 below.)

541. Epstein, Steven. "Guilds and Métiers." In *Dictionary of the Middle Ages* 6: 13-20. Ed. by Joseph R.

145

must therefore take into account the directions from which access to information within the entries is required. (p. 19)

'What is known' is, of course, the alphabet (or numbers, if the entries are arranged chronologically); but we also know the principles of selection for the bibliography, the subject breakdown in the listing, and whatever other details are explained in the introduction. That is why a clearly written and thorough introduction is so essential. And the designer must determine whether to use more of one type of coding than the other. Spencer, Reynolds, and Coe conclude:

> The final choice of design must depend on the relative frequency of use of the two search strategies, the maximum permissible length of the copy, and the production facilities available, but ideally if both search strategies are used the material should be typeset as opposed to typewritten to give the necessary range of typographic variation. (**219**, p. 19)

This was written, as I have said, before the boom in personal computers, which today will allow just about every kind of spatial and typographic coding desirable.

Some of their results are worth noting. But while their conclusions are based on scientific research, the results were predictable, especially for anyone who has been trained in book design, or who has a good eye for the logical layout of materials. The hanging indent produced the most effective means of locating the first elements in entries. Since the first element was already coded in such a way that it stood out spatially, it was redundant to add typographic coding as well; that could be saved for successive elements. And, as I have already said, if the second element (usually the title) is put into italics or quotation marks, these typographic features are distinctive enough to separate the titles from the authors' names; italics and quotation marks are eminently visible on a page, and are immediately locatable and recognizable as indicators of titles. They also carry generations of tradition; therefore, a reader need not learn anything new in order to use a bibliography which uses these typographic features. As soon as the quotation marks are closed or the italics end,

readers know they are entering the publication-data field. Once a date (for books) or page numbers (for articles or chapters) end in the publication-data field, readers know they are into whatever next element the bibliographer has provided – either other data about the book (ISBN, pagination, size, price, etc.), or annotations. And in well-designed bibliographies, annotations are spatially divided from the main part of the entry, and therefore no other spatial or typographic coding is necessary.

I refer the reader again to the sample page from my own drama bibliography (Figure 3, p. 42). This is a practical and clean design which may serve as a model. However, for bibliographies in other disciplines or for lists which aim to offer other, different kinds of data, this model might be an abomination of design. As I have stated, there is no single *right* or *best* way. If I had an infinite amount of time and money available to produce my work, I might have designed it differently. For example, I might have used facsimiles of title pages or set the text using more varied fonts of type. But I believe that for my readers' needs those options were not necessary. The point is that the simple physical variations that can be achieved with spatial and typographic coding are probably all that a designer or compiler needs to produce a clean, well-designed, functional page.

Page orientation

With respect to the use of microforms, Spencer and Reynolds (**216**) say, 'Avoid changes in page orientation; 90° rotations require a higher reduction ratio or an image rotation facility on the [microform] reader' (p. 19). Of course, they are not talking specifically about bibliographies, but about texts in microform. But the issue that they raise is important.

Book designers generally follow tradition – in this case the tradition of having a portrait format with the spine of the book on the left when it is closed face up. Work areas are even designed to hold books of that shape. And, as creatures of habit, we prefer that shape and orientation. (One book dealer sends all of his catalogues out with the spine on the 'top', so that the pages open upwards. My library's pull-out shelves, onto which these catalogues must be placed, are not shaped correctly for the catalogues [or vice versa]. And a library I have used a good deal in the production of this book has a serials list with the same orientation. There is a special place in purgatory for the designers of these things. The design itself is so peculiar that it calls attention to itself and will certainly be a distraction for the reader.)

An ordinary portrait format is best. And if there are to be any illustrations, tables, or charts in the bibliography, they should be printed with the same page orientation. I have used several books that print illustrative matter at a right angle to the normal page orientation. This is uncomfortable and awkward. It is better to reduce the image and print it 'upright' (if the image can still be read when it is reduced) than to print it with a 90° shift in orientation. If an image *is* reduced, the amount of reduction should be stated. I have even seen books with illustrations or charts rotated 90° on facing pages, so that the book must be turned 90° for the verso page, and then 180° for the recto (that is, the top of each image is at the inner margin of the page). This is particularly annoying.

Binding

This is an extremely broad subject, which I will reduce to a few simple statements only, because my focus here is bibliographies, not the exceptionally complex world of binding. And bindings are part of the overall design of bibliographies.

Reference books are designed to be used. And since bibliographies are reference books, we can be sure that readers will take notes from them. Note-taking requires two hands. Therefore a bib-liography that springs shut when it is put down is not only poorly designed, it is a headache as well.

The most important requirement is that the book open flat and the pages stay open, if such a binding is economically feasible for the publisher. And the book should be designed for *long use*, not a single reading, unlike many books today which barely make it through one reading, and are then ready for the conservator or the dustbin. Sturdy, acid-free materials cost little or no more than the spit and mucilage that go into many books today. A good bibliography should serve for one generation or ten. Some publishers now use acid-free, 250-year-life paper, sew the signatures or use a state-of-the-art, double-fan adhesive binding, and put the book into sturdy boards with a flexible spine. If this costs more (and the extra cost would be minimal), consumers would probably not complain in view of the superior product.

This chapter has looked at the content and shape of bibliographies. It does not pretend to be comprehensive, and it is not prescriptive. I simply try to raise issues and describe possibilities, with the advantages and drawbacks of these, as I see them. It is easy to criticize the work of others. It is not so easy to see one's own defects: errors, omissions, inaccuracies, biases, stupidities. My aim is to make compilers and designers aware of what choices they have, and how those choices can affect the final product.

The next chapter takes us into the 1990s with a discussion of computers and desktop publishing.

4
COMPUTERS AND
DESKTOP PUBLISHING

The 'microfiche book' is a development that has come to stay.
(S. John Teague, 'Microform Publication', in Hills, **106**, p. 139)

Teague's statement was written only ten years ago, and it is already suspect, if not outright wrong. Looking at current technology, he made one of those embarrassing predictions that, ten years later, he might hope were forgotten. Microfiche books may still be with us, but so are slide rules and the telegraph: relics of outmoded technology.

When I began writing this book, only two and a half years ago, I compiled a bibliography of over 100 items on desktop publishing, containing state-of-the-art data. It is now ready for the slide-rule heap. Advances in computer technology are racing along so fast that the computer itself can barely track them, and today's marvels are tomorrow's flotsam and quaint memories.

When I wrote my Ph.D. dissertation 20 years ago I used a main-frame computer. What a miracle it was, and how elephantine it was too. It was slow, cumbersome, and limited. It required a separate card-punch machine for its raw data. It required someone to feed stacks of cards into it and wait until the machine digested them all. I thought that this was the ultimate writing tool, that it would never be improved upon. And now it too is barely a memory.

By the time this book is in print, readers will be saying, how antiquated! this chapter needs updating. What I aim to do here is not to describe the most recent hardware and software, but to say in some general terms what computers can do, how they can be used in the compilation of a bibliography, and what they cannot do, at least at present.

Before discussing computers, I want to say something about other technology. Bibliographies can be produced on a variety of microforms: microfiche, microcard (now an obsolete technology), or microfilm. Some of the problems computers present are the same as for these microforms. For example, what will bibliographies look like on a screen? How can their legibility and readability be maximized? (Most microform readers present serious legibility and readability problems.) Will they allow a page format or will they be in a scrollable text? Will there be page or frame numbers? How can items be indexed and otherwise be locatable? In brief, the use of microforms has always been a last resort for most researchers. They offer availability of texts, but with none of the convenience that printed or computerized texts permit. One cannot make marginal notes in them or move around freely and quickly in their texts. Computers permit fast and thorough searches; books offer margins and indexes and portability. If someone is producing a bibliography for commercial sale today and does not wish to do it in a printed form on paper, she or he will want to do it in a computer format, not in a microform.

Fifteen years ago Altick (3) said that computers 'can compile bibliographies of books and articles on any topic as well as break down, under any desired system of classification, the contents not only of the bibliographies themselves but of the individual books and articles they list' (pp. 144–5). This may be true, but the casual optimism expressed in this sentence must be tempered by an understanding of the process.

Before a computer 'can compile a bibliography', the raw data must be on-line first. That is, there must be a fairly sizable database for the computer to tap. Major bibliographic utilities like OCLC and RLIN in the United States, along with databases in many individual disciplines like medicine and law, already contain vast amounts of information, with more pouring into them daily. With the proper software, a bibliographer could instruct the computer to compile from the database a chronological (or alphabetical) list of all entries which contain the words 'Italian', 'Renaissance', and 'art'. If the database – like the library utilities – contains only titles, this poses the problem of the article titled 'Looking for Mr Goldbar', but which is about the use of gold on Renaissance triptychs. None of the key words that the computer will search for to build the bibliography is in the title.

In some disciplines entire texts are in the database. In such cases, bibliographers searching for key words may have the opposite problem of the person searching for works on Renaissance art: they might be overwhelmed by the number of items the computer turns up, even though many of the items would not be appropriate for their bibliography. In other words, the casual remark that Altick made about how much the computer can do for us with respect to building a bibliography must be understood in the context of the amount of work human beings must do before and after the computer offers its assistance.

The data must be input in the first place. Then they must be proofread and checked for accuracy. They must be formatted in some way – the formatting presumably being decided upon before any of the inputting takes place. The format may be as simple as a three-line bibliographical entry, offering only author, title, and publication data; or it may be as complex as the OCLC or RLIN entries generating elaborate records in numerous MARC fields. Then it must be extracted by someone who has thought out carefully what data, what key words, what ideas are to be searched for. That person must also input the form in which the retrieved data are to be organized, something else that has to be worked out before the computer makes its search. Once the data – that is, the bibliographic entries – are printed out, the bibliographer must check each one to verify that it is appropriate for the bibliography being compiled. Many times key-word searches will produce completely inappropriate entries. 'Renaissance in the Art of Tooth Decay Prevention Used in Italian Dental Clinic' would have to be eliminated from a bibliography on Renaissance Italian Art. And someone

searching for items on the Federal Bureau of Investigation (FBI) would find inappropriate: 'Investigation of Federal Style Bureau Reveals Extensive Repair'.

The bibliographer must also assume, since all the data were input by human beings, that there are errors in the output. Therefore every entry must be checked in some way to verify its accuracy. Also, can the bibliographer assume that the record thus obtained is complete?

Finally, once the entire bibliography is complete – all the entries gathered and verified, other sources checked, each entry assessed for its pertinence to the bibliography – the bibliographer or someone else must design a form in which this list will be available to others (or to the compiler alone, if that is its purpose). Will it be on paper or in some electronic format? Will it be arranged by author, title, subject, or some other way? If it is to remain only in electronic form, it need not have any one of the standard arrangements since the data are accessible by internal searching. But the entries must be encoded in such a way that each data field is distinctive. For example, if the researcher asks for a list of authors, how will the computer discriminate between, say, Charles Dickens and David Copperfield?

Therefore, the bibliographer, in compiling the on-line list, has to code each part of each entry to enable the computer to distinguish between author, title, publication data, and so on. This, of course, is not a problem for the computer or the programmer. It is simple to put the data going into the computer into their own distinct fields. It is not even a problem when we have Sigmund Freud as the author instead of as the subject.

And if the product of all this is to be a printed list, the compiler must create a physical format for the individual entries and the page, the sections, and the entire book. 'Book' here is possibly an inaccurate term, for the printed pages could be in a three-ring binder, simply left in a long computer printout, or put into some other physical form. All this is the responsibility of the compiler.

This brings up an important issue – one which I have already touched on. Traditionally, there were authors and there were typographers. One wrote the books, the other designed them and sometimes even saw them through the printer and binder. But with the tremendous capabilities that computers give us, texts can now be produced completely on-line. Authors with no training as book designers are being asked by publishers to turn in camera-ready copy. The results are sometimes excellent, sometimes quaint; then there are the others. I need not say what 'the others' are, since most readers of this book will have seen an author-designed book that is prepared with all the typographic knowledge that went into the end product of a tornado.

Publishers realize that their authors may not be familiar with the printing theories of Aldus Manutius, Nicolas Jenson, John Baskerville, William Morris, Frederic Goudy, or Harry Duncan. Hence, many publishers have their own style manuals for their authors to follow. I have seen some of these documents, and while they help the authors to produce a perfunctorily decent page, the manuals themselves are not always written by expert typographers. Furthermore, no single manual can serve the needs of every text – each presents its own typographic challenge, its own graphic peculiarities. And bibliographies are special cases, for all the reasons and because of all the variables that I have been discussing in this book.

A computer-assisted bibliography is only as good, aesthetically pleasing, and useful as its human creators make it.

There is another vast area of computer research pertaining to the physical appearance of texts on video display terminals (VDTs). One line of research covers how to make cathode-ray-tube (CRT) texts legible. Another deals with the actual typefaces that are available for CRT displays – their legibility and the ways they are composed (with line segments, full characters, or dot matrices – and even if the dots in the dot matrix should be round, square, rectangular, or oval), their width-to-height ratio, and other features that concern 'traditional' typeface designers. There are also the issues of the colour of the screen and the text; the nature of the text with respect to 'pages' on the screen or continuous texts; copyfitting; contrast; the percentage of active area on the screen; the brightness, or luminosity, of the screen; the spacing of symbols; the viewing angle of the reader; fatigue factors of working at a CRT; cost benefits of producing texts 'at home' (even for commercial presses); the comfort of the work station of the computer user; the drawbacks and advantages of computerized texts (see especially Eisenberg, **63**); image quality on the screen; and so on.

One thing for the bibliographer to consider is whether the work will eventually be printed out or be available only on a screen. Each alternative presents its own problems. If the bibliography is to be available on a VDT, will the units be 'pages' or will the bibliography be a continuous, scrollable text? What effect will a scrollable text have on the reader who is accustomed to texts in pages? What capabilities (that are available on paper) do screens lack? For instance, some programs do not permit the image on the screen to show special characters, boldface or italic types, variations in interlinear or interletter spacing, and other typographic features of printed texts. Will the reader lose some of the meaning (say, with the loss of diacritical marks or typeface variants)? Many computers, however, especially recent models with the latest software, *will* allow all kinds of typographical niceties (maybe even more than the printer can offer).

This 'new' technology has brought a new generation of scholars and researchers out of the walls. One of the more thoughtful and comprehensive treatments is that in Reynolds's 'Designing for the New Communications Technology: The Presentation of Computer-Generated Information' (**186**). And as a perusal of the index to the present volume indicates, just about every imaginable approach to computer use is being covered in today's literature.

The biggest impact of computer technology is in the development of the personal computer. PCs running off batteries are now turning up in libraries; they are small enough to weigh only a few pounds, but powerful enough to memorize Brobdingnagian masses of information and drive all kinds of printers. Pretty soon they will be pocket size, but in the meantime the so-called laptop computer (a peculiar neologism – is there any other place on the lap?) has revolutionized research. (This is one of those statements that will seem quaint and trite fairly soon.)

Compiling a bibliography on a computer may require some old-fashioned techniques, the same kind of perseverance that I spoke of earlier, and a decent software package.

Though some bibliographies can, as I have said, be compiled right at a computer, drawing sources from a large, remote database, others may have to be done in the old way: going to the library; looking up titles, authors, and subjects; and entering data either directly into a computer, or onto index cards and then into the computer (depending on the portability of the hardware one has). Software today is becoming more and more sophisticated. I hesitate to talk about it because I do not want to sound like a fossil to my readers in a year. However, I should mention a few things.

A few years ago a software program came out which had two components, each with a different name: Bibliography and Notebook. Notebook, as I understood it, was the part of the program in which the gathered data were stored; Bibliography was the part which formatted the bibliographical data in a pre-shaped package. There were fields for author, title, and subject; publication data of all kinds; and room for notes. One could search in any of several fields, and the fields could be rather large, if the compiler desired. The final output was a compartmentalized listing, with data fields spatially distinct from each other. It was a clever concept, and apparently worked well.

But other word-processing programs also can be used, and some of them have tremendous power; that is, they offer a very great variety of operations that the computer can perform: opening up windows to allow the writer to work on several parts of the text at once; moving chunks of text from one place or file to another; alphabetizing; automatically inserting footnotes and keeping track of all the note numbers; deleting, moving, inserting, copying, making the coffee, and paying the bills. My own primitive computer (a desktop, non-portable, four-year-old behemoth), which still amazes me (and yet I know it is a relic of a bygone time), can perform, with my recent, updated software, many sophisticated operations in the production of a bibliography. I can produce what my software calls a 'Style Sheet', which permits me any kind of automatic spacing, indentation, or typeface styling, and more.

But all this talk about new and state-of-the-art equipment does not alter the fact that typewriters or primitive computers can still produce excellently designed bibliographies. One needs the fairly simple capability to indent, to use upper- and lower-case letters, to space between entries, to use italics or – for typewriters – underlining, to print in a legible typeface, and a few of the other things I mentioned above.

In other words, it is not the equipment that makes the difference; it is how you use what you have.

I should add, however, that the new ink-jet and laser printers are excellent, giving sharp, clear images. Most of the old dot-matrix printers do not produce clean copy – though some of those with 24-pin printers do produce letter-quality texts.

Computers can also be used to produce indexes for bibliographies. They can automatically check spelling and insert hyphens, and do many of the laborious things that we once had to do for ourselves. But the final product is not the creation of a computer. It is the product of a human being who gathers the data, manipulates it, designs the output, and sees the bibliography through to completion.

This last notion, however, can be modified, for if the bibliography remains in an electronic format, it does not necessarily reach 'completion'. It can be updated, augmented, corrected, or refined at any moment. Computers have made it possible for texts to remain alive, and not be entombed on static pages which grow more obsolete with every tick of the clock.

In the end, however, the quality and beauty, the legibility and usefulness of a bibliography are the results of an amalgam of many kinds of human efforts, efforts which have developed over many centuries. The information explosion demands better and more access to the multitude of data produced today. Classical typography and modern technology, combined with an understanding of human physiology and psychology, can help us produce eminently useful bibliographies. Compilers and designers, printers and publishers owe their customers the best bibliographies they can produce at a reasonable expenditure of effort and funds. Bibliographies are not only the doors to scholarship; they are works of scholarship themselves. The compiler is not a harmless drudge, but a contributor to the world's wealth of knowledge.

BIBLIOGRAPHY

The following is a list of some of the works consulted in the writing of this book. Since the range of topics pertaining to book design is broad, so is the coverage here. I have read all of the works cited below except those marked 'Not seen'.

1 Alouche, F. X., and J. M. Perriault. 'Mechanical Typesetting of Bibliographies with the Aid of a Sophisticated Information Retrieval Program.' In *Advances in Computer Typesetting: Proceedings of the 1966 International Computer Typesetting Conference*: pp. 146–7. London: The Institute of Printing, 1967.

Examines a method of writing 'a typesetting program which would organize the retrieval data so that it could be composed by any printing device' (p. 146). A fairly simple retrieval and print-out system, not at all concerned with the *design* of the printed bibliographical data. (The word *sophisticated* in the article's title is no longer appropriate.)

2 Alston, R. C. '"The Grammar of Research": Some Implications of Machine-Readable Bibliography.' *British Library Journal* 11.2 (Autumn 1985): 113–22.

Calls for standardization in bibliographical techniques – for a 'basic grammar' (p. 113). Talks about the flood of information emerging today. Stresses the importance of a 'grammar' for on-line recording of bibliographic data. Looks at the computer's potential. 'The bibliographical record [has] to be structured in such a way as to facilitate different kinds of search' (p. 117). Mentions the indexing value of computers. Points out that recent 'bibliographical analysis . . . has led to a recognition that many features of early printed books deserve particular notice in methodical descriptions' (p. 119). Mentions binding (material, colour, construction, finishing, ornament, provenance, date); paper (sheet size, quality, mould, watermark); typography; layout; illustration. Says that machine-readable bibliographies can provide much more information than can manually compiled ones.

3 Altick, Richard D. *The Art of Literary Research*, rev. ed. New York: W. W. Norton & Co., 1975.

Considers the computer's use in the compilation of bibliographies (see esp. pp. 143 ff.) and also the great value to scholarship of well-done bibliographies (pp. 146 ff.).

4 *American National Standard for Bibliographic References.* New York: American National Standards Institute, 1977. (ANSI Document No. Z 39.29–1977.)

Sets out standards for the two main kinds of bibliographical entries: author-first and title-first. Says that the preferred order has author-first or title-first, followed by edition, imprint, physical description, series statement, and notes. 'Within any bibliographic group, a decreasing order of hierarchy is used for the individual bibliographic elements' (p. 1). Points out that the bibliographic entry must provide 'the unique identification of the work' (p. 3). Contains much information on different bibliographic levels, sources of bibliographic elements, contents of the references, and essential, recommended, and optional elements. Has a short section on 'Representation of Data' (pp. 30–2). Says that the data 'should be represented in the same alphabet [i.e. typeface] as is used in the original document' (p. 30). Discusses capitalization, typography (use only one size of typeface, with underlining 'or differences in type style, size or weight' if necessary), use of abbreviations, and pagination. Gives many sample entries. More on the 'design' of the content of the bibliography than on its physical design.

5 Anderson, I. H., and C. W. Meredith. 'The Reading of Projected Books with Special Reference to Rate and Visual Fatigue.' *Journal of Educational Research* 41 (Feb. 1948): 453–60.

Considers the difference between reading printed texts and reading microfilmed texts; the latter read about 12% slower than the former. Anticipates by at least two decades the scholarship on computer VDTs. Shows that microfilm was read more rapidly without surrounding light.

6 Armitage, Merle. *Notes on Modern Printing*. New York: William E. Rudge's Sons, 1945.

'Through the centuries, book design has followed a tradition of poise, grace and good manners, within the limitations imposed by type, ornament and binding' ([p. v]; from the anonymous Foreword). Advocates designing 'a book which is easy to read and which utilizes the format to enhance or interpret the text' (p. 4). 'One thing a designer must not do: he must not become obvious, for when he does he interferes with the principal purpose . . . the readability of a book' (p. 49). (As a transition from the subject of legibility to the next subject:) 'Mere legibility is to a book as mere shelter is to architecture' (p. 69).

7 Armstrong, Don. *D. Armstrong's Complete Book Publishing Handbook*. Houston, TX: D. Armstrong Co., 1989.

A general handbook on self-publishing, book design, the publishing world, etc. On the 'design' of a bibliography, says only what it should contain, in what order, with what punctuation. Ignores the physical layout.

8 Arps, R. B., R. L. Erdmann, A. S. Neal, and C. E. Schlaepfer. 'Character Legibility Versus Resolution in Image Processing of Printed Matter.' *IEEE Transaction, Man-Machine Systems* 10.3 (September 1969): 66–71. Cited in Foster, *Legibility Research Abstracts 1970*, p. 5. (Not seen)

Aims 'to determine optimum resolution requirements for digital facsimile systems' (Foster, p. 5). Looks at several sizes of upper- and lower-case characters.

9 *The Author Looks at Format*. Ed. by Ray Freeman. N.p.: AIGA [American Institute of Graphic Arts], 1951.

Contains 11 short pieces by various authors. E.g., John Steinbeck urges innovation in typography, binding, and overall presentation ('Some Random and Randy Thoughts on Books', pp. 27–34). Pearl Buck wants books to be affordable ('Cheap Enough to Buy', p. 17). John Hersey says that 'the appearance of a book, particularly . . . its paper, typography, and page design, can help the author in the process of communication far more than the author would like to admit' ('Format and Meaning', p. 22). William Carlos Williams wants books to fit easily onto a bookshelf ('No Pretense Anywhere', pp. 39–40).

10 Bartz, Barbara S. 'An Analysis of the Typographic Legibility Literature: Assessment of Its Applicability to Cartography.' *Cartographic Journal* 7.1 (1970): 10–16. Cited in Foster, *Legibility Research Abstracts 1970*, p. 6. (Not seen)

Surveys legibility studies. Defines legibility in two ways: '(1) certain forms of type are physiologically optimal, in that they do not disrupt the motor habits involved in reading, (2) for some type variations readers have strongly developed habits' (Foster, p. 6).

11 Barzun, Jacques, and Henry F. Graff. *The Modern Researcher*. Rev. ed. New York: Harcourt, Brace & World, 1970.

Contains a brief section on the variety and forms of bibliographies. Distinguishes between the general and the selected bibliography. Also deals with classified and critical bibliographies, especially those presented in essay form. Says that before one can draw up a bibliography, she or he must be thoroughly familiar with its subject.

12 Bates, Marcia J. 'Rigorous Systematic Bibliography.' *RQ* 16.1 (Fall 1976): 7–26.

Considers the requirements for a reliable, useful bibliography and the means of compiling one. Has a section on 'Requirements for a Good Systematic Bibliography' (pp. 9 ff.). Defines 'bibliography'. Gives the two requirements: 1) that the work be 'a list or sequence of descriptions of graphic materials on a given subject or area' (p. 9); 2) 'that a bibliography state in an introduction its own specifications' (p. 9). Says these two requirements are essential for the users and for bibliographic control. On the aim or function of a bibliography, says it 'should be so designed as to perform the elementary control function of collocating materials defined by a given subject or area' (p. 12). The work's aim is to give 'a person armed with the bibliography . . . effective access to some portion of the bibliographic universe' (p. 12). All areas of inclusion and exclusion in the bibliography should be clearly specified in the introduction. Considers 'the development and description of specifications in both comprehensive and selective bibliographies' (p. 13). Cites Patrick Wilson (*Two Kinds of Power* . . ., q.v., 271 below), who enumerates five essential pieces of information in an introduction to a bibliography: 1) 'Domain'; 2) 'Selection Principles'; 3) 'Bibliographic Units'; 4) 'Information Fields'; 5) 'Organization' (see

Wilson for an expansion of these, pp. 59 ff.). Adds to these 'Scope'.

13 Beach, Mark, Steve Shepro, and Ken Russon. *Getting It Printed: How to Work with Printers and Graphic Arts Services to Assure Quality, Stay on Schedule, and Control Costs.* Portland, OR: Coast to Coast Books, 1986.

A general text on all aspects of book production, including planning to print, type selection and faces, creation of camera-ready copy, use of illustrative matter, preparing proofs, selecting paper and ink, types of printing processes, binding, etc. Nothing specifically on bibliographies.

14 Becker, D., J. Heinrich, R. von Sichowsky, and D. Wendt. 'Reader Preferences for Typeface and Leading.' *Journal of Typographic Research* 4.1 (Winter 1970): 61–6.

'. . . investigates the influence of typeface and leading on perceived appealingness of a printed page' (p. 61). Deals with four different faces in justified and unjustified texts, and with 0-, 1-, 2-, 3-, 4-, and 5-point leading. Shows that justification had no bearing on the results, but that 'different typefaces required different amounts of leading to allow most appealing composition' (pp. 61, 66). Also claims that 'sans-serifs and italics may need one point more leading than roman types' (p. 66); 'unjustified composition requires neither more nor less leading than justified composition' (p. 66). Does not deal extensively with legibility, but does comment on the relationship between legibility and attractiveness in print.

15 Beldie, Ion P., Siegmund Pastoor, and Elmar Schwarz. 'Fixed versus Variable Letter Width for Televised Text.' *Human Factors* 25.3 (June 1983): 273–7.

Recommends the use on CRT displays of variable-matrix characters. Letters with variable width were more easily read than were letters of fixed width. Claims that 'Variable-matrix text appears clearer and more distinct . . . [and] subjects were more accustomed to reading with variable-matrix character design' (p. 276); fixed-matrix character design was read 6% more slowly.

16 Bentley, Madison. 'Leading and Legibility.' *Psychology Monographs* 30, no. 136 (1921): 48–61.

Basic findings show that unleaded text is slower and less comprehensible to read than leaded text. Text

leaded up to 7 points (1/10 inch; 2.5 mm) increased legibility. (This ignores type size, and is therefore superseded by Paterson and Tinker's studies. See, e.g., *How to Make Type Readable* [**167**].)

17 Betts, Emmett A. 'A Study of Paper as a Factor in Type Visibility.' *Optometric Weekly* 33.9 (9 Apr. 1942): 229–32.

Summarizes scholarship. Compares the visibility of print on 16 different papers, 'in a controlled light situation' (p. 230). Concludes that a new paper (made by the company which funded this study) 'appears to produce as much type visibility as the "white" paper now used in basal readers' and that 'The tinted experimental paper . . . appears to produce substantially better results than the other "white" experimental paper . . . used in this study' (p. 232). With a 45-item bibliography.

17a *Bibliographical Style Manual.* New York: Dag Hammarskjold Library, United Nations, 1963. [There is also a French version: *Manuel de rédaction des bibliographies.* New York: Bibliothèque Dag Hammarskjold, Organisation des Nations Unies, 1963.]

This is typical of the many style manuals available, each done for its own audience. In this case, the audience is the United Nations Secretariat. The manual tries to accommodate 'the international and multilingual nature of the Secretariat's work' (p. iii). It covers books and pamphlets, periodicals and newspapers, parts of books, government publications, U.N. documents, and League of Nations documents.

The booklet summarizes the basic purpose of bibliographies: 'Whatever its content, size or arrangement, the purpose of a bibliography is to make it possible for the reader to refer to the publications which the bibliographer has recorded. It follows from this that each publication listed in a bibliography must be so described that the reader can identify it without mistake' (p. 1). Points out that 'the practices here recommended are [not] the only acceptable ones, [nor are they] exactly suited to every bibliography; however, they are all supported by logic as well as by widespread usage among bibliographers, and they have the advantage of familiarity to most people who work with books' (p. 1). Urges the uniform use of bibliographical form because uniformity yields familiarity, which allows easier use of the bibliography. Offers one standard presentation of data, including: (1) author, editor, or compiler; (2) title and subtitle; (3) identification of edition; (4) imprint (including place, publisher, date); (5) number of volumes; (6) illustrations, maps, charts, etc.; (7) [where applicable] title of series; (8) notes on the contents of the work. [It should be noted for item 1 (author, editor, or compiler) that since the publication of *AACR2* (*Anglo American Cataloguing Rules*, 2nd ed. Prepared under the direction of the Joint Steering Committee for revision of AACR. . . . Ed. by Michael Gorman and Paul W. Winkler. Chicago: American Library Association, 1988), in cataloguing materials, the editor or compiler is no longer the first (or filing) item in an entry. Only authors are in that position.]

18 Bigelow, Charles. 'Aesthetics vs. Technology: Does Digital Typesetting Mean Degraded Type Setting?' *The Seybold Report on Publishing Systems* 10.24 (24 Aug. 1981); 11.11 (8 Feb. 1982); 11.12 (22 Feb. 1982).

On digitized type design.

19 _____, and Donald Day. 'Digital Typography.' *Scientific American* 249.2 (Aug. 1983): 106–19.

Discusses how digital typesetters create new letterforms, and also the construction of electronic alphabets with respect to space, 'fundamental rhythmic patterns in the letterforms' (p. 115), familiarity and its effect on readability, and economic pressures on the design of the printed page. Also talks of the importance of high-resolution dot-matrix density on a CRT screen, the factors of proportion and thickness of letters, and the notion that it is not individual letters we see when we read, but words, groups of words, and a whole page of text.

20 _____, and Kris Holmes. 'The Design of Lucida®: An Integrated Family of Types for Electronic Literacy.' In *Text Processing and Document Manipulation: Proceedings of the International Conference, University of Nottingham, 14–16 April 1986*, 1–17. Ed. by J. C. van Vliet. Cambridge and London: Cambridge University Press, on behalf of The British Computer Society, 1986.

Discusses what needs to be done to create legible typefaces for digital readouts. Points out the need to look at typeface weight and style for CRT presentation. Considers form, pattern, texture, weight, contrast, joins, serifs, x-height, capital height. (See note at entry 33, by Victoria A. Burrill.)

21 _____, and Lynn Ruggles, eds. *The Computer and the Hand in Type Design: Proceedings of the Fifth ATypI Working Seminar, Part I. Visible Language* 19.1 (Winter 1985).

A special issue of the journal devoted completely to aesthetic and technical issues in the design of digital types. Contains essays on type design, with historical perspectives and predictions about the trends in type design. Only the essays by Zapf and Knuth (qq.v. 274, 123) are germane to this study and are cited here.

22 Biggs, John R. *Basic Typography*. New York: Watson-Guptill, 1968.

Considers such elements of book design as letter forms; word spacing ['As in all spacing the eye is the final arbiter, which must be on the alert for optical illusions of space (or lack of it)' – p. 32]; line length and justification ('The length of a line in a page of a book or other mass of continuous text must be related to the size of the type and the amount of leading between the lines. Many authorities have laid it down that lines should, on average, have ten to twelve words per line; twelve words must normally be regarded as a maximum' – p. 40); line spacing (i.e. leading); margins; and the book as a whole. Presents several classical page layouts: 'the Golden Typographical Module' (p. 56), the rectangle with a ratio of 1 to the square root of 2, the rectangle 'in the proportion of the Golden Section' (p. 58), and others. Recognizes the importance of good design in a bibliography, but chooses not to elaborate on this. Discusses paper, printing processes, binding, headlines, etc.

22a Blumenthal, Joseph. 'The Fitting of Type.' *The Dolphin* 2 (1935): 71–81.

Classic study of how type is designed so that lower-case letters need not be individually letterspaced. Contains much information on the appearance of a printed page based on the type's fitting.

22b _____ *The Printed Book in America*. Boston, MA: Godine, in Association with the Dartmouth College Library, 1977.

23 Borko, Harold, and Charles L. Bernier. *Indexing Concepts and Methods*. New York, San Francisco, and London: Academic Press, 1978.

Though not on bibliographies, contains much useful

information on structuring data, editing, typesetting, proofreading, computer compilation of data. Also has a section on alphabetization ('alphabetical order is the most common one for all kinds of indexes . . .', p. 42); shows the differences between letter-by-letter and word-by-word alphabetization. Contains a discussion of type. Says that while '8- to 12-point type is usual for setting text, indexes commonly use 6-point type or smaller' (p. 43). Says, 'The smaller type sizes are economically attractive' (p. 43). Points out that it is acceptable to have such a small typeface for a text which is only consulted, not read. Warns against type of 4 points and smaller. Points out that 'The typeface used conveys an impression of the care that has gone into' the work (p. 43). Mentions how different typefaces can be employed to differentiate between different parts of entries (e.g. boldface, italic, roman). Considers line length, indentations, use of running heads, special symbols, codes, abbreviations (usually use only ones recognizable to the reader), paper ('gloss interferes with the visibility of the type'; strive for the optimum opacity and bulk, p. 46).

24 Bowers, Fredson. *Principles of Bibliographical Description*. Princeton, NJ: Princeton University Press, 1949.

Not on bibliographies, but on the study and description of books. Says, 'A bibliographer must always make certain adjustments within any standard system according to the characteristics of his material and the purpose and scope of his work' (p. viii). Focuses on analytical or critical bibliography, and thus has nothing on designing bibliographies.

25 Breimer, A. J., H. Timmers, and K. G. Van der Keen. 'The Legibility of Televised Text.' *IPO Annual Progress Report* 13 (1978): 58–63. Eindhoven, the Netherlands: Institute for Perception Research. Cited by Foster, *Legibility Research 1972–1978*. (Not seen)

26 Breslauer, Bernhard H., and R. Folter. *Bibliography: Its History and Development*. New York: Grolier Club, 1984.

Defines 'bibliography', which includes lists of books such as dealers' catalogues, book-fair catalogues, and publishers' and printers' lists (but excludes catalogues of manuscripts, 'indeed . . . the whole field of palaeography', p. 14). This is basically a catalogue of an exhibit of 169 items, all bibliographies of one sort or another. Nothing on their design.

27 Brown, Bruce. *Browns Index to Photocomposition Typography: A Compendium of Terminologies, Procedures and Constraints for the Guidance of Designers, Editors and Publishers*. Ed. by S. W. Greenwood. Minehead, Somerset, England: Greenwood Publishing, 1983.

Has sections on 'Spacing type in photocomposition' (pp. 119 ff.), 'Photocomposition systems' (pp. 135 ff.), typefaces, and copyfitting. In one of the sections displaying different typefaces, Brown has the following passage (36 times): 'Legibility, in practice, amounts simply to what one is accustomed to. But this is not to say that because we have got used to something demonstrably less legible than something else would be if we could get used to it, we should make no effort to scrap the existing thing. This was done by the Florentines and Romans of the fifteenth century; it requires simply good sense in the originators and good will in the rest of us' (pp. 122–33).

28 Brown, W. S. 'Speed-reading Made Easy.' *Journal of Typographic Research* 4.1 (Winter 1970): 73–5.

Advocates vertical typography (*c.* five columns of type per page, with one or two words per line) to try to increase speed of reading. (Printed in this vertical style – very annoying; will need some getting used to.) Suggests 'that computers be used to prepare text in this form' (p. 73). Cites Coleman and Hahn's 'Failure to Improve . . .' (q.v., **48** below).

29 Bryer, Jackson R. 'From Second-Class Citizenship to Respectability: The Odyssey of an Enumerative Bibliographer.' *Literary Research Newsletter* 3 (1978): 55–61.

For bibliographies, calls for accuracy, near 'completeness', and careful organization (see p. 58). Criticizes the appearance of many bibliographies.

30 Buckler, Andrew T. *A Review of the Literature on the Legibility of Alphanumerics on Electronic Displays*. Aberdeen Proving Ground, MD: U.S. Army Engineering Laboratory, May 1977. Technical Memorandum 16–77.

Considers various features of letter forms affecting legibility, including techniques of generation of the text on VDTs, the font design, the percentage of the active area on the screen, contrast, the symbol-width-to-height ratio, the stroke-width-to-height ratio, spacing of the symbols, viewing angle, edge displayed symbols, and colour. Compares 'dot-matrix generation with symbols obtained through strokes of the electron beam' (p. 2). 'The relative advantages of CRT versus dot-matrix-generation techniques are still in question' (p. 2). Calls for more research. Talks of efforts being made to improve legibility on electronic displays. 'It has been demonstrated with CRT displays that increased active versus inactive bandwidth results in improved legibility' (p. 6). Points out that 'With dot-matrix displays, research has also found that decreasing the space between active elements results in improved legibility' (p. 6). Also mentions the attempt to improve legibility by varying the shapes of the dots: 'Square and circular dots have been found to be superior to rectangular and elongated dots respectively' (p. 6). Says it is important 'to produce an illusion of continuity of symbol form. . . . The symbol should give the illusion of being composed of solid, continuous lines' (p. 6). With respect to contrast, light symbols against a dark background seem more practical than the reverse. Also considers the brightness or luminosity of the work area with respect to that of the VDT. While a symbol-width-to-height 'ratio of 3:4 was found to be of greatest legibility on non-electronic display media' (p. 7), no such ratio has yet been determined for VDTs. Has similar observations about the other features of alphanumerics on electronic displays. Has a table summarizing results. Contains a useful 56-item bibliography focusing on CRTs and legibility.

31 Burbidge, P. G. *Notes and References.* Cambridge: Cambridge University Press, 1952. Cambridge Authors' and Printers' Guide IV.

Considers the *content* of bibliographical entries and their order (either alphabetical or chronological [p. 17]), the use of abbreviations in the entries, the importance of consistency of entry content. Nothing on the design of the bibliography.

32 Burnhill, Peter. 'The Case for a Standard Word Space.' *Journal of Typographic Research* 4.2 (Spring 1970): 146.

Briefly notes the importance in typography of consistency in the width of letters and words. Mentions 'the irrational practice of horizontal justification'. Contains no data on the results of any investigation or experiment.

33 Burrill, Victoria A. 'VORTEXT: VictORias TEXT Reading and Authoring System.' In *Text Processing and Document Manipulation: Proceedings of the International Conference, University of Nottingham, 14–16 April 1986*: pp. 43–57. Ed. by J. C. van Vliet. Cambridge and London: Cambridge University Press, on behalf of The British Computer Society, 1986.

Discusses the basic idea of presenting texts on a computer screen rather than on paper. Points out that the 'physical position' and 'typographic factors' (p. 44) of a text can give it optimum 'recognition' (p. 44). Talks of ways to adapt 'a paper book onto the computer screen' (p. 47). Says that her own program has the advantage of producing an image on the screen that resembles a page in a book.

Note: Other essays in this book consider computer-based page design, computer retrieval and document manipulation, electronic organization of texts, editing and formatting on-line, etc. See, e.g., articles by Bigelow and Holmes and by Suen and Komoda (**20 and 228**, in the present bibliography).

34 Burt, Sir Cyril. *A Psychological Study of Typography.* Cambridge: Cambridge University Press, 1959.

General discussions of typographical problems (pp. 1–2), legibility (pp. 3–18), aesthetic preferences and the classification of type faces (pp. 18–29). Nothing specifically on bibliographies.

35 Burtt, Harold E. 'Typography and Readability.' In *Readability*, pp. 26–35. Ed. by Edgar Dale. Chicago: National Conference on Research in English, 1949.

Surveys others' studies. Considers length of time a person looks at words, distance, blinking rate, type styles, capital versus small letters, line length, leading, spatial arrangement on the page, 1- or 2-column arrangements, colour, paper, illumination, etc. Almost no citation of sources. 12-item bibliography.

36 _____, and Coryne Basch. 'Legibility of Bodoni, Baskerville Roman, and Cheltenham Type Faces.' *Journal of Applied Psychology* 7.3 (Sept. 1923): 237–45.

'The legibility of individual letters was determined separately using upper and lower case and fourteen point. . . . Greatest legibility was found on the average for Cheltenham, followed by Baskerville, with Bodoni the least legible' (p. 245). This is for upper- and lower-case printing. Not a study of *words* or *text*.

37 Campbell, Frank [Francis Bunbury Fitz-Gerald Campbell]. *The Battle of Bibliography: Being an Extended Summary of Part of a Paper read before The Library Association, February, 1893. . . .* London: n.p., 1893.

Talks about the overwhelming number of publications there are. The problem: locating, cataloguing, having access to all the books in the British Museum. The solution, in part, is indexing. Advocates the 'Alphabetical Catalogue' (p. 3), and 'a chronological list of ALL the books on any given subject' p. 4). Wants a periodical list of all books published in a given year (a 'Periodical National Register of Books', p. 4). Enumerates the contents of this national register. His specimen 'Book-Registration Form' requires: title, number of volumes or parts, pagination, publisher, place of publication, size, etc.

38 _____. *The Theory of National and International Bibliography. With Special Reference to the Introduction of System in the Record of Modern Literature.* London: Library Bureau, 1896.

'The subject of "Works of Reference" is by no means an easy one to write upon, for two reasons: (1) That there are so many Works of Reference in existence which are unscientific *compromises*, whose existence has tended to obscure the course of inquiry; (2) That there is, at present, no code of defined terms agreed upon among librarians, as there are so many *general* terms in use, and so many different aspects of the subject possible, that no one can discuss the subject with any certainty that his companion interprets his words in the same manner intended' (p. 29). Discusses, in general, works of reference, a record (of literature), universal catalogues, general catalogues, national catalogues, territorial catalogues, bibliographies, book lists, etc. Looks at author catalogues, title catalogues, subject catalogues, indexes. Calls for 'Uniformity in the Sectional arrangement of certain Documents' (p. 133).

39 Carey, G. V. *Making an Index.* Cambridge: Cambridge University Press, 1951. Cambridge Authors' and Printers' Guides III.

Considers the content, not the shape or design, of back matter.

40 Carmichael, Leonard, and Walter F. Dearborn. *Reading and Visual Fatigue.* New York: Houghton-Mifflin, 1947.

Defines visual fatigue, explains the visual task of reading and its relation to fatigue, talks about the problems of lighting and eye movement, discusses comprehension. Says, 'The readable page . . . may be printed in any of several styles of type, preferably those which are fairly simple in design. The width of the lines of the type design may be medium to bold in thickness. The majority of the letters will be lower case and not italicized. The lines of print may be around 80 millimeters or 19 picas in length, solidly set or with up to two points of leading. The printing ink should be black on a cream-tinted paper of dull finish' (p. 124). This is 'one of the good formats and certainly a page that will in general be read with ease' (p. 125). Here and elsewhere these writers summarize the research of others.

41 Carter, Rob, Ben Day, and Philip Meggs. *Typographic Design: Form and Communication.* New York and Wokingham, England: Van Nostrand Reinhold, 1985.

Has sections on the evolution and the anatomy of typography, syntax and communication, legibility, technology, typographic design education, and examples. Looks closely at letterforms. Shows various page layouts which offer maximum legibility and usefulness. Explains their notion of hierarchy in typographic arrangement, 'the study of the relationships of each part [of the hierarchy] to the other parts and to the whole' (p. 52). Considers contrasting and parallel elements in the data presentation of a page. (Calls these two elements counterpart and counterpoint – p. 52.) The counterpoint elements 'do not complete the whole; rather, they function as a rhythmic support, bringing unity and integration between parts' (p. 52). [Though the authors are talking about all visual elements, specifically pictorial and typographical, this notion is useful in the design of a page of a bibliography. Coordinating elements in a bibliography must be distinct from one another; counterparts of separate entries must be presented in equivalent and clearly delineated patterns.] Talks about the physical presentation of data. 'Visual hierarchy is more clearly understood with [the] juxtaposition of opposites in mind' (p. 56). 'As a writer uses standard punctuation marks to separate words and clarify meaning, a designer introduces visual punctuation (space intervals, rules, or pictorial elements) to separate, connect, and emphasize words or lines. Visual punctuation stresses a rhythmic organization' (p. 56). 'Typographic joinery is the visual linking and connecting of elements in a typographic composition through structural relationships and form repetition' (p. 56). [This notion is particularly useful in the design of a page and the entries of a bibliography.] Discusses 'typographic space . . . defined by form and void relationships that determine a composition's underlying spatial order. . . . optical adjustment is the precise visual alignment of typographic elements in space. The designer's understanding and use of optical adjustment is necessary for visual clarity' (p. 60).

Talks of the use of a grid in the design of a page. Stresses the importance of the study of legibility, especially focusing on letterforms, the use of full capitals, all lower case, and mixed fonts, interletter and interword spacing, type size, line length, weight of the typeface, use of colour, justified and unjustified typography, paragraphs and indentation, and thought-unit typography. Opts for 'normal' letter and word spacing, upper- and lower-case types, type of average weight (use boldface only for emphasis), moderate use of italics, type set flush left, ragged-right and distinguishing one paragraph from the next (either with indentation or with extra space between the paragraphs). ['If properly used, flush-left, ragged-right typography provides visual points of reference that guide the eye smoothly down the page from line to line. Because each line is either shorter or longer than the next, the eye is cued from one to another. In a justified setting, all lines are of equal length. Lacking are visual cues that promote easy reading' (p. 88); also points out that ragged-right yields more even word spacing, line breaks are more controlled, and line breaks need not be forced, but may enhance meaning.]

42 Carver, R. P. 'Effect of a "Chunked" Typography on Reading Rate and Comprehension.' *Journal of Applied Psychology* 54.3 (1970): 288–96. Cited in Foster, *Legibility Research Abstracts 1970*, p. 8. (Not seen)

Studies the speed of reading a text presented in logical phrases. Similar text lacking punctuation was read more slowly than normally presented prose; but with regular punctuation there was essentially no difference in speed or comprehension.

43 _____, and C. A. Darby. 'Analysis of the Chunked Reading Test and Reading Comprehension.' *Journal of Reading Behaviour* 5 (1972): 282–96.

Cited by Foster, *Legibility Research 1972–1978*. (Not seen)

44 *The Chicago Manual of Style.* 13th ed., rev. and expanded. Chicago and London: University of Chicago Press, 1982.

Says, 'Each item in a bibliographical list should begin flush left (with no paragraph indentation). In entries requiring more than one line, runover lines should be indented three or four spaces' (p. 45). Suggests double spacing throughout -- especially between entries. 'Authors' names in an alphabetical list are typed last name first. If several works by the same author are listed, a dash (three typed hyphens) is used in place of the author's name for each item following the first. If a period follows the author's name in the first item, a period follows the dash as well' (p. 45). This volume contains a comprehensive treatment of how to construct bibliographical entries, with the focus primarily on content, not on form. See especially Chapter 15, from which the following notes are taken. 'The bibliography arranged in a single alphabetical list is the most common and usually the best form for a work with, or without, notes to the text' (p. 423). 'A long bibliography may be broken into sections if division into categories would really make it more useful to the reader' (p. 425). Says that in long bibliographies, articles and books may sometimes be listed separately. Also separate may be newspapers and manuscript sources. Discusses annotations, the use of a bibliographic essay rather than the standard bibliographic form, the arrangement of entries (the best is alphabetical). Has a section on bibliographic forms for many kinds of sources. Discusses the two main forms of bibliographic entries, 'One, favored by writers in literature, history, and the arts. . . . The other, favored by writers in both the natural and social sciences' (p. 439), though amalgamated and other forms are possible. One spells out names and gives full titles and more publication data, along with other differences. [Neither is preferable to the other. Choosing a style familiar to one's audience is the best rule.] Also to be considered is whether space is at a premium – then the shortened version (lacking full names, subtitles and even full titles, and other publication data) may be used. Opts for arabic numerals throughout. Asserts that only upper- and lower-case roman and italic should be used: 'Other typefaces sometimes used in bibliographies . . . – for example, caps and small caps for authors' names or boldface for volume numbers of journals – raise costs without raising clarity' (p. 440). [N.B. Other style manuals offer their own advice and 'rules' – sometimes idiosyncratic, often drawing heavily on the *Chicago Manual*.]

45 Cleland, T. M. [Thomas Maitland]. *Harsh Words: An Address Delivered at a Meeting of the American Institute of Graphic Arts, in New York City, February 5, 1940, on the Occasion of the Opening of the Eighteenth Annual Exhibition of the Fifty Books of the Year.* Newark, NJ: The Cartaret Book Club, 1940.

Discusses his sensitivity to current typographic practices. Warns designers to be wary of originality (see esp. pp. 12–13). Discusses Functionalism, in which design is related to function; also considers simplicity and restraint in the artistic design (esp. *vis-à-vis* ornamentation). Warns against anything that distracts from the primacy of the text (in decoration and type design).

46 Cobden-Sanderson, Thomas James. *The Ideal Book or Book Beautiful: A Tract on Calligraphy, Printing & Illustration and on The Book Beautiful as a Whole.* Berkeley, CA: Arif Press, 1972.

Contains a clear discussion of the importance of clear, unobtrusive typography. See p. 5 above.

47 Colaianne, A. J. 'The Aims and Methods of Annotated Bibliography.' *Scholarly Publishing* 11.4 (July 1980): 321–31.

Points out that bibliographies might be on single authors, a group of authors (e.g. Renaissance pamphleteers, the Bloomsbury Group), a single work (*Beowulf*, *The Waste Land*), a literary movement (neoclassicism, Expressionism), a genre (science fiction), a literary form (the sonnet), or a literary theme (racism, feminism). [Not to mention the many bibliographies outside the humanities.] Emphasizes the need for precision in presenting data. Discusses the economic, practical elements of publishing annotated bibliographies. Talks of the many types of bibliographies. Looks at scholars' uses of annotated bibliographies. 'The most important requirement for a bibliography . . . is usefulness – the ease with which accurate and complete information may be retrieved from its listings. The chief responsibility of the bibliographer is therefore to ensure that the user of his volume will be able to find dependable information quickly and efficiently' (pp. 323–4). Says that the bibliographer should have a clear aim of the parameters of the work he or she is compiling. That is, what will be included and what excluded? Any exclusions should be manifestly justifiable, or should be accounted for in the introduction. And 'the compiler should carefully spell out the kinds of items he has included' (p. 325).

Titles should be given in full, and all sources should be checked against the originals where possible. Avoid *passim* and *ff*. 'The organization of a bibliography should be simple and straightforward; a highly subdivided body of publication can be annoying' (p. 327). Subdivisions 'must be dictated by the contours of the material itself, not by a desire for bibliographic tidiness. And topical divisions can sometimes confuse readers; a critical study, for example, may bridge several categories, and the decision where to place it may appear arbitrary to the reader' (p. 327).

Author, title, or subject indexes may be necessary. A chronological arrangement of entries 'benefits the user who is interested in tracing the progress of critical thought or advances in the reputation of an author. An alphabetical arrangement may appear practical, but a good author index will satisfy the needs of the user in search of the contributions of an individual scholar' (p. 328). It is probably best not to separate books from articles. Use the simplest numbering system possible for entries; avoid complex coded entries with roman and arabic numbers, letters, and decimal divisions. Avoid value judgements in annotated entries. The technical apparatus used in the bibliography, along with the arrangement of all of the entries in the work and all its ancillary parts (glossary, appendixes, indexes, list of abbreviations [editor's abbreviations, abbreviations for frequently cited works or periodical titles]) should be carefully delineated in the introduction and/or in the introductions to the individual parts. 'The most important part of the introduction is the description of the technical apparatus used in the volume, for it is here that the bibliographer delineates the scope of his compendium and provides keys to its most efficient use' (p. 330).

Contains nothing specific on the actual physical design of bibliographies – their layout or the order of the data the entries should contain.

48 Coleman, E[dmund] B., and S. C. Hahn. 'Failure to Improve Readability with a Vertical Typography.' *Journal of Applied Psychology* 50.5 (Oct. 1966): 434–6.

Points out that Coleman and Kim (**49**) reported that for short passages, a vertical typography can be read 'more accurately than the same sentences presented in the conventional horizontal style' (p. 434). Coleman and Hahn's experiments deny the advantage of vertical typography. Concludes – from their own experiments – 'The conventional horizontal typography was significantly superior to vertical in all three experiments' (p. 436). (See W. S. Brown, 'Speed-reading Made Easy', 28.)

49 _____, and Insup Kim. 'Comparison of Several Styles of Typography in English.' *Journal of Applied Psychology* 45.4 (Aug. 1961): 262–7.

This experiment arranges type in various formations on the page, including single-phrase lines, 'square-span' arrangement, 'thought unit' arrangement, and vertical style (one phrase to the line). Established reading habits were difficult or impossible to suppress (p. 266), even though 'vertical, spaced, and square span [styles] were all significantly superior, vertical being the most superior' (p. 266) in terms of speed. [See the articles by Coleman and Hahn, North and Jenkins, and Nahinsky.]

50 Collison, Robert L. *Indexes and Indexing*. 4th rev. ed. London: Ernest Benn; New York: John De Graff, 1972.

Discusses the layout and style of an index (pp. 84–93), information not particularly useful or applicable to a bibliography. Has a section on 'Compiling and Arranging a Bibliography' (pp. 130–2) which says nothing at all about the physical presentation of a bibliography.

51 Conner, Martha. *Practical Bibliography Making, with Problems and Examples*. New York: H. W. Wilson Co., 1933.

Contains chapters on definitions; varieties; procedure (for compiling); criteria (e.g. accuracy, completeness, absence of repetition, consistency of form, critical value); bibliographic description (e.g. content of each entry – author, title, edition, translator, illustrator, imprint, price, collection, form of card [i.e. layout of each part of entry]), etc. Mentions the different kinds of bibliographies (dictionary, chronological, subject, regional). Gives examples of how various libraries have styled their catalogue cards: some with italics, full caps for names, indentation variations, boldface types, main entry on separate lines from the rest of the entry, smaller type for annotations, etc.

52 Cornog, D. Y., and F. C. Rose. *Legibility of Alphanumeric Characters and Other Symbols: II. A Reference Handbook*. Washington, DC: National Bureau of Standards Miscellaneous Publication 262-2, 10 Feb. 1967.

Vol. I is the index (compiled by Cornog, Rose, and J. L. Walkowicz). Vol. II contains abstracts and extracts

In several books (1943) Lillian Lieber attempted to aid understanding by printing only a single phrase on each line.	Single phrase per line
In square span is arranged the material in double-line blocks.	Square-span typography
In the vertical style the fixations would overlap and maximally exploit peripheral vision.	Vertical-style typography

Figure 4. From Edmund B. Coleman and Insup Kim. 'Comparison of Several Styles of Typography in English.' *Journal of Applied Psychology* 45.4 (1961): 262–7; p. 262.

of articles and books on the subject of legibility. Contains extracts from many general articles on legibility, but none specifically on bibliographies. Sample articles extracted (and not included in this bibliography): Curt Berger, 'Some Experiments on the Width of Symbols as Determinant of Legibility.' *Acta Ophthalmologica* 26.4 (1948): 517–50. Curt Berger, 'Experiments on the Legibility of Symbols of Different Width and Height.' *Acta Ophthalmologica* 28.4 (1950): 423–34. Emmett A. Betts, 'A Study of Paper as a Factor in Type Visibility.' *The Optometric Weekly* 33.9 (9 Apr. 1942): 229–32. C. S. Bridgman and E. A. Wade, 'Optimum Letter Size for a Given Display Area.' *Journal of Applied Psychology* 40.6 (Dec. 1956): 378–80. George R. Klare, *The Measurement of Readability*. Ames, IA: Iowa State University Press, 1963. Katherine D. Young, *Legibility of Printed Materials*. Memorandum Report no. TSEAA-8-694-1A (10 June 1946). Cornog and Rose cite many more articles and books, but none apparently on the physical design of bibliographies.

53 _____, _____, and J. L. Walkowicz. *Legibility of Alphanumeric Symbols: I. A Permuted Title Index and Bibliography.* Washington, DC: National Bureau of Standards Miscellaneous Publication 262–1, 15 Dec. 1964.

See note to Cornog and Rose, previous entry.

54 Creesy, Charles L. 'Desktop Publishing, Seriously.' *Scholarly Publishing* 21 (Oct. 1989): 3–9.

On Princeton University Press's use of in-house software and hardware in publishing books. Discusses marketing applications, the production process, and cost benefits.

55 Cropper, A. G., and S. J. W. Evans. 'Ergonomics and Computer Display Design.' *Computer Bulletin* 12.3 (1968): 94–8. Cited by Foster, *Legibility Research Abstracts 1970*, p. 9. (Not seen)

Examines 'the application of ergonomics to computer visual displays' (Foster, p. 9).

56 Crosland, H. R., and Georgia Johnson. 'The Range of Apprehension as Affected by Inter-letter Hair-Spacing and by the Characteristics of Individual Letters.' *Journal of Applied Psychology* 12 (1928): 82–124.

The experimenters conclude that '½-point inter-letter spacing in 10-point lower case Caslon . . . does not very appreciably affect the legibility of the letters' (p. 121), though there is an increase in legibility with interletter spacing for 'letters whose shapes do not contrast greatly [e.g., *p*, *b*, *d*, and *g*]' (p. 121); also, serifs on letters seem to increase legibility over sans serif letters (p. 121). This article contains a useful 31-item bibliography.

57 Dair, Carl. *Design with Type.* New York: Pellegrini & Cudahy, 1952.

Considers only general areas of legibility (size, weight, structure, form, colour, etc.); no specific analysis of bibliographies.

58 Dearborn, Walter F., Philip W. Johnston, and Leonard Carmichael. 'Improving Readability of Typewritten Manuscripts.' *Proceedings of the National Academy of Science* 37.10 (Oct. 1951): 670–2.

Discusses means of 'increasing the speed and especially the accuracy of comprehension in the reading of manuscripts' (p. 670). Focuses primarily on typed texts but also considers the printed page. Also aims to show what, in print, will enhance stressed words or passages *vis-à-vis* oral stress. Demonstrates 'that the ability of a reader to understand a prose passage may be expressed in quantitative terms by his indicating which words he would stress were he to read the passage aloud' (p. 670). Postulates that the key word(s) would best be displayed on a typewriter if the word or words were typed in full caps. Also considers two-column format, single-spaced lines, and blackening some text (i.e. creating boldface type) by overtyping. Concludes that full caps or other altering of a simple page presentation will focus a reader's attention on that which needs to be stressed.

59 DeVinne, Theodore Low. *Correct Composition: A Treatise on Spelling, Abbreviations, . . .* New York: Oswald Publishing Company, 1921.

Opts for the use of italics for titles in bibliographies (as opposed to quotation marks – pp. 102–3; 225–6). Such a distinction does not obtain today in bibliographies; the present practice is to use italics for book and periodical titles and quotation marks for titles of articles and component parts of books.

60 Didelot, Marie. 'What Type Size and Measures Offer the Maximum Legibility?' *Inland Printer* 88.3 (Dec. 1931): 35–7.

Focuses mostly on advertising media; summarizes the findings of Tinker and Paterson (q.v.). (This is an interesting example of 'piggy-back' publication: Didelot republishes in a 'popular', non-scholarly journal the already published findings of scholars whose work appeared in the scholarly series of articles in the *Journal of Applied Psychology* [see Paterson and Tinker in this bibliography]. Other than mentioning Tinker and Paterson's names, Didelot hardly credits them for their extensive work, and never cites a source. Though the data here are clearly useful for readers of *Inland Printer*, this article, nonetheless, borders on plagiarism.)

61 Dowding, Geoffrey. *Factors in the Choice of Typefaces.* London: Wace & Co., 1957. Primers for Students of Typography, 2.

Covers many topics, including legibility, readability, the nature of the work, the printing process, paper, illustrations, lettering, 'The Shape and the Size of the Space' (p. 69), combinations of type, suitability of the typeface to the text, and the method of composition of the type. The first chapter on legibility defines that term. Looks at the individual letterforms – their features which distinguish them from one another. Compares text types and display types; the latter may catch the eye but are not as legible as text types. Says that white printing on a black background 'entails a 27% loss of legibility' (p. 3). Also points out that black ink on white paper yields the greatest legibility, while other colours reduce legibility. Compares legibility with readability – 'the most legible of types can be made unreadable if it is set in too wide a measure, or in too large or too small a size for a particular purpose' (p. 5). Considers among the factors of readability such things as the typeface design, line length, leading, 'The Quality of the Setting' (p. 8), and 'The Arrangement of the Setting' (p. 8). For bibliographies, mentions only reference books and 'large catalogues like the *British National Bibliography*' (p. 13). Says, 'bold faces will be needed' (p. 13). Also mentions the uses of sans serif types. Nothing else of substance on bibliographies. Mentions narrow-, medium-, and wide-set typefaces, body size, x-height, the length of the text, and so on.

61a _____. *Finer Points in the Spacing and Arrangement of Type*. London: Wace & Co., 1954.

Considers spacing between words, line lengths, leading, letterspacing, word spacing, and setting of display matter. Also considers optical (as opposed to actual) centring of lines (and of line ends in asymmetrical layouts), line division by sense, use of quotation marks and apostrophes, hyphens, dashes, parentheses, brackets, ampersands, various means of displaying emphasis (underlining, boldface, etc.), unnecessary punctuation, the effective use of white space, and illustrations. Looks at many other features: ligatures and logotypes, spacing before and after punctuation, word division, and much more on actual typeface features (body size, x-height, design).

62 Dreyfus, John. 'Printing as Industry and Craft: Victor Hammer's Example.' *Kentucky Review* 5 (Winter 1984): 3–18.

Says that 'research into the legibility of type has proved very little of value that printers have not already discovered by experience' (p. 8). Talks of the importance of having accent marks and punctuation an appropriate weight for visibility; also the need for balance and proportion in letter forms. Expresses his disappointment with studies of legibility; says, 'We read most easily the types that we are most used to reading. Beyond that . . . there is often no statistically significant difference between our ability to read type

faces seriffed or sans serif' (p. 9). Also talks of our being able to adapt to new type styles.

63 Eisenberg, Daniel. 'Problems of the Paperless Book.' *Scholarly Publishing* 21 (Oct. 1989): 11–26.

Discusses the many drawbacks of having or putting texts on-line, along with the advantages. The advantages include savings of time, space, money, and paper; 'There will be no printer or typewriter, no inventory or warehouse' (p. 11); also, no binding or paper to deteriorate. Texts will stay 'in print' and can be easily updated. They will be more searchable and manipulable. The drawbacks are many, however: cost of equipment and its obsolescence; lack of uniformity or standardization in personal computers and software; problems in distribution and copyright (who will distribute the text? and to whom? i.e., will it be possible to keep some texts out of the wrong hands? [specifically mentions literature and literary criticism that some adults want to keep away from children]); sale of the texts; the fact that typography is not as easy to control on-line. Mentions the use of upper- and lower-case letters, italics, boldface, particularly 'desirable' typefaces and type sizes, special alphabets and characters. Talks of the process of 'converting a manuscript into a printed book' (p. 22). Emphasizes the great expertise needed in programming for the on-line production of bibliographies, notes, and headings.

63a *Electronic Composing System: A Guide for Its Utilization*. Washington, DC: US Government Printing Office, 1966.

An early document proclaiming the miracles of the new technology. Looks at the computer's potential, and its 'sacrifices in quality and readability', because 'The typical computer-printer or tabulating machine produces monospaced upper case characters [resulting in] a monotonous-looking product with no typographic variations between captions and body. There is little reader appeal and the eye must work overtime to find what it wants from the printed page' (p. 5).

64 Erdmann, R. L., and A. S. Neal. 'Character Legibility and Digital Facsimile Resolution.' *Human Factors* 10.5 (1968): 465–74. Cited in Foster, *Legibility Research Abstracts 1970*, p. 12. (Not seen)

Examines CRT legibility with respect to scan direction, use of upper- and lower-case letters, pitch and distance, and character height.

65 _____, _____. 'Word Legibility as a Function of Letter Legibility, with Word Size, Word Familiarity, and Reduction as Parameters.' *Journal of Applied Psychology* 52.5 (1968): 403–9. Cited in Foster, *Legibility Research Abstracts 1970*, p. 12. (Not seen)

Compares word legibility to letter legibility, using variations in character size and resolution. 'Word legibility was found to increase with resolution and with character size' (Foster, p. 12). Also examines legibility with respect to word length and familiarity.

Esdaile, Arundell. See Roy Stokes, *Esdaile's Manual of Bibliography*.

66 Evers, C. H. 'Adjustment to Unjustified Composition on the *Rotterdamsch Nieuwsblad*.' *Journal of Typographic Research* 2.1 (Jan. 1968): 59–74.

On the printing of newspapers. Discusses problems and benefits of ragged-right composition in general. Points out that much depends on the skill of the compositors to minimize problems. E.g., 'Exaggerated short lines . . . tend to emphasize the ragged end and irritate the reader' (p. 74). But mentions 'production advantages' (pp. 65, 72).

67 Fabrizio, Ralph, Ira Kaplan, and Gilbert Teal. 'Readability as a Function of the Straightness of Right-Hand Margins.' *Journal of Typographic Research* 1.1 (Jan. 1967): 90–5.

Another experiment proving that the shape of the right-hand margins does not affect readability. 'All measures of reading performance applied in this study gave essentially equal scores for three different right-hand margins: irregular, irregular with a printed guideline, and justified' (p. 94). 'Neither speed of reading nor level of comprehension . . . differed significantly' (p. 94). The seven-entry bibliography for this article does not mention any earlier study which comes to this conclusion, though there are a few.

68 Feinberg, Hilda. 'Sample Book Catalogs and their Characteristics.' In *Book Catalogs*, pp. 381–511. By Maurice F. Tauber and Hilda Feinberg (**231** below).

[Since book catalogues are lists of books held in a given collection, they are essentially bibliographies. The presentation of data in a book catalogue – the order of information and contents of each entry and the physical layout of data on the page – create the same problems and present the same challenges as does the presentation of data in, say, a subject bibliography.] This essay presents photocopies of the bibliographic data in book catalogues of 32 libraries. The samples reflect a very wide variety of designs.

Catalogues which are simply photocopies of a library card catalogue – such as the *National Union Catalogue* in the United States – exhibit the typical variations one comes to expect from cards produced for a library over many decades and through many changes in cataloguing rules and practices. Such variation makes locating particular elements in an entry somewhat slow and frustrating. Some of the entries show typical design solutions for the presentation of different elements in entries: the use of full caps, hanging indentation, hyphens or dashes for second and subsequent works by a given author, italics for book and periodical titles, boldface type, quite small type (also a problem with the reproduction of catalogue cards), and other peculiarities of indentation and type weight variation to make one part of an entry stand out. Some of the resulting catalogues are particularly difficult to use. The essay preceding the examples discusses input procedure and hardware, software, means of printing the output, legibility, etc. On legibility, the author cites the standard studies, summarizing the work of Tinker, Cornog and Rose, Tinker and Paterson, and others.

69 Ferguson, John. *Some Aspects of Bibliography*. Edinburgh: George P. Johnston, 1900.

Says, 'Bibliography is the science or the art, or both, of book description' (p. 3). Bibliographies may include any or all of the following data: date, place of publication, printer, material, type, size, illustrations, language, subject, authors or groups of authors, etc. They may be about any subject, person, unique item, anonymous and pseudonymous books, 'curiosa' (p. 21), 'facetiae' (p. 21), suppressed books, etc. Mentions also individual presses, printers, etc. 'The bigger the bibliography is, the more flaws it is likely to contain' (p. 25). Nothing specifically on the layout or design of all this information.

70 Finney, D. J. 'On Presenting Tables and Diagrams.' *Scholarly Publishing* 17.4 (July 1986): 327–42.

Concentrates on tabular and diagrammatic illustration of text. Calls for simplicity (p. 335) and consistency. Some characteristics for tables also apply to an annotated bibliography: 'a) the facts must be correct, but not exaggeratedly detailed in relation to purpose; b) the arrangement must be designed for easy comprehension by the reader, rather than for the pleasure of the author; c) the information content should be high . . . and unnecessary distractions to eye and brain should be avoided' (p. 336). Also, 'no one will succeed [in producing truly useful tables] without taking trouble, without seeking to understand the needs of the class of reader for whom the writing is intended' (p. 342).

71 Fisher, Paul. 'History of Type Readability Studies Discloses No "Perfect" Type Face.' *Inland Printer* 133.3 (June 1954): 66–7.

General comments on legibility of type, with some historical views. Recounts the work of Roethlein, Walter Dill Scott (a 1910 *Delineator* article; Scott opts for Cheltenham and Cheltenham Bold), Carl P. Rollins (1911 study; Rollins opts for Garamond, Scotch, and Baskerville types, in that order), Paterson and Tinker (who opt for 'any commonly used modern or ultramodern type face' [p. 66]), and Goudy (who assumes the familiarity of his readers with any typeface). Also looks at the findings of Luckiesh and Moss, who seem to have the last word in that 'all standard romans are about equal in readability' (p. 67). Fisher concludes 'that in various attempts to grade types as to their readability or to find *the* readable type there has been "much ado about nothing". But a lot of people have had fun' (p. 67). [So much for scientific investigation.]

72 Foster, Jeremy J. 'Directional Consistency in Form Identification.' *Journal of Typographic Research* 4.2 (Spring 1970): 139–45.

Comments on and agrees with Paul A. Kolers ('Clues to a Letter's Recognition', **125** below), and others; 'more accurate responses occur when scanning direction and stimulus direction are consistent' (p. 141). Cites several other studies pertaining to the direction of eye movement in reading as related to recognition.

73 _____. *Legibility Research Abstracts 1970*. London: Lund Humphries, 1971.

Offers abstracts of 234 articles which deal in some way with legibility, broken down into 17 categories; e.g. visibility of alphanumeric characters; legibility of words and text; reader preference for typographic designs; comprehension of diagrams, maps, computer displays; symbol design and symbol systems; colour coding; reviews of legibility research; etc. A number of articles from this volume are included in the present bibliography.

74 _____. *Legibility Research 1972–1978: A Summary.* N.p.: Graphic Information Research Unit, Royal College of Art, Oct. 1980.

Offers an extensive discussion about legibility relating to many of its aspects: research methods, eye movements, letter and digit identification, reading, typography, graphic displays, etc. Considers character size and form, upper and lower case, contrast, spacing, orientation, colour, typeface, layout, etc. Essentially reviews the scholarship on these subjects for this seven-year period. With a 424-entry bibliography on the subject.

75 _____. 'A Study of the Legibility of One- and Two-Column Layouts for BPS Publications.' *Bulletin of the British Psychological Society* 23 (1970): 113–14. Cited in Foster, *Legibility Research Abstracts 1970*, p. 13. (Not seen)

Considers typeface, type size, leading, and single-column versus double-column format. The single column of $5^{5}/_{16}$ inches (135 mm) was read more slowly than two columns of $2^{3}/_{16}$ inches (55 mm).

76 Frutiger, Adrian. 'Letterforms in Photo-typography.' *Journal of Typographic Research* 4.4 (Autumn 1970): 327–35.

Anticipates the personal-computer boom in calling for attention to computer-generated on-screen legibility. 'Differentiation must be made between material designed for sustained and for reference reading' (p. 327). Looks at the internationality of communication and the concomitant need for fewer, more universally recognizable typefaces: 'Today we are experiencing a stabilization toward internationally accepted text types based on the roman alphabet . . .' (p. 328). (Distinguishes movements in text types from those in display types.) Looks at type sizes with respect to their use in reference materials and with respect to their fatigue in use. Says that since reference matter is read for much shorter periods of time than is text matter, the former may be set in smaller sizes. Calls this '"reference" typography' (p. 330).

77 Gaskell, Philip. *A New Introduction to Bibliography.* New York and Oxford: Oxford University Press, 1972.

Like the work of McKerrow before him (*An Introduction to Bibliography for Literary Students*, Oxford: Clarendon Press, 1927), Gaskell's work focuses more on historical and textual issues than on the physical layout or suggested contents of bibliographies. It has a wealth of information on printing types, composition, paper, imposition, presswork, binding, storing of books, decoration and illustration, and so on – all of a historical nature.

78 Gibaldi, Joseph, and Walter S. Achtert. *MLA Handbook for Writers of Research Papers.* 2nd ed. New York: Modern Language Association, 1984.

Contains a thorough discussion of how to put together research papers, including how to compile and present a bibliography. With respect to the actual presentation of the bibliographic text, this volume gives only the simplest examples, showing a five-space indentation of second and succeeding lines and the use of underlining to indicate italics. The aim here is to show how the bibliography can be produced on a typewriter. Much information is offered on what each entry should contain, which abbreviations and punctuation are preferred, and so on. This manual is designed for use primarily in the humanities. Gibaldi and Achtert recognize that the styles of other disciplines are not necessarily the same; they list the bibliographic data for manuals in other disciplines (e.g. biology, chemistry, geology, linguistics, mathematics, medicine, physics, psychology). They also cite the guide by John Bruce Howell, *Style Manuals of the English-speaking World* (Phoenix, AZ: Oryx, 1983). [See also *The Chicago Manual of Style*, **44** above; and Turabian, **253** below.]

79 Gibney, T. K. 'Legibility of Segmental Versus Standard Numerals: The Influence of the Observer's Task.' *USAF AMRL Technical Report* 68 (1968): 124, 20. Cited by Foster, *Legibility Research Abstracts 1970*, p. 13. (Not seen)

Looks at different kinds of display techniques of alphanumeric characters: 'e.g. electroluminescence, miniature-light matrices, fiber optics, T.V.' (p. 13); many displays use segmented characters, which are not as easy to read as standard figures. Says that legibility seems to be partly a function of the kind of reading the person is doing. In some cases, 'segmented numerals . . . can be used in place of Arabic numeral displays without compromising performance' (Foster, p. 13).

80 Gill, Eric. *An Essay on Typography.* Boston, MA: David R. Godine, 1988.

Says that a book should have a design appropriate to its time and place. Chapter 2 discusses letters. Chapter 3 is on typography: use of alphabets; letter forms; roman, italic, and sans serif types. Chapter 5 covers paper and ink. Prefers handmade to machine-made papers; but for machine-made papers, advocates a good smooth surface. Also considers line length, word spacing, justified setting. Says that 'the best [line] length for reading is not more than 12 words' (p. 89). Also, says that ragged-right, which allows for even word spacing, is desirable. [Uses the phrase 'the tyrannical insistence upon equal length of lines' (p. 92).] Encourages the use of common contractions to help the typesetter get well-proportioned lines. Has a brief section on selecting types and physical sizes of books appropriate to the books' content and intended use. Looks also at type sizes for different page dimensions, the design of a title page, the bulk and binding of the book, the number of copies to be printed, etc.

81 Glanville, A. D., G. L. Kreezer, and K. M. Dallenbach. 'The Effect of Type-Size on Accuracy of Apprehension and Speed of Localizing Words.' *American Journal of Psychology* 59 (Apr. 1946): 220–35.

Uses the dictionary as a source of data. Considers 6- and 12-point types. Concludes that 12-point boldface is more congenial to the reader than is 6-point boldface – especially for spotting words on a page.

82 Goel, Arjman Chand. *Theory & Practice of Composition: (A Practical Approach).* Allahabad, India: Saroj Prakashan, n.d. (preface dated 11–25–63).

Says that the bibliography is to be set 'in 2 point smaller type than the text' (p. 284). No reason is given. No other details of format or styling mentioned.

83 Goudy, Frederick W. *Typologia: Studies in Type Design & Type Making, With Comments on the Invention of Typography, The First Types, Legibility and Fine Printing.* Berkeley and Los Angeles, CA, London: University of California Press, 1940; rpt. 1977.

Chapter XII is on 'Legibility of Type' (pp. 123–55). Defines the term. Discusses the use of upper- and lower-case letters, letters in isolation and in harmony with other letters, etc. Says that type should not call attention to itself, but should be unobtrusive, not a ' "typographical impertinence" ' (p. 128). Also considers leading, word spacing, size of the characters, line length, etc. Says legibility depends on simplicity, contrast, proportion; explains these.

Points out how legibility and beauty of design are related. Also says that in some respects, legibility is a personal matter – what is legible to one person may not be to another. Says that legibility is partly a function of how well letters fit together in groups; also that people form habits in their perception of words and phrases in reading. Discusses the inconclusiveness of the 'scientific tests of the legibility of individual letters' (p. 139). Reviews the Clark University (i.e. Miles Tinker) experiments in legibility (see esp. pp. 142–4).

Looks at several experimental typefaces – even one for which he speculates that its designer 'seems to have had the idea that type is beautiful only as it defies easy reading' (p. 150). Says that 'the greatest obstacles to easy reading are non-conformity, over-refinement, high finish, too great regularity of curves and lines, and the elimination of the natural irregularities and deficiencies of handling which the designer disregards' (p. 152). Points out that legibility depends on the clarity of the typefaces and, equally, their arrangement on the page. Good on general principles and practices – but not specific on the selection of a typeface for different kinds of printing and texts.

84 Gould, J. D. 'Visual Factors in the Design of Computer-Controlled CRT Displays.' *Human Factors* 10 (1968): 359–76. Cited in Foster, *Legibility Research Abstracts 1970*, p. 14. (Not seen)

Considers image quality of figures on CRT displays, especially with respect to such factors as screen colour, luminescence, resolution, the flickering of some displays, contrast, and character size.

85 Gould, John D., Lizette Alfaro, Vincent Barnes, Rich Finn, Nancy Grischkowsky, and Angela Minuto. 'Reading Is Slower from CRT Displays Than from Paper: Attempts to Isolate a Single-Variable Explanation.' *Human Factors* 29.3 (June 1987): 269–99.

Summarizes ten experiments and other analyses to explain why reading from paper is faster than reading from CRT displays. Concludes 'that the difference is due to a combination of variables, probably centering on the image quality of the characters themselves' (p. 269).

86 _____, _____, Rich Finn, Brian Haupt, Angela Minuto, and Josiane Salaun. 'Why Reading Was Slower from CRT Displays Than from Paper.' *Human Factors in Computing Systems and Graphic Interface. CHI & GI 1987: Conference Proceedings*, 7–11. Special Issue of the SIGCHI Bulletin. Ed. by John M. Carroll and Peter P. Tanner. Toronto: The Association for Computing Machinery, 1987.

Argues that the slowness of reading on CRT displays as opposed to reading on paper is caused by 'the image quality of the CRT characters' (p. 7). Says, 'Reading speeds equivalent to those on paper were found when the CRT displays contained character fonts that resembled those on paper (rather than dot matrix fonts, for example), had a polarity of dark characters on a light background, were anti-aliased (e.g. contained grey level), and were shown on displays with relatively high resolution' (p. 7).

87 _____, and Nancy Grischkowsky. 'Does Visual Angle of a Line of Characters Affect Reading Speed?' *Human Factors* 28.2 (Apr. 1986): 165–73.

Says that the angle of the line is not a source of difference in reading speed at the distances from which screens and books are read. Points out that lines on CRT screens are wider than equivalent lines on paper, and the longer lines may require 'more eye fixations' (p. 165). Cites many other sources which deal with the same subject.

88 _____, _____. 'Doing the Same Work with Hard Copy and with Cathode-Ray Tube (CRT) Computer Terminals.' *Human Factors* 26.3 (1984): 323–37.

Compares the effects of the two media. Concludes that any differences between the perceptions of the two media 'were unaffected by whether participants used CRT in their work', but 'were due to the work itself' (p. 334). But 'participants [in the experiment] read the hard copy from 20 to 30% faster' (p. 335). Says that there is 'no evidence that the CRT *itself* contributes to feelings of fatigue or affects visual functions' (p. 336). (Subjects were looking for typographical or spelling errors in a prose text.) Cites 16 other studies.

89 Grandjean, E., U. Bräuninger, Th. Fellmann, and R. Gierer. 'Lighting Characteristics of VDTs.' *Proceedings of the Human Factors Society 25th Annual Meeting*, Rochester, NY, 1981: 687–9. Ed. by Robert C. Sugarman. Buffalo, NY: Calspan Corp., 1981.

Analyses the lighting characteristics of eight different brands of VDTs in terms of their different levels of oscillation, sharpness, and stability of characters. Argues that some differences may be a source of eye strain to operators. The differences in the quality of the displays 'are relevant for the luminance contrasts between screen and source document . . . [and] are also substantial for all the physical characteristics determining legibility: sharpness and stability of characters' (p. 689).

90 Greene, E. B. 'The Legibility of Typewritten Material.' *Journal of Applied Psychology* 17 (Dec. 1933): 713–28.

Sees no difference in reading speed with 7-, 10-, 12-, and 14-point typewriter types. Leaded texts were read 3.3% faster than text set solid; 21-pica line was read 1.1% faster than 41-pica line. [Data similar to those given in his article 'The Relative Legibility of Linotyped and Typewritten Material.' *Journal of Applied Psychology* 18 (Oct. 1934): 697–704.]

91 Gregory, Margaret, and E. C. Poulton. 'Even versus Uneven Right-hand Margins and the Rate of Comprehension in Reading.' *Ergonomics* 13.4 (1970): 427–34. Cited in Foster, *Legibility Research Abstracts 1970*, p. 14. (Not seen)

For reading short lines, 'The style of printing made no difference for good readers, but for the poor readers, the justified style resulted in significantly worse performance' (Foster, p. 14). The problem for them disappeared when the same text was set with about 12 words per line. Blames the result on 'irregularities in spacing introduced by justification when the line length is short' (Foster, p. 14).

92 *Guidelines for the Compilation of a Bibliography.* Ottawa, Canada: National Library of Canada, Committee on Bibliography and Information Services for the Social Sciences and Humanities, 1987.

Urges the careful selection and delineation of a topic for the bibliography and the clear formulation of a title; considers the purpose, audience, and scope of bibliographies. 'Choose a standard accepted bibliographic form of citation and follow a style manual suitable to the topic and purpose of the bibliography' (p. 9). Says the 'citation should provide sufficient information for users to identify and locate the work described by each entry' (p. 9). Things to consider are elements of the citation (author, title, publication data, etc.), 'arrangement of elements within the citation' (p. 9), punctuation, spacing, capitalization, indentation, etc. Mentions some style manuals and also the organization of entries, based on various organizational principles (e.g. subject, date, author or title, form, language, geographic area). Says the compiler should also consider indexes, annotations or abstracts, numbering the entries, front matter (title

page, contents, preface or foreword, acknowledgments, introduction). The front matter should define the subject, state the purpose, identify the audience, specify the scope, explain the procedures followed in the compilation of entries, cite sources consulted, identify the 'bibliographic form or style manual used, with sample citations' (p. 11), explain the organization, give a key to abbreviations used, and mention any additional features. Has only two sentences on layout (p. 12), mentioning line length, margins, space between entries, running heads, and typefaces.

93 Haber, R. N., L. Standing, and Judith Boss. 'Effect of Position and Typeface Variation on Perceptual Clarity.' *Psychonomic Science* 18.2 (1970): 91–2. Cited in Foster, *Legibility Research Abstracts 1970*, p. 14. (Not seen)

On the perception of letters in 'well spaced repetitions, even if the position and/or the typeface changed' (Foster, p. 14).

94 Hackman, R., and A. M. Kerschner. 'The Determination of Criteria of Readability.' Office of Naval Research of the University of Maryland, n.d. Technical Report 153. (Not seen)

95 Hague, René. *Reason and Typography with Particular Reference to Typographic Layout.* [London]: Central School of Art and Design, 1978. Originally published in *Typography* 1 (Nov. 1936): 8–9.

Briefly mentions the usual elements of layout and design: type size, margins, leading, line length, page size, legibility, type weight, etc.

96 Happ, Alan J., and Craig W. Beaver. 'Effects of Work at a VDT-Intensive Laboratory Task on Performance, Mood, and Fatigue Symptoms.' *Proceedings of the Human Factors Society 25th Annual Meeting*, Rochester, NY, 1981: 142–4. Ed. by Robert C. Sugarman. Buffalo, NY: Calspan Corp., 1981.

Shows that intensive work at VDTs increases the number of complaints, 'but performance was unaffected' (p. 142); however, there was a 'strong association between visual stress and fatigue' (p. 142). [Not on bibliographies, but, like other studies, this shows the interest – nearly ten years ago – in the effects of VDTs on reading / comprehension / comfort. Almost consistently, the data show that VDTs produce more fatigue and less legible texts than are possible with paper copies.]

97 Harmon, Robert B. *Elements of Bibliography: A Simplified Approach.* Metuchen, NJ, and London: Scarecrow Press, 1981.

Discusses the various terms used for bibliography: enumerative, analytical, historical, textual, descriptive, selective or elective (75–6). Points out that bibliographies are usually arranged by author, title, or subject; also chronologically; often with a combination of these. Quotes the ideas of Robert L. Collison (*Bibliography, Subject and National*, 3rd ed. New York: Hafner, 1968, p. xiii) that 'The finished product, if good, reads so easily that few give thought to the arduous and exacting nature of the task that confronts every bibliographer anew' (p. 24). [The point can be enlarged to the design of bibliographies: if the design is good, it does not call attention to itself and lets the reader concentrate on the text.] Nothing on design or layout.

98 Harner, James L. *On Compiling an Annotated Bibliography.* New York: Modern Language Association of America, 1985.

Looks at methods of compilation. Does not consider the physical presentation in typographic terms.

99 Hartley, James. *Designing Instructional Texts.* London: Kogan Page; New York: Nichols, 1985.

Considers page size; planning; type sizes, typefaces, and spacing; space and structure; use of illustrations; tables and graphs; diagrams, charts, and symbols; etc. Chapter 13 has a section on bibliographies (pp. 117–30). Points out that bibliographies are often 'scanned rather than read word for word, but detailed reading does take place when an appropriate entry is found' (p. 117). A good design uses a 'judicious mixture of typographic and spatial cues' (p. 117) to help the reader in retrieval of main and sub-elements. Says, 'The difficulty for the designer is . . . to avoid the overuse of cueing . . . and to avoid its under-use (which could lead to materials being difficult, if not impossible, to use)' (p. 117). [Overuse of cueing can be found in the Tauchnitz bibliography of William B. Todd and Ann Bowden. See the sample pages from this bibliography in Appendix I, Examples 23a–e.] Considers bibliographies in depth on pp. 120–5. Cites many sources, including Spencer and Reynolds (see below). Displays the two main types of bibliographical entries: the vertically grouped (a new piece of information

[author, title, publication data] beginning on a new line) and the run-on. Concludes that readers prefer vertically grouped entries with typographic cueing (e.g. indentation, use of boldface and italic types, etc.). Also has a chapter on 'Designing electronic text' (Chapter 14, pp. 131–8), considering legibility of VDTs and CRTs, the limitations of VDUs, problems with legibility, problems with fatigue and with search and retrieval, and the benefits (speed, searching capabilities, etc.).

100 _____, and Peter Burnhill. 'Experiments with Unjustified Text.' *Visible Language* 5.3 (Summer 1971): 265–78.

Compares the results of tests of reading unjustified text. 'No significant differences in reading speed were found in any of the three experiments' (p. 265), though one form of unjustified text (double-column formats of different widths) revealed a significant sex difference: 'the women students scoring significantly more than the men' (p. 275). Concludes that right justification has no bearing on legibility or retention. 'Perhaps more attention should now be focused on general layout, relative to the kinds of material being printed, and, in particular, attention should be drawn to the relative position of the *beginning* of textual elements' (p. 277). [This suggests Hartley's discussion of cuing; see previous entry].

101 Hayman, E. 'Design Criteria for CRT Alphanumeric Displays.' *Proceedings of the IEEE-GMMS ERS International Symposium on Man–Machine Systems, Cambridge, England* (8–12 Sept. 1969), p. 4. Cited in Foster, *Legibility Research Abstracts 1970*, p. 15.

For maximum legibility CRT typeface designs must consider 'display brightness, flicker-free presentation, minimum operator fatigue, character legibility, and precise character presentation' (Foster, p. 15).

102 Heppner, Frank H., John G. T. Anderson, Alan E. Farstrup, and Nelson H. Weiderman. 'Reading Performance on a Standardized Test Is Better from Print than from Computer Display.' *Journal of Reading* (Jan. 1985): 321–5.

Subjects clearly preferred print to CRT displays; 'computer familiarity does not alter the relative differences in performance scores' (p. 324). That is, even if a reader has a good deal of experience at a CRT, she or he still reads a printed text more quickly.

103 Higgins, Marion Villiers. *Bibliography: A Beginner's Guide to the Making, Evaluation and Use of Bibliographies.* New York: H. W. Wilson, 1941.

Looks at capitalization, the order of elements in entries, indentation, consistency, underlining. A fairly detailed treatment, with little attention to the aesthetics of the page design. E.g., 'As a means of making prominent items stand out, underlining is often used in typed manuscripts [*sic*]. In a printed work this is accomplished by the use of contrasting type such as bold face or italic types' (p. 17). Nothing else on underlining. Points out the several types of bibliographies (general, national and regional, trade, author, subject, form [e.g. by genre], period). [There is also the bibliography of a given collection: e.g. wine books in a person's collection.]

104 Hill, C. 'An Experiment in the Reactions of Divergent Groups to Different Typefaces.' Bournemouth and Poole College of Art (England), n.d. Cited in Foster, *Legibility Research Abstracts 1970*, p. 15.

Seeks 'to find variations in attitudes of different groups of people to 4 typefaces' (Foster, p. 15). Students in art and engineering had different attitudes toward the different typefaces. [When designing a bibliography, the typographer should consider her or his audience.]

105 Hill, Mary, and Wendell Cochran. *Into Print: A Practical Guide to Writing, Illustrating, and Publishing.* Los Altos, CA: William Kaufmann, Inc., 1977.

Contains a brief section on bibliographies (pp. 101–2). Distinguishes between *works cited* and a more comprehensive bibliography. Also points out the different ways bibliographies are used in books (or at the end of each chapter, at the beginning or end of a book; broken down by some subject listing or all in one list). 'In any case consistency is essential' (p. 102). Cites the elements in 'preferred' order: author(s) or editor(s), title, date, kind of publication (e.g. abstract, editorial, photograph), series title, volume number, publisher's name and address, pagination. Suggests that no abbreviations be used: 'abbreviations save some space but they sacrifice much time spent in checking and translating' (p. 102).

106 Hills, Philip, ed. *The Future of the Printed Word: The Impact and the Implications of the New Communications Technology.* Westport, CT: Greenwood Press, 1980.

Contains 13 essays on various aspects of document storage, presentation, and retrieval; reading and the production of data; the presentation of data on video display screens; and so on. See individual works by Linda Reynolds ('Designing for the New . . .'; see **186** below) and others. E.g., those by Donald W. King ('Electronic Alternatives to Paper-Based Publishing in Science and Technology', pp. 99–110), Franco Mastroddi and Serge Lustac ('Euronet DIANE – A Precursor to Electronic Publishing?', pp. 111–21), and Yuri Gates ('Present and Future Printing Techniques', pp. 123–34) indicate the need to consider the use of non-paper, non-book media in the presentation of texts.

107 Holmes, Grace. 'The Relative Legibility of Black Print and White Print.' *Journal of Applied Psychology* 15 (1931): 248–51.

Results show 'that when ten point type is employed the legibility of words printed in black type on a white background is 14.7 per cent. greater than white type on a black background' (p. 251).

108 Houghton, Bernard, ed. *Standardization for Documentation.* Hamden, CT: Archon Books; Great Britain: Clive Bingley, 1969.

Six essays, none of which focuses on the physical design of bibliographies; stresses the importance of standardization in format, content, design, etc.

109 Hovde, H. T. 'The Relative Effects of Size of Type, Leading and Context, Part I.' *Journal of Applied Psychology* 13 (Dec. 1929): 600–29.

Says that context is more important than sensory materials. Nothing specifically applicable to the design of bibliographies.

110 _____. 'The Relative Effects of Size of Type, Leading and Context, Part II.' *Journal of Applied Psychology* 14 (Feb. 1930): 63–73.

Says that readers tend to prefer larger types and more leading, but their preferences and opinions about legibility differ from amount of reading as measured by the reading rate (p. 71). 46-item bibliography contains no study on bibliographies; all are general studies of readability, legibility, etc.

110a Hurlburt, Allen. *The Grid*. New York: Van Nostrand Reinhold, 1978. (Not seen)

111 _____. *Layout: The Design of the Printed Page*. New York: Watson-Guptill, 1977.

Looks at many aspects of typographic layout: art styles (e.g. Art Nouveau, Cubism, Dada, Surrealism, Art Deco, De Stijl, Bauhaus, etc.), symmetry and asymmetry, contrast, balance, free form, etc. Considers some elements of typography, including letter forms, style, and legibility. Says, 'Perhaps too much thought has been given to the appropriateness of a typeface to the message' (p. 106). Mildly calls into question the many studies of legibility, and says that 'the best solution is to use . . . material in such a way that it arouses interest and invites reading' (p. 107). Has nothing on bibliographies, or on other specific parts of books.

112 Hurt, Peyton. *Bibliography and Footnotes*. 3rd ed. Rev. and enlarged by Mary L. Hurt Richmond. Berkeley and Los Angeles, CA, and London: University of California Press, 1968.

Focuses on what data go into the citations and not the physical layout of the page. Reiterates the common organization of information in a bibliographical entry: author, title, publication data (with all the refinements and variations possible in these three areas). Deals with italics, capitalization, underlining, full caps, and other typographical means of designating variant parts of entries. Presents these more as conventions than as aesthetic considerations linked to legibility or ease of identification of elements. For books, cites 1) author; 2) title; 3) series and number; 4) edition; 5) imprint (place, publisher, date); 6) main pagination. For periodicals, cites 1) author; 2) title; 3) name of periodical; 4) volume number; 5) number of the issue; 6) date; 7) pagination. For both styles, authors' names are given in the sequence last name first, comma, first name or initials, etc. Also gives styles for government documents (United States and British) and reference works.

113 *Information Transfer: Handbook on International Standards Governing Information Transfer*. N.p.: ISO Information Centre, 1977. ISO Standards Handbook 1.

Contains a great amount of information on many aspects of information presentation: 'an aid and an introduction to international standardization in the field of information transfer' (p. v). The first section is on 'Bibliographic references and descriptions, abstracts and indexing' (pp. 1–166). Concerns the content and order of bibliographic entries, use of abbreviations and symbols, various kinds of documentation. Nothing on the design of bibliographies, but offers practical standards for the presentation and content of many kinds of information.

114 Jacobi, Charles T[homas]. *Some Notes on Books and Printing: A Guide for Authors, Publishers & Others*. New and enlarged ed. London: Charles Whittingham & Co., 1902.

Chapter III is on 'Types and Margins' (pp. 22–32). Nothing on legibility, except to mention that the body of the text should not be in the centre of the page. Also touches on papers, sizes of books, and binding. Nothing on bibliographies.

115 Jennett, Seán. *The Making of Books*. London: Faber & Faber, 1951; 3rd ed., 1964.

Part 2 is on 'The Design of Books' (pp. 183–459). Looks at type design, some of the parts of the book (chapter heads, part-titles, pages of the text, title pages, endpapers, etc.). Hardly mentions the bibliography except to say that it 'is placed near the end of the book' (p. 316). In section on 'End Matter' (pp. 323–7) mentions seven items (appendixes, bibliography, notes, indexes, etc.), but says 'There is little point in dealing with these in detail' (p. 323). Says the bibliography should be 'set in the text type, with headings after the manner of the chapter heads' (p. 323).

Mentions the attitude many authors have toward compiling bibliographies for their own works. Lists the items that belong in bibliographic entries. 'It is necessary to get these items in some reasonable order, and to maintain it throughout the bibliography' (p. 324).

116 Kak, Anita V. 'Relationships Between Readability of Printed and CRT-Displayed Text.' *Proceedings of the Human Factors Society 25th Annual Meeting*, Rochester, NY, 1981: pp. 137–40. Ed. by Robert C. Sugarman. Buffalo, NY: Calspan Corp., 1981.

Assesses 'the effects of CRT display upon reading, rather than lebibility [*sic*] test performance' (p. 137). Concludes that 'the notion that legibility criteria may be excessively strict when applied to tasks involving reading of connected prose text was supported' (p. 139). Also says that 'the relatively close match between reading scores in standard paper format and when presented via a CRT display suggest that CRT reading levels can, when conditions are optimized further, equal those obtained with printed text' (pp. 139–40). Not specifically on bibliographies, but shows the awareness of the issue of effective, comfortable reading on video display terminals. The claim is that they can be read as effectively as paper copies of the same text.

117 Kindersley, David. 'Space Craft.' *Visible Language* 7.4 (Autumn 1973): 311–24.

Urges the careful and 'proper' spacing of letters now that computer typesetting is here. 'Optically adjusted text spacing will require attention to the subtleties of each letter's optical centre and the inner forces involved in our eyes' perception of these letterforms' (p. 311).

118 Kinross, Robin. 'Large and Small Letters: Authority and Democracy.' *Octavo: Journal of Typography* 5 (1988): 2–5.

Justifies the use of capital and lower-case letters, especially with respect to the English use of caps for proper names and beginnings of sentences. Shows an awareness of the proper and careful use of upper-case letters.

119 Knight, G. Norman. *Indexing, the Art of.* London and Boston, MA: George Allen and Unwin, 1979.

Though not on bibliographies, covers many topics germane to the compilation of bibliographies. Considers headings and subheadings, use of punctuation, choice and styling of proper names and repeated names, compound surnames, when and what to cross-reference, etc. Has a whole chapter on alphabetical arrangement (Chapter 7, pp. 115–31) – how to use it and when to abandon it. Covers proofreading.

120 Knight, James L., Jr. 'Alternative Character-Spacing Algorithms for CRT-Displayed Text.' [Abstract.] *Proceedings of the Human Factors Society 25th Annual Meeting*, Rochester, NY, 1981: p. 141. Ed. by Robert C. Sugarman. Buffalo, NY: Calspan Corp., 1981.

Abstract of paper which notes the difference between the display of letters centred in equal-sized spaces and letters arranged with proportional spacing. The latter 'can result in significantly greater display densities of textual information than with traditional centered-spacing'. This brief abstract does not go into the issue of legibility, but it does discuss VDT-presented texts.

121 Knuth, Donald E. *Computers & Typesetting / A: The TEXbook.* Reading, MA: Addison-Wesley Publishing Co., 1986.

Essentially a computer manual designed to show how to use hardware to set mathematical texts. Shows briefly how the software may help in the display of some parts of entries in a bibliography (see, e.g., pp. 74, 93, 340–1). The last of these three examples is a printout in software TEX symbols and the resultant printed bibliographic entry. The entry looks like this:

> [1] D.E. Knuth and M.F. Plass, 'Breaking paragraphs into lines,' . . . .

If this were in a bibliography, the fact that it is not alphabetized would make it difficult to locate. It is probably to be linked with a bracketed number in the text. This is not uncommon for styling in scientific publications.

122 _____. *Computers & Typesetting / E: Computer Modern Typefaces.* Reading, MA: Addison-Wesley Publishing Co., 1986.

Considers 'Greek and Roman letterforms, together with punctuation marks, numerals, and a large collection of mathematical symbols' (p. v). Aims to show how many typefaces can be generated by the programs the book presents. Presents again the author's METAFONT ideas (see next entry). Focuses on the means of reproducing (with perfect clarity and using computer technology) the fine lines of modern typefaces. Presents ways of designing, on the computer, calligraphic caps, ligatures, upper- and lower-case letters in Roman and Greek alphabets, etc. Focuses primarily on the printing of mathematical texts. Useful in demonstrating that computer-generated texts can be legible. With bibliography containing citations to works on same subject (i.e. computer displays).

123 ———. 'Lessons Learned from METAFONT.' In *The Computer and the Hand . . .*, pp. 35–53. Ed. by Charles Bigelow and Lynn Ruggles (see **21** above).

On author's work in digital alphabet design. Explains how his METAFONT works and the problems it posed in its creation of all shapes of letterforms. Says that designers of typefaces for VDTs should consider the computer a completely new medium and should design typefaces for the screen, not try to adapt old faces to the new technology.

124 Knuth, Donald Ervin. *Mathematical Typography.* Stanford, CA: Computer Service Department, Stanford University, 1978. Josiah Willard Gibbs Lecture, given under the auspices of the American Mathematical Society, 4 Jan. 1978.

Discusses the typography of mathematics and conversely how mathematics can help typographers: 'mathematical ideas can make advances in the art of printing' (p. 1). Examines typefaces, spacing, and the over-all impression of the page. Concentrates on computer-assisted composition (now a dated discussion). Talks of designing an alphabet with a computer. Discusses TEX, 'a system which takes manuscripts and converts them into specifications about where to put each character on the page; and . . . METAFONT, which generates the characters themselves, for use in the inkier parts of the printing business' (p. 15). [See Knuth, *TEX and METAFONT: New Directions in Typesetting.* Bedford, MA: American Mathematical Society and Digital Press, 1979.] Talks of computer-based type design, but ignores legibility. In *TEX and METAFONT*, Knuth greatly expands on the two modes of computer use.

125 Kolers, Paul A. 'Clues to a Letter's Recognition: Implications for the Design of Characters.' *Journal of Typographical Research* 3.2 (Apr. 1969): 145–68.

Looks at the 'orientation of letters and direction of reading' (p. 145). Points out that readers tend to view the right sides of letters as their eyes scan a text. 'This finding suggests that typefaces might be redesigned to avoid bold strokes weighted on their left or heavy strokes that are all of equal weight' (p. 145). Also concludes that 'typefaces that emphasize bold downstrokes for the Roman alphabet . . . impede their smooth visual processing' (p. 164). Cites two other works 'in press' by him and D. N. Perkins, to be published in the journal *Perception and Psychophysics*, on letter orientation, speed of reading, and legibility.

[See his own follow-up remarks in the same journal, 4.1 (Winter 1970): 87–90. See also Jeremy J. Foster, 'Directional Consistency . . .', 72 above.]

126 Koopman, Harry Lyman. *Booklover and His Books.* Boston, MA: Boston Book Co., 1917.

Chapter [2] is on 'Fitness in Book Design' (pp. 9–13). Does not talk specifically about the individual elements in book design. Mentions in passing the size of type, the thickness of the paper, book size, thickness of the volume, and 'that all the elements of a book [must] be honest, sincere, enduring' (p. 12). Has chapters on book sizes (pp. 19–27), paper (pp. 92–6), bindings (pp. 97–101, 102–3), types (pp. 120–7, 128–33), etc. Chapter [20] touches on legibility (pp. 134–8), but is sketchy and not on bibliographies.

127 ———. 'Printing Page Problems with Geometrical Solutions.' N.p.: n.p., n.d.: 353–6. [Article removed from an unspecified journal (*The Printing Art?* 27 Jan. 1911?); from the collection at Brown University.]

Discusses the optimum placement of text matter on a page. Points out that mathematical calculations 'are never more than approximate' while 'geometric solutions are exact' (p. 353). Shows how 'to construct rectangles of the two most approved proportions for the page; [and] to construct a similar rectangle of any desired ratio to a given rectangle; and . . . to construct proportional margins' (p. 353). Talks of 'the ideal book page' (p. 353), the so-called 'printer's oblong' with a diagonal twice the width, or the '"golden oblong," in which the width is to the length as the length is to the sum' (p. 353). Points out how 'extremely pleasing' (p. 355) these page designs are, with 'an agreeable balance between slenderness and squareness in the page' (p. 355). Talks impressionistically about the resulting beauty of the page. But never analyses why it is beautiful or particularly congenial to a reader.

128 Krummel, Donald W. *Bibliographies: Their Aims and Methods.* London and New York: Mansell, 1984.

Defines the field; offers a history of bibliographies; discusses their scope, annotation, organization, and presentation. Points out that Besterman's *Bibliography of Bibliographies* lists 117,000 bibliographies and that at least 7,000 more are produced each year. Delineates the method for delimiting the scope of a bibliography. 'A bibliography on a chosen topic should be complete and comprehensive within the limitations that need to be understood by the compiler and reader alike. Omissions are inexcusable' (p. 24). Says that exclusions should be fully explained in the introduction. Looks at the 'five considerations associated with physical form' (p. 26): 1) the medium (i.e. the types of things the bibliography includes, such as books, pamphlets, newspapers, anthologies, government documents, dissertations and theses, reports, unpublished materials, conference proceedings, etc.); 2) the bibliographic level of the entries – how analytical the bibliography entry is with respect to describing the content and physical form of an item; 3) the circumstances of production (i.e. the time, place, and circumstances under which the item was produced); 4) features of the physical object; 5) citation of locations. Also mentions 'five criteria concerning intellectual and artistic content' (p. 30) which might go into a bibliographic entry: 1) subject matter; 2) circumstances of creation; 3) language(s); 4) objective (to educate, entertain, exhort); and 5) endorsement of quality. Adds that 'When a work is cited, it should be cited either in all presentations, or in only the most authoritative and canonical presentation' (p. 34). Chapter VII, on presentation (pp. 125–41), offers data on the various ways to present titles, introduction, and other features (e.g. table of contents; list of abbreviations, symbols, or acronyms; 'directory of addresses of issuing agencies of current publications' [p. 128]); indexes; appendixes; glossary; etc.).

Pages 130–5 are on layout, the most germane to the present study. 'The possibilities are vast' (p. 130), considering how many options there are in what will be included in any bibliographic entry. Says, 'Since a bibliography is consulted strategically but very rarely read through, it follows that the more entries per page the better. As a medium to be scanned, the ideal bibliography might aspire to the appearance of a map, although the sensible restrictions of largeness in page size and smallness in type serve to remind us that the ideal may be quite a long way ahead' (p. 130). Says that type sizes over 14 points are wasteful and could seem pretentious; under 8 points they are difficult to scan. 'Because of the density of information, it is more important for the lines to be short, between 65 and 100 mm (approximately 2.4–4 inches) wide; in a normal book typeface, 65 mm would provide about 40 characters in 11-point or 43 in 10-point, whereas 100 mm would allow some 60 characters in 11-point or 65 in 10-point' (p. 130). Says that two or even three columns may be acceptable. Talks of 'the manipulation of white space' (p. 131) on the page, indentation (especially the use of hanging indentation), where to

place the entry number (if the entries are to be numbered), type sizes (especially mixing sizes) and styles (roman, italic, boldface, sans serif, etc.), use of different colours for the separate elements within each entry, the styling of the annotations (if there are any), etc.

'While the day when authors will be their own compositors of text is just around the corner and basically to be welcomed, its implications for the compiler are both drastic and promising: it will be an added responsibility to be more conversant with and sensitive to matters of book design, typography, and graphic layout' (p. 134). Talks also of the advantages of on-line bibliographies (pp. 135 f.). Appendix A is 'Criteria for Evaluating a Bibliography' (pp. 143–6) – 'A statement prepared by the Bibliography Committee of the Reference Services Division, American Library Association' (p. 143), published in *RQ* 11 (1972): 359–60.

129 Kumar, Girja, and Krishan Kumar. *Bibliography*. New Delhi, India: Vikas Publishing House, 1976.

A thorough study of the *content* of bibliographies, with chapters on compiling, organizing, mechanics, arrangement, etc. Nothing on the design of the printed page of a bibliography, even though it gives sample bibliography pages (pp. 235–47).

130 Labuz, Ronald. *Typography & Typesetting: Type Design and Manipulation Using Today's Technology*. New York: Van Nostrand Reinhold, 1988.

Has sections on typography today, anatomy of type, 'The Art and Science of Legible Pages' (p. 59), book design, layout, copyfitting, etc. On legibility, looks at typeface designs, type sizes, line spacing (e.g., 'Spacing between display and body should be at least six points larger than the display type size, so as not to cramp the text' [p. 64]; also, 'In general, leading should be about 20 percent of the type size' [p. 62]), line length ('As with leading, the correct line length depends on the type size and x-height. The measure should be set from between approximately 1½ to 2½ alphabets long. To convert this into useful figures, *the line length should generally be 1½ to 3 times the type size*' [p. 67]), the space between words and between letters, and other features of the printed page. Discusses legibility research, display type, the use of figures, indentation, justified and unjustified texts, ligatures, lower-case versus upper-case letters, black paper and white print, serifs versus sans serif types, etc. On bibliographies, says that the opening page of a bibliography 'should be consistent with the opening page of the glossary and index' (p. 96). Advocates the use of the *MLA Handbook* (by Gibaldi and Achtert, 78) and *The Chicago Manual of Style* (44). Also for bibliographies, says, 'The type size may be one or two points smaller than the body copy size' (p. 96).

130a Lawson, Alexander. *Printing Types: An Introduction.* Boston, MA: Beacon Press, 1971.

Covers a full range of subjects pertaining to type: its history, mechanized typesetting, photo- and computerized typesetting, display types, small caps, numerals, typeface nomenclature and classification, etc. Discusses the parts of typefaces in detail.

131 Lee, Marshall. *Bookmaking: The Illustrated Guide to Design/Production/Editing.* 2nd ed., completely revised and expanded. New York: Bowker, 1979.

The only comments specifically on bibliographies are: 'Some bibliographies may have descriptive paragraphs for each title. These should have a separate character count, while the book titles can be counted line for line' (p. 214). This follows the statement: 'Any line of copy that will definitely begin a new line on the printed page and will definitely not extend beyond one line may be counted as *line-for-line* copy' (p. 214). In a section on 'Reference Books' is the following:

'The main consideration here is convenience in locating items, so the running heads and/or folios are of primary importance. . . . Subheads and alphabetical indicators should be made prominent also, as they are the guides followed by readers who are not inclined to use running heads or folios.

'In directories, encyclopedias, and other reference books in which the user will be reading brief passages, the text type may be quite small, particularly where 2- or 3-column composition results in a narrow measure' (p. 364). Nothing more specifically on bibliographies.

132 *The Legibility of Type.* Brooklyn, NY: Merganthaler Linotype Co., 1935. [Rpt. in 1947 under the title *The Readability of Type.* See also from the same company, *Researches in Readability,* **185** below.]

Recounts various features of letters and printed pages which affect legibility – type size; line length; use of 1- or 2-column layout; typeface; word spacing; leading; serif versus sans serif type faces; use of capitals and lower-case letters; 'the position of initials with relation to text matter' (p. 17); type weight; and use of ornamentation, paper, and ink.

133 Legros, Lucien Alphonse. *A Note on the Legibility of Printed Matter: Prepared for the Information of the Committee on Type Faces.* London: His Majesty's Stationery Office, 1922.

Considers the reader, reading abilities, typography, etc. Under 'the features presented by the printed surface' (p. 1), the author lists type size; thickness of the strokes of characters; 'the amount of white between the mean strokes or in the counters of the characters' (p. 1); 'the amount of dissimilarity between characters of pairs commonly misread' (p. 1); space between lines; line length; use of kerns; use of rule; 'similarity of form or figure' (p. 1); figure widths; type height; paper quality and colour; reflectivity of paper; 9 ink colour; etc. Examines these and other features individually.

134 _____, and J. C. Grant. *Typographical Printing-Surfaces: The Technology and Mechanism of Their Production.* London: Longmans, Green, and Co., 1916.

Contains an enormous amount of information on many aspects of book production: typecasting, printing, typography, typefaces, composing, etc. Chapter XI is on legibility (pp. 156–92). Covers size of characters; leading; typeface design; line length; 'the resemblance of some characters to others' (pp. 156, 160 ff.); 'the presence of unnecessary lines or marks, ornamental or otherwise' (p. 157); frequency of kerns; paper quality and colour; colour of ink; the reflectivity of the paper; illumination; and irradiation. Contains many observations and suggestions; e.g., 'It is recommended that the length of the line should not usually exceed 4 inches in books of 10-point type and upwards, and that this maximum should be reduced in proportion to the body if smaller sizes are used' (p. 157). Typefaces should be used in which similarly shaped letters are as distinguishable from one another as possible (e.g. *e, o, c; n, u; i, l; h, b; a, s*). Speaks strongly against Fraktur types. Nothing specific about bibliographies, but a great compendium of information on book production.

135 Level, Jeff G. 'Dear Gentle Reader.' *Journal für Druckgeschichte/Journal of Printing History/Journal de l'Histoire de l'Imprimerie* 2 (1989): 11–12.

Discusses many of the studies of legibility and questions 'whether the legibility and readability studies conducted by psychologists were really relevant to typographic design' (p. 11). Uses newspapers as his principal medium for this discussion. Says, 'What matters most about a type is that it be designed and used in a form fit to be read' (p. 12). [This short summary of Level's views is followed by a forum titled 'My God, What Do They Want?' (p. 12). Matthew Carter and Paula Scher spoke on designing types for digital typography. They and many other speakers are summarized in this issue, which contains a survey of Type '87: The International Conference on Typography and Design. Also present were James Mosley, who spoke on sans serif types; Jack Stauffacher, who spoke on Nicholas Kis and his types; and others who spoke on types, desktop publishing, and the future of type design.]

136 Lewis, R. A. 'Legibility of Capital and Lower Case Computer Printout.' *Journal of Applied Psychology* 56 (1972): 280–1. Cited by Foster, *Legibility Research 1972–1978*. (Not seen)

137 Lipsett, F. R., and F. D. Blair. 'Bibliography Preparation by Computer.' *Journal of Chemical Documentation* 8.1 (Feb. 1968): 26–9.

Points out the obsolescence of the compilation of bibliographies on 3 × 5 inch note cards and on edge-punched cards, and propounds a method of computer-assisted filing and searching procedures. Uses keypunched cards – describes the method of producing a machine-assisted bibliography, with little or no attention to the actual design of the bibliography. Concentrates more on the possible content of the bibliographic entry than on its form. A fairly unaesthetic and primitive article. [This is one of the typical early articles on computer use that takes the attitude that computers can solve all your problems. It scoffs at the use of 3 × 5 inch note cards, but, in 1968, it could not offer another way to get the data from the library to the computer.]

138 Luckiesh, Matthew. 'The Perfect Reading Page.' *Electrical Engineering* 56.7 (July 1937): 779–81.

Shows that visibility depends on size, contrast, brightness of object and background, and time available to the reader. The 'ideal printed page results from' type size and legibility, paper, illumination, and time (p. 779). Recommends type of about 12 points; white or (preferably) yellow-tinted paper; dull (i.e. not glossy) paper; c. 1,000 foot-candles of light.

139 _____, and F. K. Moss. 'Boldness as a Factor in Type-Design and Typography.' *Journal of Applied Psychology* 24 (Apr. 1940): 170–83.

Medium typefaces seem to be more readable than light- or boldface.

140 _____, _____. 'The Effect of Line Length on Readability.' *Journal of Applied Psychology* 25 (Feb. 1941): 67–75.

Says that for 10-point type – set in 13-, 17-, 21-, 25-, and 29-pica lines – readability increased as line widths increased from 13 to *c.* 21 picas.

141 _____, _____. 'Effects of Leading on Readability.' *Journal of Applied Psychology* 22 (Apr. 1938): 140–60.

All speed-of-reading criteria failed to show any significant differences with variations in leading. The practical optimum in readability was with 3-point leading.

142 _____, and Frank K. Moss. *The Science of Seeing.* New York: D. Van Nostrand, 1937.

Considers typography from a variety of perspectives. Discusses 'non-glossy colored and tinted papers' (p. 443) in terms of visibility, identification by colour, aesthetic factors, and other psychological factors (p. 444). Though many combinations of paper and ink colours have been tested, the basic unit of legibility emerges from visibility, which comes from high contrast. 'This means the use of so-called white or near-white papers' and black ink (p. 446). 'Even the grayish newsprint commonly used in newspapers, catalogues and directories measurably reduces contrast and visibility' (p. 446). 'Visibility is not necessarily the entire matter, but generally it is the overwhelmingly important factor. It does not seem that much sacrifice in visibility of printed and reading matter can be justified for the sake of vague and unmeasured so-called benefits' (p. 446). Discusses other, specific variations of paper colours and legibility (pp. 446–53), typography (pp. 455–68), reading distance and posture (pp. 469–70), eye movements (pp. 470–9), etc. Nothing specifically on bibliographies. One section is on type size and visibility (pp. 457–60), but is inconclusive in its findings other than to mention that the larger the type the more visible it is (see esp. chart, p. 459). Also, not applicable specifically to bibliographies.

143 _____, _____. 'The Visibility and Readability of Printed Matter.' *Journal of Applied Psychology* 23 (1939): 645–59.

Visibility is a product of contrast and brightness (p. 646). Readability considers the actual clarity of the typeface, line length, leading, margins, etc. (p. 653). Greater boldness of a typeface seems to yield greater legibility (p. 655); 'it appears that the readability of type is enhanced by increasing its boldness' (p. 656).

144 _____, _____. 'The Visibility of Print on Various Qualities of Paper.' *Journal of Applied Psychology* 25 (1941): 152–8.

Examines nine different papers of varying colours and weights. Results show 'that the degrees of visibility obtained with various grades and finishes of so-called "white" papers are not radically different when the quality of the printing is optimum in each case' (p. 157). Contrast seems to be the most important factor.

145 _____, _____. 'Visibility and Readability of Print on White and Tinted Papers.' *Sight-Saving Review* 8 (1938): 123.

Shows that tinted papers are no better than white papers in terms of decreased eye strain or increased ease of reading. In fact, the deeper the tint, the less visible the printed matter.

146 McCrum, Blanche Prichard, and Helen Dudenbostel Jones. *Bibliographical Procedures & Style: A Manual for Bibliographers in the Library of Congress.* Washington, DC: Library of Congress, Reference Department, 1954; rpt. 1966.

A 'handbook of standard practices and techniques, so far as standardization is possible or desirable', aiming to stress 'the unity of principles underlying the preparation of bibliographical entries and of Library of Congress catalog cards' (p. v). Contains sections on planning and procedures for preparing the bibliography, and on bibliographical style for different types of materials. Also gives instructions for compiling a bibliography. Has sections on preparing the entries and arranging them. Entries may be arranged in five ways: 1) alphabetical; 2) in a classified arrangement; 3) chronological; 4) regional; 5) arrangement by type of material. Says, when drawing entries from many sources with their own bibliographic styles, they should all be presented in one style. Part Two covers bibliographical style: the styling of each entry.

Mentions various style manuals and presents Library of Congress practices in detail for books, pamphlets, other monographic materials, documents, and serials. Says nothing about layout or page design.

147 McKerrow, Ronald B. *An Introduction to Bibliography for Literary Students.* Oxford: Clarendon Press, 1977.

Nothing on the actual physical layout of a bibliography, but useful for the terminology of the parts of a book, etc.

148 McLean, Ruari. *The Thames and Hudson Manual of Typography.* London: Thames and Hudson, 1988.

Has a chapter on legibility. 'To try to make something legible, the designer must know *what* is to be read, *why* it is to be read, *who* will read it, and *when* and *where* it will be read. "Where" includes the quality of light . . .' (p. 42). Discusses the legibility of typefaces (made possible by having letters clearly distinguishable from one another). Says, 'Sans-serif type is intrinsically less legible than seriffed type' (p. 44). 'Well-designed upper- and lower-case type is easier to read than any of its variants' (p. 44) – e.g., italic, boldface, full caps, condensed or expanded. 'Words should be close to each other (about as far apart as the width of the letter "i"); and there should be more space between the lines than between the words' (p. 45). Discusses the research done on legibility and debunks it: 'Research in legibility, even when carried out under the most "scientific" conditions, has not yet come up with anything fundamental that typographic designers did not already know . . .' (p. 47). Says that 'the normal principles of book readability' call for 'about 10–12 words a line and with some interlinear spacing' (p. 48).

Also has chapters on 'Letters for Printing' (pp. 57–78); paper (pp. 93–108); layout (pp. 109–18); book design (pp. 119–46) – all covering a wide range of issues. Considers centred or asymmetric typography, margins, shape and size of the page (landscape or portrait), page grids. Also contains a section on 'The parts of a book' (pp. 147–76) which covers half-title, copyright page, dedication, acknowledgements, preface, contents, list of illustrations, text pages, registration (or 'backing up'), running heads, page numbers, quotations, justified and ragged-right setting, footnotes, chapter openings, captions, appendixes, index, endpapers, case, and dust jacket.

For the bibliography, says that it should contain, at the very least, author, title, and publication data. Opts for upper- and lower-case italics for book titles, not quotation marks. Article titles should be in roman type in quotation marks. Has other suggestions for the *content* and *styling* of the entries, but nothing on the physical layout of the bibliography as a whole or of each entry.

149 Madan, Falconer. 'On Method in Bibliography.' *Transactions of the Bibliographical Society* 1 (1893): 91–106.

'The bibliographer must be a master of the subject of which he treats before he can really estimate the place and importance of each book which comes before him' (pp. 91–2). Calls for uniformity in the principles of compiling, and the methods of presenting, bibliographies. Warns against '*inaccuracy and scantiness of information*' (p. 93); '*superfluity of information*' (p. 94); the overuse of symbols and abbreviations, which inhibit the smooth use of bibliographies; and 'a want of perspective, a deficiency of the sense of balance and proportion' (p. 95). Also calls for '1. The use of capitals when the original title has them; 2. The mention of the first words of page 11 (and occasionally 101 or 501) to identify imperfect copies and to separate different issues; 3. The mention of the principal type of the work' (p. 96). Says the bibliography should include such elements as title, imprint, date, size, number of pages, etc. [Clearly, these notes pertain to bibliographical description for scholarly bibliographies which are designed to help scholars compare different exemplars of the same work.]

149a Major, Alexander Gregory. 'Readability of College General Biology Textbooks and the Probable Effect of Readability Elements on Comprehension.' Ph.D. diss., Syracuse University, Syracuse, NY, 1955.

Discusses the scholarship on readability and reading skills. Looks primarily at the *content* of the reading, not at its physical form. Concludes that the writing level should be appropriate for the audience. [Note: The conclusion here applies as well to bibliographies. The compiler should not present anything that will send a reader to other books to understand; i.e., terms, abbreviations, or references that are not fully explained in the bibliography itself.]

150 March, Marion. *Creative Typography*. Oxford: Phaidon, 1988.

Has a section on type – styles, use, and use with lettering, with colours, and with images.

151 Marcus, Aaron. 'A Prototype Computerized Page-design System.' *Visible Language* 5.3 (Summer 1971): 197–220.

'. . . describes a prototype system devised to investigate both the problems and capabilities of using computers for page design' (p. 197). Anticipates the personal computer and desktop publishing. Deals with all the things today's personal computers can handle: moving text blocks, manipulating type sizes and typefaces, formatting of various sorts (italics, boldface, etc.), searching for text, setting in columns, selecting line length, doing graphics, justifying lines, and so on. [This is a fairly sophisticated presentation of things which have become commonplace and trivial in the present PC world.]

152 Menapace, John. 'Some Approaches to Annotation.' *Scholarly Publishing* 1.2 (Jan. 1970): 194–205.

Asks three crucial questions: 'What is to be conveyed? To whom? How will it be used? The answers to these should determine the form of the book' (p. 194).

Discusses internal citation of sources as an alternative to note numbers and footnotes (or end-notes), and the use of footnotes for authorial commentary, rather than for bibliographical citation. Though this article does not discuss the actual layout of bibliographies, it does anticipate by about a dozen years the style of internal, parenthetical documentation adopted by many publishers (and by the Modern Language Association).

153 Mergler, H. W., and P. M. Vargo. 'One Approach to Computer Assisted Letter Design.' *Journal of Typographic Research* 2.4 (1968): 299–322. Cited in Foster, *Legibility Research Abstracts* 1970, p. 21. (Not seen)

Not on legibility but on the design of typefaces on a computer.

154 Miles, John. *Design for Desktop Publishing: A Guide to Layout and Typography on the Personal Computer*. London: Gordon Fraser, 1987.

Contains much useful information on typefaces, typesetting, page grids, symmetry and asymmetry, layout, emphasis, indenting, the use of rules and boxes, using tabular settings, notes, illustrations, colours, etc. 'Typographic design and layout are very agreeable activities. There is great pleasure to be had from bringing order out of disorder, from giving authority and style to a document that has up to then been just another anonymous typescript. But it is important to remember that it is only a means to an end; the imparting of a message from the printed page into an individual mind. Anything which gets in the way of that process is a mistake' (p. 7). In reference books (e.g. parts lists, dictionaries, timetables, [bibliographies]), 'the first requirement is easy access to a key word or number . . . . Key words have to be emphasised' (p. 13). Advises on avoiding widows, getting the proper line length, justifying the text ('There is no evidence to suggest that unjustified [ranged-right] setting is any more or less readable than justified,' p. 27); also mentions page depth, margins, use of columns, and many other typographic elements (main headings and titles, use of full caps or upper and lower case, small formats, subheads, boldface and italic types, underlining, letterspacing, indentation, etc.). Nothing specific on bibliographies.

155 Miller, Irwin, and Thomas W. Suther, III. 'Preferred Height and Angle Settings of CRT and Keyboard for a Display Input Task.' *Proceedings of the Human Factors Society 25th Annual Meeting*, Rochester, NY, 1981: 492–6. Ed. by Robert C. Sugarman. Buffalo, NY: Calspan Corp., 1981.

Only peripherally on the subject of the present text, but showing the human factors in the issue of reading texts on VDTs. Considers seat height, keyboard height and slope, and CRT height and tilt angle. Concludes 'that adjustability of keyboard slope is essential to accommodate individual preferences' (p. 493). With references to 13 other studies on this subject. [Like other entries in the present bibliography, this article, though not on bibliographies, addresses the issue of texts presented on VDTs.]

156 Morison, Stanley. *First Principles of Typography*. Cambridge: At the University Press, 1951. Cambridge Authors' and Printers' Guides I.

Like the work by Cobden-Sanderson (see **46** above), a frequently cited work on simplicity and clarity in typography. (See p. 5 above.)

157 _____. *Typographic Design in Relation to Photographic Composition*. Intro. by John Carter. San Francisco: The Book Club of California, 1959.

Generally about book design; nothing specifically on bibliographies.

158 Murray, David. *Bibliography: Its Scope and Methods*. Glasgow: James Maclehose and Sons, 1917.

[See note in entry for Roy Stokes, ed., *Esdaile's Manual*, **226** below.]

'The number of bibliographies in existence is enormous. In the Bibliothèque Nationale there were in 1897 74,601 volumes falling under this description . . .' (p. 48).

159 Nahinsky, Irwin D. 'The Influence of Certain Typographical Arrangements upon Span of Visual Comprehension.' *Journal of Applied Psychology* 40.1 (Feb. 1956): 37–9.

Another article considering the square-span and the spaced-unit forms of typography (see North and Jenkins, and Coleman and Kim). Contradicting North and Jenkins, Nahinsky states, 'The square-span style yielded comprehension spans significantly superior to both of the other styles investigated' (p. 39).

160 North, Alvin J., and L. B. Jenkins. 'Reading Speed and Comprehension as a Function of Typography.' *Journal of Applied Psychology* 35.4 (Aug. 1951): 225–8.

Compares square-span, spaced-unit, and standard typography in terms of reading speed and comprehension. The first two types arrange phrases on the page, in two-line blocks:

This is the square-span presentation.
an example of style of

or arrange the words in phrases:

This is an example of the spaced-unit style of presentation.

Contradicts Nahinsky: 'Spaced unit typography was superior to either square span or standard typography' (p. 227) in speed and comprehension. (See Coleman and Kim, and Nahinsky.) The theory is 'that spaced unit typography facilitates reading by providing auxilary [*sic*] cues for the organization of the thought' (p. 228). Generally ignores the fact that the unfamiliarity of the reader with these variant forms of typography would retard speed and comprehension. Also seems to ignore the additional drawback of the higher cost (because of the added space and resulting use of paper). Not really applicable to the physical layout of bibliographies; designed more for prose. (But see pp. 24ff. above.)

161 Oakman, Robert L. *Computer Methods for Literary Research.* Columbia, SC: University of South Carolina Press, 1980.

162 Ofer, Kurt D. 'A Computer Program to Index or Search Linear Notations.' *Journal of Chemical Documentation* 8.3 (Aug. 1968): 128–9.

An early article showing computer capabilities for indexing. Not useful for the actual *design* of bibliographies.

Operbeck, H. See [G. W. Ovink], 'The Effect of Paper and Ink Gloss on Legibility,' **164** below.

163 Orth, B., H. Weckerly, and D. Wendt. 'Legibility of Numerals Displayed in a 4 × 7 Dot Matrix and Seven-Segment Digits.' *Visible Language* 10 (1976): 145–55.

Cited by Foster, 74. (Not seen)

164 [Ovink, G. W.] 'The Effect of Paper and Ink Gloss on Legibility.' *Journal of Typographic Research* 4.2 (Spring 1970): 187–8.

This is Ovink's abstract of an article by H. Operbeck in the Institut für Medizinische Optik der Universität München. Operbeck's study used five kinds of paper (two high-gloss, two medium-gloss, and one matt), each printed in three kinds of ink (high-gloss, medium, and matt). The conclusion is that the highest scores were made on all papers printed in matt ink. Scores were lowest on all papers printed in glossy ink. 'Going from the glossiest paper to the matt paper, the scores for glossy ink become higher' (p. 187). The high reflectivity of the glossy papers was disturbing. '. . . matt papers gave the best results' (p. 188).

165 _____. 'Fashion in Type Design.' *Journal of Typographic Research* 3.4 (Oct. 1969): 371–7.

On the general topic of design of type. Looks at how styles change: 'Fashion seeks novelty' (p. 371). Analyses the difference between *styles* and *fashions*. Points to various uses of type: 'as a mere sign to activate dormant ideas and images and to call forth reactions . . . . as a magnet for the eye, to direct the attention to what really matters . . . . as a decorative filling of a plane' (p. 375). In some 'cases optimal legibility or recognizability is unimportant . . . . For certain purposes type may be illegible, irrational, . . . unsympathetic, ugly, repulsive' (p. 375).

166 _____. *Legibility, Atmosphere-Value and Forms of Printing Types.* Leiden, the Netherlands: A. W. Sijthoff's Uitgeversmaatschappij N.V., 1938.

Deals exclusively with types, not with (specialized) page layouts. Has a good bibliography on legibility, etc. (pp. 246–53).

166a Parnau, Jeffrey R. *Desktop Publishing: The Awful Truth.* New Berlin, WI: Parnau Graphics Inc., 1989.

Points out that the phrase 'desktop publishing' is a misnomer since what can be done at the desk is really the printing and copy preparation; the publishing must be done by a publisher. Shows that there are many hidden costs to such publishing. Considers the problems one might face with such things as compatibility of hardware, loss of detail, colour, tints, the use of art, typesetting devices, lithographic reproduction, the training one needs to do things right, the software.

167 Paterson, Donald G., and Miles A. Tinker. *How to Make Type Readable: A Manual for Typographers, Printers and Advertisers.* New York and London: Harper & Brothers, 1940.

Considers many features of typography, including speed of reading, kinds of type, size of type, width of line, size of type in relation to width, leading, leading and line width in relation to type size, spatial arrangements of the printed page, black versus white print, colour of print and background, etc. With extensive bibliography. Though not specifically focusing on the design of bibliographies, this volume presents many observations about legibility applicable to typography in general.

One conclusion is 'that type faces in common use are equally legible' (p. 18). Roman type is fractionally more legible than italic (p. 21). A mixture of upper- and lower-case types is more legible than the use of all upper-case types (p. 23). [Therefore, for bibliographies, it is probably not useful to present the first element in the entry (i.e. the name of the author or the work's title) in all upper-case letters, as is common; the spatial arrangement on the page is all one needs to make this first element stand out.] Regular types are more legible than boldface types (pp. 26–7). Slightly bold regular types are more legible than slightly thinner regular typefaces (p. 27).

This study (later than the authors' essay 'Studies in Typographic Factors . . . II. Size of Type') concludes that 10-point type is not necessarily the best for speed of reading; 11-point is better; so is 9-point (though 11-point seems best) (p. 35). Various line lengths are more readable depending on the size of the type used. For 10-point type, a line width of 17–28 picas is best (p. 52), with a 19-pica line the optimum (p. 58); with 2-point leading, 10-point type is equally legible in line widths between 14 and 31 picas. For 10-point type, 2-point leading yields the greatest legibility (p. 65). With 12-point type, leading was not a factor (pp. 66–7). For 8-point type, 2-point leading yields maximum readability (p. 67). Optimal is 10-point type, 2-point leading, and a 19-pica line (p. 71); also satisfactory is 11-point type, 2-point leading, and a 22-pica line (p. 81).

The actual 'size of the page is a matter of whim' (p. 84) and seems unrelated to legibility; this holds also for the size of the printed page (pp. 84–5). As for margins, they should compose about 50% of the page area (pp. 91–2). There are various methods for determining the size and shape of the margins. One method is described here: 'The vertical position is determined mechanically by a clever procedure which provides that the type page should be centered on a diagonal of the total page drawn from the inner top (center of the two-page unit) to the outer bottom corner. This means that the upper inner corner and the lower outer corner of the type page should be on the diagonal' (p. 93; for other treatments of the shape and positioning of the margins, see the Tschichold article, **251** below). But the experiments determine 'that margins do not promote greater legibility' (p. 98).

Double-column arrangements are preferred by readers over single-column formats (pp. 100–2). If a 2-column format is used, an intercolumnar rule is preferable to blank space between the columns, with ½-pica space on each side of the rule. The second preferred arrangement is to have a 2-pica space with no rule between the columns (pp. 105–6).

Indentation of paragraphs speeds up reading and therefore increases legibility (pp. 108, 110). (The indentation is not really an issue for a bibliography since all lines after the first will be indented in the standard bibliographical format.) [But see Example 22 in Appendix I, Malcolm Andrew's bibliography of the *Gawain*-Poet, which uses no indentation.]

Black ink on white (or light-coloured) paper is more legible than the reverse (pp. 112–17). Black on white or near white backgrounds is preferable to other colour combinations (e.g. green on white, orange on black, red on blue or white, etc.) (pp. 120–1). Other good, legible combinations are lustre blue on white, black on yellow, and grass green on white (p. 128). The basic issue is 'brightness contrast' (p. 129).

Either glossy or dull paper stock yields the same legibility, but because of the 'opinions and prejudices of the overwhelming majority of readers who believe that they can read material printed on dull finished paper more rapidly than material on glazed paper', the recommendation is for dull-finished paper (p. 136). 'It is good business to give the readers what they want' (p. 136).

Combining all the characteristics of retardation to speed of reading and comprehension, Paterson and Tinker can thus 'specify an optimal printing arrangement' (p. 145) composed of many factors: 1) use a *common*, familiar, modern typeface (Bodoni, Caslon, Old Style, Garamond, Cheltenham, Antique, Scotch Roman, for example); 2) a slightly bolder typeface is fractionally more legible than a regular typeface (e.g. Antique or Cheltenham); 3) use upper- and lower-case types, not full caps or italics; 4) 10-, 11-, or 12-point type seems to be optimum; 5) for 10-point type set solid, a line width of 17–28 picas is best; for 10-point type with 2-point leading, equal legibility is achieved between 14 and 31 picas; 6) 2-point leading seems to be most legible; 7) 10-point type at 19-pica widths seems best [much more detail on leading, line width, and type size on pp. 148–52]; 8) double-column format seems to be preferred with ½-pica open space between columns, and no rule (this contradicts what they said earlier; see above); 9) black print on white background yields the greatest legibility; 10) for longer texts, paper with no glaze is recommended. Avoid small sizes of type, long lines, and text set solid (with no leading) (pp. 146–55).

168 _____, _____. 'The Part-Whole Proportion Illusion in Printing.' *Journal of Applied Psychology* 22 (1938): 421–5.

'Printing rules and printing practices utilize only 50 per cent of available page space for the printed text' (p. 425), while readers believe that the text takes up about 75% of the page. Hence, margins should be adjusted accordingly.

169 _____, _____. 'Studies of Typographical Factors Influencing Speed of Reading. VI. Black Type Versus White Type.' *Journal of Applied Psychology* 15 (1931): 241–7.

Black ink on a white background is read faster than white type on a black background. No 'adequate theoretical explanation' (p. 247) can be given for this.

170 _____, _____. 'Studies of Typographical Factors Influencing Speed of Reading. XII. Printing Surface.' *Journal of Applied Psychology* 20 (1936): 128–31.

A re-examination of earlier studies of legibility on papers of various glossinesses (with glares of 22.9%, 85.8%, and 95.1%). Results show 'that all three paper surfaces produce printing material that is equally legible' (p. 130), and that 'slight differences in color of printing surface and striking differences in degree of gloss do not influence speed of reading' (p. 131).

171 _____, _____. 'Studies of Typographical Factors Influencing Speed of Reading. II. Size of Type.' *Journal of Applied Psychology* 13 (1929): 120–30.

An article representative of the work of Paterson and Tinker, dealing with legibility, readability, reading speed, reading facility, etc. The general results show 'that in every comparison the 10 point standard was read more rapidly than any other size of type' (p. 126); and, furthermore, '6, 8, 12, and 14 point type are all read slower than 10 point type' (p. 128). This is for a line length of 80 mm (*c.* 3⅛ inches). The conclusion is that '10 point type yields the fastest reading [with no loss of comprehension] and is thus the optimum size of type (in comparison with other sizes used) for efficient reading' (p. 130). (Contains references to many other studies.)

172 _____, _____. 'Studies of Typographical Factors Influencing Speed of Reading. Part VIII. Space between Lines or Leading.' *Journal of Applied Psychology* 16 (1932): 388–97.

'2 point and 4 point leading definitely increase speed of reading . . . with a slight advantage in favor of 2 point' (p. 395). This is for 10-point type at 19-pica line length. But 'it is probable that optimal leading will vary somewhat with type size, being smaller for small type and larger for large type' (p. 395). 'Text material printed with 2 point leading is read 7.5 per cent faster than text set solid' (p. 397).

173 _____, _____. 'Studies of Typographical Factors Influencing Speed of Reading. X. Styles of Type Face.' *Journal of Applied Psychology* 16 (1932): 605–13.

Ultimate results: 'Type faces in common use are equally legible' (p. 613). (But see the authors' later findings in *How to Make Type Readable* – summarized above.)

174 Phillips, R. M. 'The Interacting Effects of Letter Style, Letter Stroke-Width and Letter Size on the Legibility of Projected High-Contrast Lettering.' Ed.D. diss., Indiana University, 1976. See *Dissertation Abstracts International* 37A (1977): 4796. Cited by Foster, *Legibility Research 1972–1978.* (Not seen)

175 Poffenberger, A. T., and R. B. Franken. 'A Study of the Appropriateness of Type Faces.' *Journal of Applied Psychology* 7.4 (Dec. 1923): 312–29.

Discusses the appropriateness of typefaces for the commodities they are used for in advertising. Discusses typefaces in terms of their 'pleasantness or unpleasantness' (p. 328), and with respect to the 'atmospheres' (p. 328) which may be created by the various faces. These types were mainly used in advertising.

176 Pollard, Alfred. 'The Arrangement of Bibliographies.' *The Library*, 2nd ser. 10 (1909): 168–87; rpt. in *Alfred William Pollard: A Selection of His Essays*, pp. 130–43. Comp. by Fred W. Roper. Metuchen, NJ: Scarecrow, 1976. The Great Bibliographers Series, No. 2.

Deals with the two main problems of the compiler, finding the items to include in the bibliography and arranging them. Says the bibliographer needs to know his subject well. Cites some general principles for bibliographical construction. 1) 'Whatever arrangement be adopted it must be easily Intelligible [*sic*] to those for whose use the bibliography is intended. An arrangement which no one is likely to understand, save its author, stands self-condemned. The idea to be aimed at is a system which explains itself' (p. 32). Says that if there is any doubt as to the clarity of the arrangement, there should be a clear statement on the bibliography's arrangement in an introduction. 2) The 'method of arrangement . . . should be always and constantly Visible [*sic*]' (p. 133). 3) 'A principle of arrangement to be permanently satisfactory must rest on facts definitely ascertained, and not liable to be upset' (p. 133). Concludes that the arrangement should be 'Intelligible, Visible, Certain, and Permanent' (p. 133). The three possible arrangements, according to Pollard, are alphabetical, chronological, and logical. Analyses these three methods; justifies the first two more than the third.

176a _____. 'Margins.' *The Dolphin* 1 (1933): 67–80.

Lays out some 'rules' about the appearance and construction of margins (especially with respect to old manuscripts), but 'the variations which may be played upon it [the design of the page] are numberless' (p. 80). Reiterates the old notion that the inner margins should be smallest, the top larger, etc., and questions whether this is 'artistic rather than utilitarian' (p. 67). Talks of 'the appeal to tradition' (p. 68) espoused by William Morris and others who opted for this pattern. Holding the book for reading requires that the outer and lower margins be wide enough for our fingers not to cover up the text. Says that with manuscripts it was easier for the scribes to write at the top than at the bottom of the page. Also points out that the tradition of wide margins in manuscripts (and later in printed books) may have come from the need for space to write annotations. Discusses the proportions of margins.

176b Pottinger, David T. 'The Characteristics of a Good Book Type,' *The Dolphin* 1 (1933): 58–66.

Points out how serifs affect legibility, as do type proportions, letterspacing, and the overall balance of colour produced by an evenly inked page.

177 Poulton, E. C. *Effects of Printing Types and Formats on the Comprehension of Scientific Journals.* Cambridge: Cambridge University Press, 1959.

Does not consider bibliographies. Looks at type styles and single- versus double-column formats.

178 Pratt, C. C. 'A Note on the Legibility of Items in a Bibliography.' *Journal of Applied Psychology* 8 (Apr. 1924): 362–4.

The optimal 'position for a suffix to dates in bibliographical references' for quick legibility was found to be the one in which 'the letter-suffix is above the line and separated from the date by a space' (p. 364) (our present practice for footnotes).

179 Preston, Katherine, Howard P. Schwankl, and Miles A. Tinker. 'The Effect of Variations in Color of Print and Background Legibility.' *Journal of Genetic Psychology* 6 (1932): 459–61.

Investigates 'the effect of variations in color of print and paper on perceptibility of isolated words' (p. 459). Determines legibility 'by the distance method' (p. 459). Result: 'the greater the luminosity or brightness differences between symbol and background, the greater the legibility of print' (p. 461). [Same results as in Tinker and Paterson, 'Studies of Typographical

Factors . . . . VII. Variations in Color of Print . . . .' See 246 below.]

180 Pugno, G. A. 'Physical Size of a Printed Text in Relation to Its Legibility.' (In Italian) *Graphicus* 9 (1969): 17–21. Cited by Foster, *Legibility Research Abstracts 1970*, p. 23. (Journal abstract, translated.) (Not seen)

Looks at size, illumination, contrast, reflection, and glossy paper as factors in legibility.

181 Pyke, R. L. *Report on the Legibility of Print.* London: His Majesty's Stationery Office, Medical Research Council, 1926.

Considers many scientific experiments and studies on legibility, including such things as paper, impression of the printed type, type styles, illumination, contrast of type strokes, size of type, margins, indentation, etc. Nothing specifically on the design of bibliographies.

182 Ranganathan, S[arada] R. 'Depth Classification, Tools for Retrieval, and Organisation for Research.' In *Documentation and Its Facets,* being a Symposium of Seventy Papers by Thirty-Two Authors, 604–24. Ed. by S. R. Ranganathan. Bombay, Calcutta, New York . . .: Asia Publishing House, 1963.

In this collection of 70 essays (26 by Ranganathan and two by him and a co-author), this essay is on the Universal Decimal Classification of books; but it mentions the importance in documentation of a 'consistent sequence' in the presentation of data. This is an essential feature of a well-designed catalogue as well as a well-designed bibliography.

182a Ratcliffe, F. W. 'Margins in the Manuscript and Printed Book.' *Penrose Annual* 56 (1966): 217–34.

Looks at margins with respect to justified and unjustified setting. Quotes A. W. Pollard (*The Printing Art* 10.1 [1907]: 17–24) as writing that 'the chief object of margins is to give pleasure to the eye' (Ratcliffe, p. 218). Talks extensively of the many uses to which margins were put through the centuries. Says that with computers, justified right setting is never a problem. Expresses a preference for justified margins because they look best on versos, which are separated from the even left margins of rectos by the pair of small white spaces (the inner margins) that separate them.

183 Reichl, Ernst. 'Designing the Physical Book.' In *What Happens in Book Publishing*, 2nd ed., pp. 80–91. Ed. by Chandler B. Grannis. New York and London: Cambridge University Press, 1967.

A general discussion about book design, emphasizing the things a designer should know and take into account (length of text, page size, types, illustrations, binding, dust jacket, etc.).

184 _____. *Legibility: A Typographic Book of Etiquette*. Brooklyn, NY: George McKibbin & Son, 1949.

Considers 1) Type size – points out differences in what is considered legible in Europe and the United States. Says, 'A large-faced 10 point type – such as Baskerville or Janson – is the smallest that can be used for straight reading matter in the U.S.A.' (p. 10).

2) Leading – 'Machine faces should never be set solid unless they are . . . designed for just such use' (p. 12). Advocates a 'single point of leading . . . [which] increases legibility to a considerable degree by making it easier to find the next line' (p. 12). Over-generous leading . . . distorts the type face nearly as much as too little leading would' (p. 14).

3) Line measure – reiterates 'the old printer's rule that type should be set to a line 1½ times the length of its lower case alphabet' (p. 16). Points out that custom allows for a line length as much as 2½ times the width of the lower-case alphabet, 'but beyond that width, reading speed is interfered with, and our eyes have difficulty returning to the next line. The longer the line, the more leading is required to restore legibility, and the pace gained in width is therefore lost in depth' (p. 16). Also advocates paragraph indentations of sufficient depth. 'Large, wide-running type set to a narrow measure loses its rhythm and gives a nervous picture. Big holes and rivers appear on the page because short lines do not permit tight word-spacing. Many words have to be divided, hyphens at the end of consecutive lines cannot be avoided and disturb the evenness and balance of the page still further.' Also, 'To avoid holes between words on a page of this kind, compositors not familiar with book composition will sometimes letterspace bad lines. This must not be tolerated; holes are still the lesser evil' (p. 18).

4) The length of the type page – advocates good margins all around. 'The length of a page considered harmonious by contemporary standards will be found by taking twice its width as the diagonal measure' (p. 20).

5) Margins – 'Due to the technical possibility of printing bleed illustrations, as well as to the modern trend to asymmetrical arrangements, a large variety of margin treatments is acceptable to our eyes' (p. 22). Mentions the optical function 'the white area around the type page has . . . warning the eye of the approach of the end of the line' (p. 22). A small margin 'detracts from reading ease' (p. 22). 'A standard page will be found to contain about 10% more unprinted than printed area' (p. 22). Margins too wide (and those out of proportion) detract as much as do margins too narrow.

Also contains sections on paper and running heads, and other elements of typography.

185 *Researches in Readability*. New York: Merganthaler Linotype Co., 1947. [See also this company's *The Legibility of Type*, **132** above.]

Discusses 'What Makes Type Readable' (p. 3). Reviews scholarship, particularly the work of Matthew Luckiesh. Considers typefaces, 'readability vs. legibility' (p. 8), and the many other factors which affect legibility (type size, leading, word spacing, paper, ink, etc.).

186 Reynolds, Linda. 'Designing for the New Communications Technology: The Presentation of Computer-Generated Information.' In *The Future of the Printed Word*, pp. 81–98. (See under Philip Hills, **106** above.)

Deals with the computer's role in the display of texts. Discusses various kinds of visual media and shows that each 'has its own possibilities and limitations in terms of typography and layout' (p. 81). Points out the design constraints imposed by computer-generated information. Says, 'Although some of the basic design principles established in relation to the printed word can still be applied [to the design of texts on a video display], some cannot' (p. 81). The presentation on the screen is important because it will affect the user's attitude and approach to the data and 'the ease, speed and accuracy with which the information can be used' (p. 83).

Discusses the need 'to emphasize important items, to divide items which are functionally unrelated to one another or which are different in kind, and to relate items which do have a functional relationship or which are of the same kind' (p. 83) – [especially important in the presentation of bibliographical data]. Since there is a limited number of characters that one can present on a screen, it is important to code data spatially, and this is not easy in the restricted space of the screen. Considers letterspacing, rivers on the page, the problems with right justification, the limited character sets available on most screens and printers, the use of italics and boldface, the use of capitals and other characters which code special features of data (e.g. asterisks, pareus, daggers). Advises that the use of full caps 'should be kept to a minimum' (p. 86). 'Research has shown that words in capitals are less easily recognized than words in lowercase because they lack the distinctive outline created by the ascenders and descenders of lowercase letters' (p. 86). [Cites H. Spencer, *The Visible Word*. See **214** below.]

Also says, 'Underlining should also be avoided where possible, because interlinear spacing is often minimal and the underlining may fuse with the letters above and below. It is also likely to interfere with the perception of the word shapes, and for this reason it should not be used with capitals' (p. 87). Adds, 'Double underlining should never be used, as it is extremely ugly' (p. 87).

Says that with some terminals and programs, colour coding might be useful in distinguishing one entry from another, or one part of an entry from another. But 'only the most legible colors' (p. 87) should be used, 'to convey the structure of the information' (p. 87).

Adds, 'The possibilities for information layout in many kinds of computer-generated display are considerably restricted by unsuitable line lengths and inflexible line spacing' (p. 87). Points out that 'The optimum line length for conventionally printed materials has been shown to be between 50 and 60 characters and spaces' (p. 87) – citing H. Spencer, *The Visible Word*, q.v. Explains this in terms of legibility and eye movements. Discusses the importance of adequate line spacing, the difference between single-page displays and the display of continuous text (which requires, optimally, a 60- to 70-character line), the possible use of columns, justified and unjustified text, the use of hyphens, and irregular word spacing – all affecting legibility. Also mentions the proper use of upper- and lower-case letters, setting a text solid, spacing between paragraphs, the number of paragraphs per page and per screen, the use of headings (which should be numbered to show the reader where she or he is in the text), the placement of section numbers ('in the margin if possible', p. 89), the use of upper- and lower-case letters in the headings, the use of the left-hand margin, subheadings, boldface type, the consistent use of spacing as a code for where the reader is in the text, the possible use of two columns, and in continuous texts whether to display

the data in terms of pages. Says that for library catalogues (and therefore in bibliographies) it is important 'to distinguish between the different elements within each entry [and] . . . to emphasize that element of each entry which determines its place in the alphabetical or numerical sequence' (p. 90).

Asserts that the designer should avoid unnecessary abbreviations and computer jargon (p. 97). Talks also about the design of lists, indexes and tables; the use of columns and the best distance between columns, how to use column headings, line spaces, horizontal rules every five entries, leader dots, vertical rules ('should be avoided in tabular materials', p. 92), etc.

187 _____. 'Results of Tests Comparing the Performance of Six Versions of Keyword Catalogue Presentation.' In *Keyword Catalogues and the Free Language Approach: Papers Based on a Seminar Held at Imperial College, London, 19th October 1983*, pp. 55–85. Ed. by Philip Bryant. [Bath]: Bath University Library, 1985.

Appropriate primarily for texts like concordances. For the purposes of bibliographies, the keyword is the author's last name or whatever element is in a consistent placement on the page – the item one would look for in an alphabetical list (or in a list organized in some other, non-alphabetical, way). Reiterates the standard idea that there must be consistency in the spatial arrangement of the elements in bibliographic entries. Raises the issue of single-column or double-column presentation. Also gives examples of centre-aligned or left-aligned elements.

188 _____. *The Presentation of Bibliographical Information on Prestel*. N.p.: Graphic Information Research Unit, Royal College of Art, 1980.

[Prestel is a computer library catalogue system considered for use by the British Library. This is a report advising the library on its use.] Discusses the 'limited character set and relatively small number of character positions available on each Prestel frame' (p. 2). Especially discusses how such a limited system could be used to present bibliographical data. Considers typography, layout, colour, legibility, content of entries, content of data fields, etc. Recommends 'that layout should be kept as simple as possible, and the number of colours used should be restricted to two in most cases' (p. 2). Also has recommendations about indentation and use of emphases. 'It is important that the visual presentation of bibliographic information should both reflect its logical structure and facilitate its use' (p. 4).

189 _____. *Visual Presentation of Information in COM Library Catalogues: A Survey*. Vol. I. London: British Library, Research and Development Report 5472, 1979.

190 _____. *Visual Presentation of Information in COM Library Catalogues: A Survey*. Vol. II, appendixes. London: British Library Research and Development Reports, 1979.

Gives examples of 'Frame layouts' for computer output microform catalogues. Contains the examples for which volume I (probably) contained the commentary. Discusses briefly the effective and attractive presentation of data, given the available computer equipment. Discusses legibility and the typographic variations available. Considers one-column and two-column formats – also the continuous text versus the framed (i.e. paged) text. Also looks at microfiche indexes.

[Note: While much of Reynolds's work cited here is not specifically on bibliographies (though see below under Spencer and Reynolds), it covers areas germane to our purposes here. She is among the scholars with foresight enough to see the importance of applying our knowledge of typography and legibility to the whole new world of problems the computer presents – with its many kinds of texts: printouts, texts on screens of various types, and other microformats.]

191 Rice, Stanley. *Book Design: Systematic Aspects*. New York & London: Bowker, 1978.

Contains basic considerations on many aspects of book design (e.g. editing, typesetting options, page make-up, adjustment of book length, etc.), but nothing specifically on the design of bibliographies.

192 _____. *Book Design: Text Format Models*. New York & London: Bowker, 1987.

Has a brief chapter (the text of which is two-thirds of a page) on bibliographies. Offers five options: 1) humanities or science style; 2) annotated or unannotated; 3) numbered or not numbered; 4) items spaced (3 points) or not spaced; 5) annotations flush or indented. Points out that 1–3 are editorial concerns. Suggests that, 'For numbered bibliographies . . . hanging indent list form is used. For unnumbered bibliographies, the first line of each item is flush left and the rest indented. A 1 em indent is used for most of the models [in this volume], but 2 ems may be used if

the line is long, or if this is preferred to the use of added space when item separation is felt to be necessary' (p. 95). 'Space is commonly added between items only if items average more than 2 lines and space is available in paging' (p. 95). Under 'Paging Considerations': 'Items should not be broken in such a way that less than 3 lines of bibliography appear at the top or bottom of any page. Widow rules apply . . . . "Continued" lines for an item broken from recto to verso are not generally considered necessary' (p. 95).

193 Riche, C. V., Jr., and G. C. Kinny. 'Studies in Display Legibility.' *AGARD Displays for Command and Control Centres* (July 1969): 99–103. Abstract in *Scientific and Technical Aerospace Reports*, Report No. N70–154.16. Cited in Foster, *Legibility Research Abstracts 1970*, p. 23. (Not seen)

Concerns legibility of data on CRT displays.

194 Robinson, A. M. Lewin. *Systematic Bibliography: A Practical Guide to the Work of Compilation*. Hamden, CT: Archon, 1966.

Contains a two-page chapter on layout (pp. 66–7), which considers book form or card form. 'The essentials of good bibliographical layout are a) clear distinction of one item from another; b) the standing out for easy reference of all headings, both those for sections of the work and those for individual items; and c) the clear distinction of the component parts of the entry. . . . These may be satisfactorily produced by the effective use of spacing and . . . varied forms of letter' (p. 66). Considers standard typewriter layouts and typography, emphasizing the need to double-space between entries. Asserts that 'the first word of the author heading should be in capitals' as follows (p. 67):

> HUNT, Sir John
> The ascent of Everest. London, Hodder & Stoughton, 1953.

Other variants are discussed. 'Double column is not recommended' (p. 67). Nothing else on the physical presentation of bibliographies. [N.B. The 4th ed. rev. of this work, 1979, adds nothing to these recommendations.]

195 Robinson, David Owen, Michael Abbamonte, and Selby H. Evans. 'Why Serifs Are Important: the [*sic*] Perception of Small Print.' *Visible Language* 5.4 (Autumn 1971): 353–9.

Considers briefly the history of the use of serifs. Suggests 'that the neurological structure of the human visual system benefits from serifs in the preservation of the main features of letters during neural processing' (p. 353). Reviews the work of others.

196 Roethlein, Barbara Elizabeth. 'The Relative Legibility of Different Faces of Printing Types.' *American Journal of Psychology* 23.1 (Jan. 1912): 1–36.

Finds that 'certain faces of type are much more legible than other faces; and certain letters of every face are much more legible than other letters of the same face' (p. 33). But the legibility of letters is partly dependent on whether the letters are shown in isolation or in groups. 'Legibility is a product of six factors: 1. the form of the letter; 2. the size . . .; 3. the heaviness of the face . . .; 4. the width of the white margin which surrounds the letter; 5. the position of the letter in the letter-group; 6. the shape and size of the adjacent letters' (p. 33). Other findings: heavier faces are more legible than light ones; initial positions are more legible than medial ones; final positions are second in legibility; neighbouring letters play an important role in legibility of single letters; quality of paper is not a very important factor (p. 34). Contains a 40-item bibliography.

[Paterson and Tinker (*How to Make Type Readable*) claim that Roethlein's findings are suspect since she 'merely investigated the relative legibility of isolated letters at a distance' (p. 13); her study considers 'meaningless groups of letters, and therefore fails to duplicate ordinary reading conditions' (p. 17).]

197 Rogers, Walter Thomas. *Manual of Bibliography, Being an Introduction to the Knowledge of Books, Library Management, and the Art of Cataloguing.* New York: Scribner and Welford, 1891.

Says that in a library catalogue entry, the following data should be recorded on each book: author, title, translator, annotator (where applicable), number of volumes, size, number of pages, illustrations, city, publisher, date, location (he means location in the library, but many bibliographies cite locations of copies in various libraries). Deals with each of these at length (see esp. Chapter IV, pp. 98–148).

198 Rollins, Carl Purington. 'Gilding the Lily: In the Designing of Books There's No Sin Like Complacency.' In *Bookmaking & Kindred Amenities*, pp. 21–31. Ed. by Earl Schenck Miers and Richard Ellis. New Brunswick, NJ: Rutgers University Press, 1942.

On the designing of books, especially from the commercial standpoint of the printer who needs to make a profit. Focuses on the relationships the printer has with the author, the text, the types she or he must choose, and the book designer. Says the printer's job is 'to make the book clear and distinct and quiet' (p. 30).

199 _____. 'The Printing of Bibliographies.' *Papers of the Bibliographical Society of America* 16 (1922): 107–17.

'A decent respect for the uses to which such books are put should govern the printer in determining the shape of his volume' (p. 111). The book should be 'a workable size' (p. 111) – e.g. octavo – *c.* 6½ × 9½ inches or as small as 5½ × 8½ inches (p. 111). This should allow for (and even demand) a 2-column format. The standard octavo is 'too wide for the type running the full width of the type page' (p. 111). Recommends that the bibliography should be kept to a single volume. Each entry must be 'clear and distinct' (p. 112). Rarely or never use boldface type (p. 112). Suggests 'abbreviated references in brackets in the running heads, topical running heads, and folios [i.e. page numbers] at the bottom of the page' (p. 112). Many other suggestions about spaces between entries, number of lines and entries per page, word spacing, indentations ('almost a necessity' [p. 113]), varying type sizes, the sparing use of italics and small capitals, the careful choice of typeface (preferably handset – p.114), the use of a good rag-content paper carefully and properly folded, and a sound, appropriate binding (p. 116).

200 _____. *Some Trifles Which Make for Perfection: A Brief Discourse on the Details of the Setting-up of Footnotes, Bibliographies, and Indexes. Applicable to Any Kind of Type and Any Size of Book.* Brooklyn, NY: George McKibbin & Son, 1949.

'In the printing of bibliographies or bibliographical lists, the desirability of compactness should be emphasized. . . . One really needs to see as much on each page as can be put there without hampering easy reading' ([p. 6]).

'Most scholars prefer a narrow column to a broad one,

because the eye has difficulty in traveling across a broad measure. This matter of the proper length of line is important, and the recent tendency to undue length of line is to be guarded against' ([p. 6]).

'In setting a bibliographical list there is much to be said for the use of hanging indention' ([pp. 6, 9]).

'In narrow measure it is sometimes best to put the author's name on a separate line, thus bringing the title of the book over to the left. But in any case the eye can catch the desired name more easily than if the regular indention is followed' ([p. 9]). Mentions the difficult and sometimes unachievable practice of trying to reproduce the typography of the original title pages of books ([p. 9]). 'If the true look of a title page is desired, photography is the only way to get it' ([p. 9]). [But even photography will not show what the paper is like.]

'In bibliographical listings the use of capitals for titles sometimes makes the words in capitals stand out with too much emphasis. An interesting variant is to use a large size of small caps. Sometimes capitals of a smaller point size can . . . be successfully employed' ([p. 12]).

'The general effect of the type page should be that of pleasant and even texture, without spottiness or vulgar mixtures of heavy and light patches of color' ([p. 14]).

201 Romano, Frank J. *The TypEncyclopedia: A User's Guide to Better Typography*. New York and London: Bowker, 1984.

Contains a broad discussion on typography covering such issues as the use of accents, alignment of text, ascenders and descenders, biform ('the intermingling of modified small-cap and lowercase characters in the formation of a lowercase alphabet', p. 12), black-letter types, borders, use of calligraphy, etc. Looks at line spacing, tabular composition, letterspacing, pagination, type selection, and so on. Says, 'Legibility is related to the way we read. The human eye makes a fixation each quarter of a second and takes in a group of words. It then jumps to the next fixation, etc. . . . [L]egibility research teaches us that narrower line lengths, consistent word spacing, and well-designed typefaces will aid in more efficient reading' (p. 79). 'Text copy should adhere to certain time-tested rules for length of line in order to achieve maximum readability' (p. 86). Gives following table (p. 86):

Type size	Minimum line length	Optimum line length	Maximum line length
6	8	10	12
7	8	11	14
8	9	13	16
9	10	14	18
10	13	16	20
11	13	18	22
12	14	21	24
14	18	24	28
16	21	27	32
18	24	30	36

Says, 'A line should have 55 to 60 characters, or 9 or 10 words, for optimum legibility. Also, as line length increases, paragraph indentations should increase, too' (p. 87). Says to use short lines for 'lively design', long lines 'for prolonged reading' (p. 87). 'Short lines are often best unjustified' (p. 87). Avoid widows and orphans (p. 107). 'Frequent paragraphs are important for good legibility' (p. 107).

201a Rothenberg, Randall. 'Revolution in Type Makes Headlines.' *New York Times*, Monday, 23 July, 1990: Business, p. 1, D6.

Discusses typefaces; their number, history, families, etc. Looks at computer technology and its impact on the development of new typefaces.

202 Rubenstein, Richard. *Digital Typography: An Introduction to Type and Composition for Computer System Design*. Reading, MA: Addison-Wesley Publishing Co., 1988.

Notes the boom in desktop publishing. Warns that new printers (using computer technology) should familiarize themselves with classical typography. Aims to show how to use computer technology to produce legible, beautiful books. Subsumes under his title all notions of 'desktop publishing, electronic publishing, demand publishing, computer typesetting, and prepress imaging' (p. 4). Considers individual letters (legibility, the construction of digital letter forms, serif versus sans serif typefaces, etc.), human psychology, the physiological act of reading, good typeface design, and a means of producing legible typefaces on VDTs. Also considers space – between letters, between words, between lines, margins, separation of text from illustration, rivers, etc. [Shows the importance of separating one entry from another in a bibliography, and also of coding each entry so that different elements in each entry stand out from other elements.] Shows how the computer-typeset text can eliminate rivers and optimize the use of hyphens. Has a section on 'Reading from Screens versus Reading from Paper' (pp. 189 ff.). Says, 'Typefaces and layouts on screens are frequently inferior to those on paper. . . . Similarly, screen layouts are seldom designed by graphic designers or book designers for clarity or aesthetic quality' (p. 192).

Points out the importance of good use of type, space, hyphenation, columns, margins ('Good page design allocates about 50% of the space on the page to margins. This practice contrasts with the norm on screens of having negligible margins in windows', p. 193). Cites studies which indicate that reading speeds are '20% to 30% slower from CRT displays than from paper' (p. 189). [See studies by Gould; Gould *et al.*; Heppner; Kak; respectively, entries **84**, **85**, **102**, and **116** above.]

Contains a chapter on what one sees on a screen in preparation for what one will eventually see on paper. Discusses resolution, font differences, letterspacing, line breaks, type sizes, margins, relation of text to graphics, scripts, page layout, pagination, and the balancing of facing pages. With a useful, partially annotated bibliography, citing many items of a highly technical nature (pp. 297–310).

203 Ryder, John. *The Case for Legibility*. London: Bodley Head; New York: Moretus Press, 1979.

Says that legibility implies, for him, 'not just a readable page but a complete book produced in such a way that it is easy to use and to read' (p. 7). With respect to computerized texts, says, 'Recent startling changes in techniques have not invalidated the canons of good typographical arrangement, though they have made sympathetic understanding between designer and printer more difficult to establish and maintain' (p. 9).

Points out the three stages of 'the process of design for legibility' (p. 9): '1. knowing and understanding the author's and editor's intention, 2. translating this intention into typographical signs and instructions so that setting and proofreading may be done, 3. arranging the typographical material on proof into a sequence of pages which . . . reflects the author's intention' (p. 10).

Considers selection of a typeface, type size, format, paper, margins, line length, word and letterspacing, page size, use of page numbers, headlines, shoulder titles, footnotes, and anything else outside the basic text area. Even considers binding.

[Note: There is an emphasis here on the role of the designer and printer. But this role is minimized with the production of camera-ready copy by the author. Authors must therefore become educated about those typographic matters that Ryder and others write about.]

Speaks of 'the present terror of being overcome by illiteracy and blinded by illegibility' (p. 16). 'You must present an author's work to the reader without fuss and with design techniques as invisible as possible' (p. 16). Looks at page layout and examines, at length, title pages, contents pages, and dust jackets.

204 Sanford, E. C. 'The Relative Legibility of the Small Letters.' *American Journal of Psychology* 1.3 (1887–8): 402–35.

Considers individual letters in isolation, not in a prose text. Looks minutely and scientifically at the individual characteristics of letter forms, and calls for clear delineation of each stroke.

205 Schneider, Georg. *Theory and History of Bibliography*. Translated from the German by Ralph Robert Shaw. New York: Columbia University Press, 1934.

Extensive treatment of content and form, but with little consideration of the typographical form of entries. '. . . orthography must be uniform' (p. 119); 'chirography must also be uniform' (p. 120).

'"Stressing of certain parts" of the entry by use of different type faces or by some other means is related to the excerpting of headings only to a limited extent' (p. 120).

206 Shurtleff, D. A. 'Studies of Display Symbol Legibility: XXII, Relative Legibility of Four Symbol Sets Made with a Five by Seven Dot Matrix.' Abstract in *U.S. Government Research and Development Reports* (Report No. AD-704 136). Cited by Foster, *Legibility Research Abstracts 1970*, pp. 24–25. (Not seen)

Uses 'Optimal viewing conditions' (Foster, pp. 24–25) and 'degraded viewing conditions' (Foster, p. 25) to observe the legibility of dot-matrix displays. Concludes 'that new symbols designs are needed to improve the legibility of present 5 × 7 dot symbol sets' (p. 25).

207 Shurtleff, Donald. 'Relative Legibility of Leroy and Lincoln/MITRE Fonts on Television.' *Journal of Typographic Research* 3.1 (Jan. 1969): 79–90.

Analyses specifically two typefaces; but does so in general remarks on 'how to improve symbol design for more legible television displays' (p. 79). Written before the advent of the personal computer; but contains observations relevant to the reading of texts on computer monitors. One conclusion is that 'a minimum resolution of 10 lines per symbol height is required for a 90% or better accuracy of identification' (p. 85). Also, for television screens, 'increasing symbol width' (p. 88) might increase legibility, while 'decreasing the stroke-width of symbols' (p. 88) should also increase legibility. Contains a useful bibliography on other studies of television legibility.

208 Shurtleff, Donald A., William F. Wuersch, and James G. Rogers. 'How to Make Large Screen Displays Legible.' *Proceedings of the Human Factors Society 25th Annual Meeting*, Rochester, NY, 1981, pp. 149–53. Ed. by Robert C. Sugarman. Buffalo, NY: Calspan Corp., 1981.

Evaluates legibility with respect to changing variables in VDT texts. The variables are 1) luminance adaptation level; 2) symbol contrast ratio; 3) symbol visual size; and 4) off-axis viewing angle. Anticipates many later studies of legibility on VDTs. Cites earlier studies; e.g. M. N. Crook, J. A. Hanson, and A. Weisz, 'Legibility of Type as Determined by the Combined Effect of Typographical Variables and Reflectance of Background' (WADC Technical Report 53–441, Mar. 1954).

209 Silverman, Robert A. 'Desktop Publishing: Its Impact on the Academic Community.' *Scholarly Publishing* 21 (Oct. 1989): 57–63.

Considers the process of electronic submission of texts and its implications. E.g., review of electronic texts can be done widely on-line only hours after the texts become available. This allows updates and corrections, and indicates the malleable condition of the text, unlike printed texts, which are static. Also, reviews and criticism can accompany the text, presenting corroboration or criticism to other readers. The on-line process 'can enhance conversation [if] a large number of peer commentators are invited to react' (p. 59).

210 Simon, Oliver. *Introduction to Typography*. London: Faber and Faber, 1945.

'The minimum data for entries of a Bibliography comprise title of book, name of author, date and place of publication, and the name of the publisher. The printer should differentiate clearly between the title of the book and the name of the author by the use of italic, capitals, or small capitals for the former' (p. 83). Offers one sample – not very useful for the design of bibliographies.

211 Simpson, G. C. 'A Comparison of the Legibility of Three Types of Electronic Digital Display.' *BISRA* – The Inter-Group Laboratories of the British Steel Corporation, London, Operational Research Department, 1970. Abstract in U.S. Government Research and Development Reports (Report No. PB-188 760). Cited in Foster, *Legibility Research Abstracts 1970*, p. 25. (Not seen)

Compares legibility among cold-cathode, side-illumination, and straight-projection forms of display. The side illumination form is inferior to the other two, which are of approximately equal legibility.

212 Skillin, Marjorie E., Robert M. Gay, *et al. Words into Type*. New York: Appleton-Century-Crofts, 1948.

Contains a section on the compilation of bibliographies (pp. 32–8). Says, 'The arrangement of bibliographies is usually alphabetical, but chronology or value may determine the order. The author should make his intention so clear in this matter that no question of it can arise' (p. 36). Also deals with the proper contents of bibliographical entries (p. 33) and their styling. Looks as well at many elements of book design (e.g. running heads, widows, page length, columns, ditto marks, illustrations, typography, type, etc.).

213 Southall, Richard. 'Visual Structure and the Transmission of Meaning.' In *Document Manipulation and Typography: Proceedings of the International Conference on Electronic Publishing, Document Manipulation and Typography, Nice (France), April 20–22, 1988*, 35–45. Ed. by J. C. van Vliet. Cambridge, New York, Melbourne . . .: Cambridge University Press, 1988.

Points out how the visual structure of a document 'provides an encoding of the structure of relationships between content objects that exists in the message the document carries' (p. 35). Says that different specialities look at texts from their own perspectives, each looking for the emphasis of different elements in the texts. Applied to computer structuring of texts. 'Part of the content of an author's message can indeed be realized in ways that are independent of any particular written document' (p. 40). Talks of 'the graphic structure of the document' (p. 41). 'The relationship between graphic objects in an actual document can be exploited to realize the relationships between content objects that make up the structure of an author's message' (p. 41). [Highly prolix and 'scientific' language in this essay obfuscates the basic meaning, which seems to be that structure in a text conveys part of the meaning.] Talks of 'content structure encoding' (p. 42): 'The relationships between content units that make up the content structure of the message are encoded by graphic relationships between the blocks of word images that realize the content units in the actual document [*sic*]' (p. 42). [The point seems to be, for example, with bibliographies, that the structure of an entry contains in a particular order and shape all of the individual elements that the bibliographic entry contains; that shape will be a cue to the reader to look for equivalent elements in the same places in other entries. It is what Reynolds *et al.* have called 'spatial coding'.]

214 Spencer, Herbert. *The Visible Word*. London: [Lund Humphries in Association with] The Royal College of Art; New York: Hastings House, 1969.

Basically on legibility – 'greater reading efficiency' (p. 6). Urges book designers to heed the large body of research on legibility. Aims to prepare readers to familiarize themselves with 'the photo-electronic letter' (p. 10). Reviews studies of legibility at length, most of which are covered in the present volume (above and below). Considers all the usual topics – type styles, eye movements, length of ascenders and descenders, rate of reading, distance from the text, visual fatigue, capitals versus lower-case, boldface and italic types, the printing of different styles of numerals, punctuation marks, type size, line length, leading, justified versus unjustified setting, boustrophedon and vertical type arrangements, paragraphing, indentation (indention), margins, and page size. Summarizes: full caps is less legible than words in upper and lower case; italics reduces legibility; bold type, 'provided the counters of the letters are open' (p. 55), does not reduce legibility; excessively long or short lines are not desirable, but leading allows 'line length to be extended without loss of legibility' (p. 55); black ink on tinted paper of at least 70% reflectance is perfectly legible; black text on white paper is more legible than the reverse; high- or low-gloss paper yields the same legibility, 'but well

diffused illumination is important' (p. 55); unjustified lines are as legible as justified ones; horizontal type arrangement – the norm – yields maximum reading efficiency. Looks at proposals for new alphabets. Points out that we must now redesign texts with the new television screen or with the microfilm reader in mind.

215 _____, and Linda Reynolds. *The Effects of Show-Through on the Legibility of Printed Text*. London: Royal College of Art, Readability of Print Research Unit, 1977.

'Show-through effectively reduces the contrast between the type images and the paper and is therefore likely to impair legibility' (p. 2). Examines 'five different printing conditions on four different papers' (p. 2). Concludes 'that legibility is not greatly affected either by printing conditions or by paper opacity until paper opacity falls below about 2.0. At opacities below this figure, double sided printing is significantly less legible than single sided, and interlinear show-through causes significantly more impairment than show-through which is aligned with the type image being read' (p. 2).

216 _____, _____. *Factors Affecting the Acceptability of Microforms as a Reading Medium*. London: Readability of Print Research Unit, Royal College of Art, 1976.

Talks of the psychological and physiological effects of reading from microforms. Discusses, *inter alia*, typography and layout for source documents, COM, and organization of information content. Considers many types of microforms. With respect to printed materials, comes to many conclusions, including: 1) use of microfiche does not impair reading performance; 2) readers of microfilm and printed books read at about the same speed; 3) in some cases hard copy is slightly better than microforms, and vice versa; 4) some students take more notes from microfiche than from hard copy (pp. 7–8).

Discusses printing processes; paper ('paper should preferably be smooth blue-white, opaque, and gloss coated for maximum contrast; textured and tinted papers should be avoided' [p. 9]); ink; graphics (background colour, background tint, image colour, quality of half-tone illustrations and diagrams); character size ('characters should be 8 pt or larger, not 6 pt or smaller' [p. 13]); character style ('sans serif or square serif faces are preferable; avoid fine serifs and thick/thin body strokes; avoid italic seriffed faces and scripts; sans serif numerals are preferable for tables' [p. 14], etc.); upper- versus lower-case letters; character weight and spacing; line spacing; line length; column spacing; page layout and format ('an 8.5 × 11″ [inches] page is suitable for most readers; avoid oversize formats' [p. 18]); page orientation ('avoid changes in page orientation; 90° rotations require a higher reduction ratio or an image rotation facility on the [microform] reader' [p. 19]); location of figures and tables; location of notes, references, and indexes; continuity between microfiche; roll film versus microfiche; frame progression on roll film and microfiche; horizontal versus vertical frame progression on microfiche; the notion of 'page' for a text published only in microform; frame numbering systems; indexing on microforms; recording and copying equipment; film type; uses of positive versus negative images; reduction ratio and resolution and contrast; etc. With more data on equipment, screen angle, size, reflectance, colour, curvature, and transmission, luminescence, magnification ratio, resolution, focus, and so on. Also talks about printout options and quality, work-station design, etc. A thorough and informative treatment. Includes a 78-entry bibliography and an index.

217 _____, _____. *The Study of Legibility.* London: Royal College of Art, Readability of Print Research Unit, [1976]. [Date taken from St Bride's Library card catalogue.]

Discusses legibility in general, the reading process, earlier scholarship, speed of perception, perceptibility at a distance, peripheral vision, visibility, reflex blink rate, visual fatigue, eye movements, rate of work, letters and numerals and punctuation marks, variations in character forms (capitals versus lower case, typeface variations, type weight, italics, type size), line length, leading, use of more than one column on a page, justified and unjustified setting, margins, page size, and 'the relation between form and content' (p. 13). Also looks at paper, ink, and printing processes. Covers authors' own and other research.

218 _____, _____, and Brian Coe. *A Comparison of the Effectiveness of Selected Typographic Variations.* London: Royal College of Art, Readability of Print Research Unit, Sept. 1973.

Points out that texts – especially bibliographies – are made up of logical units. 'In materials which have a clearly defined logical structure, such as bibliographies, it is especially important that the elements within each logical unit should be clearly distinguishable from one another' (p. 2). Says, 'There are at least 6 typographic variations which might be used singly or in combination to make the required distinctions: size change; weight change; changes between upper and

lowercase; type style change; change in linear spacing; change in letter spacing' (p. 2). This study concentrates only on type weight and type style. Looks at 'medium', and 'bold' types, along with serif (Times Roman, Goudy Old Style), slab serif (Fortune Light, Rockwell Medium), and sans serif (Univers Medium, Futura Medium) faces. Concludes that 'differences in type weight are more effective than differences in type style or typeface' (p. 11). Also, 'style differences are stronger than face differences' (p. 11).

219 _____, _____, _____. *The Relative Effectiveness of Spatial and Typographic Coding Systems within Bibliographical Entries.* [Part 2; see next entry for Part I.] London: Royal College of Art, Readability of Print Research Unit, 1974. (See Appendix I, Example 4.)

This and other tests done by these same researchers are the only ones I know that focus specifically on the shape and design of bibliographies. Unfortunately, they were published in short runs and never distributed widely on a commercial basis. Furthermore, they concentrate on only two aspects of bibliographical entries, spatial coding and typographic coding. The former refers to the physical layout of the page – one entry's shape and its relation on the page to the entries around it. For example, 1) entries running together like prose, one entry picking up in the same line as the previous entry; 2) entries beginning flush left on a new line, but with no space between entries, and the full text of each entry running margin to margin; 3) entries beginning flush left, with no space between entries, and with each element in each entry (author, title, publication data, price, classification, numbers of publication) beginning on a new line; 4) entries beginning flush left, with one element on each line, and each succeeding line indented about 1 em from the line above; 5) entries running margin to margin like prose, set flush left, ragged-right, with a line space between entries; 6) entries set flush left, one element per line (long titles running onto a second line also flush left), with a space between entries. These six spatial arrangements were combined with three typographic coding systems, employing such differences as the use of full caps, italics, and boldface types. Thus, some entries were set completely in one type; some used full caps for authors' names and italics for titles; some used italics for authors' names and boldface for titles. This yielded 18 different styles.

This volume reproduces sample pages of these 18 styles, in the format in which they were given to test subjects. It also reproduces the question sheets which the subjects filled out, along with a full explanation of the procedures and test materials, and the results based on all accumulated data and showing which styles were most legible and yielded up information the most efficiently.

Shows 'that spatial coding was more effective than typographic coding where the target entries [those to be located in the bibliography by the subjects who took the test] were identified by their alphabetically listed first elements, whereas typographic coding was more effective than spatial coding where subjects were scanning the second element of each entry' (p. 14).

The authors raise the significant issue that 'These results emphasise the necessity for a pragmatic as opposed to a purely aesthetic approach to the design of lists and indexes. The design must not only reflect the logical structure of information, it must also facilitate its retrieval' (p. 19). They discuss retrieval of data from indexes, looking at alphabetical and other arrangements and at spatial and typographic coding.

[Note: if a bibliography is chronological rather than alphabetical, some arrangement under each date would be useful. The bibliography by Stratman (Carl J. Stratman, *Bibliography of Medieval Drama*. 2nd ed., rev. and enlarged. 2 vols. New York: Frederick Ungar, 1972), which is arranged by genre of medieval plays, subdivided by individual plays, is further subdivided by a chronological arrangement of criticism for each play. When there are only a few scholarly works on a given play, locating a specific critic is easy. But for plays such as *Everyman* or for Stratman's sections on 'General Studies' (pp. 554–67 and 255–306 in the two volumes), there are hundreds of entries listed in chronological order. To find the work of a single critic, one must know the date of her or his work. A good index would help; but Stratman is in two volumes. The index is in volume 2, while the citations fill volume 1 and part of volume 2. This is a particularly time-consuming bibliography to use. Probably more efficient would be an alphabetical arrangement, by author, though the chronological arrangement makes some sense, too, for those studying the history of the criticism.]

'For bibliographical material such as the author indexes used in this study, it would appear that if the information within the entries is to be accessed only via the authors' surnames, then spatial coding is more effective than typographic coding' (p. 19). The authors point out that certain arrangements take up more space than others, and are thus more expensive to produce. 'If, however, users are likely to want to scan the titles

of the entries as well as referring to entries relating to specific authors, then strong typographic coding within the entries . . . is necessary in addition to spatial coding' (p. 19). Discusses at length the two basic search strategies (spatial and typographic), and whether typewriters will do, or if typesetting is better.

[Note: This was written in 1974. Today the personal computer and printer allow just about any kind of spatial and typographic variation necessary. Only the base economic considerations of how much space can be saved should affect the final product.]

220 _____, _____, _____. *The Relative Effectiveness of Ten Alternative Systems of Typographic Coding in Bibliographical Material.* London: Royal College of Art, Readability of Print Research Unit, July 1973. (Part I of a two-part study; see previous entry.)

'. . . compares the effectiveness of ten alternative systems of typographical/spatial coding which might be used in the presentation of highly structured information such as bibliographical material' (p. 2). Uses spatial and typographic elements to distinguish between elements in a single entry, and between separate entries. Allows for simple machinery in the creation of the entries (these various styles could be produced on a typewriter). 'The most effective system tested was a two-unit left extension of the first line of each entry' (p. 92). The systems employ variations in capitalization, upper- and lower-case print, bold face, underlining, use of 'a single-unit dash in the margin' (p. 5), entries beginning two spaces into the left margin, and different line spacing. The best styles 'make a clear distinction between successive entries and between the first word of each entry and the rest of the entry' (p. 47). This can be achieved on a typewriter and even on a computer printer which gives only upper-case characters. [As this final comment suggests, this article appeared quite early in the computer boom. The importance of this study is in its recognition of the need for a careful analysis of the spatial and typographic elements in bibliographical entries which contribute to ease of use of the bibliography.]

221 _____, _____, _____. *A Report on the Legibility of Alternative Letter Shapes.* [London]: Royal College of Art, Readability of Print Research Unit, July 1973.

Not focused on the traditional areas of legibility study (legibility of letters of the alphabet, capitals versus lower case, etc.), but aiming 'to establish . . . the relative legibility, at four different levels of image quality, of the alternative signs currently employed to represent the same letter' (p. 2). Considers size, capitalization, etc. of letters in varying clarified or 'fuzzy' presentations. Explains the legibility of the 160 characters tested at varying levels of clarity. '. . . with only one exception, capital letters performed better than their lowercase equivalent where the latter are without ascenders or descenders, but . . . lowercase letters with ascenders and descenders generally proved superior to capitals' (p. 4).

222 _____, _____, _____. 'Spatial and Typographic Coding in Printed Bibliographical Materials.' *Journal of Documentation* 31.2 (June 1975): 59–70.

This is essentially a re-presentation of the very same experiment the authors wrote about in 'Typographic Coding in Lists and Bibliographies' (see entry **223**) – even reproducing large sections of prose verbatim and identical tables. The only two references cited in this article are two other essays by the same three authors: 'The Relative Effectiveness of Ten Alternative Systems of Typographic Coding in Bibliographical Material', and 'The Relative Effectiveness of Spatial and Typographic Coding Systems within Bibliographical Entries'.

222a _____, _____, _____. 'Spatial and Typographic Coding with Bibliographical Entries.' *Programmed Learning* (March 1975): 95–101.

Presents their findings about the 18 coding styles reported on in *The Relative Effectiveness of Spatial and Typographic Coding Systems within Bibliographical Entries* (see entries **219** and **220** above). Offers the same data and conclusions.

[Note: The work of these scholars, as my bibliography shows, is presented in several publications, often drawing on a single large research project. Their initial findings were published by their own organ: the Royal College of Art's Readability of Print Research Unit. Subsequent publication in various journals did the scholarly world the service of making these findings available to a wide audience in several disciplines.]

223 _____, _____, _____. 'Typographic Coding in Lists and Bibliographies.' *Applied Ergonomics* 5.3 (Sept. 1974): 136–41.

Uses single-column format. Offers 10 coding systems (see Appendix I, Example 3). 'The coding systems with the highest mean scores were Systems 7 and 9. . . . The

two-unit left extension of the first line in these two systems apparently distinguished very effectively between successive entries. . . . Possibly the additional half line space between entries in System 9 made this comparison of names slightly more difficult, though the difference between the two systems was not significant' (pp. 140–1). 'Capitals were not especially helpful' (as in Systems 1, 3, and 10) (p. 141). The initial hyphens in System 6 were 'not especially helpful' (p. 141), nor did the space between entries seem to be helpful (as in Systems 8, 9, and 10). 'The results of this study suggest that the most effective coding systems for highly structured information such as bibliographic material are those which make a clear distinction between successive entries and between the first word of each entry and the rest of the entry' (p. 141). System 7 seemed to be the best (most effective); it is as effective as number 9, and uses less space. N.B. All systems are compatible with typewriters and most computer printers. (See previous entry.)

224 S[perison], A[lbert]. [Untitled item.] *The Book Club of California Quarterly News-Letter* 55.1 (Winter 1989): 11–12.

In a brief entry about a new journal (*The California Book Collector*), points out the existence and quality of the new periodical, mentions that it was produced fully on computers, but complains, 'The production cries for a capable designer' (p. 11). Adds, 'Why can't someone realize that design is essential and that design cannot be produced on a machine?' (p. 12).

225 Stanton, Frank N., and Harold E. Burtt. 'The Influence of Surface and Tint of Paper on the Speed of Reading.' *Journal of Applied Psychology* 19 (1935): 683–93.

This is another 'piggy-back' study, simply repeating the findings of Paterson and Tinker (see their study on 'Printing Surface', **170** above). The findings are consistent with Paterson and Tinker's, though this study uses seven papers from Warren's Paper Company. Stanton and Burtt also find that 'no differences between mean scores on two papers are statistically significant', and that 'surface and yellowish tint of paper do not influence speed of reading to a significant degree' (p. 693).

225a Stern, Philip Van Doren. 'How to Look at a Book.' *The Dolphin* 4.3 (Spring 1941): 243–8.

Looks at various aspects of bookmaking. Points out the importance of good choice of paper, type, etc. Says,

'The subject of book margins is obscured by mathematical mysticism, vague references to the Greek law of the golden mean, and other well-meaning but often impracticable terms. . . . Margins should be wide enough to be pleasant and proportioned so that the inside margins are smallest, the top margins larger, the outside still larger, and the bottom margins largest of all' (p. 246). Offers a diagram showing the 'classical' 2:3:4:5 margins, with the author's own commentary. Says that consistency in all elements is essential to achieve coherence in style.

226 Stokes, Roy, ed. *Esdaile's Manual of Bibliography*. London: George Allen & Unwin, 1967. [This is Stokes' edition of Arundell Esdaile's work.]

Chapter 11 deals with 'The Arrangement of Bibliographies' (pp. 277–91). Sorting 'the titles into the alphabetical order for authors . . . is mere intellectual laziness or want of imagination' (p. 277). Suggests subject divisions. Also describes the '"library catalogue arrangement"' (p. 278), and chronological arrangement. Notes the differences among the bibliography of an author and his works, that of a historical person, and that of a locality. [To these one could add the bibliography of a subject area. . . . For other types of bibliographies, see Marion Villiers Higgins, *Bibliography: A Beginner's Guide*, **103** above. David Murray, in *Bibliography: Its Scope and Methods* (**158** above), divides bibliographies into the following categories: general, special, particular, personal, local.] Points out that in any one of these categories, arrangement may need to differ from one volume to the next: '. . . few authors present quite the same problems' (p. 280) as do others.

227 Stokes, Roy [Bishop]. *The Functions of Bibliography*. London: André Deutsch, 1969.

Defines 'bibliography'. Has chapters on enumerative, analytical or critical, descriptive, textual, and historical bibliography. Talks of how inclusive or exclusive bibliographies should strive to be; mentions many conflicting ideas in selectivity in compiling a bibliography. Has a useful discussion of Short Title Catalogue titles, how to compress much data into a small space, and why leaving out possibly useful data is justifiable (pp. 48–54). Also looks at classical ways of organizing data in a bibliography. Chapter 5 is on 'Arrangement of a Bibliography' (pp. 118–29). Says, 'The material must be ordered if it is to serve any purpose other than that of a purely preservative record' (p. 118). Adds that there are many arrangements

possible, but the three most common and useful are alphabetical, chronological, and subject. In quoting Pollard, the author points out that with an alphabetical arrangement, 'The principle of arrangement will be continuously visible' (p. 119; see Pollard, 'The Arrangement of Bibliographies', **176** above). Emphasizes the problems with the rules of alphabetization (the 'letter-by-letter' and the 'all-through' methods, the placement of the *Mc*, *Mac*, and *O*' patronymics, non-roman alphabetical symbols, rules for transliteration, etc.). Says the use to which the bibliography is to be put by readers should help one decide on the most appropriate arrangement. [Note: In a bibliography alphabetized by author, title and subject access can be obtained with a good index.] Discusses chronological arrangement. Points out its scholarly advantages for the person studying the history of the subject of the bibliography, and also the problems this raises (should the entries also be arranged as they would be in a classified arrangement on a library shelf? and what sub-arrangements are necessary [i.e. by printer, town, month, author, subject, etc.]?).

Also looks at the problems inherent in determining 'the basis on which . . . subject groupings shall be organized' (p. 127). Emphasizes that 'The compiler of a bibliography needs foremost to be a specialist in that subject field rather than primarily a bibliographer' (p. 128). [This book covers the realm of the design of the *intellectual content* of bibliographies rather than their *physical* content.]

228 Suen, C. Y., and M. K. Komoda. 'Legibility of Digital Type-fonts and Comprehension in Reading.' In *Text Processing and Document Manipulation: Proceedings of the International Conference, University of Nottingham, 14–16 April 1986*: pp. 178–87. Ed. by J. C. van Vliet. Cambridge and London: Cambridge University Press, on behalf of The British Computer Society, 1986. (See also entries for Burrill and for Bigelow and Holmes, **33** and **20** above.)

Examines 'the effects of font-styles on legibility and on reading proficiency' (pp. 178–9). Shows that on a screen, some letters in some fonts are easily confused for similarly shaped letters. Calls for a redesign of such letters.

229 Sumner, F. C. 'Influence of Color on Legibility of Copy.' *Journal of Applied Psychology* 16 (1932): 201–4.

Considers the legibility of single letters and digits, not of general printed matter. Uses only five subjects (with

42 colour combinations); so test results are suspect for prose on a printed page. Determines 'that legibility depends on brightness – difference between color of lettering and that of background' (p. 202), and 'that dark colored lettering on a light colored background is more legible than the reverse in daylight' (p. 202). Also, grey was 'the best background for the legibility of colored lettering' (p. 202). Inconclusive for prose.

230 Tabachnick, Sharon. 'Reviewing Printed Subject Bibliographies: A Worksheet.' *Journal of Academic Librarianship* 15.5 (Nov. 1989): 279–84.

'. . . proposes a worksheet that will enable reviewers of printed subject bibliographies to address the needs of librarians' (p. 279). Says, 'without good bibliographies, the world would resemble a library without catalogs: a hodge-podge of inaccessible ideas and knowledge' (p. 280). Focuses more on *reviews* of bibliographies than on bibliographies themselves. Some of the factors of bibliography review are germane here: Is the publisher 'known for publishing this type of material'? (p. 280). Is the compiler an expert on this subject? and known to be a 'quality' scholar? Is the purpose of the bibliography clearly articulated? and the scope fully defined and justified? Is the methodology used in compiling entries clearly indicated and justified? Are the limitations of the bibliography noted? Is the organization of the bibliography explained? and the indexing explained and justified? Does the bibliography avoid jargon and use clear language? Does it contain extraneous entries? Are entries under proper headings? Is this a real contribution to the field? Are locations of items noted? What are the quality and extent of the annotations? If there is a classification scheme, is it proper for the subject? Is proper bibliographical form used and applied consistently? Is a clear, simple bibliographical form used? Are there a good introduction and index? Is the print legible? Is there a good distinction between main headings and subheadings? and between main entries? Is the text 'relatively free of typographical errors' (p. 283) and grammatical mistakes? Is there good spacing of type? Are full entries given only once? Also mentions the appropriateness of binding, print quality, and good paper. Abbreviations should be adequately and conveniently explained. The table of contents should lead readers clearly to the main sections of the text. [Most of the issues here are presented in the author's worksheet for reviewers.]

231 Tauber, Maurice F., and Hilda Feinberg. *Book Catalogs.* Metuchen, NJ: Scarecrow Press, 1971.

Looks at many kinds of book catalogues listing libraries' holdings. Contains more than two dozen essays on a wide range of issues. Compares book and card catalogues; considers computerization, catalogue costs, and the many different kinds of catalogues there are for many kinds of libraries (colleges and universities, medical, county, public, etc.). The essay by Feinberg is the most germane for the present study (see Feinberg, 'Sample Book Catalogs . . .', **68** above).

232 Taylor, Insup, and M. Martin Taylor. *The Psychology of Reading.* New York: Academic Press, 1983.

Contains sections on the reading process, units of reading, letter and word recognition, etc. The sections on letter recognition and word recognition look at shapes of words and letters, letters and words in isolation versus in context, the ability of readers to discriminate different letters from one another, word length and contour, the importance of initial letters, word frequency and familiarity, and many other elements affecting one's ability to read.

233 Teal, G. E., I. T. Kaplan, D. E. Payne, and F. Hollstein. 'Readability as a Function of the Straightness of Righthand Margins.' Abstract in U.S. Government Research and Development Reports (Report No. AD-425 150). Cited by Foster, *Legibility Research Abstracts 1970*, p. 26. (Not seen)

Offers data on readability of justified text versus unjustified text with a vertical line beside it. 'It was concluded that text with an uneven right margin is as easy to read as text with a straight right margin' (Foster, p. 26). [It is surprising how often similar experiments are conducted – apparently with no knowledge of the fact that they have been done before – with identical results. More thorough bibliographical research before conducting a 'new' experiment might save some scholars much time and effort – and embarrassment.]

234 Thompson, Bradbury. *The Art of Graphic Design: With Contributions by Noteworthy Designers, Critics, and Art Historians.* New Haven, CT, and London: Yale University Press, 1988.

Contains many chapters on aspects of typography and book design (also the design of posters, advertisements, etc.). Looks at various uses of type. Mentions 'the logic behind the proposal to employ consistent graphic symbols for each of the 26 letters of the alphabet' (p. 75). The reasoning was as follows. Most letters have two symbols (*A*, *a*; *B*, *b*; etc.). Only seven have the same symbol for upper and lower case (*C*, *O*, *S*, *V*, *W*, *X*, *Z*) for most typefaces. To speed identification, only a single symbol was to be used (as proposed by the Westvaco Paper Company in 1950) – to 'provide a readable and practical simplified alphabet' (p. 73). Upper- and lower-case letters were selected on the basis of their having ascenders or descenders, their fit with other letters, or their angularity. The final selection contained caps, small caps, and lower-case letters. The original idea behind this was Thompson's; it was called the Monalphabet. Thompson recognizes the 'degree of unfamiliarity' (p. 79) the alphabet presents (especially in its bucking centuries of tradition).

Also has chapters on logos; art and typography; photography and typography; the use of paper; graphic design on postage stamps, in magazines, and in books; and so on. Useful in making designers think of the legibility of the alphabets they choose to print books in.

235 Tinker, Miles A. *Bases for Effective Reading*. Minneapolis, MN: University of Minnesota Press, 1965.

[Note: Herbert Spencer calls Tinker 'the most prolific writer on legibility research' (*The Visible Word*, p. 118 – see **214** above), and Spencer in his bibliography lists no fewer than 98 works by Tinker on the subject (22 of which are co-authored – one with A. Frandsen, 21 with D. G. Paterson). See Spencer's bibliography, pp. 101–5.] Also see Appendix I, Example 35.

Part 1 is on reading, perception, and comprehension. Part 2 is on eye movements in reading. Part 3 is on 'Scientific Typography: Printing for Easy and Efficient Reading'. Has sections on legibility, type for adult books and for children's books, 'Color and Surfaces of Printing Paper' (p. 157), 'Newspaper Typography' (p. 169), 'Spatial Arrangement and Position of the Printed Page' (p. 181), and 'Special Typographical Arrangements' (p. 192). Contains only one short paragraph on bibliographies (p. 198), citing Pratt ('A Note on the Legibility . . .', see **178** above).

Looks at the legibility of letters (pp. 125 ff.); upper and lower case; italics (pp. 134–5); boldface (pp. 135–6); full caps versus lower-case type (pp. 136–8); size of type (pp. 138–41); line width (pp. 141–5); leading (pp. 145–6); 'Leading and Line Width in Relation to Type Size' (pp. 146–8). Says that each of these factors has an optimal use and that the optimal uses

should be combined for greatest legibility. For example, a 6-point type set 14 picas should be leaded 2–4 points; 6-point type set 21 picas should be leaded 1–4 points; 6-point type set 28 picas should be leaded 2–4 picas. (Gives similar figures for type of 8, 9, 10, 11, and 12 points; see p. 147.)

Considers various colours of ink on various coloured papers. Says black ink on white or 'a lightly tinted or an antique wove finish printing paper' (p. 162) is excellent. Also considers printing surfaces (pp. 166–8), illumination, and much more. With a 356-entry bibliography.

236 _____. *The Effect of Color on Visual Apprehension and Perception. Genetic Psychology Monographs* 11.2 (Feb. 1932): 61–136. Worcester, MA: Clark University, 1932.

Looks at various kinds of printed matter, on different coloured stocks, and in different coloured inks. Considers span of attention, light sources, the influence of letter position on visual apprehension (letters on the left of lines seem to be more easily recognized than letters to their right), the effect of colour on the apprehension of letters (especially with respect to people's colour preferences, 'attention value' [p. 89], and luminosity), differences between the sexes in apprehension (orange, for example, had a higher attention value for women), homogeneous versus heterogeneous colours (the use of homogeneous colours rates higher apprehension scores), etc. The data here are especially relevant for advertising and posters, but are applicable to books as well. Cites many studies.

237 _____. 'Influence of Simultaneous Variation in Size of Type, Width of Line, and Leading for Newspaper Type.' *Journal of Applied Psychology* 47.6 (1963): 380–2.

'Results revealed that 7-, 8-, and 9-point type in a 12-pica line width with 2-point leading were read most rapidly and equally fast. But text in relatively long lines, very short lines, and small type size, or combinations of these with little or no leading were significantly slower than the standard' (p. 380). Points out that readers preferred '8- or 9-point type with 2-point leading in a line width of 12 picas (12 or 18 picas for 9-point type)' (p. 380).

238 _____. *Legibility of Print*. Ames, IA: Iowa State University Press, 1963.

'Items in Bibliographies' covered on pp. 225–6. Here 'bibliographies' means 'footnotes'. Discusses the placement of the note numbers – essentially summarizing Pratt's findings (q.v., 178 above). Discusses legibility of letters and digits, kinds and sizes of types, line width, leading, arrangement of the printed page, colour of ink and paper, printing surfaces, etc. Contains an annotated bibliography of general treatments of legibility (pp. 267–322; 238 items), only one of which focuses on bibliographies (the Pratt item).

This is perhaps the most fully elaborated study on legibility, drawing on the author's own scholarship and a very wide range of the work of others (as the bibliography indicates). Has a section 'Special Printing Situations', which discusses typewritten material, Linotype text, manuscript presentation, stencil-duplicated materials, print in comic books, projected materials (anticipates computers and VDTs, but focuses on microfilm and filmed text projected on ceilings for bed patients), dictionary printing, items in bibliographies (i.e. footnotes; see above), telephone directories, Library of Congress Catalog cards, timetables, and printing on spines of books.

Among many other things here, shows the legibility of each individual letter with respect to others in the alphabet and of each number (considering roman and arabic numerals). Points out the effect on legibility of serifs, heaviness of stroke, delineation of distinguishing characteristics, simplification of outline, white space within a letter, and width of the letter. In the chapter on kinds of type (Chapter 4), relates typefaces with the texts they are suited for.

Reviews the extensive scholarship. Looks at several faces, italic versus roman, upper- versus lower-case letters, boldface, mixed type forms. Concludes that 'Type faces in common use are equally legible'; 'Readers prefer a type face that appears to border on boldface'; 'A serifless type . . . is read as rapidly as ordinary type, but readers do not prefer it'; 'Italic print is read somewhat more slowly than ordinary lower case'; 'All-capital print greatly retards speed of reading in comparison with lower-case type'; 'Boldface type is read at the same rate as ordinary lower case'; and 'Speed of reading seems to be the most satisfactory measure of legibility of type faces' (pp. 64–6).

Summarizes the large body of scholarship on the size of type. Concludes that 10- or 11-point type is probably the most legible. Considers width of line and the optimum line lengths for the different type sizes. Points

out that the median line width for magazines is from 17 to 18 picas; for scientific journals, it is from 25 to 26 picas; for textbooks, it is from 21 to 22 picas. 'For 10-point type set solid, results . . . show that materials in line widths between 17 and 27 picas are equally legible' (p. 86). Gives similar data for other type sizes. Has a coordinating chapter on leading between lines, considering it with different sizes of type and line lengths. The smaller the typeface, the more leading is needed for legibility: 10-point type set solid is as legible as 8-point type leaded 2 points, though readers preferred the 10-point type.

Talks of page sizes, margins, single versus multiple column printing, use of rule between columns, arrangement of paragraphs, vertical versus horizontal printing (see his 'Perceptual and Oculomotor Efficiency . . .', next entry), and even curvature of printed material caused by too small an inner margin and too tight a binding.

The book goes on to cover a great variety and number of other factors affecting legibility: colour of ink and colour of paper, texture and thickness of paper, newspaper typography, printing of formulas and mathematical tables, illumination for reading, angular alignment of the reading material, vibration of the printed matter, length of reading period, etc.

239 _____. 'Perceptual and Oculomotor Efficiency in Reading Materials in Vertical and Horizontal Arrangements.' *American Journal of Psychology* 68.3 (Sept. 1955): 444–9.

Discusses which arrangement of text is 'more efficient' (p. 444), horizontal or vertical. Considers habit due to practice, which allows subjects to read more quickly horizontally. Even after much practice, subjects read more quickly horizontally than they did vertically. Shows that 'the vertical reading required fewer fixations, fewer regressions, a longer pause duration, and more words were read per fixation' (p. 447). Says that with more practice, subjects would probably read equally well in both directions, and possibly even faster vertically. Cites as a reason for this the 'increased efficiency in perceiving larger groups of words per fixation due to the shape of the area of clear vision' (p. 448). But concludes that 'the efficiency of vertically arranged printing is apt to remain largely a matter of theoretical interest' (p. 449). (See also Coleman and Kim, Nahinsky, and North and Jenkins.)

240 _____, and Donald G. Paterson. 'Influence of Type Form on Speed of Reading.' *Journal of Applied Psychology* 12.4 (Aug. 1928): 359–68.

Text set all 'in lower case letters was read 13.4 per cent faster than that in all capitals' (p. 368), and '2.8 per cent faster than the italics' (p. 368). Regular upper- and lower-case roman types yield greatest legibility – especially in familiar typefaces.

241 _____, _____. 'Readability of Mixed Type Forms.' *Journal of Applied Psychology* 30 (Dec. 1946): 631–7.

Medley arrangements retarded reading speeds 8.35% and 11.39%. Recommends that the printer use one typeface throughout to maintain speed of reading and the sense of legibility.

242 _____, _____. 'Studies of Typographical Factors Influencing Speed of Reading. III. Length of Line.' *Journal of Applied Psychology* 13 (1929): 205–19.

Cites studies asserting that (usually for 10-point type – presumably the most legible) a line length of between 3.6 and *c.* 4 inches is optimum for speed of reading. The '80 mm. [3⅛ inches] line yielded faster reading than any of the other line lengths employed . . . [therefore] it is evident that the optimum for 10 point type lies somewhere between 59 and 97 mm.' (p. 213). Especially efficient is a line length 'within the limits of 75 to 90 mm.' (p. 213). In general, 'short lines are favored over long ones' (p. 219). Final recommendation is 10-point type and line 80 mm. in length.

243 _____, _____. 'Studies of Typographical Factors Influencing Speed of Reading. XIII. Methodological Considerations.' *Journal of Applied Psychology* 20 (1936): 132–45.

This general article explains methods used by Paterson and Tinker in all their experiments on speed of reading; it justifies the accuracy of their findings in their preceding studies.

244 _____, _____. 'Studies of Typographical Factors Influencing Speed of Reading. XI. Role of Set in Typographical Studies.' *Journal of Applied Psychology* 19 (1935): 647–51.

Verifies earlier findings that 10-point type in 19-pica lines set solid show 'a retarding influence on speed of

reading' (p. 650), but not when leading is used between lines.

245 _____, _____. 'Studies of Typographical Factors Influencing Speed of Reading. V. Simultaneous Variation of Type Size and Line Length.' *Journal of Applied Psychology* 15 (1931): 72–8.

Reconfirms earlier tests that 10-point type set in 19-pica lines yields best reading speed. Also quite acceptable is 8-point type in 17-pica-long lines (p. 78). The final results show that 'within certain limits, neither size of type nor line length as single variables can be relied upon in determining optimal typographical arrangements. Both factors . . . work hand in hand and must be properly balanced to produce a printed page which will promote a maximum reading rate' (p. 78).

246 _____, _____. 'Studies of Typographical Factors Influencing Speed of Reading. VII. Variations in Color of Print and Background.' *Journal of Applied Psychology* 15 (1931): 471–9.

The best legibility results from 'Black on white, grass green on white, lustre blue on white, and black on yellow' (p. 478). Fair legibility results from 'Tulip red on yellow, tulip red on white' (p. 479). Poor legibility results from 'grass green on red, chromium orange on black, chromium orange on white, tulip red on green, black on purple' (p. 479). The final recommendation: 'Care must be taken to produce a *printed page* which shows a maximum *brightness contrast* between print and background' (p. 479).

247 Tracy, Walter. *Letters of Credit: A View of Type Design.* Boston, MA: Godine, 1986.

Contains a brief section on 'Legibility and readability' (pp. 30–2). Distinguishes between these two, and points out that different typefaces must be used for different kinds of text. Speaks of 'the proper balancing of the functional and the aesthetic' (p. 32) aspects of type.

248 Trevitt, John. *Book Design.* London, Cambridge (England), and New York: Cambridge University Press, 1980.

Has sections on printing processes, choice of page size, typesetting, typefaces, margins, justified and unjustified setting, centred and asymmetrical layouts, subheadings, running heads, titles, quotations, footnotes, endnotes, bibliographies, indexes, preliminary pages, illustrations, paper, binding, and jackets and covers.

On bibliographies, there is only one 67-word paragraph. Says that they 'should be set in the same type size as endnotes (which is likely to be the size chosen for small-type quotations), probably unjustified, with turnovers indented two ems' (p. 21). Footnotes should be set in the 'smallest [type] that can be read' – 8- or 9-point – and endnotes 'in type slightly larger than would be used for footnotes' (p. 21). Says, 'The old habit of listing names in small capitals was rather prettifying for all but the most elegant of literary monographs; but small capitals for frequent short-form author references can be useful.'

With respect to choice of page size, the author says that the designer must consider many things, including the use to which the book will be put, the size of the press and paper available, whether a reprint in a small run is contemplated, whether there need be illustrations in the text, the length of the text, etc. Says the paper should be matched to the type and vice versa; e.g., older faces should not be used on coated stock (p. 8).

Considers the reading public's attitudes to short and long texts. Contains a sensible discussion of type styles, their appearance on the page in various sizes, and so on (see especially pp. 8–11). Advocates the standard 1½:2:3:4 or 2:3:4:5 margins; talks of the 'optical centre' of the page (p. 12). Also points out that small-format, low-budget books will necessarily have narrower margins. Discusses the advantages and drawbacks of justified typesetting. On this topic, as in his discussion of asymmetry versus centring the text, the author opts for neither side. As for subheads and running heads, he says, 'Occasionally the decision, centred or asymmetrical, may rest on these: centred they are formal, prominent, even dominant, whereas they become much less insistent when ranged to the left of an asymmetrical page' (p. 15).

Discusses these with respect to the numbering of parts of the text, indentation, use of small capitals, bold and italic type. . . . Also warns that running heads should be kept short. Talks of the use of ornamentation and decoration, chapter or section titles, and the design of tables.

249 Trollip, Stanley R., and Gregory Sales. 'Readability of Computer-generated Fill-justified Text.' *Human Factors* 28.2 (1986): 159–63.

Fill-justified text has straight left and right margins. Shows that text set ragged-right is read faster than fully justified text which contains the same words on each line. Text flush left and right 'slows reading speed . . . significantly' (p. 162). [Note that this study measures texts which have the same number of characters on a line, and the means of right justification is the insertion of extra spaces between words. It does not consider proportional spacing.] Comprehension is not affected in a fill-justified text, but reading time increases (i.e., reading speed slows down.)

250 Tschichold, Jan. *Asymmetric Typography*. Trans. by Ruari McLean. London: Faber and Faber; Toronto: Cooper & Beatty; New York: Reinhold, 1967.

Covers a rich array of subjects – decorative typography; functional typography; types; hand versus machine composition; words; lines; leading; line length and grouping; indentation and line endings; type size, headings, and type mixtures; the use of space; tables; rules; colours; paper; posters; typography, photography, and drawings; etc.

Says that 'Good typography depends only secondarily on types, primarily on the way they are used' (p. 16). The aim of this typography is simplicity ('We aim at simplicity', p. 28); hence the stress on 'simple and clear type faces' (p. 28). 'Sans serif, although it is no longer new, is so simple and clear that it is by far the best all-purpose type for today and will remain so for a long time to come' (p. 28; the footnote to this statement says, 'this being the author's opinion in 1935', p. 28). [Note: Tschichold later reversed many of the views expressed in this book.]

Points out that sans serif is not tied to older practices of typography, and because of the many thicknesses of stroke the sans serif faces offer, they can express the 'New Typography' in an uninhibited way (see especially p. 28). Urges the use of a variety of types. Type set in upper and lower case 'is the most legible and should be regarded as the norm. Words should rarely be set in capitals' (p. 38). 'Too much letter spacing will . . . diminish legibility' (p. 38).

[Contains much information on typography, but focused primarily on pages of text, secondarily on pages with headlines, posters, and title pages. Nothing on the setting of indexes or bibliographies.]

'Good setting . . . must be leaded. . . . Matter set solid tends not to look clear. . . . The amount of leading depends on the amount of white around the type and the general colour required' (p. 44). Indentation is the best way of designating a new paragraph. It should be 1 em, except with long, heavily leaded lines (p. 48).

Comments on appropriate type size and mixtures, and the use of space. Has a section on tables – discussing the use of rule, the overall appearance of the table, table headings, and ditto marks. Also discusses the colour of ink and paper. 'The choice of paper plays an important part in successful typography. It is seldom right to use coated paper if there are no halftone engravings' (p. 68). Explains the notion of functionalism with respect to the 'New Typography'.

251 _____. 'Non-Arbitrary Proportions of Page and Type Area.' In *Calligraphy and Palaeography, Essays Presented to Alfred Fairbank on His 70th Birthday*, pp. 179–91. New York: October House, 1966.

See illustration in text (p. 14).

252 Tufte, Edward R. *The Visual Display of Quantitative Information*. Cheshire, CT: Graphics Press, 1983.

Looks at charts, tables, graphs of various kinds, data maps, time-series, space-time narrative designs, and relational graphics. With respect to the aesthetic presentation of data, says, 'Graphical elegance . . . has two key elements: . . . simplicity of design and complexity of data' (p. 177). Also says that the subject matter is important: 'The best graphics are about the useful and important, about life and death, about the universe. Beautiful graphics do not traffic with the trivial' (p. 177). Offers these seven points in creating an aesthetic page: 1) 'have a properly chosen format and design'; 2) 'use words, numbers, and drawing together'; 3) 'reflect a balance, a proportion, a sense of relevant scale'; 4) 'display an accessible complexity of detail'; 5) 'often have a narrative quality, a story to tell about the data'; 6) have 'a professional manner, with technical details of production done with care'; 7) 'avoid content-free decoration' (p. 177). Says to avoid contractions and abbreviations where possible, as well as excesses and peculiarities in typography. Type should be 'clear, precise, modest' (p. 183). Says to use seriffed types. Pick a typeface in which the letters are most differentiated from one another. Avoid 'the fashionable preference for sans-serif' types (p. 183).

Adds that the designer should establish principles of design, but 'the principles should not be applied rigidly or in a peevish spirit . . .; it is better to violate any principle than to place graceless or inelegant marks on paper. Most principles of design should be greeted with some skepticism' (p. 191). 'The task of the designer is to give visual access to the subtle and the difficult –

that is, the revelation of the complex' (p. 191). Though not on bibliographies, offers some practical considerations on layout and design.

253 Turabian, Kate L. *A Manual for Writers of Term Papers, Theses, and Dissertations*. 4th ed. Chicago and London: University of Chicago Press, 1973.

Presents the standard 'style manual' type of information on the content and order of bibliographical entries. On the physical layout, says only, 'Entries may be typed single space, double space, or one and one-half space. If single spacing is used, there should be a double space between entries. Each item should begin at the left margin and succeeding lines should be indented a definite number of spaces. . . . If desired, the authors' names may be typed in capitals throughout. Annotations should begin a new line and should be typed single space' (p. 199).

254 *Typography and Design*. Washington, [DC]: United States Government Printing Office, 1951. Apprentice Training Series, Intermediate Period.

Contains much information on book design. Covers printing types, use and kinds of illustrations, principles of design, determining format, printing processes, paper, binding, layouts, etc. With respect to legibility, discusses word spacing and letterspacing, leading, indentations, ink, paper, and selection of typefaces. Nothing specifically on bibliographies.

255 Updike, Daniel Berkeley. *In the Day's Work*. Cambridge, MA: Harvard University Press, 1924.

Contains three chapters: 1) 'On the Planning of Printing' (originally printed in *The Fleuron* 2: 13–27); 2) 'Style in the Use of Type' (originally issued in *Handcraft*, a publication of The Society of Arts and Crafts, of Boston); 3) 'Seven Champions of Typography'.

255a _____. 'On the Planning of Printing.' *The Fleuron* 2 (1924): 13–27.

'There is . . . the tendency to strive for undue originality . . . [in typography]. Most experiments, wise and otherwise, have already been tried, and the sure way – which is not very original, now – is on the whole the best way, unless it can be so much improved that its utility can be recognized at once' (p. 23).

256 Urban, F. M. 'A Remark on the Legibility of Printed Types.' *American Journal of Psychology* 23.3 (July 1912): 454–6.

Discusses Roethlein's suggestion that slightly yellowed paper is preferable – in terms of legibility for numerical tables – to white paper (see **196** above). Comments that tables should be broken up into groups of 3 – not 10 – lines (p. 455), and considers leading in such tables as well as the breaking up of logarithmic sets of figures into groups of 6 – to aid memory. Nothing on legibility of prose.

257 Van Hoesen, Henry Bartlett, and Frank Keller Walter. *Bibliography: Practical, Enumerative, Historical: An Introductory Manual.* New York and London: Charles Scribner's Sons, 1928.

Contains chapters on many aspects of bibliographies. Chapter 2, 'Practical Bibliography', contains a short section on 'Format': 'The publisher will, of course, know the fashions in books, the trade conditions, etc., and, accordingly, suggest the proper format, but the author will have certain requirements. . . . The public for whom the book is intended, the uses for which it is designed, and the price at which it is to be sold, are considerations affecting the selection of format as well as the selection of literary style and illustrations, type-face, etc. . . . Also the subject-matter itself often seems to demand a certain format and style' (p. 39).

Also discusses handset versus machine-set types and justification. Suggests 12-point as the 'standard', and vaguely talks about margins, leading, and number of lines to the page. 'The size of the type and the amount of "leading" between lines are the prime factors in legibility' (p. 40). Mentions also size of type for notes, selection of typeface, paper, and even the cover material.

Says that the bibliography may use abbreviations. 'The capitalization of every noun in the titles of books, as prescribed by most style manuals, makes the page of a bibliography appear absurdly and confusedly "peppered" with capitals' (p. 29). Mentions the use of ellipses, square brackets, semicolons to separate the main from the explanatory title, colons between independent titles, and so on.

258 Waern, Yvonne, and Carl Rollenhagen. 'Reading Text from Visual Display Units (VDUs).' *International Journal of Man-Machine Studies* 18 (1983): 441–65.

A psychological look at reading texts from video displays. The 'VDU situation may lead to fatigue and stress, which may decrease performance' (p. 441). Focuses on reader comprehension. Considers such factors as character size and shape, spacing, stability of image on the screen, resolution, luminance, contrast, chromaticity, screen angle, posture, environment, and personal characteristics of the reader. Also looks at the content and form of the text, the reading purpose, the physiological act of reading. Draws only general conclusions on how to do research on the psychological factors in reading on VDT screens. With a bibliography of 106 related entries.

258a Warde, Beatrice. *The Crystal Goblet: Sixteen Essays on Typography.* Ed. by Henry Jacob. Cleveland, OH, and New York: World Publishing Co., 1956.

Contains her well-known statement that typography should be as invisible for its text as a crystal goblet should be for the wine it contains. See p. 5 above.

259 Webster, Helen A., and Miles A. Tinker. 'The Influence of Paper Surface on the Perceptibility of Print.' *Journal of Applied Psychology* 19 (1935): 145–7.

Comes to the same conclusions as do earlier researchers 'who investigated the influence of paper surface on speed of reading. Variation in paper surface had no differential effect on the speed of reading' (p. 146). However, illumination should not allow glazed paper to create a glare for the reader over prolonged reading times. 'Eye-strain from reading material printed on glazed paper must be due entirely to continuous reading in light not uniformly dispersed rather than to inability to see the print satisfactorily' (p. 147).

260 _____, _____. 'The Influences of Type Face on the Legibility of Print.' *Journal of Applied Psychology* 19 (1935): 43–52.

Summarizes earlier findings which conclude that 'type faces in common use are equally legible' (p. 44). This study aims to 'get more comparable data' (p. 44) to explain the differences in the earlier findings (of Pyke, Roethlein, Burtt and Basch, and Paterson and Tinker). The present study adds to Paterson and Tinker's normal reading situation the additional factor of distance used by the other experimenters. Results show 'that legibility of letters is increased when the size of the letter is increased, when the lines in the letter are widened, when the area of white space around or within the outline of the letter is increased, when the contrast of shading or hair lines is lessened, and when the outline of the letter is made simpler' (p. 49). However, 'certain factors which increase *perceptibility* of words at a distance reduce *speed* of reading' (p. 52). Such results do not apply to normal book-reading distance, especially for bibliographies.

261 Wendt, Dirk, and Hans Weckerle. 'On Effects of Indentation and Underlining in Reference Work.' *Visible Language* 6.2 (Spring 1972): 167–71.

Aims to assess the usefulness of these two typographic features, especially with respect to the 'ease of search in reference works' (p. 167). Concludes that 'indentation of key words makes reference work about 8% faster than the usual arrangement' (p. 171), while 'underlining does not help' (p. 171).

262 White, Jan V. *Graphic Design for the Electronic Age.* New York: A Xerox Press Book, Watson-Guptill Publications, 1988.

Contains sections on type, elements of a page, and the physical features of books. Reviews some of the typical issues about legibility (sans serif or serif types, justified or ragged-right setting, line length, caps or lower case, roman or italic faces, and ink and paper colours). Considers also columns, the format for lists, titles, headlines, headings, initial letters, etc. Suggests the usual arrangement of a bibliographic entry (author, title, publication data – see p. 138). Has only one short paragraph on bibliographies. Advocates use of *The Chicago Manual of Style* for the form of entries, and says only, 'the type style should be similar to that of the notes' (p. 161). Talks also of paper and binding, and of getting a well-proportioned page.

263 _____. *Mastering Graphics.* New York and London: R. R. Bowker, 1983.

Chapter 3 is on layout and typewriter 'typography'. Considers line length; typeface appropriate for needs; and the relationship between line length and things such as subject matter, size of type, line spacing, number of lines per page, use of subheads, colour of ink and paper, size of page, number of pages, number of columns on a page, etc. Looks also at ragged-right or justified typing, 'the problem of creating emphasis in typewritten copy' (p. 34), the use of headlines and marginal notes, etc. Has a similar chapter (Chapter 4) on type use. Nothing specifically about bibliographies, but much data on paper, ink, reproduction methods, general page layout, use of illustrations, printing methods, and other technical data on book production.

264 _____. *On Graphics: Tips for Editors: A Miscellany of Practical Fundamentals.* Chicago: Lawrence Ragan Communications, Inc., 1981.

Has sections on styling text with a typewriter, the use of rules and grids, how to achieve legibility (especially with proper choice of type), etc. Nothing on bibliographies, but has some useful comments about page design.

265 White, Lewis Felix. *The Art of the Book, A Talk . . . Given under the Auspices of the Type Directors Club of New York City.* New York: The L. F. White Company, 1951.

Speaks of the requirements – in a good book designer – of an 'enthusiasm for type, papers or decoration' and a love for books [p. 5]. Also needed is a 'knowledge of the tradition of bookmaking' [p. 5]. Cites Cobden-Sanderson's *Ideal Book* (q.v.). Says we must design books with a sensitivity to current typographic practices.

266 Wiggins, Richard H. 'Effects of Three Typographical Variables on Speed of Reading.' *Journal of Typographical Research* 1.1 (Jan. 1967): 5–18.

Summarizes the findings of many earlier researchers (Pyke, Tinker and Paterson, Roethlein, etc.). Considers mostly line length (column width), lower-case alphabet lengths, and the question of uneven versus even right margins (p. 6). No findings related to bibliographies.

267 Wilkinson, Tim. 'Book Margins.' *Book Design and Production* 1.2 (Spring 1958): 44–5. London: Printing News Ltd.

Says that many designers settle on margins 'by eye', but the author's own method uses a simple scale. Usually, 'the proportion of gutter 2, head 3, fore-edge 4, and tail 5 [is] most useful (for more extravagant work the classical 1½:2:3:4 is perhaps better)' (pp. 44–5). Has diagrams on how to construct the 'perfect' page with ideal margins.

268 Williams, Rodney Don. 'Design Considerations for Distance Viewed Dot-Matrix Displays.' *Proceedings of the Human Factors Society 25th Annual Meeting*, Rochester, NY, 1981: 26–9. Ed. by Robert C. Sugarman. Buffalo, NY: Calspan Corp., 1981.

Discusses the results of research on 'a systematic analysis and extension of the human design considerations for dot-matrix displays' (p. 26). Looks at CRT literature and considers the factors which affect legibility – character factors, viewer factors, and environmental factors. Character factors include such things as font, matrix size, symbol shape, symbol colour, symbol orientation (slanted and vertical characters), symbol motion, definition, and so on.

Raises the issues of computer technology as applied to the presentation of texts, and human interaction with computers. The use of dot-matrix CRT displays and dot-matrix printouts affects the legibility of any text.

269 Williamson, Hugh. *Methods of Book Design: The Practice of an Industrial Craft*. 3rd ed. New Haven, CT, and London: Yale University Press, 1983.

Covers many aspects of book design, from typescript to final bound product (including dust jacket, price, cover, etc.). For bibliographies, recommends a 'type size appropriate for appendixes and notes' (p. 182), but this is for a bibliography in a book – not for a volume-length bibliography. 'Precedence is usually alphabetical order of authors' surnames, with which each entry begins. Small capitals, with or without initial capitals, are often used for authors' names, but this can look clumsy; a combination of capitals and small capitals is out of fashion, and if small capitals are letterspaced as they should be, the names appear to be over-emphasized at the expense of the titles. Roman upper and lower-case will prove clear enough for names' (p. 182). On the styling of bibliographies for texts in the sciences, author makes not very practical suggestions (e.g., dates should follow the authors' names, boldface figures should be used for volume numbers).

270 Wilson, Adrian. *The Design of Books*. Salt Lake City, UT, and Santa Barbara, CA: Peregrine Smith, 1974.

This volume contains many excellent suggestions about how to design books, covering a wide range of topics.

About bibliographies, says, 'If the bibliography is not of great length it should be set in a type intermediate between that of the extracts and the footnotes (e.g., text 12/14, extracts 10/12, footnotes 8/9, bibliography 9/10). If space and budget permit it is agreeable to add 2 points extra space between entries. Subheadings are best handled in the same type size as the body in a descending scale with capitals, small capitals, italic, etc. The major heading should follow the style of the appendix and the notes' (p. 85). These remarks pertain to a bibliography in a book, not to a whole volume which is a bibliography. [Note: The designation of type size as '10/12' means a 10-point typeface on a 12-point body; this ensures a 2-point space between lines, and takes the place of leading.]

Though there is nothing else specifically about bibliographies in this book, it is still one of the more honoured and appreciated books about book design available.

271 Wilson, Patrick. *Two Kinds of Power: An Essay on Bibliographical Control*. Berkeley and Los Angeles, CA: University of California Press, 1968. Contributions to Librarianship, 5.

Looks at the world of 'bibliographical control'. Chapter I is on 'The Bibliographical Universe' (pp. 6–19): 'the things over which one might have bibliographical control' (p. 6). Chapter IV is on 'bibliographical Instruments' (pp. 55–68). Looks at various types of bibliographical works, separate volumes as well as bibliographies at the ends of books. Talks of the importance of a clear explanation of how to use the bibliography. Calls the need a 'knowledge of the Specifications of the instrument, the rules according to which it was constructed. . . . My knowledge of the power given me by an instrument depends on the clarity of the rules according to which it was constructed' (p. 59).

Lists the five elements in bibliography specifications that are essential for the best use of the work. 1) The domain of the volume, 'the set of items from which the contents of the work, the items actually listed, are drawn' (p. 59). 2) Principles of selection for items in the bibliography. Says these principles should be logically formulated and clearly delineated in the volume. 3) The bibliographical units that will be listed and described; 'the size of the listable unit has a profound effect on the value of a' bibliography (p. 61). 4) Information fields: 'We must . . . know what information we can expect to find about an item, [and] what conclusions we can draw from the absence of a piece of information' (pp. 61–2). 5) The organization of the bibliography; a good, logical organization, explained carefully, should allow 'immediate and direct identification of items that fit some description without the necessity of scanning all the descriptions of the items listed' (p. 62). Also says, 'Any index to a bibliographical instrument is part of its organizational scheme' (p. 62). Adds that the rules for the organizational scheme must be set forth precisely. Has a chapter on indexing. [See article by Marcia J. Bates, 'Rigorous Systematic Bibliography', **12** above.]

272 Wrolstad, M. E. 'Adult Preferences in Typography: Exploring the Function of Design.' *Journalism Quarterly* 37.2 (1960): 211–23.

Considers symmetry and five principles of typographic design ('balance, contrast, proportion, rhythm, and unity' – p. 212). Subjects were given title pages to respond to.

272a Wroth, Lawrence C. 'Formats and Sizes.' *The Dolphin* I (1933): 81–95.

Shows how the sizes of books traditionally were linked to the sizes of the sheets of paper available. Discusses the standard formats (folio, quarto, octavo, duodecimo, etc.). Explains how the different formats are produced.

273 Zachrisson, Bror. *Studies in the Legibility of Printed Text.* Stockholm, Göteborg, and Uppsala: Almqvist & Wiksell, 1965.

A careful and extensive treatment (225 pp.) of all aspects of typography: printing, typography, reading, legibility, 'congeniality' of types and typography, familiarity with typographic elements, etc. With a 277-item bibliography. A highly scientific and thorough study of the physiological and psychological responses to various kinds of typography – basically for reading texts. Very little here applicable to the specialized problems of (annotated) bibliographies. A few fairly obvious findings may be appropriate.

'Burtt (1949) found that the usual arrangement of indented paragraphs promotes legibility' (p. 43). 'Several experiments have shown that lower case is more legible than capitals' (p. 43). 'No particular advantage seems to be attached to' the use of italics (p. 42). Leading may or may not affect speed of reading, which itself is not necessarily a measure of comprehension (p. 47). Bound books are preferred to unbound (i.e. paperback) books, but this probably has little effect on comprehension or legibility (p. 92), for these characteristics are not even mentioned. Results of one experiment 'show that typographic arrangement is not in itself the decisive factor in legibility' (p. 143). Says, 'We have long felt that there is a superstition in dividing text and putting in headings, colour, etc. Our belief is that such typographic variation is suitable in informative texts of the registering and dictionary kind. It is obviously necessary in most programmed material' (p. 144).

Ragged-right texts have no retarding (or hastening) effect on reading (pp. 144–55). Ragged-right is immaterial in legibility or comprehension.

274 Zapf, Hermann. 'Future Tendencies in Type Design: The Scientific Approach to Letterforms.' In *The Computer and the Hand* . . .: pp. 23–33. Ed. by Charles Bigelow and Lynn Ruggles (**21** above).

Explains why many typefaces, designed for letterpress printing, do not 'transfer' to computerized displays. Speaks of the mistakes type designers are making 'in the digitizing of some old alphabets' (p. 28).

A P P E N D I X I
F A C S I M I L E E X A M P L E S

Note Every effort has been made to secure copyright permission for the pages reproduced here. Some were out of copyright; for some permissions are gratefully acknowledged. For the rest, permission is still pending.

Bradley, Will M. *Will Bradley, His Chap Book*. Typophile Chap Book, no. 30. New York: The Typophiles, 1955.

Bradsher, Earl L. *Mathew Carey, Editor, Author, and Publisher*. Columbia University Studies in English, ser. 2, no. 19. New York: Columbia University Press, 1912.

Cary, Melbert B., Jr. *A Bibliography of the Village Press, 1903–1938*. New York: Press of the Woolly Whale, 1938.

Cave, Roderick. *The Private Press*. New York: Watson-Guptill, 1971.

Chappell, Warren. *A Short History of the Printed Word*. New York: Knopf, 1970.

Cleland, Thomas Maitland. *Harsh Words*. Typophile Chap Book, no. 2. New York: The Typophiles, 1940.

Daniel Berkeley Updike and the Merrymount Press. New York: American Institute of Graphic Arts, 1940.

De Vinne, Theodore Low. *The Invention of Printing*. New York: Francis Hart & Co., 1876.

Duncan, Harry. "The Cummington Press." *New Colophon* 2 (1949), pp. 221–234.

Dwiggins, William Addison. *Mss., by WAD: Being a Collection of the Writings of Dwiggins on Various Subjects*. Typophiles Chap Book, no. 17. New York: The Typophiles, 1947.

Edelstein, David S. *Joel Munsell: Printer and Antiquarian*. Columbia University. Faculty of Political Science. Studies in History, Economics and Public Law, no. 560. New York: Columbia University Press, 1950.

Exman, Eugene. *The House of Harper: One Hundred and Fifty Years of Publishing*. New York: Harper & Row, 1967.

Gilliss, Walter. *Recollections of the Gilliss Press and Its Work during Fifty Years, 1869–1919*. New York: The Grolier Club, 1926.

Goudy, Frederic W. *The Alphabet and Elements of Lettering*. Rev. & enl. Berkeley: University of California Press, 1942.

Goudy, Frederic W. *A Half-century of Type Design and Typography, 1895–1945*. Typophiles Chap Book, no. 13–14. 2 vols. New York: The Typophiles, 1946.

Grabhorn, Edwin. *The Fine Art of Printing*. San Francisco: E. & R. Grabhorn, 1933.

Haas, Irvin. *Bruce Rogers: A Bibliography*. Mount Vernon, N.Y.: Peter Pauper Press, 1936.

Hamill, Alfred E. *The Decorative Work of T. M. Cleland*. New York: The Pynson Printers, 1929.

Hammer, Carolyn R. "Victor Hammer." In *Heritage of the Graphic Arts*, edited by Chandler B. Grannis. New York: Bowker, 1972.

Haraszti, Zoltán. *The Enigma of "The Bay Psalm Book."* Companion volume to *The Bay Psalm Book*, a facsimile reprint of the first edition of 1640. 2 vols. Chicago: University of Chicago Press, 1956.

Example I

Joseph Blumenthal. *The Printed Book in America*. Boston, MA: Godine, 1977. Courtesy David Godine, Publishers.

Blumenthal himself designed this book, and it shows. This bibliography is clear and legible, with the minimum of typographic (only italics break up the roman type used throughout) and spatial coding (the entries themselves use only a hanging indent). The entries are well laid out, clearly printed, and fully accessible.

Also, the designer knew that the size of the page required the printing of a long measure, which would not have been appropriate for bibliographic data set in about 12-point type. Therefore he shortened the measure by using a shoulder note, 'Selective Bibliography', throughout.

My only quibble is that the word 'selective' seems wrong; I would have preferred 'selected'. Otherwise, this is a model of a legible and pleasing bibliography.

Example 2a, b

Patricia Lockhart Fleming. *Upper Canadian Imprints, 1801–1841: A Bibliography*. Toronto: University of Toronto Press, 1988. Courtesy University of Toronto Press.

Here is a bibliography that uses rule to separate entries. The method is quite effective. It also uses a two-column format and ragged-right setting. As I mentioned above, ragged-right is quite practical when the line is set to a short measure.

The amount of information that this book gives is impressive: author, title, publication data, collation of signatures, paper, typography, binding, notes, copies examined, and references. Each of these data fields is set off at the left margin (not completely distinctly) by the use of small caps. The fields could have been made more distinct with either typographic coding (labelling each in boldface type) or spatial coding (indenting second and subsequent lines of each field). But with all lines running flush left, it is not always easy to locate different data fields.

The use of full caps for the titles is satisfactory, though it does not indicate what the original styling was; and the use of a thin vertical line to separate lines of type on the title page is not completely successful since the lines are too small and thin. The quasi-facsimile works fairly well, and is enhanced by the use of boldface type for authors' names and 'Toronto' in entries 1105 and 1106.

With the rule separating entries, it is easy to spot entry numbers and authors' names. In general, this is a relatively successful page design.

COPIES EXAMINED: OOA, OOP, OTAR, OTMCL (2 copies), OTUTF, QMMRB

REFERENCE: Casey 1533, TPL 2008

1052   Upper Canada. Parliament (12th, 2nd session: 1836). House of Assembly
IMPORTANT DEBATE ǀ ON THE ADOPTION OF THE ǀ REPORT OF THE SELECT COMMITTEE ǀ ON THE DIFFERENCES BETWEEN ǀ HIS EXCELLENCY AND THE LATE EXECUTIVE COUNCIL: ǀ IN THE ǀ HOUSE OF ASSEMBLY, APRIL 18th, 1836. ǀ [rule 29 mm] ǀ TORONTO, U.C. ǀ JOS. H. LAWRENCE, PRINTER, GUARDIAN OFFICE. ǀ MDCCCXXXVI.
COLLATION: 8° (19.6 × 13 cm), A^8 B–D^8 [$1 signed], 32 leaves, pp *1–3* 4–63 *64* (page numbers flanked by section marks)
CONTENTS: *1* title; *2* blank; *3–62* text; *63* vote; *64* blank
PAPER: Wove, unmarked
TYPOGRAPHY: *Text*: long primer, modern face. *Display*: thickened romans and short french rule
47 ll., 160 (167) × 94; 67 mm for 20 ll.
BINDING: Wrapper of (light) grayish yellowish pink (32) wove paper, the upper printed within frame of printers' flowers with corner rosettes and lozenges [166 × 112 mm] IMPORTANT DEBATE ǀ IN THE ǀ HOUSE OF ASSEMBLY, APRIL 18, 1836, ǀ ON THE ǀ DUTIES AND RESPONSIBILITY [egyptian] ǀ OF THE ǀ EXECUTIVE COUNCIL. [fat] ǀ [rule 31 mm] ǀ [imprint as title]. Wove endpapers (QMMRB); rebound retaining wrapper (OSTCB, OTMCL); QQS copy with wrapper brownish pink (33)
COPIES EXAMINED: OKQ, OLU, OOA, OSTCB, OTMCL (2 copies), QMBM, QMMRB, QQS
REFERENCES: Casey 1538, Gagnon I–1733, Lande 857, TPL 2009

1053   Upper Canada. Parliament (12th, 2nd session: 1836). House of Assembly
JOURNAL [egyptian] ǀ OF THE [fat] ǀ HOUSE OF ASSEMBLY [egyptian] ǀ OF [fat] ǀ UPPER CANADA, [fat] ǀ FROM THE ǀ 14th DAY OF JANUARY TO THE 20th DAY OF APRIL, 1836. [fat] ǀ (*BOTH DAYS INCLUSIVE*.) ǀ IN THE SIXTH YEAR OF THE REIGN OF ǀ KING WILLIAM THE FOURTH: ǀ BEING THE ǀ SECOND SESSION OF THE TWELFTH PROVINCIAL PARLIAMENT. ǀ [double rule 36 mm] ǀ MARSHALL SPRING BIDWELL, ESQ. Speaker. [fat] ǀ [double rule 36 mm] ǀ SESSION 1836. [italian] ǀ [royal arms 23 × 64 mm] ǀ [double rule 35 mm] ǀ SIR FRANCIS BOND HEAD, K.C.H. ǀ LIEUTENANT GOVERNOR. ǀ [double rule 35 mm] ǀ 𝕿oronto: ǀ PRINTED BY M. REYNOLDS. ǀ [french rule 10 mm] ǀ 1836.

COLLATION: 2° (29.7 × 18.3 cm), πA^2 B–C^2, A–I^2 K–$2B^2$ $\chi 2$B–$2I^2$ 2K–$3I^2$ 3K–$4I^2$ 4K–$4W^2$ $\chi 4$W–$4Y^2$, $5A^2$ 5B–$5F^2$ $\chi 5$F–$5I^2$ 5K–$5U^2$ 5X–$6H^2$, $^2A^2$ B^2 ($B2$ + $B2$), C–H^2 [$1 signed, missigning M4 as L4], 287 leaves, pp [2] *i–iii* iv–x, *1* 2–531 *532*, ^2i ii–xxx; STATE: misprinting iv, v as 4, 5
CONTENTS: [*1*] half-title [double rule 147 mm] ǀ JOURNAL. [egyptian] ǀ HOUSE OF ASSEMBLY. [fat] ǀ [ornamental dash 17 mm] ǀ SESS. 1836. [fat] ǀ [double rule 148 mm]; [*2*] blank; *i* title; *ii* blank; *iii–viii* rules; *ix–x* proclamation; *1–531* text; *532* blank; ^2i–xxx index with viii a printed cancel pasted over verso of vii
PAPER: Wove, unmarked; varied
TYPOGRAPHY: *Text*: pica, modern face. *Display*: thickened and fat romans, swash italic, open black letter, and ornamental dashes
57 ll., 254 (266) × 121 (147); 85 mm for 20 ll.
BINDING: Half dark yellowish green leather edged in blind with trefoil wave and bead roll and light brown marbled paper. Spine divided into five compartments by gold rule, repeated at tail. Lettered JOURNAL ǀ OF ASSEMBLY. ǀ 2ND SESS. 12TH PARL. ǀ U. CANADA. ǀ in second; 1836 at tail. Edges sprinkled red. Marbled and wove endpapers (OOA); with quarter leather, lettered not decorated, and pale blue paper. Wove endpapers (OLU); OTL copy in half very dark red leather and gloster paper finished as OOA; OTUTF copy rebacked with pale yellowish pink paper.
COPIES EXAMINED: OLU, OOA, OTAR, OTL, OTMCL, OTUTF

1054   Upper Canada. Parliament (12th, 2nd session: 1836). House of Assembly
APPENDIX ǀ TO THE ǀ JOURNAL [fat] ǀ OF THE ǀ HOUSE OF ASSEMBLY ǀ OF ǀ UPPER CANADA, ǀ OF THE ǀ SECOND SESSION OF THE TWELFTH PROVINCIAL PARLIAMENT. ǀ VI. WILLIAM IV. ǀ [double rule 58 mm] ǀ MARSHALL SPRING BIDWELL, ESQ. SPEAKER. ǀ [double rule 58 mm] ǀ SESSION 1836. [egyptian] ǀ Vol. 1. [fat] ǀ [thick-thin rule 52 mm] ǀ [royal arms 23 × 63 mm] ǀ [double rule 97 mm] ǀ SIR FRANCIS BOND HEAD, K.C.H. LIEUTENANT GOVERNOR. ǀ [double rule 95 mm] ǀ TORONTO: [fat] ǀ WILLIAM LYON MACKENZIE. ǀ OFFICE OF THE CONSTITUTION. ǀ [thick rule 12 mm] ǀ 1836.
IMPRINTS: ^{4}8 R. Stanton; ^{5}10 J.H. Lawrence, Guardian Office; ^{7}6 W.J. Coates; ^{10}44 Guardian Office, J.H. Lawrence; ^{11}24 R. Stanton; ^{13}8 R. Stanton; ^{14}20 Mackenzie
COLLATION: 2° (30 × 17.8 cm), π^2 A–I^2 K–O^2, $^2A^2$ B–F^2, *1–2²*, ^{2}*1–2²* *3¹*, ^{3}A–D^2, ^{3}*1² 2¹*, ^{4}*1–3²*, $^4A^2$ B–I^2 K–L^2, $^5A^2$ B–F^2, ^{5}*1–2²* *3¹*, $^6A^2$ B^2, $^7A^2$ B–E^2, $^8A^2$ B–F^2, $^9A^2$ B–D^2, ^{10}A–F^2, ^{6}*1–9²*, ^{7}*1²*, ^{11}A–C^2, ^{8}*1–5²*, ^{12}A–C^2 H–I^2 K–T^2 V^2 W–$2E^2$ $\chi 2E^2$ 2F–$2I^2$ 2K–$2U^2$ $\chi 2U^2$

Handbill: photomechanical reproduction
CONTENTS: 3 ll. heading; 4 ll. verse; 1 l. salutation; 52 ll.
text; 3 ll. signature
NOTES: Gowan explained 'I have not time to correct the
press, and hurry off this short Address, before I leave
for the country, to enroll ... loyal Volunteers'; his vol-
unteer company was called the Brockville
Invincibles.
EXAINED: OTMCL

1104   Hepburn, William

COURT OF CHANCERY, UPPER CANADA. [rule
13 mm] | THE | SOLICITOR'S MANUAL: [fat]
CONTAINING AN OUTLINE | OF THE |
EQUITABLE | JURISDICTION OF THE
COURT | WITH | PRACTICAL DIRECTIONS
FOR THE | INSTITUTION AND
PROSECUTION | OF A | SUIT THROUGH ITS
SEVERAL STAGES. | [rule 35 mm] | BY WM.
HEPBURN, ESQ., REGISTRAR. | [rule 35 mm]
TORONTO: | PRINTED AT THE PATRIOT
OFFICE. | [rule 8 mm] | 1837.
COLLATION: 8° (21.4 × 14 cm), 1^4 $2-3^4$ 4^2 [\$1 signed], 14
leaves, pp *1–5* 6–27 *28* (pagination in ( ))
CONTENTS: *1* title; *2* blank; *3* author's note dated at To-
ronto, August 1837; *4* blank; *5–11* introductory ob-
servations; *12–27* 'Practical Directions'; *28* blank
PAPER: Wove, unmarked
TYPOGRAPHY: *Text:* pica, modern face. *Display:* swash
italic
40 ll., 171 (183) × 104; 84 mm for 20 ll.
BINDING: Wrapper of (grayish) light blue (181) wove
paper (OTAR)
NOTES: Ten years after discussions began a Court of
Chancery was established in Upper Canada (418);
Hepburn was registrar of the court.
COPIES EXAMINED: OTAR, OTMCL
REFERENCE: TPL 2078

1105   Higham, Robert

REPORT [shadowed tuscan] | OF THE | ENGINEER
[egyptian] | ON THE SURVEY OF THE |
TORONTO & LAKE HURON [shadowed egyptian] |
RAIL-ROAD. [shadowed] | [rule 38 mm] | Toronto:
Printed at the Albion Office, S.E. corner Market
Buildings. | 1837.
COLLATION: 12° (16.7 × 10.3 cm), B^6 $C–D^6$ [B3 signed
2], 18 leaves, pp [2] *1* 2–32 *33–34*
CONTENTS: [*1*] title; [*2*] blank; *1–32* text signed R. High-
am, civil engineer, at the office of the Toronto and
Lake Huron Rail Road Company, Utica, 1 February
1837; *33–34* blank
PAPER: Wove, unmarked; machine-made
TYPOGRAPHY: *Text:* long primer, modern face. *Display:*
medium ornamental dash

39 ll., 137 (143) × 74; 68 mm for 20 ll.
BINDING: Rebound retaining wrapper of bluish gray
(191) wove paper (OTMCL)
COPIES EXAMINED: OOA, OTMCL (2 copies)
REFERENCE: TPL 2079

1106   Home District Mutual Fire Insurance
Company

BYE-LAWS | AND | REGULATIONS | OF
THE | HOME DISTRICT | MUTUAL FIRE
INSURANCE COMPANY, [sans serif] | TORONTO,
UPPER CANADA, | AS APPROVED BY | THE
BOARDS OF DIRECTORS, [egyptian] | WITH |
TARIFF OF INSURANCE. | [double rule 44 mm] |
INCORPORATED BY ACT OF PARLIAMENT. |
[double rule 44 mm] | Toronto: | PRINTED BY W.J.
COATES. | [rule 11 mm] | 1837.
COLLATION: 8° (17.7 × 10.3 cm), π^2 A^8 [A1 signed], 10
leaves, pp *1–5* 6–20
CONTENTS: *1* title; *2* blank; *3* officers; *4* blank; *5–15* text;
16–20 tariff of rates
PAPER: Wove, unmarked; machine-made
TYPOGRAPHY: *Text:* small pica, modern face. *Display:*
condensed and fat romans, sans serif, and black letter
38 ll., 138 (149) × 79; 73 mm for 20 ll.
BINDING: Wrapper of (grayish) moderate blue (182)
wove paper. Binder's leaf front and back
COPIES EXAMINED: OTMCL (2 copies)
REFERENCE: TPL 2080

1107   Hopkins, Robert, plaintiff

INTERESTING TRIAL. | [swelled rule 21 mm] |
HOPKINS AGAINST GOWAN. | [swelled rule 21
mm] | WEXFORD SPRING ASSIZES, MARCH 14,
15, 1827; | BEFORE THE | HON. JUDGE
BURTON, AND A SPECIAL JURY. | [in three
columns separated by rules, to left:] BENJAMIN
WILSON, | EDWARD TURNER, | HIGATT
TENCH, | JOHN SHEPPARD, | [middle:]
CHARLES JACOB, | WILLIAM TOOLE, |
CHARLES HEWSON, | ROBERT HUGHES, | [to
right:] WILLIAM RICHARDS, | BENJAMIN
WHITNEY, | EDWARD WATSON, | JOHN
NICKSON NUNNE. | [rule 26 mm] | COUNSEL
FOR THE PLAINTIFF: [fat] | MESSRS. SCOTT,
DIXON, HATCHELL & HAMILTON. |
AGENT – H.P. WOODROOFE. | FOR THE
DEFENDANT: [fat] | MESSRS. DOHERTY,
M'KANE, MOORE & BREWSTER. | AGENTS –
HOPE & DOWSE. | [rule 26 mm] | This extraordinary
Trial lasted two entire days; the Jury retired at ten
o'clock, and consulted for a few | minutes, when they
returned a verdict for the Plaintiff, thereby
establishing the Will of the late JOHN | HUNTER GOWAN,
and invalidating the Deed endeavoured to be set up

System 1

PAGE, MICHAEL FITZGERALD. FORTUNES OF WAR. HALE. £1.90.
823.91F (B72-10444) ISBN 0 7091 2803 7
PALLAS, NORVIN. CODE GAMES. STERLING; DISTRIBUTED BY WARD
LOCK. £1.05. 001.5436 (B72-09950) ISBN 0 7061 2328 x

System 2

Allman, Michael. Geological laboratory techniques.
Blanford Press. £8.50. 550.28 (B72-17338) ISBN 0 7137 0559 0
Allsop, Kenneth. Adventure lit their star. Revised ed.
Penguin. £0.35. 823.91F (B72-17562) ISBN 0 14 003446 3

System 3

HAIGH, Basil. Organic chemistry of nucleic acids. Part A.
Plenum Press. £9.00. 547.596 (B72-10819) ISBN 0 306 37531 1
HAINING, Peter. The Channel Islands. Revised ed. New
English Library. £1.50. 914.2340485 (B72-12211)

System 4

Barrett, Edward Joseph. Essentials of organic chemistry.
Holt, Rinehart and Winston. £5.00. 547 (B72-17335)
ISBN 0 03 080348 9
Barrow, Charles Clement. A short history of the S.

System 5

Bartlett, Kathleen. Lovers in Autumn. Hale. £1.30. 823.91F
(B72-10379) ISBN 0 7091 2329 9
Bassett, Michael Gwyn. Catalogue of type, figured & cited
fossils in the National Museum of Wales. National Museum

System 6

-Cartland, Barbara. A ghost in Monte Carlo. Arrow Books
Ltd. £0.25. 823.91F (B72-12081) ISBN 0 09 906180 5
-Cartwright, Frederick Fox. Disease and history. Hart-Davis.
£2.50. 904.5 (B72-11136) ISBN 0 246 10537 2

System 7

Edson, John Thomas. Wagons to Backsight. Hale. £1.10.
823.91F (B72-10401) ISBN 0 7091 2394 9
Efemey, Raymond. The story of the parish church of St
Thomas, Dudley. 5th ed. British Publishing. Unpriced.

System 8

Cadell, Elizabeth. Bridal array. White Lion Publishers
Ltd. £1.80. 823.91F (B72-17578) ISBN 0 85617 622 2
Cafferty, Bernard. Spassky's 100 best games. Batsford.
£2.50. 794.159 (B72-16145) ISBN 0 7134 0362 4

System 9

Manessier, Alfred. Manessier. Adams and Dart. £10.50.
759.4 (B72-10983) ISBN 0 239 00098 6
Mangalam, J J. Mountain families in transition: a case
study of Appalachian migration. Pennsylvania State

System 10

FARNHAM, Ann. Action mathematics. 5. Cassell. £0.65. (non-net)
372.73045 (B72-15925) ISBN 0 304 93803 3
FARQUHAR, Ronald M. The earth's age and geochronology.
Pergamon. £2.50. 551.701 (B72-17343) ISBN 0 08 016387 4

3

Example 3

Herbert Spencer, Linda Reynolds, and Brian Coe. 'Typographic Coding in Lists and Bibliographies.' *Applied Ergonomics* 5.3 (Sept. 1974). Courtesy of the authors.

These authors are among the very few ever to consider the physical form of bibliographies. Their work focuses on how to make such lists legible using a typewriter. This prevents typographic coding such as italics, but it does not preclude boldface types created by overtyping, or underlining.

The ten systems they list vary in capitalization, boldness of type, underlining, indentation, and the use of a hyphen at the beginning of a line to signal the new entry. Another work by these authors, *The Relative Effectiveness of Spatial and Typographic Coding Systems within Bibliographical Entries* ([London]: Readability of Print Research Unit, Royal College of Art, Oct. 1974), presents 18 different styles, made up of combinations of six spatial and three typographic coding systems. (See Example 4 and entry **219** in the bibliography.) All of their work clearly shows that the two areas of variability (spatial and typographic) do make a difference.

In the present example, it is clear that System 2 is not as effective as System 7. My only criticism of these ten variations is that not one distinguishes the title typographically from the rest of the entry. Since underlining and boldface were available, I would have preferred the use of one of them for titles, to separate author fields from publication data fields. Nonetheless, the use of indentation or boldface (as in Systems 7–9 and 4, respectively) works better, for me, than the other ones, though the underlining of System 5 is also effective. And the use of a space between entries combined with full caps for the author's name (System 10) is perfectly reasonable and legible.

As I have said many times throughout my book, no one system is necessarily better than any other; a good one, consistently applied, is all we need.

Example 4

Herbert Spencer, Linda Reynolds, and Brian Coe. *The Relative Effectiveness of Spatial and Typographic Coding Systems within Bibliographical Entries.* [London]: Readability of Print Research Unit, Royal College of Art, Oct. 1974. Courtesy of the authors.

(See Example 3. See also entry **219** in bibliography.)

The 18 systems of bibliographic display presented here are far more sophisticated than those in the earlier works of these writers. As they show, there are variations in caps and lower-case roman, caps and lower-case italic, and in the use of boldface types with these other features. At the same time, there are variations in line spacing (i.e., leading), indentation, and run-on lines. These are selected from the many other possibilities that these spatial and typographical variables offer.

As I mentioned for the previous entry, if one selects a legible, serviceable format and uses it consistently, readers will quickly accustom themselves to it and should have no trouble finding what they seek.

The authors point out that some of these styles take much less space than others, and thus are more economical to print. But economics should be only one of the criteria a publisher considers in designing a bibliography. For more commentary on this work, see entry **219** in the bibliography.

Figure 1
The combination of 6 spatial and 3 typographic coding systems to give 18 styles

A. (1) Roman caps & lowercase
   (2) Roman caps & lowercase
   (3) Roman caps & lowercase
   (4) Roman numerals

1. Copy runs on. 3 space units between each entry.

ISBN 0 85292 069 5.   Bajin, Boris. Olympic gymnastics for men and women. Prentice-Hall. £5.50. 796.41 ISBN 0 13 633925 5.   Baker, C D. Lepard's metric reckoner: for cost per thousand sheets given price per kilogramme and weight in kilogrammes. Pitman. £4.00. 338.4367620942 ISBN 0 273 25242 9.   Baldwin, Brenda. Skid prevention and control. R.W. Noon. £0.30. 629.283 ISBN 0 9502394 0 2.   Ball, Alan. Alan Ball's international soccer annual No. 4. Pelham. £1.00.

2. 1st element of each entry begins a new line. 2nd, 3rd and 4th elements run on.

Pettman, Dorothy. Oral embryology and microscopic anatomy: a textbook for students in dental hygiene. 5th ed. Lea and Febiger; Kimpton. £3.80. 611.314 ISBN 0 8121 0376 9.
Philips, Francis Edward. Greek philosophical terms: a historical lexicon. New York University Press; University of London Press. £3.80. 180 ISBN 0 340 09412 5.
Piatek, Clare Gray. Perspectives in surgery. Lea and Febiger; Kimpton. £9.45. 617 ISBN 0 8121 0279 7.

3. All elements begin a new line.

Learmonth, Peter.
The houses we build.
Central Committee for the Architectural Advisory Panels.
£0.25.
721.0942 ISBN 0 9502302 0 0.
Leary, Harold W.
The PL/1 machine: an introduction to programming.
Addison-Wesley. £5.60.
001.6424 ISBN 0 201 05275 x.

4. All elements begin a new line. 1st element of each entry full out. 2nd, 3rd and 4th elements successively indented.

Emmet, Louis Emanuel.
    Emmet's notes on perusing titles and practical
    conveyancing. 2nd (cumulative) supplement. 15th ed.
        Oyez. £3.00.
            346.420438 ISBN 0 85120 124 5.
Emsden, Leo.
    Sound of the sea.
        White Lion Publishers Ltd. £1.80.
            823.91F ISBN 0 85617 894 2.

5. Line space between entries. 2nd, 3rd and 4th elements run on.

Fielding, A J. Internal migration in England and Wales: a presentation and interpretation of 'city-region' data. Centre for Environmental Studies. £0.50. 301.3260942 ISBN 0 901350 52 4.

Figes, Eva. Konek landing. Panther. £0.35. 823.91F ISBN 0 586 03638 5.

Fincher, Norah M. Mingling, and other poems. Stockwell.

6. Line space between entries. Each element begins a new line.

Serraillier, Ian.
The clashing rocks: the story of Jason and the Argonauts.
Carousel Books. £0.20.
823.91J ISBN 0 552 52022 5.

Seuffert, Muir.
Devil at the door.
Hale. £1.40.
823.91F ISBN 0 7091 2907 6.

B. (1) Roman caps
   (2) Italic caps & lowercase
   (3) Roman caps & lowercase
   (4) Italic numerals

C. (1) Italic caps & lowercase
   (2) Bold caps & lowercase
   (3) Roman caps & lowercase
   (4) Italic numerals

Hutchinson and Co. (Publishers) Ltd. £6.00. *230.01 ISBN 0 09 108850 x.* WALTERS, PATRICK GORDON. *The Cabinet. Revised ed. Heinemann Educational. £1.00. 354.4205 ISBN 0 435 83915 2.* WALTON, BRUCE. *Essays in social biology. Vol. 1: People, their needs, environment, ecology. Prentice-Hall. £4.00. 301.3108 ISBN 0 13 656835 1.* WARD, WILLIAM F. *Electronics testing and measurement. Macmillan. £4.50. 621.381 ISBN 0 333 12544 4.* WARNATH, ARTHUR WILLIAM.

GILL, JOHN. *The tenant.* Collins. £1.50. *823.91 F ISBN 0 00 221843 7.*
GILLARD, R D. *Essays in chemistry. Vol. 3: 1972.* Academic Press. £1.80. *540 ISBN 0 12 124103 3.*
GILLEN, LUCY. *Dangerous stranger.* Mills and Boon. £0.80. *823.91F ISBN 0 263 05021 1.*
GILLESPIE, IAN ERSKINE. *Gastroenterology: an integrated course.* Churchill Livingstone. £1.50. *616.3 ISBN 0 443 00854 0.*

SALT, JOHN.
Parents - participation and persuasion in primary education. University of Sheffield Institute of Education. £0.15. *372.1103 ISBN 0 902831 07 0.*
SANDERS, ED.
The family: the story of Charles Manson's dune buggy attack batallion.
Hart-Davis. £2.50.
301.4494 ISBN 0 246 10528 3.

MELLISH, E MUDGE.
   Rust and rot and what you can do about them.
   Angus and Robertson. £1.25.
      620.11223 ISBN 0 207 95436 4.
MENDELSOHN, JACOB.
   Decision and organization: a volume in honor of Jacob Marschak.
      North-Holland Publishing. Unpriced.
      330.1 ISBN 0 7204 3313 4.

BAKER, HILARY. *Oakes Park, Sheffield: the historic home of the Bagshawe family since the year 1699.* English Life Publications. £0.15. *914.2746 ISBN 0 85101 057 1.*

BALDWIN, CECIL HENRY. *Teaching science to the ordinary pupil. 2nd ed.* University of London Press. £3.45. *507.12 ISBN 0 340 15583 3.*

BALL, GEORGE SAYERS. *Who is a white-collar*

CERVINE, JO.
X-Ray diagnosis positioning manual.
Glencoe Press; Collier-Macmillan. £1.50.
616.07572 ISBN 0 02 473270 2.

CHADWICK, ANGELA.
The infernal desire machines of Doctor Hoffman: a novel.
Hart-Davis. £1.95.
823.91F ISBN 0 246 10545 3.

Bristol and Gloucestershire. Darwen Finlayson. £3.20. *914.241 ISBN 0 85208 065 4.* Ramchand, Kenneth. **The West Indian novel and its background.** Faber and Faber Ltd. £1.70. *823.009 ISBN 0 571 10139 9.* *Ramsay, Anna Augusta Whittal.* **Sir Robert Peel.** Constable. £3.25. *942.0810924 ISBN 0 09 458290 4.* *Randall, Christine.* **Creating with papier-mache.** Crowell-Collier; Collier-Macmillan. £1.05. *745.54 ISBN 0 02 767190 9.* *Ranis, Gustav.* **The gap between rich and poor nations:**

Perraton, Jean. **Urban systems: collection and management of data for a complex model.** University of Cambridge Department of Architecture. Unpriced. *301.36094229 ISBN 0 903248 29 8.*
Perry, Eric Akers. **The Parish Church of Holy Trinity, Wickwar. New ed.** British Publishing. Unpriced. *914.241 ISBN 0 7140 0677 7.*
Perryman, Albert Charles. **Life at Brighton locomotive works, 1928-1936.** Oakwood Press. £0.90. *625.261*

Hindmarch, Jack.
Multiple choice questions for intermediate economics.
Macmillan. £0.50.
330.076 ISBN 0 333 13570 9.
Hislop, George.
Let history judge: the origins and consequences of Stalinism.
Macmillan. £5.75.
947.08420924 ISBN 0 333 13409 5.

Medlen, Wolf.
   The Samson riddle: an essay and a play, with the text of the original story of Samson.
   Vallentine, Mitchell and Co. Ltd. £2.25.
      822.914 ISBN 0 85303 152 5.
Mehmet, George Byron.
   A.B.C.'s of transistors. 2nd ed. reprinted.
   Foulsham. £1.25.
      621.381528 ISBN 0 572 00579 2.

Adams, Arlon T. **Topics in intersystem electromagnetic compatability.** Holt, Rinehart and Winston. £12.00. *621.38411 ISBN 0 03 085342 7.*

Adeney, Carol. **This morning with God: a daily devotional guide for your quiet time. Vol. 1.** Hodder and Stoughton. £0.40. *242.2 ISBN 0 340 15997 9.*

Adkins, Arthur William Hope. **Moral values and political**

Chamberlain, Peter.
German army semi-tracked vehicles, 1939-45.
Model and Allied Publications. £0.40.
623.747 ISBN 0 85344 136 7.

Chance, June E.
Applications of a social learning theory of personality.
Holt, Rinehart and Winston. £6.05
155.2 ISBN 0 03 083183 0.

Haley, F. E.
   1933.   The green gold of the tropics. 8 p., illus. Hawaiian
               Avocado Co., Honolulu.

Hansen, F. J.
   1927.   Avocado villas in class one belt. 8 p., illus. F. J.
               Hansen Organization, La Mesa, California.

   1929.   Independence and happiness await you at the Mt. Helix
               Calavo Gardens. 3 p. Mt. Helix Calavo Gardens, San Diego,
               California.

   1929.   What about this avocado income? 4 p., illus. Mt. Helix
               Calavo Gardens, San Diego, California.

   1932.   Contentment—a story of promises fulfilled. 8 p. Mt.
               Helix Calavo Gardens, San Diego, California.

Hanson, E. F.
   1922.   The avocado and the development of avocado park groves.
               24 p., illus. Square Deal Land and Development Co.,
               Miami, Florida.

Hart, E. G.
   1921.   The avocado as a commercial fruit. 4 p. Edwin G. Hart,
               Inc., Los Angeles.

   1926.   Profit with safety—avocados. Edwin G. Hart, Inc., Los
               Angeles. (Three circulars: Vista, 12 p., illus.; North
               Whittier, 6 p., illus.; La Habra Heights, 12 p., illus.)

   1927.   Take this one hour scenic drive through famous Avocado
               Empire. 4 p. Edwin G. Hart, Inc., Los Angeles.

   1933-34.   The avocado—your questions answered. 16 p., illus. Sub-
               urban Home and Income Lands, La Habra Heights, California.

Hart, E. G., and T. U. Barber.
   1916.   Varieties which we recommend for commercial planting. 6
               p. Hart and Barber Avocado Co., Los Angeles.

Harvey Machine Co.
   1931.   Harvey champion avocado clipper. 3 p., illus. Harvey
               Machine Co., Los Angeles.

Henry, C. C.
   1937.   Henry's select,—commands respect! Why? 3 p. Escondido,
               California.

Knapp Investment Co.
   1927.   La Colina Farms. 12 p., illus. Knapp Investment Co., Los
               Angeles.

1934.   Cleaning scale from avocados. California Avocado Assoc.
          Yearbook 1934:140-41.

Merrill, G. B., and Jeff Chaffin.
1923.   Scale insects of Florida. Florida State Pl. Bd. Quart.
          Bul. 7(4):177-298, illus. (Avocado, p. 188, 223, et al.)

Miller, N. C. E.
1932.   A preliminary list of food-plants of some Malayan insects.
          Fed. Malay States and Straits Settlements Dept. Agr. Bul.
          38. Suppl:1-54. (Avocado pear, p. 13, 16.)

Moreira, Carlos.
1921.   Entomologia Agricola Brasileira. Bol. No. 1, Ser.
          Divulgacao, Inst. Biol. Defeza Agr., Minist. Agr., Rio de
          Janeiro. (Cited by Barbosa, 1933.)

Moulton, D.
1928.   New Thysanoptera from Formosa. Trans. Nat. Hist. Soc.
          Formosa 18(98):287-328, 4 pl. (Taeniothrips on P.
          gratissima, p. 292.)

Moznette, G. F.
1919.   Annotated list of the injurious and beneficial insects
          of the avocado in Florida. Florida Buggist 3:45-48.

1920.   Dusting vs. spraying for the control of avocado insect
          pests. Florida Grower 21(14):8, 17, 2 figs. April 3.

1920.   The red spider mite and leaf thrips on the avocado and
          how they may be controlled. Florida Grower 21(5):8-9,
          2 figs. Jan. 31.

1920.   A blossom-destroying beetle of the mango. Florida State
          Pl. Bd. Quart. Bul. 4(3):95-98. (Avocado, p. 97.)

1920.   Some important insects which attack the avocado in Florida.
          California Avocado Assoc. Ann. Rept. 1919-20:76-78.

1920.   The dictyospermum scale on the avocado, and how it is
          controlled. Florida State Pl. Bd. Quart. Bul. 5(1):5-11,
          5 figs.

1920.   Pyriform scale on avocado leaf. Florida Grower 22(8):5,
          1 fig. Aug. 21.

1920.   Insects which attack the avocado in Florida. Florida
          State Hort. Soc. Proc. 33:73-76.

1921.   Injurious insects of the avocado. California Citrogr.
          6(5):152, 184, 6 figs.

5b

Example 5a, b

Ira J. Condit. *A Bibliography of the Avocado (Persea americana Miller).* Riverside, CA: University of California, Citrus Experiment Station, [1941].

This bibliography presents its data first alphabetically by author, then, under each author, chronologically, the dates being entered as a hanging indent, and the other bibliographic data typed at a tab (five letter spaces) further in from the dates. Under each author and date there is a further arrangement which is not apparent, despite the author's statement, 'It is hoped that the arrangement of references under subjects will make the bibliography more useful to specialists' (p. 2). The separation by subject is good (along with the author index at the end of the volume), but the arrangement of entries within each subject is the problem.

The system of indentation and tab separates the information and the individual entry fields distinctively. Since the text was produced on a typewriter, no italics were used, either for book or article titles; and the compiler chose not to underline the titles, believing the spatial coding was enough to distinguish titles from other data.

Though I find peculiar some of the spacing of the numbers and abbreviations, the entries are nonetheless easy to understand. This is a perfectly acceptable design for a typewritten bibliography.

Example 6a, b

Fred Lewis Pattee. 'Bibliography of Philip Freneau.' *The Bibliographer: A Journal of Bibliography and Rare Book News* 1.3 (Mar. 1902): 97–106.

This bibliography has adopted a peculiar layout in that it lists items by the year, and, within each year, barely distinguishes one entry from another. Thus, for the year 1772, the spacing between the title *The American Village*, the note about it, and the next work ('A Poem . . .') is identical. It is difficult to see that two separate items are being listed here. This is true as well for the two entries under the year 1786 on page 102.

The quasi-facsimile effort in the title-page transcription (using the solidus [/] between lines) is informative, but it looks peculiar in the 1772 entry when six of them are used in succession, interspersed with a like number of ellipses. There is no typographic coding; does this indicate that all the title pages listed used no italics, boldface, or other typographic variation? The lack of any information preceding the bibliography is thus annoying. As I have said, a good introduction helps the reader to understand the parameters and layout of the bibliography.

One other quibble is that the designation of book sizes given in the listing is by format (i.e. octavo, duodecimo), not by inches or centimetres. This tells us more about the number of times the original sheet of paper was folded or how many leaves there are to a signature than about the actual dimensions of the books. This is a bare-bones bibliography, with a minimum of information.

BIBLIOGRAPHY OF PHILIP FRENEAU.

by FRED LEWIS PATTEE.

1772.

The American Village.

No copy is known to be extant.   The only mention of it is in a letter from Freneau to Madison dated November 22, 1772: "I have printed a poem in New York called *The American Village,* containing about 450 lines, also a few short pieces added.   I would send you one if I had a proper opportunity. The additional poems are, 'A Poem to the Nymph I Never Saw,' 'The Miserable Life of a Pedagogue,' and 'Stanzas on an Ancient Dutch House on Long Island.'   As to the main poem it is damned by all good and judicious judges. My name is in the title page."

A / Poem / on the / Rising Glory / of / America / being an / Exercise / Delivered at the Public Commencement at / Nassau Hall, Sept. 25, 1771 . . . / . . . / . . . / . . . / . . . / Philadelphia / Printed by Joseph Crukshank, for R. Aitken / Bookseller, opposite the London-Coffee- / House in Front Street. / MDCCLXXII.

12mo, 27 pp.

Written in collaboration with H. H. Brackenridge.

1775.

American Liberty / a / Poem / . . . / . . . / . . . / New York / Printed by J. Anderson, at Beekman-slip / MDCCLXXV.

General Gage's Soliloquy.

No copy of this is known.   A manuscript copy was made, probably by Du Simitière, now in the Library Company of Philadelphia.   On this is endorsed, "Printed in New York, August 1775 by Gaine."

New Travels / through / North America / In a Series of Letters / Exhibiting the History of the victorious Campaign / of the Allied Armies; under his Excellency / General George Washington, and the Count / de Rochambeau, in the Year 1781 / Interspersed with political and philosophical Observations / upon the genius, temper and customs of the Americans. / Also, Narrations of the Capture of General Burgoyne / and Lord Cornwallis, with their Armies; and a va / riety of interesting particulars, which occurred in the course of the / War in America / Translated from the original of the Abbé Robin; / One of the Chaplains to the French Army in America / . . . . . / Philadelphia / Printed and sold by Robert Bell in Third Street / MDCCLXXXIII. Price two thirds of a dollar.

1784.

New Year's verses for those who carry the Pennsylvania Gazette to the Customers.

See Pennsylvania Imprints, 4524.

New Year's Verses addressed to the Customers of the Freeman's Journal by the lad who carries it.

See Pennsylvania Imprints, 4524.

Reprint of "New Travels through North America." Boston / Printed by E. E. Powars and N. Willis for E. Battelle / and to be sold by him at his Book-store, State Street. / MDCCLXXXIV. /

1785.

New Year's verses addressed to Customers of the Freeman's Journal by the lad who Carries it.

1786.

Newsman's address written for the Carriers of the Columbian Herald. [Charleston, S. C.]

The / Poems / of / Philip Freneau. / Written Chiefly During the Late War. / Philadelphia / Printed by Francis Bailey, at / Yorick's Head, in Market Street. / MDCCLXXXVI. /

Sm. 8vo, pp. xxii, 362.

6b

1787.

A / Journey / from / Philadelphia to New York / by way of Burlington and South Amboy / by the late / Mr. Robert Slender. / . . . / . . . / . . . / Persons of the Play.

8vo, pp. 28.

Published in Philadelphia. Princeton University, Brown University, Library of Congress and New York Historical Society have copies.

1788.

Newsman's Address.

In one of his collections, but no hint as to the paper.

The / Miscellaneous / Works / of / Mr. Philip Freneau / containing his / Essays / and / additional Poems / Philadelphia / Printed by Francis Bailey, at Yorick's / Head, in Market Street. / MDCCLXXXVIII.

12mo, pp. xii, 429.

1794.

The / Village Merchant / a / Poem / To which is added the / Country Printer / . . . / . . . / . . . / . . . / Philadelphia / Printed by Hoff and Derrick / MDCCXCIV. /

Sm. 8vo, pp. 16.

1795.

Poems / written between the Years 1768 and 1794 / by / Philip Freneau / of / New Jersey / A New Edition, Revised and Corrected by the / Author; including a considerable number of / Pieces never before Published. / Monmouth / N. J. / Printed / at the press of the Author, at Mount Pleasant, near / Middletown Point; MDCCXCV, and of / American Independence / XIX. /

8vo, pp. xv, 448.

1797.

Means / for the / Preservation / of / Public Liberty / an / Oration / Delivered in the New Dutch Church / on the / Fourth of July 1797 / Being the Twenty-First / of our Independence / By G. J. Warner. / 'Columbia Hail! Immortal be thy reign,'

Example 7

William M. Bowsky. *A Medieval Italian Commune: Siena under the Nine, 1287–1355.* Berkeley and Los Angeles, CA, and London: University of California Press, 1981. Courtesy William M. Bowsky.

Here is another example of a fairly original design which works – up to a point. The placement of the filing elements into the left margin is quite good, for it helps the reader to distinguish new entries instantly. This is also facilitated by the use of a slightly larger space between entries than between lines within each entry. The styling of the content of the entries in the right column is idiosyncratic but perfectly clear, once readers familiarize themselves with the order of data (and that takes just a few seconds). Perhaps some of the names in the left column are rather far from the coordinating elements in the right column, but this is possibly too subtle a thing to complain about.

A few entries might be puzzling. For example, the entry for DR which gives only 'ASS, Diplomatico Riformagioni', does not explain what ASS means, nor where the reader can find items with this designation. The answer is that earlier in the list of abbreviations we are told that these letters mean Archivio di Stato di Siena. It is not unprecedented for an abbreviation to refer to another abbreviation, but it is disconcerting the first time one looks at the letters.

I should point out that this section of the book is called 'Abbreviations'. It is not really a bibliography *per se*. But since the book contains no section designated 'Bibliography', this must be considered one.

This is not a model for bibliographies that I would advocate others using; but it is a perfectly acceptable and fairly legible layout.

Example 8

Catalogue of the John Carter Brown Library in Brown University, Providence, Rhode Island. Vol. I. Providence, [RI]: Published by the Library, 1919.

This bibliography offers a quasi-facsimile presentation; that is, it does not give photocopies of the original pages, but it does present line-by-line and paragraph-by-paragraph information. Hence, a double upright line shows line breaks, and the stylized paragraph sign shows paragraph breaks.

Authors' names, printed in full caps and small caps, distinguish the beginnings of entries. Full title-page transcriptions fill the first paragraph of each entry, followed in smaller type by descriptive data. Perhaps the smaller type is too small for the line length, especially for notes that run several lines (such as the Prudentius note on page 55).

The arrangement is by date, and under dates, alphabetically by author. Part of the running head of each page is the date of the books presented below, a clever device to show where one is in the volume. A glance at a page quickly reveals the organization of the bibliography and of each entry. The generous margins and good paper of the volume show fine taste. Daniel Berkeley Updike at the Merrymount Press designed and produced the bibliography, and it shows.

Caleffo Vecchio	Giovanni Cecchini, ed., *Il Caleffo Vecchio del comune di Siena*, 3 vols. (Florence, 1932–34; Siena, 1940)
CG	ASS, Consiglio Generale, Deliberazioni
Cherubini, *Signori*	Giovanni Cherubini, *Signori, contadini, borghesi* (Florence, 1974)
Const. 1262	Lodovico Zdekauer, ed., *Il constituto del comune di Siena dell'anno 1262* (Milan, 1897)
Const. 1309–10	Alessandro Lisini, ed., *Il costituto del comune di Siena volgarizzato nel MCCCIX–MCCCX*, 2 vols. (Siena, 1903)
Const. 1337–39	ASS, Statuti, Siena, 26
C.S.	Alessandro Lisini and Fabio Iacometti, eds., *Cronache Senesi*, in *Rerum Italicarum scriptores*, n.s., XV, pt. VI (Bologna, 1931–1937)
Davidsohn, *Geschichte*	Robert Davidsohn, *Geschichte von Florenz*, 4 vols. (Berlin, 1896–1927)
DR	ASS, Diplomatico Riformagioni
Guida	Ministero dell'Interno, Pubblicazioni degli Archivi di Stato, V, VI, *Archivio di Stato di Siena: Guida-inventario dell'Archivio di Stato*, 2 vols. (Rome, 1951)
Repertorio	Paolo Cammarosano and Vincenzo Passeri, "Repertorio," in Vol. II of *I castelli del Senese: Strutture fortificate dell'area Senese-Grossetana*, 2 vols. (Siena, 1976) [N.B.: Repertorio is to be consulted when no other reference is given for a place in the Sienese state.]
Roncière, *Florence*	Charles M. de la Roncière, *Florence: Centre économique régional au XIVe siècle*, 5 vols. (Aix-en-Provence, [1976])
Senigaglia, *Mercanzia*	Quinto Senigaglia, ed., *Lo statuto dell'arte della Mercanzia Senese, 1342–1343* (Siena, 1911), first published in *BSSP*, XIV–XVII (1907–1910)

dis: per Henricum Stephanū in formularia litterarū arte opifi-‖cē / illius
maxima cura & diligentia / necnō eiusdē & Iodoci ‖ Badij in hoc opere
sociorum paruis expensis An-‖no ab incarnatione domini cuncta guber-‖
nantis Millesimo quingen-‖tesimo duodecimo. ‖ Idibus ve-‖ro Iu-‖nij.

19 unnumbered leaves, 173 numbered leaves, and 1 unnumbered at end. 197 × 150 mm.
Harrisse, *Bib. Am. Vet.*, No. 71, and *Add.*, No. 43. John Carter Brown, I. 46. MS. annotations. Bought of J. W. Bouton, New York, June, 1875. On 172ᵇ is the passage
probably referring to the Indians brought from Canada by Thomas Aubert, the Dieppe
pilot, quoted in Harrisse and translated in John Carter Brown Catalogue. Although the
last numbered leaf is 175, there are no folios 173 and 174, and the same defect appears
in the edition of 1518.

JOANNES, Stobnicensis [Stobnicza].

Introductio in Ptholomei Cosmo-‖graphiā cū longitudinibus ʒ latitudi-
nibus regio‖num ʒ ciuitatum celebriorum. ‖ ℭ Epitoma Europe Ence
Siluij ‖ ℭ Situs ʒ distinctio parcium tocius Asie per brachia Tauri mō‖
tis ex Asia Pij secundi.‖ ℭ Particularior Minoris asie descriptio ex eiusdem Pij asia ‖ ℭ Sirie compendiosa descriptio: ex Isidoro ‖ ℭ Africe
breuis descriptio: ex paulo orosio ‖ ℭ Terre sancte ʒ urbis Hierusalem
apertior descriptio: fratris ‖ Anselmi ordinis Minorum de obseruancia.
[Verses, Magister paulus: Crosnensis. Lectori studioso, 12 *lines*. Dis-
thicon, 2 *lines*.] Colophon: ℭ Impressum Cracouie p Florianū Ungleriū.
Anno dñi. M.D.xij.

2 unnumbered leaves, 40 numbered, and two maps (in facsimile). 213 × 152 mm.
Harrisse, *Bib. Am. Vet.*, No. 69, and *Add.*, No. 42. John Carter Brown, I. 45.

LASCARIS, Constantine.

In hoc libro haec habentvr. ‖ Constantini Lascaris Byzantini de octo
partibus orōnis, *etc.* Colophon: Venetiis apud Aldum mense octobri.
M.D.XII.

215 × 146 mm. Renouard, I. 135. Sussex book-plate.

MELA, Pomponius.

Cosmographia ‖ Pomponij Mele: Autho-‖ris nitidissimi Tribus ‖ Libris
digesta: puo q̊daȝ ‖ Compendio Joannis ‖ Coclei Norici ‖ adaucta ‖ quo ‖
Geographie ‖ principia ‖ genera-‖liter comprehēduntur / ‖ Breuis q̄p̄ Ger-
manie Descri‖ptio / Ad profectū Iuuētutis Lau‖rentiane Norinbergen-
sis imprimis: ‖ Dein ad Ceterorum quoqȝ in litterarum ‖ studio successus
nūc prima sui Editione in lucē pfert. ‖ Chelidonius Musophilus Ad lec-
torē ‖ [*Ten lines of verse.*]

[54]

27 numbered leaves and 31 unnumbered. Signatures A, B, D, E, F, H, and K⁶, and C, G, I, and L⁴. 210 × 149 mm. The letter from Benedictus Chelidonius to Joannes Cocleus Noricus (on 56ᵇ) is dated "Vale Norinberge. x Calendas Februarias. Anno ‖ Salutiferi partus. 1512." On 29ᵇ: Veruȝ ‖ Americus Vesputius iam nostro secolo / nouū illū mundū inue‖nisse fert / Portugalie Castilieȝ regū nauibus. Purchased, October, 1903.

ↄ Pompo‖nii Melae de Sitv or‖bis, libri tres. ‖ Cvm Indice.

Title set in an engraved border. 44 numbered leaves and 2 unnumbered. Signatures A, E, and H⁸, B, C, D, F, and G⁴, and I¹. 180 × 138 mm. The unnumbered leaf contains ↄ Ioannes Ca‖mers ordinis minorvm sacrarvm ‖ Literarvm, D. Theobaldo Offenburgensi professionis ‖ eiusdem discipulo suo charissimo, S. D., which is dated "Nonas Septembris, M.D.XII."

PRUDENTIUS.

[Escutcheon of Spain.] Prudentij opera que in hoc ‖ libro continentur. ‖ Cathemerinon. idest hymni per horas diei. ‖ Peristephanon. idest de coronis martyrum.‖Psycomachia. idest de pugna anime.‖Apotheosis. idest de diuinitate. ‖ Amartigenia. idest de origine peccati. ‖ Contra symmachum oratorem senatus. ‖ Dittocheon. idest de duplici cibo. a iiᵃ: ❡ Ad per quam reuerendum in christo iesu patrē ac nobilissimuȝ ‖ dominum Jacobum raimirum auillascusa Episcopum malacita ‖ num. ȝc. Aelij Antonij Nebrissen. regij. historiagraphi in opera ‖ Aurelij clementis prudentij prefatio. Colophon: Fuit impressum presens opus in Ciuitate Lucronij ‖ per Arnaldum guillermū dė Brocario, et finitur die ‖ secunda mēsis Septēbris Anno a natiuitate Christi ‖ Millesimo quingentesimo duodecimo. [Printer's device.]

Collation: a⁴, A–M⁸, N⁴, a–l⁸, m⁴. 196 unnumbered leaves. 195 × 145 mm. Harrisse, *Bib. Am. Vet., Add.*, No. 44. This is the Harrisse copy, from the Samuel Latham Mitchill Barlow Library, and he notes that the epistle of Ant. de Lebrija (the preliminary four leaves) is not found in all copies of this edition. In this epistle (a iiᵃ) occurs the following: hispanie fines cum indorum fronte commisisse: alterum himispherium maioribus nostris incognitum indagasse.

1513

ARISTOTLE.

Habentvr hoc Volvmine haec Theo-‖doro Gaza Interprete. ‖ Aristotelis de natura animalium, *etc*. Colophon: Venetiis In Aedibus Aldi, & ‖ Andreae Asulani Soceri ‖ Mense Februario. ‖ M.D.xiii.

312 × 217 mm. Renouard, i. 142. On fly-leaf is written, "M: Wodhull, Feb: 12th, 1778;" on 1ᵃ, "M. Maty."

Books and articles referred to in the notes and selections

Andrews, Charles M. *The colonial period of American history. The settlements, vol. I.* New Haven and London, 1964.

Arber, Edward (ed.) *The first three English books on America.* Trans. by Richard Eden. Westminster (England), 1895.

Arber, Edward (ed.) *The story of the Pilgrim Fathers, 1606–1623.* Boston, 1897.

Arber, Edward (ed.) *Travels and works of Captain John Smith.* With bibliographical and critical introduction by A. G. Bradley. Edinburgh, 1910. 2 vols. (Referred to as Arber-Bradley in notes.)

Ascensión, Father Antonio de la. *Relacion de la jornada que hizo el Generál Sevastian Vizcayno al descubrimiento de las Californias el eno de 1602.* (Manuscript in Newberry Library, Chicago: Ayer Collection 1038.) Trans. in Wagner, H. R. *Spanish Voyages to the northwest coast of America in the 16th century.* San Francisco, 1929, pp.180-272.

Ashe, Geoffrey. *Land to the west.* London, 1962.

Asher, G. M. (ed.) *Henry Hudson the navigator.* London, 1860.

Bakeless, John. *The eyes of discovery: the pageant of North America as seen by the first explorers.* New York, 1950.

Bandelier, A. F. *Contributions to the history of the Southwestern portion of the United States.* Papers of the Archaeological Institute of America. American series V. Cambridge, 1890.

Barbour, Philip L. (ed.) *The Jamestown voyages under the first charter, 1606–1609.*

Barbour, Philip L. *The three worlds of Captain John Smith.* Boston, 1964.

Baudry, René. 'Marc Lescarbot'. *Dictionary of Canadian Biography*, I, 469-71. Toronto, 1966.

Benzoni, G. *See* Bry, Theodore de.

Biggar, H. P. (ed.) *A collection of documents relating to Jacques Cartier and the Sieur de Roberville.* Canadian Archives Publication no. 14. Ottawa, 1930.

Biggar, H. P. 'Jean Ribaut's Discoverye of Terra Florida.' *The English Historical Review,* XXXII (1917) 253-70.

Biggar, H. P. (ed.) *Précurseurs de Jacques Cartier, 1497–1534: collection de documents relatifs à l'histoire primitive du Canada.* Canadian Archives Publication, no. 5. Ottawa, 1911.

Biggar, H. P. (ed. and trans.) *The voyages of Jacques Cartier.* Canadian Archives Publication, no. 11. Ottawa, 1924.

Biggar, H. P. (ed.) *The Works of Samuel de Champlain.* Toronto, 1922–36. 8 vols.

Bolton, H. E. (ed.) *Drake's plate of brass.* California Historical Society (Special Publication, no. 13). San Francisco, 1937.

Bolton, H. E. *Spanish exploration in the Southwest, 1542–1706.* New York, 1916.

Bradford, William. *The history of Plymouth Plantation, 1606–1646.* William T. Davis (ed.) New York, 1964.

Brebner, John Bartlet. *The explorers of North America, 1492–1806.* London, 1933.

Brereton, John. *A brief and true relation of the discovery of the north part of Virginia.* London, 1602.

Brereton, John. *A brief relation of the discovery and plantation of New England . . .* Published by the President and Council of New England. London, 1622.

Bry, Theodore de. *America (Historia Americæ sive Novi Orbis).* Parts I-XIII. Frankfurt, 1590–1634. Part I. Harriot, Thomas. *A briefe and true report of the new found land of Virginia.* Frankfurt, 1590. Part I. Harriot, Thomas. *Admiranda narratio . . . Virginiæ.* Frankfurt, 1590. Part II. Le Moyne de Morgues, Jacques. *Brevis narratio eorum quæ in Florida Americæ provincia Gallis acciderunt.* Frankfurt, 1591. Part IV. Benzoni, Girolamo. *Americæ pars quarta . . . historia . . . Occidentali India.* Frankfurt, 1594. (cont.: Part V, 1595; Part VI, 1596; Part X, 1618.) Part XIII. Merian, M. (ed.) *Decima tertia pars historiæ Americanæ . . . Novæ Angliæ, Virginiæ . . .* Frankfurt, 1634.

Burrage, H. S. (ed.) *Early English and French voyages, 1534–1608.* New York, 1906.

Butterfield, C. W. *History of Brulé's discoveries and explorations.* Cleveland, 1898.

Cartier, Jacques. *See* Biggar (1924).

Castañeda, Pedro de, de Najera. Trans. by G. P. Winship. *See* F. W. Hodge and T. H. Lewis (1907) pp.273-387.

Champlain, Samuel de. *Works. See* H. P. Biggar (1922–36).

Champlain, Samuel de. *Voyages. See* W. L. Grant (1959).

Christy, Miller (ed.) *The voyages of Captain Luke Foxe . . . and Captain Thomas James . . . in search of a north-west passage, in 1631–32.* London, 1894.

Churchill, Awnsham and John. *A collection of voyages and travels.* London, 1732, vol. VI.

Clissold, Stephen. *The seven cities of Cibola.* New York, 1962.

Collinson, Richard (ed.) *The three voyages of Martin Frobisher.* London, 1867.

Connor, Jeannette Thurber (trans. and ed.) *Jean Ribaut, together with a transcript of an English version in the British Museum.* Florida State Historical Society, publication no. 7. DeLand, Florida, 1927.

Conway, Sir William Martin (ed.) *Early Dutch and English voyages to Spitzbergen.* London, 1904.

'Coppie d'une lettre venant de la Floride, envoyée à Rouen, et depuis au Seigneur d'Eueron; ensemble le plan et Portraict du fort que les François y ont faict.' A Paris, pour Vincent Norment et Ioanne Bruneau . . . 1565. In Ternaux-Compans, H. *Voyages, Relations . . .* Paris, 1841. Vol. XX, pp. 233-45.

Cortesão, Armando, and Avelino Teixeira da Mota. *Portugaliæ monumenta cartographica.* Lisbon, 1960–62. 6 vols.

Crone, G. R. *Maps and their makers.* London, 1953.

Cumming, William P. (ed.) *The Discoveries of John Lederer.* Charlottesville, Va, 1958.

Cumming, William P. 'The Parreus map (1562) of French Florida.' *Imago Mundi,* XVII (1963) 27-40.

Cumming, William P. *The Southeast in early maps.* Chapel Hill, North Carolina, 1962. 2nd edition.

Davies, James (?) *The relation of a voyage unto New England. See* Burrage (ed., 1906) pp.398-417. *See also* Thayer (ed., 1892) pp.35-86.

Day, John. Letter to the 'Lord Grand Admiral' of Spain. *Archivo General de Simancas, Estado,* Leg. 2, fo. 6. *See* Williamson (1962) for text used. *See* Vigneras (1956) for first publication.

Delanglez, Jean S. J. *El Rio del Espíritu Santo.* New York, 1945.

Dictionary of Canadian Biography. Vol. I, 1000-1700. Toronto, 1966.

Dicuil. *De mensura orbis terrae* (ed.) A. Letronne. Paris, 1814.

Dodge, Ernest. *North-west by sea.* New York, 1961.

Elvas, a Gentleman of. *Relaçam verdadeira . . . feita per hũ fidalgo Deluas.* Evora, 1557.

Elvas, a Gentleman of. *The discovery of Florida.* Trans. by Buckingham Smith. *See* F. W. Hodge (1907) pp.127-272.

Final report of the United States de Soto Expedition Commission, 76th Congress, 1st Session, House Document no. 71 (J. R. Swanton). Washington, D.C., 1939.

Fink, C. G. and E. P. Polushkin. *Drake's plate of brass vindicated.* California Historical Society, special publication no. 14. San Francisco, 1938.

Fite, E. D. and A. Freeman. *A book of old maps delineating American history from the earliest days down to the close of the Revolutionary War.* Cambridge, Massachusetts, 1926.

Foxe, Luke. *North-West Fox, or Fox from the North-West Passage.* London, 1635.

French, B. F. (ed. and trans.) *Historical collections of Louisiana . . .* New York, 1846–53. 5 vols.

Ganong, W. F. *Crucial maps in the early cartography and place-nomenclature of the Atlantic coast of Canada.* With introduction, commentary, and map notes by T. E. Layng. Toronto, 1964.

Gerritsz, Hessel. *Descriptio ac delineatio geographica detectionis freti.* Amsterdam, 1612.

Gosch, C. C. A. (ed.) *Danish Arctic expeditions, 1605 to 1620.* London, 1897.

Grajales, Francisco Lopez de Mendoza. *Memoir of . . . Menéndez de Avilés.* In: *Historical collections of Louisiana and Florida . . . 1527–1702.* Second series, trans. and ed. by Buckingham Smith. New York, 1875, pp.191-222.

Hakluyt, Richard. *Collection of the early voyages, travels, and discoveries of the English nation.* London, 1809–12. 5 vols.

Hakluyt, Richard. *Divers voyages touching the discoverie of America.* London, 1582.

Hakluyt, Richard (?) *The famous voyage of Sir Francis Drake.* In *Principall Navigations.* 6 folio leaves inserted between pp. 643 and 644. London, 1589.

Hakluyt, Richard. *The principall navigations, voiages and discoveries of the English nation.* London, 1589.

Hakluyt, Richard. *The principall navigations, voiages and discoveries of the English nation.* London, 1598–1600.

Hakluyt, Richard. *The principal navigations, voyages, traffiques and discoveries of the English nation.* Maclehose for Hakluyt Society, extra series I-XII. Glasgow, 1903-5.

Hall, E. H. (trans.) *Cèllere Codex. See* Verrazzano, G. da.

Hallenbeck, Cleve. *Álvar Nuñez Cabeza da Vaca . . .* Glendale, California, 1940.

Hammond, George P. *Coronado's Seven Cities.* United States Coronado Exposition Commission. Albuquerque, 1940.

Hammond, George P. (ed.) *The discovery of Florida, by a Gentleman of Elvas.* Buckingham Smith (trans.) Grabhorn Press, Book Club of California, 1946.

Hammond, George P. (ed.) *The discovery of Florida, by a Gentleman of Elvas,* trans. Buckingham Smith. Grabhorn Press, Book Club of California, 1946.

Hammond, George P. and Agapito Rey. *Don Juan de Oñate, colonizer of New Mexico, 1595–1628.* Albuquerque, 1953. 2 vols.

Hamy, E. T. (ed.) *Le livre et la description des pays de Gilles Le Bouvier.* Paris, 1908. (pp.157-217, the Bruges Itinerary.)

Harriot, Thomas. *A briefe and true report of the new found land of Virginia.* London, 1588. *See also* Quinn (1955) I, 341-74.

Harriot, T. *See* Bry, T. de.

Heizer, Robert Fleming. *Francis Drake and the California Indians, 1579.* University of California Publications in American Archaeology and Ethnology. Berkeley, 1947.

Hodge, F. W. and Lewis, T. H. (eds.) *Spanish explorers in the Southern United States,*

Example 9

W. P. Cumming, R. A. Skelton, and D. B. Quinn. *The Discovery of North America.* London: Elek Books, 1971.

The very large format of this volume dictated a two-column printing. This was necessary, of course, but the style of layout chosen for the bibliography is unfortunate. Not only is it set in very small type, but, worse, each entry begins flush left with no lines between entries. It is practically impossible to distinguish one entry from another. And no attempt has been made to make each author's name stand out. Such a model serves to show what to avoid in the design of a bibliography.

Example 10

Marcus McCorison, compiler. *Vermont Imprints 1778–1820.* Worcester, MA: American Antiquarian Society, 1963. Courtesy American Antiquarian Society.

The date at the top of each recto of this bibliography is a good guide, but there is no way of knowing from a glance at any given recto if the entry beneath this date is the first one for the stated year. The use of full caps for the filing part of the entries is distinctive; and at *Mc* and *Mac*, the small letters are distinguished by the use of small caps.

Numbers for each entry stand out clearly because each entry is preceded by a blank line, and the first line of each entry is indented. Library locations are given in small caps in the last lines of entries, using Library of Congress abbreviations. Each entry appears as a single block on the page, and since titles are not italicized or in boldface type, the smooth reading of entries could be inhibited when one is looking for publication data, because of this block style, which lacks spatial coding. Otherwise, this is a fairly well-designed page.

Printed in Bennington, Vermont, in 1810. By Anthony Haswell. 24p. 19cm.
MWA *.

1242 WRIGHT, CHESTER, 1776–1840

The Federal Compendium : Being a plain, concise, and easy intro-
duction to arithmetic. Designed for the use of common schools. By
Chester Wright. Second edition. Middlebury, Vt. Printed by J. D. Hunt-
ington. Sold by him, wholesale & retail.—Sold also by Wm. Fessenden,
Brattleboro'; J. Parks, Montpelier; P. Merrifield & Co. and Farnsworth
& Churchill, Windsor; A. Willard, St. Albans; S. Mills, Burlington; O.
White, Middlebury, &c, &c. 1810. vi, [7]–108p. 15cm.

KARP.152 ¶ GAR; HGR; MWA; VtHi; VtMiM; VtMiS; VtU-w * ¶ Adv. *Middlebury Mercury*, Apr. 11, 1810, 'Now in the Press'.

1243 WRIGHT, CHESTER, 1776–1840

A Sermon, preached on the day of general election, at Montpelier,
Oct. 11, 1810, before the Honorable Legislature of Vermont. By Chester
Wright, A.M. Pastor of the Congregational Church, in Montpelier. Published by order of the Legislature. Randolph, (Vermont) Printed by Ser-
eno Wright. 1810. 14p. 22.5cm.

G; S105570; VE ¶ DLC; HGR; ICN; MWA; MiD-B; NN *; NhHi; OCHP; VtHi;
VtMiM; BrMus.

 1811

1244 THE ADVISER; or Vermont Evangelical Magazine for the year
1811. Volume III. ... The editors appointed by the General Con-
vention are the Rev. Messrs. Asa Burton, D.D. Gershom C. Lyman,
Martin Tullar, Leonard Worcester, John Fitch, Henry Davis, D.D.
Holland Weeks, Bancroft Fowler, Thomas A. Merrill, John Hough,
Daniel Haskel, Chester Wright. Middlebury: Published by Samuel
Swift, general agent of the editors, at whose store may be had complete
sets of The Adviser. Price one dollar each vol.—Bound $1,25. T. C.
Strong, printer 1811. viii, 376p. 21cm.

G ¶ MWA; Vt; VtHi; VtU-w *.

262

1245 ALMANACS

The Complete New-Hampshire & Vermont Almanac, for the year of our Lord, 1812. Being bissextile or leap year, and the 36th of Columbian independence.—From creation, according to the Scriptures, 5774. Fitted to the lat. & long. of the town of Windsor, but will serve without essential variation for the adjacent states. Containing lunations, eclipses of the luminaries, aspects, judgment of the weather, &c. &c. With other matter, curious, useful & entertaining. Calculations by Amos Cole, Philom. [Motto] ... Windsor, Vt. Published by Merrifield & Cochran. Sold wholesale and retail by them, in Windsor, and by the principal book-sellers and printers in New-Hampshire and Vermont. Price 7 1-2 dolls. per gross, 75 cts.per dozen, 10 cts. single. [1811] [52]p. 16cm.

G; NA ¶ DLC; MWA * ¶ Adv. *Vermont Journal*, Nov. 4, 1811.

1246 ALMANACS

The Farmer's Calender: or The New-York, Vermont, and Connecticut Almanac, for the year of our Lord 1812. Being bissextile, or leap year. The twelfth year of the nineteenth century—and of American independence, which was declared the fourth of July, 1776, (till July 4) the 36th year. Calculated for the horizon and meridian of Troy ... By Andrew Beers, Philom. Containing the usual calculations, times of setting of the courts, and a variety of useful and entertaining matter. Bennington, Vermont, Printed by William Haswell. [1811] [24]p. 17.5cm.

G; NA; Sp191 ¶ HGR; MWA *; VtBennM; Vtili.

1247 ALMANACS

Swift's Vermont Register and Almanac, for the year of our Lord, 1812; and the thirty-sixth of the indpendence of the United States. Middlebury: Published by Samuel Swift, at his theological, classical and law book-store. T. C. Strong, printer. [1811] [16], [17]-108p. 15cm.

G; NA ¶ HPM; MHi; MWA; NN *; Vtili; VtMis; BrMus.

1248 ALMANACS

The Vermont & New-York Almanack, for the year of our Lord Christ, 1812, being bissextile or leap year, and the thirty sixth of the independence of the United States of America. Calculated for the meridian of Burlington, ... Containing the necessary astronomical calculations, and a variety of useful articles. Astronomical calculations by Eben W. Judd. Burlington, Vt. Printed by S. Mills. Sold at his bookstore, wholesale and retail and by the printers and booksellers in Vermont, the west-

263

Example 11

David Farrell, compiler. *The Stinehour Press: A Bibliographical Checklist of the First Thirty Years.* Lunenburg, VT: Meriden-Stinehour Press, 1988. Courtesy Roderick Stinehour, Meriden-Stinehour Press.

This is a good example of what can be done when money is no object. At least that seems to be the case. This is a sumptuously printed, beautifully conceived volume, with colour illustrations, generous margins, beautiful endpapers and binding, fine paper, and an overall sense of wealth.

Entries are clearly distinguished from one another by the entry number and the spaces used between them. The chronological arrangement is sensible since this is not at all a subject bibliography. Alphabetical arrangement by title within years makes as much sense as anything else, and this is supplemented by a good index giving access to the entries by authors' names, and another with a listing of all the titles. Even the volume's little bibliography, called 'Writings Related to the Stinehour Press', on pages 237–8, is elegantly designed, following the simplicity of the Blumenthal layout (see Example 1 above).

Also, the 'Compiler's Note' is brief (pp. xix–xxi) and clear. We are told, for example, that the parenthetical number at the end of each entry is the Stinehour job number, where that information was available. This number is important for researchers who wish to go to the press's archives.

This is a well-designed and eminently accessible bibliography.

Example 12

C. William Miller, *Benjamin Franklin's Philadelphia Printing: 1728–1766.* Philadelphia: American Philosophical Society, 1974. Courtesy American Philosophical Society.

This very well-designed bibliography offers a facsimile for most entries in the book. It also presents a great amount of information for each item. A combination of typographic and spatial coding makes each entry and every element in the entries distinct.

The arrangement is chronological, with an alphabetical sequence within each year, a perfectly reasonable listing since most readers interested in Franklin's printing want to see his growth and development. Running heads on versos indicate the first entry on the page, not the first *full* entry. Hence, on page 64, we know that the entry we first see, which continues as a carry-over from the previous page, is for a work by Fox. Sometimes in books running heads indicate the first entry which begins on the page, making the reader flip back to identify the first entry which appears; this is not the case here.

Large numbers in the margins, a blank space between entries, and the use of full caps in the filing entry are almost overkill. All three are not necessary, but they do the job. The use of small caps and hanging indents for the notes also makes this a perfectly legible and accessible tool.

The volume also has an excellent, extensive index, affording even more accessibility to the data; it even includes references to the watermarks in the paper of all of Franklin's books, broken down by the country of origin of the paper. With 583 pages plus an 85-page apparatus at the beginning, this is a most impressive work.

755

FACT AND FANTASY: ILLUSTRATED BOOKS FROM A PRIVATE COLLECTION. Catalogue by David P. Becker. Cambridge, Mass., Harvard College Library Department of Printing and Graphic Arts, 1976.

8½×5½ inches; 32 pages + 70 pages of plates.
Smythsewn and glued into printed cream paper cover. (S37651)

756

THE FIRST HUNDRED YEARS OF WESLEYAN COLLEGE, 1836–1936. By Samuel Luttrell Akers. Macon, Ga., Wesleyan College; Savannah, Ga., The Beehive Press, 1976.

9½×6½ inches; 160 pages; illustrated; portraits; schematic plans.
Orange-brown paper over boards; gold-stamped spine; wrapper. (F127530)

757

FORTY YEARS MORE: A HISTORY OF GROTON SCHOOL, 1934–1974. By Acosta Nichols. Groton, Mass., The Trustees of Groton School, 1976.

9½×6½ inches; xviii+257 pages; illustrated.
Red cloth over boards; gold-stamped spine; wrapper. (F27608)

758

FROM FLESH IS HEIR: TWO UNPUBLISHED PARAGRAPHS. [By Lincoln Kirstein. Lunenburg, Vt., Privately printed], 1976.

Cover title: "For Lincoln Kirstein."
8×5 inches; [8] pages; frontispiece photograph tipped in.
17 copies printed on handmade Amatruda paper; handsewn into printed handmade light brown paper wrapper. (F37647)

759

FROM SEED TO FLOWER: PHILADELPHIA 1681–1876: A HORTICULTURAL POINT OF VIEW. Philadelphia, Pa., The Pennsylvania Horticultural Society, 1976.

9½×7¼ inches; 119 pages including 41 pages of plates.

[173]

distributed (Minutes of YM I, 394, 400). In an un-dated account book entry Franklin charged Pemberton and Morris the sum of £80 "For 2000 Geo. Fox Spelling Books" (Ledger A & B, p. 142). The first edition of this school book composed by Fox and Ellis Hookes was printed in London in 1673 (Wing F 1859), eventually enlarged, and frequently reprinted in England and the Colonies, Reynier Jansen, William Bradford's successor, printed the first Philadelphia edition in 1702. Evans found a titleless copy of the Boston (Rogers and Fowle), 1743 edition at NN and for some reason entered it in his bibliography under entry 4138 as a 1737 Newport-James Franklin imprint. Alden, *Rhode Island Imprints*, No. 40, corrected the error, and the editors of *STE* have reassigned the Evans number to BF's Philadelphia printing.

COPIES: PP. PU.

133　[FRANKLIN, Benjamin (1706–1790)]. Poor Richard Almanack for the Year 1738. [First and Second Impressions].　　　　　[1737]

COLLATION: Foolscap 8° in fours *A–C⁴*. Pp. *1* title, *2* preface, *3* anatomy of man's body, symbols, notes, *4* planets' motions; verses, *5* chronology, *6* explanation; observations, *7–18* January to December, *19* eclipses, *19–21* court days in Middle Colonies, *21* general meetings; fairs, *22* catalogue of European rulers, *23* BF adv.; J. Wilkinson adv., *24* roads northeastward and southwestward, T. Grew adv.

ORNAMENT: *3* No. 10.

TYPE: [within single-rule frame] BF long primer, black letter.

PAPER: American, unmarked.

LEAF: 6.8 x 3.9 in.

REFERENCES: Evans 4141, Hildeburn 561, Campbell 110, Drake 9604.

NOTES: Advertised as just published in *Pa. Gaz.*, Nov 3, 1737. In Nov., 1737, BF sent "1000 Almanacks of 1738" to Sister Ann in Newport (Ledger A & B, p. 246), and evidently the usual 400–500 copies to Fleet in Boston (*Boston Evening Post* adv., Dec. 12, 1737) and Timothy in Charleston (*S. C. Gaz.* adv., Jan. 5, 1737–38). The use of traceable series of distinctive frame rules in the formes of this almanac makes it possible to distinguish two complete machinings. The only example of the one impression is the CSmH copy, which because it exhibits one unproofed page (August) is considered the earlier; the other nine extant copies are of another and presum-

ably later impression (see Miller, *Almanacs*, pp. 100–101 and plate 3).

COPIES: PU. CSmH, CtY, DeWin, MB, MH, NN, PHi, PPAK, PPL, PPRF; NBLiHi.

Poor Richard, 1738.

AN

Almanack

For the Year of Christ

1738,

Being the Second after LEAP YEAR.

And makes since the Creation	Years
By the Account of the Eastern *Greeks*	7246
By the Latin Church, when ☉ ent. ♈	6937
By the Computation of *W. W.*	5747
By the *Roman* Chronology	5687
By the *Jewish* Rabbies	5499

Wherein is contained,

The Lunations, Eclipses, Judgment of the Weather, Spring Tides, Planets Motions & mutual Aspects, Sun and Moon's Rising and Setting, Length of Days, Time of High Water, Fairs, Courts, and observable Days

Fitted to the Latitude of Forty Degrees, and a Meridian of Five Hours West from *London*, but may without sensible Error, serve all the adjacent Places, even from *Newfoundland* to *South-Carolina.*

By *RICHARD SAUNDERS*, Philom.

PHILADELPHIA:

Printed and sold by *B. FRANKLIN*, at the New Printing-Office near the Market.

[133]

LAY, Benjamin (1677–1760). All Slave-Keepers　134 that keep the Innocent in Bondage, Apostates. Printed for the Author.　　　1737 [1738]

COLLATION: Foolscap 8° in fours *A–2M⁴* (B2, C2, 2M2 unsigned; 2G2, 2K2 signed G2, K2). Pp. *1* title, *3–5* preface, signed Benjamin Lay, Abington, Nov. 17, 1736, 6–269 text, *270–271* excerpts from *Paradise Lost*, Book XII, *272* blank, *273–277* contents, *278* errata, *279–280 blank.*

COLLATION: Foolscap oblong half-sheet. TEXT: 19 ll. 89 (124) x 237 mm.
TYPE: Caslon great primer.
PAPER: Imported, marks obscured.
LEAF: 8.9 x 14.7 (PPAmP).
REF: Evans-Bristol 11242, *Papers*, V, 451–52.
NOTES: Assumed to be from Franklin's pen and the work of his press. Hall charged Franklin "for Work done for the Post Office in 1752, 1754, and 1756" (BF and DH Settlement, Debits, item 9). The copy with the earliest date inserted by hand is that directed to Thomas Vernon, Newport, Dec., 24 1754; the one with the latest date, that to Thomas MacKreth, Charleston, S. C., July 11, 1760.
COPIES: NN-c.1. NN-c.2, PPAmP.

590 [HALL, David (1714–1772)]. Imported in the last Ships from London, and to be sold by David Hall. Book Advertisement. [no imprint]. [1754?]

COLLATION: Demy half-sheet. TEXT: 95 ll. 355 (369) x 183 mm.
TYPE: (2 cols.) Caslon long primer.
PAPER: American, unmarked.
LEAF: 14.8 x 9.5 in.
REFERENCES: STE 40686, Evans-Bristol 1649.
NOTES: Dated in the year 1754 largely because the piece was found bound into Isaiah Thomas' file of *Pa. Gaz.* after the issue of June 27, 1754. The two most recently published books on the list are Franklin on Electricity and Tobias Smollett's *Peregrine Pickle*, both dated 1751.
COPY: MWA.

591 JERMAN, John. American Almanack for the Year 1755. [1754]

COLLATION: Foolscap 8° in fours *A*–C⁴. Pp. *1* title, *2* preface, *2–5* verses on twelve months of year, *6* anatomy of man's body, symbols, notes, *7–18* January–December, *19* eclipses, *20–23* court days in Middle Colonies, *23* Quaker meetings; fairs, *24* roads northeastward and southwestward; DH adv.
ORNAMENT: *6* No. 13.
TYPE: [within single-rule frame] BF long primer; Caslon long primer, brevier.
PAPER: American, marked Penn Arms or IH.
LEAF: 6.3 x 4 in.
REFERENCES: Evans 7219, Hildeburn 1368, Campbell 520, Drake 9758.

Imported ⸱ the laſt Ships from *London*, and to be ſold by *DAVID HALL*, at the *New-Printing-Office*, in *Market-ſtreet*, *Philadelphia*, the following Books, *viz.*

FOLIO'S.

SALKELD's Reports; Jacob's Law Dictionary; Rudiments of Law and Equity; Poſtlewait's Mercantile Dictionary, firſt Volume; Swan's Britiſh Architect; Gibbs's Rules for Drawing; Malyne's Lex Mercatoria; Roberts's Map of Commerce; Engliſh and Weſt-India Pilots; Prideaux's Connection of the Old and New-Teſtament; Burkitt and Whitby on the New-Teſtament; Sidney's Arcadia; Bickham's Penmanſhip; Hughes's Natural Hiſtory of Barbados; Story's Journal; Univerſal Engliſh Dictionary; Boccalini's Advices from Parnaſſus; and Reynolds's Triumphs of God's Revenge againſt Murder.

QUARTO'S.

Hanway's Travels; Langley's Builder's and Tradeſman's Treaſury of Deſigns; Deſigns of Inigo Jones and others; Hoppus's Architecturo; Price's Carpentry; Hatton's Tradeſman's Treaſury; London Art of Building; Geography of the Antients; Dodderidge's Family Expoſitor; Ludwig's Dictionary; Boerhaave's Chymiſtry; Malcom's Arithmetick; Univerſal Library of Trade and Commerce; Stephens's Spaniſh Dictionary; Univerſal Harmony, or the Gentleman and Ladies ſocial Companion; Fitzherbert's New Natura Brevium; Biſſet on Fortification; Franklin on Electricity; and Cruden's Concordance.

OCTAVO'S.

Bailey's and Dyche's Dictionary; Jacob's Law Dictionary abridg'd; Abridgment of the Statutes, from Magna Charta, to the End of the ninth Year of his preſent Majeſty; Morgan's Modern Pleader; Jacob's Attorney's Practice; Clerk's Engliſh Tutor; Every Man his own Lawyer; General Law of Eſtates; Scrivener's Guide; Molloy de Jure Maritimo; Law of Ejectments; Law of Executions; Trials per Pais; Tradeſman's Lawyer; Student's Law Dictionary; Clerk's Inſtructor; Complete Conveyancer; Townſend's Preparative to Pleading; Livy's Roman Hiſtory; Martin's, Muſchenbroeck's, Roning's, and Graveſend's Philoſophy; Miller's Gardiner's Dictionary; James's and Quincey's Diſpenſatories; Quincey's Lexicon; Haller's Phyſiology; Robinſon on the Conſumption, Stone, Spleen, and Venereal Diſeaſe; Lobb and Glaſs on Fevers; Hillary and Thompſon on the Small-Pox; Sharp's Surgery; Mead's Medicina Sacra; Mead on Poiſons; Boerhaave's Aphoriſms, and Materia Medica; Allen's Synopſis Medicinæ; Le Dran's Obſervations and Operations in Surgery; Lind on the Scurvy; Dover's Phyſician's Legacy; Smellie's Midwifery; Cheyne's Engliſh Malady; Cheyne on Regimen; Sidney on Government; Burnet's Hiſtory of his own Time; Hammond's and Newton's Algebra; Wingate's and Hill's Arithmetick; Haſelton's Seaman's Aſſiſtant; Sellers's, Patoun's, Wilſon's and Atkinſon's Navigation; Mariner's Kallenders; Anſon's Voyage; Builder's Dictionary; Britiſh Empire in America; Complete Houſewife; Barrow's Lectures; Boccace's Novels; Cramer on Metals; Charron on Wiſdom; Critical Hiſtory of England; Chalkley's Journal: Bieler's and Bachmair's Grammars; Bailey's Eraſmus; Britiſh Antiquities; Bolingbroke's Remarks on the Hiſtory of England; Bolingbroke on Parties, and on the Study of Hiſtory: Bulſtrode's Eſſays; Barrow's Medicinal Dictionary; Chriſtian's Mazagine; Le Clerc's Hiſtory of Phyſick; Cambray on Pure Love; Chriſtianity as old as the Creation; Clergyman's Intelligencer; Cambray's Fables; Euclid's Elements; Duchall's Sermons; Drelincourt on Death; Diſſertations on the Numbers of Mankind; Dialogues on Education; Elwood's Life; Eſſay on Motion; Evans's Sermons; Female Fables; Foſter's Sermons; Gordon's Grammar; New Family Inſtructor; General Shop Book; Gibbons's Poems; Hare's Hebrew Pſalter; Deſcription of Holland; Holmes's Geography; Howe's Bleſſedneſs of the Righteous; Kennet's Roman Antiquities; Italian Grammar; Young's Love of Fame; Lambert on Education; L'Eſtrange's Eſop; Letters concerning Mythology; Locke on Government; Locke on Chriſtianity; Management of the Tongue; Mallet's Life of Bacon; Hayes's Negotiator's Magazine; Worſter's Philoſophy; preſent State of Europe; Practice of Piety; Obſervations on Minorca; Pilgrim's Progreſs; Puffendorff's Introduction to the Hiſtory of Europe; Sherlock on Death and Judgment; Shaw's Chymical Lectures; Stanhope on the Epiſtles and Goſpels; Stone's Mathematical Dictionary; Preſent State of Britain; Shuckford's Sacred and Profane Hiſtory; Starret's Projectiles; Stephens's Repreſentation of Popery; Turnbull on Education; Taylor's Contemplations; Watts's Logick and Supplement; Trowell on Huſbandry; Tillotſon's Life; Varenius's Geography; Theory and Practice of Commerce; The Librarian; Watts's Sermons; Weſt on the Reſurrection; Vertot's Revolutions of Rome; Ditto's Revolutions of Sweden; Webſter's and Mair's Book-keeping; Deſcription of the Iſlands of Scilly; Buchanan's Hiſtory of Scotland; Eſſays on ſeveral Subjects concerning Britiſh Antiquities; Eſſays on the Principles of Morality and Natural Religion; Biggs's Military Hiſtory; Jones's Introduction to the Mathematicks; Titles for a Common Place Book; Hiſtory of the Quakers; New Family Inſtructor; Nelſon's Feſtivals; and Bolingbroke's Letter to Windham.

TWELVES.

Pope's Works, with Warburton's Notes; Gordon's Tacitus; Lives of the Poets; Nature Diſplay'd, Tillotſons Sermons; Spectator, Guardian, and Tatler; Rambler; Turkiſh and Jewiſh Spies; Belles Lettres, Engliſh; Ditto French; Cato's Letters; Young's Night Thoughts; Stage Coach; Merry Fellow; Letters from Felicia to Charlotte; Apothegms of the Antients; The Actor; Attorney's Pocket Book; Abelard and Heloiſe; Don Quixotte; Addiſon's Works; Betſy Thoughtleſs; Ovid's Metamorphoſes; Conduct of a married State; Modern Characters, illuſtrated by Hiſtories in real Life; Peregrine Pickle; Pamela; Ninon's Letters; Univerſal Spectator; Rowland's Meaſuring; Law and Gee on Trade; Real Chriſtian; Law's Serious Call; Preſent State of England; Life of Prince Charles of Lorrain, and Prince Eugene of Savoy; New Pilgrim's Progreſs; Seaman's Vademecum; Tully's Offices; Paradiſe Loſt and Regain'd; Steel's Political Tracts; Salmon's Gazetteer: Short Way to know the World; Secret Hiſtory of Perſia; Pocket Farrier; Philips's Paſtorals: Fullers Proverbs; Remarks on London; Rochfaucault's Maxims; Plutarch's Lives: Pious Country Pariſhioner: Thouſand Notable Things; Houſekeeper's Pocket Book: Ruyſch's Obſervations in Surgery: Gentleman Accomptant: Moffet on Health: Lover's Secretary: Law concerning Landlords and Tenants: Life of Madam Maintenon: Manners of the preſent Age: Maxims of Chriſtina Queen of Sweden: Meditations for young People; Memoirs of Brandenburgh: Lemery on Food: Library of the Law: Law of Arreſts: Land Purchaſer's Companion: Lanſdowne's Poems: Lady's Library: Locke on Education: Law's Chriſtian Perfection: Jenks's Devotion: Hudibras: Bracken's Farriery: Barker's Novels: La Belle Aſſemblée: Britiſh Diſpenſatory: Handley's Colloquia Chirurgica: Hiſtory of Betty Barnes: Behn's Novels: Caſſandra: Blackmore's Creation: Young Clerk's Magazine: Compleat Tradeſman: Travels of Cyrus: Dryden's Virgil: Claſſical Dictionary: Eachard's Terence: Eachard's Gazetteer: Dean of Colerain: Euclid's Elements: Derham's Phyſico Theology: Gil Blas: Free Thinker: Fletcher's Political Works: Female Academy: Force of Education: Fowler's Deſign of Chriſtianity: Pope's Homer's Iliad and Odyſſey: Harvey's Meditations: Hiſtory of Birds: Human Prudence: Trapp's Confutation of Popery: Temple on the Netherlands: Trader's Companion: Trublet's Eſſays: Vernet's Dialogues: Watts's Guide to Prayer: Youth's Monitor: Young Chriſtian's Guide: Granville on the Troubles of England: Mariner's Compaſs: Select Tales and Fables: Croxall's Eſop: Quinteſſence of Engliſh Poetry: Britiſh Muſe: Schoolmaſter's Aſſiſtant; Lives of the Criminals: Parnell's Poems: Guthrie's Memoirs: Monroe's Oſteology: Preſent for an Apprentice: Craig's Poems: Shaftſbury's Letters: Account of Denmark: Sophocles: Ray's Wiſdom of God: Edinburgh Entertainer: Harvey de Motu Cordis: Moore's Dialogues: Nye's Diſcourſe on Natural and Reveal'd Religion: Barrow on Contentment: Douglaſs on the Muſcles: Life of Charles the 12th of Sweden: Man of Honour: Hubner's Geography: Shaftſbury's Characteriſticks: Henry on the Sacrament: Pomfret's Poems: Dunlop's Sermons: Dryden's Eſſays: Buckingham's Plays; The Fool: Perſian Letters, Engliſh and French: Cook's Terence: Banquet of Xenophon: Shaw's Immanuel: Fairy Tales: Nettleton on Virtue: The Aviary: Pitſcottie's Hiſtory of Scotland: Marſay's Spiritual Life: Cervantes's Novels: Danois's Novels: Addiſon on Medals: Fontenelle's Plurality of Words: Le Diable Boiteux: Gay's Fables: Longinus on the Sublime: Melcourt's Memoirs: Ludlow's Memoirs: Roſcommon's Poems: Hathornden's Hiſtory of the James's: Orrery's Remarks on Swift: Bennet's Chriſtian Oratory: Gulliver's Travels: Jamieſon on Virtue: Byſhe's Art of Poetry: Comes Commercii: Journey to the World under Ground, Shakeſpear's Works, and Joſephus.

SCHOOL BOOKS.

Boyer's and Cole's Dictionaries: French Teſtaments and Telemachus: Virgil, Horace, Juvenal, and Ovid, Delphini: Clarke's Introduction to the making of Latin, with and without the Supplement: Clarke's Salluſt, Sueton, Nepos, Eraſmus, Florus, Ovid, Eutropius, Grammar, Cordery, and Eſop: Wettenhall's and Weſtminſter Greek Grammars: Ruddiman's and Bailey's Grammatical Exerciſes: Ruddiman's Rudiments: Murphy's Lucian's Dialogues: London Vocabulary: Accidence: Hoole's Terminations: Sententiæ Pueriles: Hoole's Cato: Titus Livius, printed by Ruddiman: Longinus: Dyke's Ovid's Triſts: Iliad of Homer: Engliſh Examples: Leuſden's Compend of the New-Teſtament: Greek and Latin Teſtaments: Latin Ditto: Lilly's Grammar: Virgil, Horace, and Ovid, with Minelly's Notes: Pliny's Works: Euripides: Gray's Hebrew Grammar: Davidſon's and Watſon's Horace: Selectæ è Profanis Scriptoribus Hiſtoriæ: Selectæ è Veteri Teſtamento Hiſtoriæ: Dialogi Sacri: Ruddiman's Grammar: Poetæ Minores: Virgil, Horace, Terence, Cornelius Nepos, Quintus Curtius, Juvenal, Juſtin, and Eutropius, ſmall: Cicero's Orations; and Buchanan's Pſalms.

[590]

NOTES: Advertised in *Pa. Gaz.*, Nov. 7, 1754, as "Saturday next will be published." The verses on the twelve months printed on pp. *2–5* appeared on the identical pages in Jerman's almanac for 1751.
COPIES: PHi. CtY, DLC, NHi, PP.

[KENNEDY, Archibald (1685–1763)]. Serious Considerations on the Present State of Affairs of the Northern Colonies. 1754 (*See B 62*)

BIBLIOGRAPHY

Adams, M.J.
1969   System and meaning in East Sumba textile design; A study in tradi-
        tional Indonesian art. New Haven: Yale University.
Arndt, P.
1931   Grammatik der Sika-Sprache. Ende, Flores: Arnoldus.
1932   Mythologie, Religion und Magie im Sikagebiet (ostl. Mittelflores). Ende,
        Flores: Arnoldus.
1933a   Gesellschaftliche Verhältnisse im Sikagebiet (ostl. Mittelflores). Ende,
        Flores: Arnoldus.
1933b   Li'onesisch-Deutsches Wörterbuch. Ende, Flores: Arnoldus.
Barnes, R.H.
1972   'Solorese', in: F.M. LeBar (ed.), Ethnic groups of insular Southeast
        Asia. Vol. 1, pp. 91-4. New Haven: Human Relations Area Files Press.
1974   Kédang; A study of the collective thought of an eastern Indonesian
        people. Oxford: Clarendon.
1977   'Mata in Austronesia', Oceania 47:300-19.
Basílio de Sá, A.
1956   Documentação para a história das missões do padroado português do
        Oriente: Insulíndia. Vol. 4. (1568-1579). Lisboa: Agência Geral do
        Ultramar.
Biro Pusat Statistik
1981   Hasil pencacahan lengkap sensus penduduk 1980. Seri L No. 2, Pendu-
        duk Indonesia 1980 menurut propinsi dan kabupaten/kotamadya. Jakar-
        ta.
Brabander, A. de
1949   'Het oude adat-huwelijk in het Maoemeregebied', Het Missiewerk 28:225-
        36.
Burling, R.
1963   Rengsanggri; Family and kinship in a Garo village. Philadelphia: Uni-
        versity of Pennsylvania Press.
Calon, L.F.
1890-91 'Woordenlijstje van het dialect van Sikka (Midden-Flores)', Tijdschrift
        voor Indische Taal-, Land- en Volkenkunde (TBG) 33:501-30, 34:283-
        363.
1893   'Eenige opmerkingen over het dialect van Sikka', Tijdschrift voor
        Indische Taal-, Land- en Volkenkunde (TBG) 35:129-99.
1895   Bijdrage tot de kennis van het dialekt van Sikka. Batavia: Albrecht
        and Rusche; 's Hage: Nijhoff. [Verhandelingen van het Bataviaasch
        Genootschap van Kunsten en Wetenschappen 50.]
Cunningham, C.E.
1964   'Order in the Atoni house', Bijdragen tot de Taal-, Land- en Volken-
        kunde 120:34-68.
1965   'Order and change in an Atoni diarchy', Southwestern Journal of
        Anthropology 21:359-82.
Dagboek van de Controleurs
1879-80; 1884-85; 1887-1905   Dagboek van de Controleurs, Maoemere. [Trans-
        lated from the Dutch into Indonesian by Mo'ang Pedro Fernandes,
        1943. Unpublished manuscript.]

Example 13

E. Douglas Lewis. *People of the Source: The Social and Ceremonial Order of Tana Wai Brama on Flores.* Dordrecht, Holland; Providence [RI]: Foris Publications, 1988.

This is a fairly common layout of bibliographies published outside the United States. It is alphabetical by author, and then chronological under each author. My complaints are predictable: the dates and the authors' names have the same prominence, since both are flush left. Hence, it is not easy to see subsequent authors. This is intensified by the fact that there are no spaces between entries or between authors. Furthermore, titles, both of books and of periodicals, are printed in the same roman type as the rest of each entry. And the line length is perhaps a bit too long for the small type size.

In all, this is a rather uncongenial bibliography.

Example 14a, b

Ronald Louis Silveira de Braganza, ed. *The Hill Collection of Pacific Voyages.* San Diego, CA: University Library, University of California, 1982. Vol. II. Courtesy Ronald Louis Silveira.

This is a meticulously compiled bibliography, as the notes to each entry show. Authors' names are in full caps, which presents no problem on page 438, but is possibly ambiguous on page 483 where the always problematical *Mc*, *Mac*, and *M'* appear. By using small caps, the compiler has been able to show the lower-case *c*, though there may be some confusion about *Macgillivray*.

Spaces between entries and indentation nicely set off entries and parts of entries from one another. But the smaller type used for the notes, set at the same line length as the rest of the entries, is a little hard to read. And using roman type for titles of books – when italic type was clearly available – makes it difficult to see where the title ends and the publication data begin. This is especially so in the entry for *Hale*, for example.

The thoroughness of the work done here is reflected not only in the notes, but also in the amount of information given, including pages, maps, plates, sizes of books, and so on.

Formosa, Japan, Kamtschatka, Siberia, and the mouth of the Amoor River. By A. W. Habersham . . . Philadelphia, J. B. Lippincott & Co.; London, Trübner & Co., 1858 [c1857]

    507, [4] p. front., plates. 23 cm.

    Added engraved title page has title: My last cruise, or, where we went and what we saw.

    Publisher's advertisements: 4 p. at end.

The author was an American naval officer who later became a tea and coffee merchant. He was descended from a family of early English settlers in Georgia who became prominent rice plantation owners and merchants. This expedition, under the orders of Commander Cadwalader Ringgold, sailed in June of 1853 for the Orient via the Cape of Good Hope and Batavia. The *Vincennes* served as flag-ship to four other vessels. The ships returned, via San Francisco and Cape Horn, to the New York Navy-yard in the summer of 1856. The first edition, with the same pagination, was dated 1857.

HADFIELD, WILLIAM, 1806-1887.   Brazil, the River Plate, and the Falkland Islands; with the Cape Horn route to Australia. Including notices of Lisbon, Madeira, the Canaries, and Cape Verds. By William Hadfield . . . Illustrations by permission, from the South American sketches of Sir W. Gore Ouseley . . . and, by permission, from the drawings of Sir Charles Hotham . . . during his recent mission to Paraguay, of which country much new information is supplied; as also of the region of the Amazon . . . London, Longman, Brown, Green, and Longmans, 1854.

    1 p. *l.*, vi, 384 p. front., illus., port., maps. 23 cm.

Hadfield was for many years a resident of Brazil. He was at times secretary to the South American and General Steam Navigation Company and to the Buenos Aires Great Southern Railway, and was editor of the *South American Journal.* This book also supplies much interesting historical information on Peru and Chile. A survey of the various authorities on South America is added, including Southey, Koster, Humboldt, Dundas, Maury, and several others. The author made return trips to South America in 1868 and from 1870 to 1876; each of these voyages led to its own book, showing the progress there since his last visit.

HAIGH, SAMUEL.   (see *Viajeros en Chile, 1817-1847.*)

HALDE, JEAN BAPTISTE DU.   (see Du Halde, Jean Baptiste.)

HALE, RICHARD LUNT, 1828-1913.   The log of a forty-niner; journal of a voyage from Newbury-port to San Francisco in the brig Genl. Worth, commanded by Capt. Samuel Walton, kept by Richard L. Hale, Newbury, Mass. [Edited by] Carolyn Hale Russ. Boston, Mass., B. J. Brimmer Co., 1923.

    7 p. *l.*, 17-183 p. facsims., plates, 2 ports. (incl. front.) 25 cm.

    "Being the record of adventures by sea and shore to the California gold-fields and the Pacific Northwest, 1849-1854. Illustrated from original sketches by the author. Edited from original manuscripts; now for the first time published."

    Trade edition.

See Volume I for special edition of 1923.

HALES, STEPHEN.   (see *Histoire des tremblemens.*)

The author's survey of China in 1850 with much on Chinese cultural life and the opium trade. The ship visited Rio de Janeiro; the Cape of Good Hope twice; Christmas Island; Macao, Hong Kong, and Canton three times; Manila; Shanghai and Amoy; Formosa; Batavia, Java; and the Mascarene Islands.

McCAULEY, EDWARD YORKE, 1827-1894.   With Perry in Japan; the diary of Edward Yorke McCauley, edited by Allan B. Cole. Princeton, Princeton University Press; London, Humphrey Milford, Oxford University Press [1942]
> 4 p. *l.*, 3-124, [2] p. illus. 24 cm.
> "Illustrations from the original watercolor drawings in McCauley's diary, now in the possession of the New York Historical Society."

McCLATCHY SENIOR HIGH SCHOOL.   (see Sacramento, Calif. C. K. McClatchy Senior High School.)

M'CLINTOCK, Sir FRANCIS LEOPOLD, 1819-1907.   The voyage of the 'Fox' in the Arctic seas. A narrative of the discovery of the fate of Sir John Franklin and his companions. By Captain M'Clintock . . . London, John Murray, 1859.
> xxvii, 403, [1] p. illus., facsim. (fold.), maps (3 fold.), plates (incl. front.) 23 cm.
> First edition.
> Title vignette (port.)
> Publisher's advertisement: 1 p. at end.

M'Clintock had served in the Arctic expeditions in search of Sir John Franklin under Sir James Clark Ross in 1848, and under Captain Henry Kellett and Captain Sir Edward Belcher in 1852. From 1857 to 1859 he led this expedition, financed by Lady Franklin, for the same purpose. In 1859, M'Clintock found the log book, diaries, documents, and relics left by the Franklin expedition in 1848 on King William Island, for which he was knighted in 1860. His book is quite important, and there is an extensive geological account in the appendix. His "Meteorological Observations in the Arctic Seas," was republished in 1859 by the Smithsonian in Washington, D.C. M'Clintock's *Voyage* was well received, and there are also London editions dated 1860 as well as three American editions of that date published in Boston, Philadelphia, and New York.

M'CLUER, JOHN.   (see Hockin, John Pearce.)

McCLURE, Sir ROBERT JOHN LE MESURIER.   (see *Découverte du passage du nord-ouest*; Schmucker, Samuel Mosheim.)

MACDONOUGH CRAVEN, TUNIS AUGUSTUS.   (see Craven, Tunis Augustus Macdonough.)

MACGILLIVRAY, JOHN, 1822-1867.   Narrative of the voyage of H.M.S. Rattlesnake, commanded by the late Captain Owen Stanley . . . during the years 1846-50. Including discoveries and surveys in New Guinea, the Louisiade Archipelago, etc. To which is added Mr. E. B. Kennedy's expedition for the exploration of the Cape York Peninsula. By John Macgillivray . . . London, T. & W. Boone, 1852.
> 2 v. fronts., map, plates. 22 cm.
> "Account of the Polyzoa and sertularian zoophytes, collected in the voyage . . . by George Busk": v. 1, p. 343-402.

14b

REFERENCES

Adamson, A. W., *A Textbook of Physical Chemistry*, Academic Press, New York, 1973.

Appel, B. R. and Y. Tokiwa, "Atomspheric Particulate Nitrate Sampling Errors Due to Reactions with Particulate and Gaseous Strong Acids," *Atoms. Environ.*, **15**, 1087 (1981).

Appel, B. R., S. M. Wall, Y. Tokiwa, and M. Haik, "Interference Effects in Sampling Particulate Nitrate in Ambient Air," *Atmos. Environ.*, **13**, 319 (1979).

Appel, B. R., M., Haik, E. L. Kothny, S. M. Wall, and Y. Tokiwa, "Evaluation of Techniques for Sulfuric Acid and Total Particulate Acidity in Ambient Air," *Atmos. Environ.*, **14**, 559 (1980a).

Appel, B. R., E. L. Kothny, E. M. Hoffer, and J. J. Wesolowski, "Sulfate and Nitrate Data from the California Aerosol Characterization Experiment (ACHEX)," *Adv. Environ. Sci. Technol.*, **10**, 315 (1980b).

Appel, B. R., S. M. Wall, and R. L. Knights, "Characterization of Carbonaceous Materials in Atmospheric Aerosols by High Resolution Mass Spectrometric Thermal Analysis," *Adv. Environ. Sci. Technol.*, **10**, 353 (1980c).

Appel, B. R., E. M. Hoffer, Y. Tokiwa, and E. L. Kothny, "Measurement of Sulfuric Acid and Particulate Strong Acidity in the Los Angeles Basin," *Atmos. Environ.*, **16**, 589 (1982).

Appel, B. R., Y. Tokiwa, and E. L. Kothny, "Sampling of Carbonaceous Particles in the Atmosphere," *Atmos. Environ.*, **17**, 1787 (1983).

Appel, B. R., Y. Tokiwa, M. Haik, and E. L. Kothny, "Artifact Particulate Sulfate, and Nitrate Formation on Filter Media," *Atmos. Environ.*, **18**, 409 (1984).

Appel, B. R., Y. Tokiwa, J. Hsu, E. L. Kothny, and E. Hahn, "Visibility as Related to Atmospheric Aerosol Constituents," *Atmos. Environ.*, **19**, 1525 (1985).

Atchison, J. and J. A. C. Brown, *The Lognormal Distribution*, Cambridge University Press, London, 1957.

Ayer, H.E. and J. M. Hochstrasser, Cyclone Discussion, in *Aerosol Measurement*, D. A. Lundgren, F. S. Harris, Jr., W. H. Marlow, M. Lippmann, W. E. Clark, and M. D. Durham, Eds., University Presses of Florida, Gainesville, FL, 1979, pp. 70–79.

Bassett, M. and J. H. Seinfeld, "Atmospheric Equilibrium Model of Sulfate and Nitrate Aerosols," *Atmos. Environ.*, **17**, 2237 (1983).

Bassett, M. and J. H. Seinfeld, "Atmospheric Equilibrium Model of Sulfate and Nitrate Aerosols—II. Particle Size Analysis," *Atmos. Environ.*, **18**, 1163 (1984).

Bates, D. V., B. R. Fish, T. F. Hatch, T. T. Mercer, and P. E. Morrow, "Deposition and Retention Models for Internal Dosimetry of the Human Respiratory Tract," *Health Physics*, **12**, 173 (1966).

Berglund, R. N. and B. Y. H. Liu, "Generation of Monodisperse Aerosol Standards," *Environ. Sci. Technol.*, **7**, 147 (1973).

Biggins, P. D. E. and R. M. Harrison, "Chemical Speciation of Lead Compounds in Street Dusts," *Environ. Sci. Technol.*, **14**, 336 (1980).

Blanchard, D. C. and A. H. Woodcock, "The Production, Concentration, and Vertical Distribution of the Sea-Salt Aerosol," *Ann. N.Y. Acad. Sci.*, **338**, 330 (1980).

Bohren, C. F. and D. R. Huffman, *Absorption and Scattering by Small Particles*, Wiley, New York, 1983.

Brosset, C., K. Andreasson, and M. Ferm, "The Nature and Possible Origin of Acid Particles Observed at the Swedish West Coast," *Atmos. Environ.*, **9**, 631 (1975).

Cadle, R. D., *The Measurement of Airborne Particles*, Wiley, New York, 1975.

Cadle, R. D. and R. C. Robbins, "Kinetics of Atmospheric Chemical Reactions Involving Aerosols," *Disc. Faraday Soc.*, **30**, 155 (1960).

Cadle, S. H., P. J. Groblicki, and P.A. Mulawa, "Problems in the Sampling and Analysis of Carbon Particulate," *Atmos. Environ.*, **17**, 593 (1983).

15

Example 15

Barbara J. Finlayson-Pitts and James N. Pitts, Jr. *Atmospheric Chemistry: Fundamentals and Experimental Techniques.* New York: John Wiley & Sons, 1986.

There is nothing to criticize about this bibliography. It is well laid out; it uses type large and clear enough for the line measure; and its data are organized simply and logically. The use of boldface type for journal volume numbers is probably unnecessary, but it is unobtrusive and perfectly readable. With only roman and italic type (as well as limited use of boldface), and with a simple spatial coding, this is a model of clarity. Sometimes less is better.

Example 16a, b

Lawrence Lande, ed. *The Lawrence Lande Collection of Canadiana in the Redpath Library of McGill University: A Bibliography.* Montreal: The Lawrence Lande Foundation for Canadian Historical Research, 1965. (Courtesy Lawrence Lande.)

This large-format volume, printed on good paper, exhibits much attention to fine points. Each entry is separated from others by a generous space, and is further distinguished by the use of the entry number at the left margin and the large type used for the filing entries. Since the names are in such large type, it was not necessary to use full caps; hence, there is no problem with *Mc* and *Mac*.

Titles are printed in small caps, probably an unnecessary feature since regular roman upper- and lower-case type would stand out clearly under the large type above and the space and italics below.

With such a large format, it was sensible to use a two-column layout.

Some of the entries are quite brief. The longer ones, such as number 1966, use a line break rather than indentation to indicate new paragraphs. This is a good idea, since the prose is densely packed in the column, and the spaces between paragraphs continue the theme of sumptuousness in the book. This bibliography is well designed and quite accessible.

1322 McLean, John 1799-1890

NOTES OF A TWENTY-FIVE YEARS' SERVICE IN THE HUDSON'S BAY TERRITORY. *London, Richard Bently, 1849.*

2 v.: xii, [13]-308 p.; [viii], [9]-328 p. • 8vo • half-leather • One of the chief designs of the writer was to draw a faithful picture of the Indian trader's life with its toils, annoyances, privations, and perils, when on actual service or in a trading or exploring expedition. Most of the work is devoted to the narration of incidents of travel among the Indians of the territory, descriptions of their life, habits and character, and of their relationship with the Hudson's Bay Company.

PEEL 107; SMITH 6418; TPL 2729.

1323 McLean, William John 1841-1929

NOTES AND OBSERVATIONS OF TRAVELS ON THE ATHABASCA AND SLAVE LAKE REGIONS IN 1899. *Winnipeg, Manitoba Free Press Co., 1901.*

7 p. • 8vo • cover title • Historical and Scientific Society of Manitoba, transaction no. 58.

PEEL 1137.

1324 McLeod, Malcolm 1821-1899

PACIFIC RAILWAY ROUTES, CANADA. BY M. MCLEOD, "BRITANNICUS". A SERIES OF LETTERS PUBLISHED IN THE MONTREAL "GAZETTE". *[n.p., 1874?]*

21 p. • 8vo • stitched as issued • With the following notation by Charles Horetsky: "This pamphlet was sent to me by a friend, the notes in margin are not mine. C.H."

CAN. ARCH. I 3928.

1325 McLeod, Malcolm

PACIFIC RAILWAY, CANADA; SELECTION FROM SERIES OF LETTERS BY "BRITANNICUS", (FROM 1869-1875), ON THE SUBJECT; WITH ADDITIONAL REMARKS. *[Ottawa, 1875].*

36 p. • 8vo • printed in two columns.

CF. PEEL 328.

1326 McLeod, Malcolm

MEMORIAL TO THE GOVERNMENT AND PARLIAMENT OF CANADA OF MALCOLM MACLEOD, Q.C., &C., FOR INDEMNITY FOR SERVICE IN INITIATING THE CANADIAN PACIFIC RAILWAY, &C., &C. *Ottawa, printed by A. S. Woodburn, 1889.*

24 p. • 8vo • orig. printed wrappers • Pres. copy by McLeod to Henry J. Morgan with many annotations and corrections in his hand.

PEEL 820.

1327 McLeod, Malcolm

OREGON INDEMNITY; CLAIM OF CHIEF FACTORS AND CHIEF TRADERS OF THE HUDSON'S BAY COMPANY THERETO AS PARTNERS UNDER TREATY OF 1846. *[Ottawa], 1892.*

63 p. • 8vo • orig. printed wrappers • Author's copy, with his marginal notes and corrections.

CF. SMITH 6426.

1328 McMicken, Gilbert 1813-1891

THE ABORTIVE FENIAN RAID ON MANITOBA. ACCOUNT BY ONE WHO KNEW ITS SECRET HISTORY. *Winnipeg, Manitoba Free Press print, 1888.*

11 p. • 8vo • cover title • Historical and Scientific Society of Manitoba, transaction no. 32.

PEEL 778.

1329 McMicken, Gilbert

THE ABORTIVE FENIAN RAID ON MANITOBA. ACCOUNT BY ONE WHO KNEW ITS SECRET HISTORY. WITH OPEN CORRESPONDENCE ARISING OUT OF THE SAME BETWEEN HIS GRACE THE ARCHBISHOP OF ST. BONIFACE AND MR. MCMICKEN. *Winnipeg, The Call Printing Co., 1888.*

35 p. • 8vo • cover title • Historical and Scientific Society of Manitoba, transaction no. 32.

CF. PEEL 778.

1330 McMillan, Donald 1835-1914

LETTERS AND EXTRACTS ON THE RIEL QUESTION, WITH NOTES. *Alexandria, printed at the office of The Glengarian, 1887.*

[1] l., [3]-27 p. • 8vo • green printed wrappers • signed, "Advance copy."

CAN. ARCH. II 1094; PEEL 744.

1331 Main Street Views, Winnipeg

MAIN STREET VIEWS, WINNIPEG MANITOBA. *Winnipeg, published and for sale by Clarence E. Steele, 1892.*

Long fold. ill. • 12 ft. • 12mo • purple and gold buckram.

1332 Mair, Charles 1838-1927

THROUGH THE MACKENZIE BASIN; A NARRATIVE OF THE ATHABASCA AND PEACE RIVER TREATY EXPEDITION OF 1899 .... ALSO NOTES ON THE MAMMALS AND BIRDS OF NORTHERN CANADA, BY RODERICK MACFARLANE. *Toronto, William Briggs, 1908.*

149 p., 1 l., 151-494 p. • front., ports., fold. map, plates • 8vo.

PEEL 1308.

Condition of the United Kingdom (Halifax, 1851); *The Strong Drink Delusion* (Halifax, 1855); *On the Moral Condition of British Society* (Liverpool, 1857); *Errors Reviewed and Fallacies Exposed* (Halifax, 1859); *Sermons* (Halifax, 1862); *Answers to "Essays and Reviews"* (Halifax, 1862); *A Full Review and Exposure of Bishop Colenso's Errors* (London, 1863); *A Full Review of Bishop Colenso's Profane Fictions and Fallacies* (London, 1864); *An Examination of the Proposed Union of the North American Provinces* (Halifax, 1865); *Fictions and Errors* (Halifax, 1877); *Reflections During a Visit to my Native Place* (Halifax, 1881); and A Brief *History of Public Proceedings and Events, Legal, Parliamentary and Miscellaneous, in the Province of Nova Scotia during the Earliest Years of the Present Century* (Halifax, 1879). Under the nom de plume of "A Nova Scotian," he published *Remarks Upon the Proposed Federation of the Provinces* (Halifax, 1864) and *Confederation Considered on its Merits* (Halifax, 1867).

Reflections During a Visit to my Native Place appeared in the form of these three newspaper extracts placed within the covers of a manuscript book of the same material in Judge Marshall's own hand. His own title was completed by the phrase, *Being the First Part of an Essay chiefly designed to exhibit and explain the true causes of the Principal Portion of Human Suffering.* On the first clipping is noted, in what appears to be the author's hand, "written in youth"; we can conclude that the poem was probably written sometime before 1808 — the time Marshall was admitted to the Bar. (The paper on which the original was written is watermarked 1798.)

Reflections is probably one of the very few poems Marshall ever wrote, if not the only poem. "Written in youth," he seems to have followed it like a star throughout his life.

> "Here springs the thought, why do we ever view,
> All with such zeal, Earth's busy days pursue.
> What high design calls forth those toils and cares,
> Those swift vicissitudes of hopes and fears,
> Which agitate and pain the human breast,
> And keep it evermore devoid of rest;
> Which through all ranks of life are felt and known,
> From the rude cottage, to the splendid throne . . . ."

1967 Marshall, John George

REFLECTIONS DURING A VISIT TO MY NATIVE PLACE. *Halifax, N.S., printed at Wesleyan Office, 1881.*

22 p. • 12mo • philosophical poem • photographic facs., with original MS [Halifax, c. 1808].

1968 Martin, Benjamin

MISCELLANEOUS CORRESPONDENCE, CONTAINING A VARIETY OF SUBJECTS, RELATIVE TO NATURAL AND CIVIL HISTORY, GEOGRAPHY, MATHEMATICS, POETRY, MEMOIRS OF MONTHLY OCCURRENCES, CATALOGUES OF NEW BOOKS, &C. VOL. 3. *London, printed & sold by W. Owen, and by the author, 1764.*

v. 3. plates (part. fold.). • contemp. calf. • 20.2 x 12.5 cm. • front. of a Mohawk Warrior; plan of City of Quebec, p. 73. From Jan. 1759 to Dec. 1760. Items of Canadian interest appear on the following pages: 10, 107, 161, 212, 234, 255, 260, 277, 278,

284, 299, 310, 315, 321, 336, 481, 505, 525, 526, 556, 566, 581, e.g. "Plantation News" section in many issues; "Quebec; An hero-elegiac poem on the conquest of that place, and the death of General Wolfe (p. 310); "Extract of a letter from an officer in Colonel Fraser's regiment, Quebec, May 20," p. 480-1; news of the surrender of the French Army in Canada, p. 566-7.

1969 Maude, John

VISIT TO THE FALLS OF NIAGARA, IN 1800. *London, Longman, Rees, Orme, Brown & Green, Wakefield, Richard Nichols, 1826.*

viii p, 1 l., v, 313, xxvi, 16 p. • 8vo • orig. boards • L. P. • Printer's label on spine reads: Visit to Niagara, — 1/11/6 • Only 250 copies printed.

TPL 744.

1970 Maw, H. Lister

STATEMENTS BY H. LISTER MAW. IN REPLY TO A LETTER FROM CAPTAIN JAMES SCOTT, OF H. M. SHIP, PRESIDENT, PUBLISHED IN THE UNITED SERVICE JOURNAL, FOR APRIL, 1835. *London, published by Smith, Elder and Co., Cornhill, 1835.*

32 p. • 8vo • stitched, unbound.

1971 Mayhew, Jonathan 1720-1766

TWO DISCOURSES DELIVERED NOVEMBER 23RD, 1758. BEING THE DAY APPOINTED BY AUTHORITY TO BE OBSERVED AS A DAY OF PUBLIC THANKSGIVING: RELATING MORE ESPECIALLY TO THE SUCCESS OF HIS MAJESTY'S ARMS AND THOSE OF THE KING OF PRUSSIA, THE LAST YEAR. *Boston, N.E., R. Draper, [1758].*

1 l., [5]-57 p. • 8vo • marbled wrappers.

EVANS III 8192; SABIN 47149.

1972 Mayne, Daniel Haydn

POEMS AND FRAGMENTS. *Toronto, printed by W. J. Coats, 1838.*

vii, [9]-126 p. • 12mo • orig. boards.

TPL 2185.

1973 Medical Conference on Cholera. Ottawa 1866

MEMORANDUM ON CHOLERA, ADOPTED AT A MEDICAL CONFERENCE HELD IN THE BUREAU OF AGRICULTURE, IN MARCH, 1866. PRINTED BY AUTHORITY. *[Ottawa], printed for the Bureau of Agriculture and Statistics, 1866.*

34 p. • 12mo • orig. wrappers.

CAN. ARCH. I 3384; CF. TPL 4521.

Example 17

The Ulysses Sumner Milburn Collection of Hawthorniana.
Canton, NY: St Lawrence University, Special Collections,
1989. Courtesy Richard J. Kuhta, St Lawrence University.

Many exhibition catalogues are little more than
bibliographies. As this volume is an author list – that
is, every item in it is by the same author – there was
obviously no need to give the author's name for each
entry. So titles are the filing elements, and they are
listed in alphabetical order.

The simple features of a blank line and italics are used
to flag new items. With the italicized title flush left, the
publication information can also be flush left and not
be confused, since it is printed in roman type. And all
notes are printed with hanging indents, so there is
never any confusion among the different data fields.
This is a simple design, and for the most part is quite
effective in laying out information and distinguishing
the parts of entries.

My only quibble is that the letters and numbers at the
right margin, which apparently are designed to indicate
the placement of the items in the collection, seem to
float by themselves in many instances. In some cases it
is difficult to see which entries these finding aids go
with. This is especially true of *A 22.1*, under
Tanglewood Tales, for Girls and Boys (London:
Chapman and Hall, 1853). Since the last line of the
previous entry ends near the right margin, it looks as if
A 22.1 were attached to this previous entry rather than
to the correct one. Perhaps either using leader dots to
link the numbers with the line they are in, or moving
these numbers closer in the line to the end of their own
entries and enclosing them in square brackets would
have been better. The brackets would be a typographic
coding element that would be quite easy to spot,
allowing the numbers to link up more discernibly.
(Also, the *A 5.2* of the first line of this page is so far
removed from the title to which it belongs that the
number looks like a page number.)

Otherwise, this is an attractive, serviceable, and simple
layout that has a high legibility and good accessibility
of information.

Example 18

Robert Greenwood, ed. *California Imprints, 1833–1862: A
Bibliography.* Los Gatos, CA: Talisman Press, 1961. Courtesy
Robert Greenwood for Talisman Press.

This is another of those bibliographies which are quite
useful but not 'perfectly' designed. The entries begin
after a blank line, but similar blank lines appear within
some entries, such as entries 877 and 878 on page 271.
The numbers for the entries are in the same typeface as
the rest of the printing in that information field;
therefore, it is not easy to spot these numbers.

Authors' names or other filing elements for anonymous
pieces are given on separate lines, but, again, if the line
is long, it is lost in the rest of the entry since there is no
typographical coding except for the small type in the
lines which describe each item. The use of only roman
type throughout truly impedes one's reading. It is clear
that italic type was available (see the bottom of page
270, in which *The Settler's Guide* is printed in italics).
And since all new data fields are printed flush left along
with all the other lines of the entries, finding the
different fields is difficult.

It is a shame that the design of such a useful book was
not thought out better.

The Sister Years   A 5.2
Salem, MA: Salem Gazette and Essex County Mercury, January 1, 1892.
> Second edition. Includes an unsigned introduction by a latter-day carrier boy.

The Snow-Image, and Other Twice Told Tales   A 19.1.a
Boston: Ticknor, Reed, and Fields, 1852.
2 copies.
> First edition; first printing. Binding: brown bold-ribbed T cloth with blindstamped floral device inside ruled panels on both covers. Spine goldstamped. Pale yellow wove endpapers. Flyleaf inserted at front and rear. Bottom edge untrimmed.

The Snow-Image and Other Tales   A 19.2.a
London: Henry G. Bohn, 1851.
> Printing from the Bohn edition plates. First English edition; first printing. Issued in rose linen-like T cloth with broad blindstamped border panel. "Although the first printing of the first American edition bears a title-page date of 1852 and the first printing of the first English edition has an 1851 title-page date, they were intended for simultaneous publication and both editions appeared in December 1851. American publication probably preceded by several days." . . . Clark.

The Snow-Image; A Childish Miracle   A 19.4
New York: James G. Gregory, 1864.
> First separate and first illustrated edition. Prints title story only. Color illustrations by Marcus Waterman.

Tanglewood Tales, for Girls and Boys   A 22.2.a
Boston: Ticknor, Reed, and Fields, 1853.
> First American edition; first printing. Binding: purplish blue bold-ribbed T cloth. Blindstamped covers and plain edges. Spine goldstamped with title and author's name. Pale yellow wove endpapers. White wove flyleaf inserted front and rear.

Tanglewood Tales, for Girls and Boys   A 22.1
London: Chapman and Hall, 1853.
2 copies.
> First English edition; only printing. Includes "The Wayside-Introductory," "The Minotaur," "The Pygmies," "The Dragon's Teeth," "Circe's Palace," "The Pomegranate Seeds," and "The Golden Fleece." Binding: green herringbone-patterned cloth. Covers blindstamped with decorative lattice-framed window-like panel with central floral element, all inside single-edge rule. Spine goldstamped. White wove endpapers coated pale yellow one side. Top edge untrimmed. Bound by Bone & Son, 76 Fleet Street, London.

Tanglewood Tales   A 22.28
London: Hodder and Stoughton, 1938.
> Limited edition. Deluxe format illustrated and signed by Edmund Dulac. Our copy is number 490 of 500.

Transformation   A23.1.a
London: Smith, Elder and Co., 1860.
> First English edition; first printing. English editions have the title "Transformation; or, The Romance of Monte Beni," and all American editions have the title "The Marble Faun; or, The Romance of Monte Beni." Binding: red wavy-grain TR cloth. Covers

◆◆◆

[San Francisco: Excelsior print., 1857.]
Broadside. 27.6 cm. Illustration.
CSmH.

San Jose, California. College of Notre Dame. Prospectus and Distribution of Premiums, 1857. [Not located.]

872. Santa Clara College. Santa Clara, California.
Programme of exercises at Santa Clara College, at the sixth annual commencement. July 8th, 1857. San Francisco: O'Meara & Painter, print., [1857].
12p. 18 cm.
CHi.

873. Santa Clara College. Santa Clara, California.
Prospectus of Santa Clara College, with a catalogue of the officers and students, for the year 1856-1857. Also the exercises of the sixth annual commencement, and the distribution of premiums. San Francisco: O'Meara & Painter, printers, 1857.
Cover-title, 36p. 16 cm.
C; CStclU; CU-B; DLC; MH; MoSU; Nh.

874. Scott, William Anderson.
The pavilion palace of industry. [The Mechanics' Industrial Exhibition; or, the useful arts exponent of the nature, progress and hope of Christian civilization: a discourse delivered in Calvary Church . . . August 23, 1857.] By Rev. Dr. Scott, of San Francisco. San Francisco: Hutchings & Rosenfield, publishers, Whitton, Towne & Co., printers, 1857.
24p. 21 cm.
Description of the first industrial exhibition of the Mechanics' Institute.
Cowan 1933, p.574.
C; CLU; CSansS; CSfCW; CSmH; CU-B; NN; WHi.

875. Settlers and Miners Central Committee.
To the settlers and miners of the State of California . . . San Francisco: Commercial steam press, 1857.
Broadside. 48 cm.
CSmH.

The Settler's Guide. See no. 826.

876. Sierra Nevada Lake Water and Mining Company.
By-laws . . . Incorporated August 24th, 1854. San Francisco: Printed by B. F. Sterett, 1857.

Cover-title, 9p. 23 cm.
CU-B.

877. Simmons, Gustavus L., M. D.
Case of complex labor with remarks, etc., reported by Gustavus L. Simmons, M. D. [Etc.] Sacramento: Crocker & Edwards, Book and Job printers, Second street, between K and L, 1857.
33p. 22.5 cm.
CSt-L; MH-M; NNNAM.

Simmons, I. C. *Catechism for Sunday Schools.* See
  Appendix A, item 132.

878. Society of California Pioneers. San Francisco.
Oration delivered before the Society of California Pioneers at their celebration of the seventh anniversary of the admission of the State of California into the Union, by Hon. T. W. Freelon. Ode by Edward Pollock. San Francisco: September 9th, 1857. San Francisco: Printed by Charles F. Robbins, 1857.
1, 1, 24p. 21 cm.
Cowan 1933, p.595.
C; CHi; CL; CSfCP; CSf; CSfCW; CSfLaw; CSmH; CU-B; MB; MH; NN; RPB; WHi.

Sons of Temperance. California. Grand Division. Proceedings, 1857. [Not located.]

879. Speer, William.
An answer to the common objectives to Chinese testimony, and an earnest appeal to the Legislature of California for their protection by our law. By Rev. William Speer. San Francisco: Published at the Chinese Mission House, Printed by B. F. Sterett, 1857.
Cover-title, 16p. 23 cm. Text printed in double columns.
Cowan 1933, p.604.
CHi; CU-B; MB; PHi.

880. Stanly, Edward.
Speech of the Hon. Edward Stanly, delivered at Sacramento, July 17th, 1857, at a public meeting held in the Forrest theatre. [Sacramento, 1857.]
Caption-title, 16p. 22 cm.
Cowan 1933, p.608.
CtY; CU-B.

session, 1838. Hartford? 1839?] 7 p. CtY. 55119

----. ----. Joint Select Committee on Judiciary Expenses. Report of the committee appointed by the General Assembly, May session, 1838, on judicial expenses, to the General Assembly, May session, 1839. Hartford: Courant office, 1839. 48 p. Ct; CtSoP; CtY. 55120

----. Governor [William W. Ellsworth] Speech of His Excellency, William W. Ellsworth, governor of Connecticut, to the legislature of the state, May, 1839.... Hartford: Courant office press, 1839. 16 p. O. Ct. 55121

----. Laws, Statutes, etc. Public acts of the state of Connecticut, passed May session, 1839. Published agreeably, under the superintendence of the secretary of said state. State of Connecticut, SS: Office of the secretary of said state, June, 1839. Hartford: printed at the Courant office, 1839. 62, 136 p. Ar-SC; IaU-L; Nv; T; Wa-L. 55122

----. ----. The public statute laws of the state of Connecticut...to which is added the Declaration of Independence, Constitution of the U.S. and Constitution of the state of Connecticut.... Hartford: J. L. Boswell, 1839. 717 p. CtB; Ia; MiGr; NNLI; PU; WaU. 55123

----. ----. Resolves and private acts of the state of Connecticut, passed May session, 1839. Published agreeably to a resolve of the General Assembly, and prepared by and under the superintendence of the secretary of state. State of Connecticut, SS: office of the secretary of said state, June, 1839. Hartford: printed at the Courant office, 1839. 136 p. Ar-SC; IaU-L; Nj; T; Wa-L. 55124

----. Secretary of State. Report of the Secretary of the State relative to certain branches of industry. May session, 1839.... Hartford: 1839. 38 p. Ct; CtY; MH-BA. 55125

Connecticut almanac for 1840. Astronomical calculations by J. H. Gallup. Norwich City, Conn.: M. B. Young [1839] CtNwchA; DLC; MWA. 55126

The Connecticut annual register, and United States calendar, for 1839, to which is prefixed an almanack...No. 49. Published by Samuel Green, Durrie and Peck, and Canfield and Robins, 1839. 174 p. Ct. 55127

Connecticut College. Academical institution at New London. Catalogue, 1838-1840. D. Concord: 1838-1840. Nh-Hi. 55128

Connecticut Historical Society. The charter of incorporation and by-laws of the Connecticut Historical Society, together with a list of the officers, and an address to the public. Hartford: n. pub., Case, Tiffany and Company, printers, 1839. 11 p. CtSoP; MH; MWA; PHi; RPB. 55129

The Connecticut register: being a state calendar of public officers and institutions for 1839 [Hartford: S. Green, etc., 1839-[1868] 4 v. MnU. 55130

Consecrated life and guide to holiness? V. 1-75. July, 1839-Dec., 1901. Boston and New York, Philadelphia: 1839-1901. DLC; IEG; OCl. 55131

Considerations in regard to the application of the Shakers, for certain special privileges [Albany: 1839] 8 p. NN; OClWHi; WHi. 55132

Convention, dritte, der deutschen Burger der Vereinigten Staaten; gehalten zu Philippsburg im Bibergau, P.a. vom. 1. bis 8. Aug. 1839. Philadelphia: J. G. Wesselhoeft, 1839. pamph. PPG. 55133

Convention of American Women. Address from the Convention of American Women, to the Society of Friends, on the subject of slavery. Philadelphia: 1839. 10 p. MB; PHi. 55134

Convention of Civil Engineers, Baltimore, 1839. Address of the committee appointed at the Convention of Civil Engineers, which met in Baltimore, Maryland, February 11, 1839. Philadelphia: printed by Merrihew and Thompson, 1839. 8 p. CSmH; MB; PHi. 55135

Convention of Merchants and others, Charleston, 1839. Proceedings of the 4th Convention of Merchants, and others, held in Charleston, S.C., April 15, 1839, for the promotion of the direct trade. Charleston: A. E. Miller, printer, 1839. 64 p. DLC; GU; MH; PHi; ScU. 55136

Convention of Reformed Churches. Proceedings of the Convention of Reformed Churches, Session II. Philadelphia, September, 1839. Extracted from the minutes. New York: Craighead and Allen, printers, 1839. 15 p. NcMHi. 55137

Conversations on nature and art.... Philadelphia:

19a

----. Tourist pocket map of the state of Ohio, exhibiting its internal improvements, roads, distances, by J. H. Young. Philadelphia: Mitchell, 1839. IGK. 57329

----. Mitchell's travellers's guide through the United States...stage, steamboat, canal, and railroad routes.... Philadelphia: Thomas, Cowperthwait and Company, 1839. 78 p. Ct; IJI; KHi; MnHi; PHi. 57330

Mitchell, Thomas Duche, 1791-1865. Annual address to the College of Physicians and Surgeons of Lexington; in which the principals and practice of medical ethics are illustrated...delivered in the medical hall, January 1, 1839. Lexington: Noble and Dunlop, 1839. 32 p. DNLM; KyU; NNNAM. 57331

----. The pains and pleasures of a medical life; being an introductory to a course of lectures on materia medica and therapeutics. Lexington, Ky.: the medical class, James Virden, printer, 1839. 23 p. CSmH; DLC; KyLxT; KyU; OC. 57332

Moffat, William B. The medical manual; containing information concerning the most prevalent diseases and most approved remedies. New York: 1839. 64 p. DLC; MBAt; NcU. 57333

Mogridge, George, 1787-1854. The juvenile moralists. New York: C. Wells, 1839. 80 p. MH; MHi. 57334

Mohawk and Hudson Railroad Company. Report of the superintendent to the president and directors of the Mohawk and Hudson Railroad Company.... Albany: printed by Packard, Van Benthuysen and Company, 1839. 17 p. NNE. 57335

Money and banking, or their nature and effects considered. See Beck, William.

Monfort, David. Reply to the views of A. R. Hinkley of sermons on Christian Baptism, Indianapolis, 1830. Two sermons on Christian baptism, Cincinnati: 1839. OCHP. 57336

----. Two sermons on Christian baptism, delivered in Franklin, Indiana, July 1838. Cincinnati: 1839. 48 p. OC; OCHP. 57337

Monkland, Mrs. Elvira, the nabor's wife. By Mrs Monkland. Philadelphia: Lea and Blanchard, 1839. 2 v. MBAt; NN; PReaAT. 57338

Monson Academy, Monson, Massachusetts. Catalogue of the trustees, instructors, and students of Monson Academy, for the year ending August 6, 1839. Springfield: Merriam, Wood and Company, printers, 1839. 12 p. MB; MH; MMons-A. 57339

Montgomery, George Washington, 1804-1841. Narrative of a journey to Guatemala, in Central America, in 1838. New York: Wiley and Putnam, 1839. 195 p. CLU; MdBP; PPA; RPB; TxU. 57340

Montgomery, George Washington, 1810-1898. An essay on the law of kindness. Utica: printed by Grosh and Hutchinson, 1839. 27 p. MMeT. 57341

Montgomery, James, 1771-1854. Lectures on general literature, poetry, etc., delivered at the royal Institution in 1830 and 1831. New York: Harper and Brothers, 1839. 324 p. AMoJ; IEG; MoSpD; OAU; RNR. 57342

Montgomery, William Fetherston, 1797-1859. An exposition of the signs and symptoms of pregnancy, the period of human gestation and the signs of delivery. Philadelphia: A. Waldie, 1839. 220 p. CoCsE; KyU; MB; PU; ViU. 57343

The monthly chronicle of interesting and useful knowledge, embracing education, internal improvements, and the arts. With notices of general literature and passing events. Edited by Edward D. Mansfield. Cincinnati: A. Pugh, 1839. 568 p. MiD-W; DLC; FMU; KyU; OClWHi. 57344

The monthly law reporter. Boston: Weeks, Jordan and Company, 1839-[1866] 27 v. Ar-SC; CU; MB; NjP; OClW. 57345

The monthly miscellany of religion and letters. Boston: W. Crosby and Company, 1839-1843. 9 v. DLC; IU; MB; NIC; OOxM. 57346

Moore, Ely, 1798-1861. Remarks in the House, February 4, 1839, on presenting a remonstrance from citizens of the District of Columbia agianst the reception of abolition petitions, etc. [Washington: 1839] 16 p. MdHi; NjR; OClWHi; TNF; WHi. 57347

Moore, Jacob Bailey, 1797-1853. Biographical notice of John Farmer, late corresponding secretary of the New Hampshire Historical

Example 19a, b

Carol Rinderknecht, compiler. *A Checklist of American Imprints for 1839*. Metuchen, NJ, and London: Scarecrow Press, 1988. Courtesy Scarecrow Press.

Following the pattern set for all of the previous volumes of this series, the designer has used a two-column format, necessary because of the small type size chosen. And the relatively small page size had to conform to the size of the other volumes. The use of a dash (four hyphens) to indicate 'same author as above' also follows the pattern of previous volumes. But it is irksome to identify that author when the dash comes as the first entry on the page, since the running head indicates the first new name on the page – or does it? One must turn back to find out.

These volumes are heavily used by librarians and book dealers who are trying to identify particular nineteenth-century imprints. And the standard method of citation is something like *AI 55127* (meaning *American Imprints*, entry number 55127). That is, the item number is often used as a finding aid in catalogues. In separate quotations from booksellers, many dealers give only the imprint number, often omitting the title and author altogether.

For this reason the number should be more prominent than it is in this volume. In previous volumes the entry number was given flush right in the entry, regardless of where the last word on the line was. In this bibliography precious extra time is spent searching for items by number. I have used these volumes for years, and when this one was issued, I and other readers I queried about it had the same complaint.

The small difference in line placement of the number shows the same kind of carelessness as can be seen in the occurrence of widows and orphans, both of which appear on page 67. Also, titles are in the very same type as the rest of the entry, so one must look carefully to see where a name ends and a title begins, and where a title ends and publication data begin. The little boxes of information for each item contain no spatial or typographic coding.

While this book contains mountains of valuable information, it is a shame that it has been so carelessly presented on the page.

Example 20a, b, c

Jacob Blanck, compiler. *Bibliography of American Literature*. New Haven, CT, and London: Yale University Press, for the Bibliographical Society of America, Vol. 8, 1990. By permission of the Bibliographical Society of America.

This set of volumes is one of the monuments of scholarship. It is relied on by scholars, librarians, collectors, dealers, and others to such an extent that the citation of *BAL* holds great weight. And it contains such a wealth of information that one might feel abashed at criticizing it. But my criticism has to do with its form, not its content.

In volume 8, page 64 exhibits what I feel is the work's greatest problem: it does not distinguish clearly between entries. This particular section, showing the legal publications of William Wetmore Story, lists entries with the main bibliographic data flush left and all subsequent data indented 1 em and flush left to this 1-em indentation. The same amount of space is used to separate data fields in each entry as is given between entries. It takes especial concentration to use this page.

Page 106 presents other problems. All titles are printed in full caps. Someone wanting to know the styling in the original would be at a loss. Also, entry numbers are flush left, but so is all text after the title and publication data fields. Therefore entry numbers, while at a margin over the hanging indents, are still not immediately apparent, especially since other numbers appear at left margins (as with '<1-50>[4]' in the first column). And, as is the case throughout this set, entries and subparts of entries are separated from one another with the same amount of spacing. So finding entry numbers (i.e., the beginnings of entries) is not simple. Perhaps spatial coding could have been adjusted, or boldface or italic type could have been used.

Page 190 displays problems similar to those of page 64. The final criticism I have of these otherwise excellent volumes is that there is no index to the contents, either for author or for title. An index would be especially helpful for works published anonymously or under pen names. (A discussion I had with the current editor, Michael Winship, indicates that at present no index is planned.)

with Introduction and Notes by Gertrude Reese Hudson

Barnes and Noble   New York   ⟨1965⟩

"Letter from William Wetmore Story to Robert W. Barrett Browning (Pen)," pp. ⟨195⟩-198. "Letters Exchanged by James Russell Lowell and the Storys," pp. ⟨199⟩-347. "Poem to James Russell Lowell," pp. 366-367; uncollected.

A copy at H received June 18, 1965.

B Y H

LEGAL PUBLICATIONS

The following list contains a selection of the publications of a legal nature written or edited by Story.

Reports of Cases Argued and Determined in the Circuit Court of the United States for the First Circuit . . . Volume I.   ⟨II.⟩   ⟨III.⟩

Boston: Charles C. Little and James Brown. 1842.   ⟨1845.⟩   ⟨1847.⟩

Edited by W. W. Story.

Vol. 1 listed in NAR Oct., 1842. A new edition of Vol. 1 has title-page imprint dated 1851.

A Treatise on the Law of Contracts Not under Seal . . .

Boston: Charles C. Little and James Brown. MDCCCXLIV.

For later editions see below under 1847, 1851 and 1856.

Announced in USDR Feb., 1844. Deposited Aug. 19, 1844. London (Maxwell) edition listed in PC March 1, 1845.

Report of the Case of Washburn, et al. vs. Gould, Heard before Mr. Justice Story, in the Circuit Court of the United States for the District of Massachusetts.   At Boston, May Term, 1844 . . .

Boston: Printed by Freeman and Bolles.   1844.

Cover-title.   Printed self-wrapper.   Edited by W. W. Story.

Commentaries on Equity Jurisprudence . . . by Joseph Story . . . Fourth Edition, Revised, Corrected, and Enlarged.   In Two Volumes . . .

Boston: Charles C. Little & James Brown. London: A. Maxwell & Son, 32 Bell Yard, Lincoln's Inn, Law Booksellers to His Late Majesty; T. Clark, Edinburgh; Hodges & Smith, Dublin.   M DCCC XLVI.

Edited by W. W. Story.

Deposited May 19, 1846.

Commentaries on the Law of Bailments . . . by Joseph Story . . . Fourth Edition.   Revised, Corrected, and Enlarged.

Boston: Charles C. Little and James Brown. London: A. Maxwell and Son, 32 Bell Yard, Lincoln's Inn, Law Booksellers to His Late Majesty.   M DCCC XLVI.

Edited by W. W. Story.

Deposited May 19, 1846.

Commentaries on the Conflict of Laws . . . by Joseph Story . . . Third Edition.   Revised, Corrected, and Greatly Enlarged.

Boston: Charles C. Little and James Brown. London: A. Maxwell and Son, 32 Bell Yard, Lincoln's Inn.   M DCCC XLVI.

Edited by W. W. Story.

Deposited July 21, 1846.

Commentaries on the Law of Agency . . . by Joseph Story . . . Third Edition . . .

Boston: Charles C. Little and James Brown. London: V. and R. Stevens and G. S. Norton, 26 Bell Yard, Lincoln's Inn.   M DCCC XLVI.

Edited by W. W. Story.

A Treatise on the Law of Sales of Personal Property, with Illustrations from the Foreign Law . . .

Boston: Charles C. Little and James Brown. London: V. and R. Stevens and G. S. Norton, 26 Bell Yard, Lincoln's Inn.   M DCCC XLVII.

For 2nd edition see below under 1853.

Deposited March 10, 1847.

A Treatise on the Law of Contracts Not Under Seal . . . Second Edition, Revised and Greatly Enlarged.

Boston: Charles C. Little and James Brown. MDCCCXLVII.

Deposited Oct. 18, 1847.

20a

19480. WOMAN IN SACRED HISTORY
A SERIES OF SKETCHES DRAWN
FROM SCRIPTURAL, HISTORICAL,
AND LEGENDARY SOURCES . . .
ILLUSTRATED WITH TWENTY-FIVE
CHROMO-LITHOGRAPHS, AFTER
PAINTINGS BY RAPHAEL, BATONI,
HORACE VERNET, GOODALL,
LANDELLE, KOEHLER.⟨sic⟩ PORTAËLS,
VERNET-LECOMTE, BAADER, MERLE,
AND BOULANGER AND OTHERS;
PRINTED BY MONROCQ, FROM STONES
EXECUTED BY JEHENNE, PARIS.

NEW YORK   J. B. FORD AND COMPANY   ⟨1873; *i.e.,*
1874?⟩

Title-page in red and black.

For the English and another American edition see
preceding 2 entries. *Note*: Both the English and
the other American edition contain only 19
sketches; this edition, though printed in part from
the same plates as the other American edition, has
been extended by the additon of 6 sketches by
Stowe and verse by others.

⟨1⟩-400. Frontispiece and 24 plates inserted, each
with a printed tissue; an illuminated title-page is
inserted in some copies. 11⁷⁄₁₆″ x 8½″ full. *Note*:
Each page printed with a 2-rule red frame.

⟨1-50⟩⁴.

A subscription book and thus issued in a variety of
bindings. Noted in full leather; and, leather shelf-
back and corners, cloth sides. All edges gilt or
plain.

BAL has not been able to establish the date of publication of this extended edition, but assumes that
it follows that of the shorter 1874 dated edition. A
copy at SD inscribed by original owner Aug. 22,
1875. It is possible that this edition was originally
issued in 25 semi-monthly parts, but the only copy
in parts located (AAS) has the title-page imprint of
Fords, Howard & Hulbert and thus could not have
been published before 1878. However, the front
wrapper of 3 parts of this set has the imprint of
J. B. Ford & Co. and is dated 1874, suggesting that
such was the original form and date of publication.

H   AAS   SD   CWB

19481. "Tell It All" . . . An Autobiography: by
Mrs. T. B. H. Stenhouse . . . with Introductory
Preface by Mrs. Harriet Beecher Stowe . . .

Hartford, Conn.: A. D. Worthington & Co.
Louis Lloyd & Co., Chicago.   A. L. Bancroft &
Co., San Francisco.   1874.

"Preface," p. ⟨vi⟩.

NYPL

19482. WE AND OUR NEIGHBORS OR THE
RECORDS OF AN UNFASHIONABLE
STREET.   A NOVEL . . .

LONDON: SAMPSON LOW, MARSTON, LOW, &
SEARLE, CROWN BUILDINGS, 188 FLEET STREET.
1875.   [ALL RIGHTS RESERVED.]

For American edition see next entry.

⟨i⟩-⟨viii⟩, ⟨1⟩-390, blank leaf. 6½″ x 4⁷⁄₁₆″.

⟨-⟩⁴, A-I, K-U, X-Z, 2A⁸, 2B⁴. Leaf 2B₄ excised in
some copies.

Terra-cotta S cloth. Red C cloth. Bevelled covers.
Brown-coated end papers. All edges gilt. Publisher's catalog, paged ⟨1⟩-40 and dated Feb.,
1875, inserted at back.

Noted for *shortly* and *in advance* of the U. S. edition
in PC March 1, 1875. Advertised for April 3 in Ath
March 27, 1875. Deposited at BMU March 31,
1875. Advertised as *now ready* in PC April 2, 1875, in
Ath April 3, 1875, and in Bkr April, 1875. Listed
in Ath April 10, 1875, in PC April 16, 1875, and in
Bkr May, 1875. Reviewed in Ath April 17, 1875. A
cheap edition listed in PC May 1, 1876, and in Bkr
May, 1876.

BMU   Bodleian

19483. WE AND OUR NEIGHBORS: OR,
THE RECORDS OF AN UNFASHIONABLE
STREET.   (SEQUEL TO "MY WIFE AND
I.")   A NOVEL . . . WITH
ILLUSTRATIONS.

NEW YORK: J.B. FORD & COMPANY.   ⟨1875⟩

For English edition see preceding entry.

⟨i⟩-⟨vi⟩, ⟨7⟩-480; plus publisher's catalog ⟨1⟩-10,
blank leaf. Frontispiece and 7 plates inserted. 7¼″
x 4¾″.

⟨A⟩-I, K-U¹²; plus ⟨-⟩⁶.

FL-like cloth: terra-cotta; green; blue. Yellow end
papers. Flyleaves.

Two issues noted; no sequence established:

ISSUE A

Imprint as above.

Issue A noted in two states; the sequence is probable:

1: Short dash below imprint on title-page.

2: No dash below imprint on title-page.

Valley Forge. Proceedings on the Occasion of the Centennial Celebration of the Occupation of Valley Forge by the Continental Army, under George Washington, June 19, 1878. Also, Dedication of Headquarters, June 19, 1879. With an Appendix.

Printed by J. B. Lippincott & Co., Philadelphia. 1879.

Flower Songs for Flower Lovers. Compiled by Rose Porter . . .

New York: Anson D. F. Randolph & Company, 900 Broadway, Cor. 20th Street. ⟨1880⟩

The Union of American Poetry and Art . . . by John James Piatt . . .

Cincinnati . . . 1880

For fuller entry see No. 16006.

Harper's Cyclopædia of British and American Poetry Edited by Epes Sargent

New York . . . 1881

For fuller entry see No. 4336.

The Elocutionist's Annual Number 9 . . . Edited by Mrs. J. W. Shoemaker . . .

Philadelphia . . . 1881.

For fuller entry see No. 1247.

Gems for the Fireside . . . ⟨compiled by⟩ Rev. O. H. Tiffany . . .

Boston . . . 1881.

For fuller entry see BAL, Vol. 5, p. 610.

Indian Summer   Autumn   Poems and Sketches ⟨compiled by⟩ L. Clarkson . . .

New York . . . 1881 . . .

For fuller entry see No. 10449.

Favorite Poems, Selected from English and American Authors.

New York . . . ⟨n.d., after May 1, 1881⟩

For fuller entry see BAL, Vol. 5, p. 320.

In the Saddle . . .

Boston . . . 1882

For fuller entry see BAL, Vol. 6, p. 212.

The Cambridge Book of Poetry and Song . . . by Charlotte Fiske Bates . . .

New York . . . ⟨1882⟩

For fuller entries see Nos. 7887 and 11490.

Poems of American Patriotism Chosen by J. Brander Matthews

New-York   Charles Scribner's Sons   1882

H copy received Nov. 25, 1882. Listed in PW Dec. 2, 1882.

Tender and True.   Poems of Love . . .

Boston . . . 1882.

For fuller entry see BAL, Vol. 5, p. 112.

The Two Hundred and Forty-Fourth Annual Record of the Ancient and Honorable Artillery Company of Massachusetts.   1881–1882 . . .

Boston: Alfred Mudge & Son, Printers, No. 34 School Street.   1882.

Printed paper wrapper.

American Poems.   Selected and Edited by William Michael Rossetti . . .

Ward, Lock and Co., London: Warwick House, Salisbury Square, E. C.   New York: Bond Street.   ⟨n.d., not before 1882⟩

Surf and Wave . . . Edited by Anna L. Ward . . .

New York . . . ⟨1883⟩

For fuller entry see No. 16009.

No. 2.   Standard Recitations by Best Authors . . . Compiled . . . by Frances P. Sullivan.

. . . N. Y.   ⟨1883⟩

For fuller entry see BAL, Vol. 6, p. 213.

Brilliant Diamonds of Poetry and Prose . . . ⟨compiled by⟩ Rev. O. H. Tiffany . . .

Published for the Trade.   ⟨n.p., 1883⟩

A truncated printing of *Gems for the Fireside . . . ⟨1883⟩*.

of additions by R. Proctor. The Hague: Nijhoff, 1874-1897.

Additional notes and supplements published by L. Polain, 1897, 8 pp., and by E. Voullième, Zentralblatt für Bibliothekswesen 21 (1904): 439-450; 22 (1905): 313-315.

A23.1   Kronenburg, Maria E. Campbell's "Annales de la typographie néerlandaise au XVe siècle." Contributions to a new Edition. The Hague: Nijhoff, 1956, 168 pp.

A24   Catalogue of Books printed in the XVth Century now in the British Museum. Part I ff. In progress. London: British Museum, 1908 ff. Each vol paginated separately.

A25   Catalogue of Books in the Library of the British Museum printed in England, Scotland and Ireland, and of Books in English printed abroad to the Year 1640. 3 vols. London: British Museum, 1884, 1787 pp.

A26   Catalogue of Incunabula in St Andrews University Library. St Andrews: University of St Andrews, 1956, 101 pp.

A27   Catalogue of Manuscripts and early printed Books from the Libraries of William Morris, Richard Bennett, Bertram, fourth Earl of Ashburnham, and other Sources, now forming Portion of the Library of J. Pierpont Morgan. Early printed Books; France (End), The Netherlands, Spain and England III. London: Chiswick, 1907, 279 pp.

The incunabula were catalogued by E.G. Duff; the HORAE by A.W. Pollard.

A28   Catalogus van de incunabelen. I Italië, Frankrijk, Spanje, England. The Hague: Museum Meermanno Westreenianum, 1911, 124 pp.

A29   Check-List or brief Catalogue of the Library of Henry E. Huntington [English Literature to 1640]. New York: privately ptd, 1919, 482 pp. Rptd with additions. New York: privately ptd, 1920, 570 pp.

A30   Clair, Colin. A Chronology of Printing. London: Cassell, 1969, 228 pp.

A31   Cole, G.W. "A Survey of the Bibliography of English Literature, 1475-1640, with especial Reference to the Work of the Bibliographical Society of London." PBSA 23 (1929): 1-95.

A32   Collijn, Isak. Katalog der Inkunabeln der Kgl. Universitäts-Bibliothek zu Uppsala. Uppsala: Almqvist & Wiksell, Leipzig: Haupt, 1907, xxxviii+507 pp.

21a

5

A33   Collman, Herbert and Paternoster Brown. _The Britwell Hand-list, or short-title Catalogue of the principal Volumes from the Time of Caxton to the Year 1800, formerly in the Library of Britwell Court, Buckinghamshire._ 2 vols. London: Quaritch, 1933, xiv+1067 pp.

A34   Cook, Olan V. _Incunabula in the Hanes Collection of the Library of the University of North Carolina._ Enlarged edn. Chapel Hill: University of N. Carolina Press, 1960, xviii+125 pp.

A35   Davies, Hugh W. _Devices of the early Printers 1457-1560, their History and Development._ London: Grafton, 1935, x+707 pp. with plates.

     Contains an account of printers' marks and a catalogue.

A36   De Ricci, Seymour. _A Census of Caxtons._ Bibliographical Society Illustrated Monographs 15. Oxford: Oxford University Press, 1909, xv+196 pp. with facsimiles.

     Arranges all known copies, fragments and untraced copies of Caxton editions by author; indices of libraries and sales.

A36.1   Munby, A.N.L. "Jacob Bryant's Caxtons; some Additions to De Ricci's Census." _Library_ 5th ser.3 (1948):218-22.

A37   Dibdin, Thomas F. _Typographical Antiquities: or The History of Printing in England, Scotland and Ireland: containing Memoirs of our ancient Printers and a Register of the Books printed by them._ Begun by the late Joseph Ames, F.R. & A.SS. considerably augmented by William Herbert, of Cheshunt, Herts. 4 vols. London: William Miller, 1810-1819.

     Replaces the earlier works by Ames and by Ames and Herbert. Contains in the first volume a life of Caxton and a list of books printed by him with bibliographical and literary comments.

A38   Duff, E. Gordon. _A Century of the English book Trade 1457-1557._ Bibliographical Society Publications ser.1 no.6. London: Bibliographical Society, 1905, xxxv+200 pp.

     Arranges booksellers and printers alphabetically.

A39   Duff, E.G. "Early printed Books to 1558." _Bibliotheca Pepysiana, a Descriptive Catalogue._ Edited by J.R. Tanner, et al. London: Sidgwick & Jackson, 1914-40; pt II 1914, pp.1-82.

F1   Allen, H.E. "Wynkyn de Worde and a second French Compilation from the 'Ancrene Riwle' with a Description of the first (Trinity College Cambridge MS 883)." <u>Essays and Studies in Honor of Carleton Brown</u>. New York: New York University Press, 1940, pp.182-219.

     De Worde's <u>Tretÿse of Love</u> is translated from French in 1493, but the French source must have used <u>Ancrene Riwle</u>. The translation suggests Burgundian influence in religious works, perhaps associated with the foundation of the Franciscans of Strict Observance by Margaret of Burgundy in Greenwich in 1481.

F2   Amos, Flora R. <u>Early Theories of Translation</u>. Columbia University Studies in English and Comparative Literature. New York: Columbia University Press, 1920, xv+184 pp.

     General survey which touches on Caxton.

F3   Armstrong, C.A.J. "Verse by Jean Miélot on Edward IV and Richard, Earl of Warwick." <u>MÆ</u> 8 (1939):193-7.

     Discusses two Latin poems in Bibliothèque Nationale MS Français 17001.

F4   Atkins, John W.H. <u>English literary Criticism: the medieval Phase</u>. Cambridge: University Press, 1943, x+211 pp. Rptd London: Methuen, 1952.

     Deals in chapter 8 with Caxton, Hawes and Skelton with particular reference to their comments on style, aureation and rhetoric.

F5   Bateson, Frederick N.W. <u>A Guide to English Literature</u>. London: Longmans, 1965, xii+260 pp. Rptd 1966.

     Contains brief entry for Caxton.

F6   Bayot, Alphonse. <u>Le légende de Troie à la cour de Bourgogne</u>. Société d'émulation de Bruges, Mélanges 1. Bruges: Plancke, 1908, 50 pp.

     Shows that book 3 of Lefèvre's French version of HISTORY OF TROY is an existing French translation of Guido delle Colonne's Latin history which was added to Lefèvre's work after the earliest manuscripts were made.

F7   Beaty, Nancy L. <u>The Craft of Dying. The literary Tradition of the Ars Moriendi in England</u>. Yale Studies in English

21b

Example 21a, b

N. F. Blake. *William Caxton: A Bibliographical Guide.* New York and London: Garland, 1985. Courtesy Garland Publishing Company.

Many bibliographies published by Garland are printed from authors' camera-ready copy. As I mentioned above, subject specialists are not necessarily book designers. But in this case, the compiler has not done too badly.

Each entry is clearly distinguished by its number in the left margin. This almost completely offsets the problem of the equal spaces between main entries, notes, and subsequent entries. The widow at the top of page 4 is unsightly (to me), and could have been avoided. Titles are underlined, one of the necessities in a typed text, and not at all distracting. For a typed text, this is an eminently usable bibliography.

Another thing to note is that the content of the bibliography is broken down into different sections, as page 109 indicates. Using a different letter to separate the sections is no problem, but it does yield duplicated numbers. That is, there are a *B25* and an *E25*. This should not cause much confusion, but the possibility is there.

Example 22

Malcolm Andrew. *The Gawain-Poet: An Annotated Bibliography, 1839–1977.* New York: Garland, 1979. Courtesy Garland Publishing Company.

This volume uses running heads, a feature which is quite useful for bibliographies subdivided into several parts. The use of italics for titles separates author from publication data fields. Entries are clearly distinguished from one another by marginal numbers. Abbreviations for the *Gawain*-Poet's works (*Erk* for *St Erkenwald*; *Pe* for *Pearl*; and so on) are acceptable since there are only five works, and readers of the book will be familiar with these poems.

Also good is the use of hanging indents for book reviews. Like N. F. Blake's *Caxton* bibliography (Example 21), this is a perfectly legible and useful text.

þeod) in 108 texts, including the four poems. (Cf. item 225).

225. ————. *ME Words for "People."* GothSE, 27. Stockholm: Almqvist och Wiksell, 1973.

Contains further analysis of the material in item 224. Makes special reference to the four poems on pp. 29, 93, 167-68, 172-73, 287, 290. Expresses doubt about the theory of common authorship on p. 93: cf. item 226.

226. ————. *Did the '"Pe" Poet' Write "Pe"?* GothSE, 30. Göteborg, 1975.

Reviews the debate on the authorship of the four poems and *Erk*, and discusses various methods for establishing authorship. Specifies his own method: essentially that of setting up norms for a group of texts and observing individual deviations. Reports that the following "linguistic dimensions" were used: lexical frequency, clause length, sentence length, clause-linkage types, subordinate types, passive forms, alliteration; that *Pe* proved to be the deviant text; and that it remained so both when *Winner and Waster* was added to the group and·when *Erk* was removed. Concludes that *Pe* is not by the "*Pe* Poet." Includes many tables.

Reviews: Rima Handley, *N&Q*, 221 (1976), 480.
R.W. McTurk and D.J. Williams, *YWES*, 56 (1975), 86-87.

227. Knigge, Friedrich. *Die Sprache des Dichters von "SGGK," der sogenannten "Early English Alliterative Poems" und "De Erkenwalde,"* I. *Lautlehre.* Marburg: Elwert, 1886. Diss., Marburg, 1885.

Sets out to prove that *Erk* was written by the author of the four poems. Analyzes the occurrence of sounds in the group of five poems under the following headings: A. Germanic sounds: 1. OE: (a) vowels, (b) consonants; 2. ON: (a) vowels, (b) consonants; B. Romance sounds: OF: (a) vowels, (b) consonants. Announces plans to publish this work along with a further volume of texts. Cf. items 192, etc.

228. Körting, Gustav. *Grundriss der Geschichte der Englischen Litteratur von ihren Anfängen bis zur Gegenwart.* Sammlung von Kompendien für das Studium und die Praxis, ser. I, vol. 1. Münster i.W.: Schöningh, 1887; 5th ed., 1910.

22

Provides basic information on all four poems, together
with a brief bibliographical guide (sects. 105-08 in
5th ed.).

229. Koziol, Herbert. "Zur Frage der Verfasserschaft einiger
      mittelenglischer Stabreimdichtungen." *EStn*, 67 (1932),
      165-73.

      Argues for the common authorship of the four poems.
      Also assigns *Erk* to the poet.

230. ————. *Grundzüge der Syntax der mittelenglischen Sta-*
      breimdichtungen. WBEP, 58. Wien und Leipzig: Braumü-
      ller, 1932.

      A study of the syntax of ME alliterative verse; makes
      extensive use of examples from all four poems. Includes
      surveys of nouns of specific gender and of the pronoun
      of address in each poem (pp. 16-21, 55-57).

  *   Kuriyagawa, Fumio. See item 1296.

  *   Kuruma, Norio. See item 1297.

231. Lang, Andrew. *History of English Literature from "Beo-*
      wulf" to Swinburne. London, etc.: Longmans, Green,
      1912; 2nd, rev., ed., 1912; 3rd ed., 1913.

      General comments on *G* and *Pe*, and passing reference to
      Pat and *Cl* (pp. 72-75).

232. Lasater, Alice Elizabeth. "Hispano-Arabic Relation-
      ships to the Works of the *G*-Poet." Diss., Tennessee,
      1971. Abst.: *DAI*, 32 (1972), 4570A-71A. Cf. item 233.

233. ————, Alice E[lizabeth]. *Spain to England: A Compara-*
      tive Study of Arabic, European, and English Literature
      of the Middle Ages. Jackson: UP of Mississippi, 1974.

      (Cf. item 232). Includes sections on *Pe* (pp. 69-95),
      Cl (pp. 120-23), and *G* (pp. 168-96), as well as many
      passing references.

      Pe: Reviews the major critical debates. Suggests that
          the Maiden reflects the influence of Islamic escha-
          tological tradition (cf. pp. 67-69); emphasizes the
          combination of elegiac and eschatological elements
          within a dream vision. (Cf. item 484).

      Cl: Detects Islamic influence in lines 697-708.

Example 23a, b, c, d, e
William B. Todd and Ann Bowden, compilers. *Tauchnitz International Editions in English 1841–1955: A Bibliographical History*. New York: Bibliographical Society of America, 1988. Courtesy William B. Todd and Ann Bowden.

Like my comments about Jacob Blanck's *Bibliography of American Literature* (Example 20), the assessment below considers only physical format, not content. This bibliography is one of the most amazing gatherings of bibliographical information of the last 20 years. The Tauchnitz editions pose massive bibliographic problems, not only because of the vast number of titles the company produced, but also because of the company's long-standing use of most of them.

In order to encapsulate the great amount of information that these editors have compiled about all the Tauchnitz titles, they decided to save space by using abbreviations and symbols. As I have said in the text of this book, the use of symbols is risky at best, and positively deadly at worst. This volume is a case in point. A glance at a couple of sample pages will bear this out. Pages 228 and 229 look as if they come from some engineering or mathematics textbook. One's head fairly swims with numbers and letters, symbols and codes.

It is easy to find the beginnings of the entries, because of both the marginal numbering and the use of boldface for the filing elements (usually personal names). But what do the letters *a* through *f* and the asterisk mean just below the entry numbers? And what about the rest of the entries?

One would expect a clear listing of these abbreviations in tables at the beginning of the volume. But, unfortunately, there are so many symbols and abbreviations that they fill about nine pages, the last seven of which give full names for libraries and archives cited and bibliographical references used. Usually the abbreviations can be deciphered. For example, *LA* means UCLA, and *DB* means Deutsche

Bibliothek. Unfortunately, these scholars have gone so far afield for their data that they have researched in places not traditional or positively unfamiliar. Thus, *A* stands for Universiteitsbibliotheek, Amsterdam; *K* is for the Dr Karl H. Pressler Collection, Munich; and *MT* refers to the Bancroft Library, University of California, Berkeley, Mark Twain Papers, manuscript file. Therefore a reader cannot understand the abbreviations without constant referral to the list at the front of the volume. At least the designers had the wisdom to include abbreviated keys at the foot of each page, making use of the bibliography's abbreviations somewhat easier.

But the most perplexing part of the apparatus is the first two pages of the section called 'Summary of Descriptive Procedure' (pp. xiii–xiv), which explains the symbols. As I have said, symbols require pure memorization since nothing inherent in the symbol can indicate its meaning. A glance at these pages, accompanied by a glance at the pages of the text of the bibliography, will show why this is an almost impenetrable bibliography for a casual user. It will take dedication, time, perseverance, and a good memory to become proficient with this volume.

I should balance my critique with praise. This volume contains over 1,100 pages with fairly small print. It would have been possible to dispense with the symbols and abbreviations, but the result would have been three volumes of this length, not one. For the sake of convenience and economy, the designers and compilers have chosen a shorter and less expensive route. Scholars doing extensive work with the Tauchnitz volumes will need to immerse themselves in this bibliography; and then they will become familiar with the symbols and abbreviations. It might have been possible to have a foldout page or two to allow for a constant display of these codes; but this was not possible with nine pages of them. This is a truly magnificent reference tool, and scholars will be grateful that it has been compiled so thoroughly and carefully, regardless of its physical appearance.

SUMMARY OF
DESCRIPTIVE PROCEDURE

Ordinarily all books are described in the manner cited below. Further commentary on 'points' briefly noted here appears in the concluding Addendum Z (pp.942-956); 'points' peculiar only to certain special series are defined as they occur. For each entry the headline cites, in order, serial number of the volume, author's name as usually given by Tauchnitz, title of the book, date of imprint. A number without prefix designates a volume in the general series 1-5372; a number with an assigned prefix letter A or B etc. identifies one of the numerous special series. The original imprint date usually remains *unchanged* in all subsequent issues.

Below serial number, to the left, are alphabetical indicators: capital letters to signify settings if more than one, lower case to identify impressions within the setting. Then follows the description, based essentially on the three most variable pages, H (half-title), T (title), C (colophon). Throughout it will be understood that copies lacking any of these three leaves, and especially the first, usually cannot be defined as of a certain impression.

Typically books first impressed in the years 1859-1921 (volumes 462-4552), and all earlier books (1-461) reimpressed in that same period, conform to this pattern:

H:6, Td©2: — , *v*-vi pref, *1* 2-364 text, C3.   That is:

H:6	half-title recto with serial in arabic numbers: verso listing *six* other titles
Td	title with author's surname as *designated* in headline
©	'Copyright Edition'
2	imprint in *second* state: 'Leipzig | Bernhard Tauchnitz | [date]'
—	verso *blank,* [H-T counted by the printer as four pages]
v-vi	preface [page *v* unnumbered. 'vi' originally in small capitals but reproduced throughout this bibliography in lower case]
1 2-364	text page *1* again unnumbered
C3	colophon, here at foot of last text page, in *third* state: 'Printing Office of the Publisher'

Other symbols for variable points include:

Hr: —	half-title recto with serial number in *roman* letter [early issues of vols. 1-500 only]: verso blank
H18:2	recto statement dated *1918* [referring to poor paper]: verso listing two other titles
Ta	title no author line, *anonymous*
Tb	title — author designated only as '*By* the Author of [some other work]'
Tc	title — author's surname as given is *contrary* to that cited in entry headline

If title has no © statement, then another symbol will appear, indicating:

s	'*Sanctioned* by the Author' [early issues of vols. 51-109 only]
@	'*Authorized* Edition' [usual designation for American authors]
o	*no* indication [pirated, in public domain, or © cited on verso]

Title may also indicate:

f	'With the Portrait of the Author' [appearing as *frontispiece*]

23a

§   ornament above imprint [early issues of vols. 1-148 only]

Variant title imprints:
1   Leipzig | Bernh. Tauchnitz Jun. | [date]
2   Leipzig | Bernhard Tauchnitz | [date]
3   Bernhard Tauchnitz / Leipzig | [no date]
4   Bernhard Tauchnitz · Leipzig   [no date]
5   Leipzig | Bernhard Tauchnitz   [no date, title in ornamental frame]

Variant colophons:
C1   Printed by Bernh. Tauchnitz Jun.
C2   Printed by Bernhard Tauchnitz.
C3   Printing Office of the Publisher.
C4   Printed by Bernhard Tauchnitz, Leipzig
C5bi, hd, or rb   Printed by Bibliographisches Institut, Offizin Haag-Drugelin,
          or Réval Bros. [colophons in variant states].
C6   Printed by Oscar Brandstetter   [colophon in variant states]

Following the description are other bibliographical data, as required, concluding
with a trade periodical 'notice' of original issue. This notice and certain other
general information usually applies to all volumes of the title.

    Upon completion of the descriptive account the word 'Copies' introduces the
issues of the impression, here ordered successively in four groups, according to
their covers:
w   wrappers: as indicated in Addendum Z, these proceed chronologically
          through three sequences   (1) wl-w22 early undated variants [1841-1872],
          (2) wJun72 etc. wrappers dated by month on back cover [June
          1872-December 1934], (3) w — wb wg etc. later undated covers uncolored,
          or colored blue, green, etc. [1935-1943].
x   publisher's trade bindings xl-x12 in approximate order of manufacture.
y   publisher's gift or presentation bindings yl-y3.
z   other, undifferentiated bindings, usually supplied by early owners.
<   copy defective, cited only if available points are significant.
After the copy record the account proceeds degressively to the next succeeding
impression, there listing only the 'points' differing from the earlier description
and citing the copies located of this subsequent variant.
    Within each class of bindings, copies are identified chronologically according
to the issue-state of the cover. Immediately after location symbol (one, two, or
three capital letters) an occasional letter p will designate a poor-paper issue and
further reference in parentheses indicate that the copy also contains:
('4Jul71') manuscript date, so formalized: this entered presumably by first owner.
(May72)   Tauchnitz dated catalogue, usually included after this month.
(G09)   undated 'Gift Books' catalogue issued ca. 1909: see L8cl.
(G29)   undated 'Geschenkbücher' catalogue inserted ca. 1929: see L8c2.
    Final volume notes, introduced by an '*', may contain as many as five particu-
lars: (1) cross reference to any later volumes; (2) pertinent correspondence and
other data on early production of the Leipzig issue; (3) notation if the work is
later cited in Tauchnitz's 1939 General List [L8d5] or in '500 Best Titles' [L8c6];
(4) references in author bibliographies, however minimal; (5) citation, if any, in
Bibliography of American Literature [BAL], *New Cambridge Bibliography of English Literature* [NCBEL], and *National Union Catalog: Pre-1956 Imprints* [NUC].

23b

LIBRARIES AND ARCHIVES

A	Universiteitsbibliotheek, Amsterdam
AM	Amherst College, Amherst
AS	University of Texas at Austin: Authors' Syndicate manuscript file, Harry Ransom Humanities Research Center
AV	University of Texas at Austin: Albatross Verlag manuscript file, Harry Ransom Humanities Research Center
B	Bernhard Tauchnitz bequest, Landesbibliothek, Coburg
BLH	County Record Office, Hertfordshire: Bulwer Lytton manuscript archive
BLK	Knebworth House, Hertfordshire: Bulwer Lytton library and manuscript archive
BP	Magyar Tudományos Akadémia, Budapest
BR	Bibliothèque Royale Albert 1er, Brussels
BT	Boston Public Library, Boston (collection at New England Deposit Library)
C	Cornell University, Ithaca
CM	Biblioteca Comunale, Milan
D	Deutsche Bücherei, Leipzig
DB	Deutsche Bibliothek, Frankfurt
E	Englische Seminar, Universität München, Munich
F	Stadt-und Universitätsbibliothek, Frankfurt
FS	Folger Shakespeare Library, Washington, D.C.
G	Dr. Alexander N. Gansa collection, San Francisco
H	Ben Hutchison collection, Brighton'
HG	Koninklijke Bibliotheek, The Hague
HU	Harvard University, Cambridge (collections at Houghton, Widener, and New England Deposit Libraries)
JBS	John Bennett Shaw, Sherlock Holmes collection, Santa Fe
JW	Jan von Wendelstadt collection, Neubeuren am Inn'
K	Dr. Karl H. Pressler collection, Munich
L	British Library, London
LA	University of California, Los Angeles
LC	Library of Congress, Washington, D.C.
M	Bayerische Staatsbibliothek, Munich
MB	University of Massachusetts, Boston
MT	University of California, Berkeley: Mark Twain Papers, manuscript file
NC	University of North Carolina, Chapel Hill
NY	New York Public Library, New York
NYB	New York Public Library: Henry W. and Albert A. Berg Collection, manuscript file
O	Bodleian Library, Oxford
P	Bibliothèque Nationale, Paris
PM	Pierpont Morgan Library, New York
PR	University of Reading, Reading: Chatto & Windus and Macmillan publishers' archives
R	University of Rochester, Rochester (royal Hanover collection)
S	Bernadottebiblioteket, Stockholm
SF	San Francisco Public Library, San Francisco

SK   Pierpont Morgan Library, New York: George Bernard Shaw and Tauchnitz Firm manuscripts, Frederick R. Koch Foundation Deposit

SL   London School of Economics and Political Science: George Bernard Shaw Account Books 1928-1939 and miscellaneous manuscript file

SM   Huntington Library, San Marino

ST   University of Texas at Austin: George Bernard Shaw Account Books 1898-1928, Harry Ransom Humanities Research Center

T   University of Texas at Austin

TH   Thomas Hardy Memorial Collection, Dorset County Museum, Dorchester

TR   Metropolitan Library, Toronto

V   Österreichische Nationalbibliothek, Vienna

VA   Victoria & Albert Museum, London (Dyce and Forster collections)

VS   Rockefeller Foundation Study and Conference Center, Villa Serbelloni, Bellagio

W   University of Western Ontario, London

WB   Staatsbibliothek Preussischer Kulturbesitz, West Berlin

X   Collection of Dr. William B. Todd and Dr. Ann Bowden, Austin

Y   Yale University, New Haven

Z   Zentralbibliothek, Zurich

Note: For further information on the 46 book collections listed above see Addendum X (pp.913-20). All copies have been personally examined, excepting only certain copies reported from Amherst, Coburg, Cornell, University of California at Los Angeles, and the entire royal collection at Bernadottebiblioteket, Stockholm.

1. The Hutchison collection (H), examined in 1980, has since been sold in large part to Meisei University, Tokyo.

2. The Jan von Wendelstadt library (JW), examined in 1982, was later acquired and incorporated into Dr. Pressler's extensive collection (K).

REFERENCES

Citations from all German references are consistently quoted in English translation. The first entry cited below and other trade lists provide the volume issue notices cited successively in the bibliographical record: HB (1841-1848), BB (1849-1852, the extent of the Library of Congress file), AB (1853-1892), WV (1893-1930), and DN (1931-1941). The few exceptions to this practice are duly remarked.

AB	*Allgemeine Bibliographie für Deutschland.*
ADB	*Allgemeine deutsche Biographie.*
Adler	Betty Adler. *H. L. M. The Mencken Bibliography.* Baltimore: Johns Hopkins Press, 1961.
Ath	*The Athenaeum: A Journal of English & Foreign Literature.*
Author	*The Author. The Organ of the Incorporated Society of Authors, Playwrights and Composers.*
Babington	Percy L. Babington. *Bibliography of the Writings of John Addington Symonds.* London: John Castle, 1925.
BAL	Jacob Blanck and Michael Winship. *Bibliography of American Literature.* New Haven: Yale University Press, 1955–
Barnes	Warner Barnes. *A Bibliography of Elizabeth Barrett Browning.* Austin: University of Texas, 1967.
BB	*Börsenblatt für den deutschen Buchhandel.*
Bennett	Arnold Bennett. *The Journal of Arnold Bennett 1896-1928.* New York: Viking Press, 1933.
Beswick	Jay W. Beswick. *The Work of Frederick Leypoldt.* New York: R. R. Bowker, 1942.
BLC	*The British Library General Catalogue of Printed Books.*
Broughton	Leslie N. Broughton *and others. Robert Browning: A Bibliography, 1830-1950.* Ithaca: Cornell University Press, 1953.
Brussel	I. R. Brussel. *Anglo-American First Editions.* London: Constable, 1935-1936.
Carr	Lucile Carr. *A Catalogue of the VanderPoel Dickens Collection at The University of Texas.* Austin: University of Texas, 1968.
Clark	C. E. Frazer Clark, Jr. *Nathaniel Hawthorne: A Descriptive Bibliography.* Pittsburgh: University of Pittsburgh Press, 1978.
Cline	C. L. Cline (ed.). *The Letters of George Meredith.* Oxford: Clarendon Press, 1970.
Coleridge	Ernest H. Coleridge. *The Works of Lord Byron.* London: John Murray, 1898-1905.
Collie(1)	Michael Collie. *George Meredith: A Bibliography.* Toronto: Dawson 1974.
(2)	— —. *George Gissing: A Bibliography.* Toronto: University of Toronto Press, 1975.
Cowan	Robert E. Cowan *and others. The Library of William Andrews Clark, Jr. Wilde and Wildeiana.* San Francisco: John H. Nash, 1922-1931.
Crane	Joan Crane. *Willa Cather: A Bibliography.* Lincoln: University of Nebraska Press, 1982.
Crisp(1)	Jane Crisp. *Jessie Fothergill, 1851-1891: A Bibliography.* St. Lucia: University of Queensland, 1980.
(2)	— —. *Mary Cholmondeley 1859-1925: A Bibliography.* St. Lucia: University of Queensland, 1981.

   *   The publication of this work, discussed by Robert Browning in earlier letters to Tauchnitz (cf. 1197), is again mentioned on 1 January 1872, when the agreement was returned and a 'good photograph' of an appropriate portrait duly promised — a promise, it seems, not early fulfilled (VT p.68). Cited in 1939 General List. Barnes E76, NUC:4.

1249   **Mac Donald, George.** *The Vicar's Daughter An Autobiographical Story.* 1872.
       H:3, Td©2: −, *5* 6-302 text, *303* C3. AB notice: 19Sep72. Copies wAug72: H, wFeb88:C, wOct02:BRp, z:B HU LA Mp S V WB.
   *   [Vol.2 = 1250]   NUC:5.

1250   [1249,vol.2] 1872.
       H: −, Td©2: −, *5* 6-312 text, C3. Copies wSep95:C, wSep03:BRp, z:B HU LA Mp S V WB.

1251   **Yates, Edmund.** *A Waiting Race. A Novel.* 1872.
       H:quote, Td©2: −, *5* ded, *6*−, *7* cont, *8*−, *9* 10-320 text, C3. AB notice: 19Sep72. Copies wFeb84:Cp, wOct91:BR W, z:B S V W WBp.
   *   [Vol.2 = 1252]   NUC:2.

1252   [1251,vol.2] 1872.
       H:9, Td©2: −, *5* cont, *6*−, *7* 8-303 text, *304* C3. Copies wDec88:C W(Sep96), wSep96:BR, z:B S V W WBp.

1253   **Black, William.** *In Silk Attire. A Novel.* 1872.
  a H:1, Td©2: −, *5* quote, *6*−, *7* cont, *8*−, *9* 10-303 text, *304* C3. AB notice: 19Sep72. Copies z:AM M S X('23May85').
  b H:9. Copies wMar78:P, z:HU V.
  c H:18. Copies wJun93:C, w after 29Sep19:BR, z:B WB.
   *   [Vol.2 = 1254]   NUC:3.

1254   [1253,vol.2] 1872.
       H: −, Td©2: −, *5* cont, *6*−, *7* 8-288 text, C3. Copies wMar76:P(Sep78), wJan95:C, wApr06:BR, z:B M S V WB X('23May85') AM(Aug72).

1255   **Hardy, Iza Duffus.** *Not Easily Jealous. A Novel.* 1872.
       H:quote, Ta©2: −, *5* cont, *6*−, *7* 8-296 text, C3. AB notice: 19Sep72. Copies wJan86:Cp, wMar06:BRp, z:Ap B CMp M V WBp.
   *   [Vol.2 = 1256]

1256   [1255,vol.2] 1872.
       H: −, Ta©2: −, *5* cont, *6*−, *7* 8-303 text, *304* C3. Copies wJan80:Cp, wJan23:BRp, z:Ap B CMp M V WBp.

1257   **Blagden, Isa.** *The Woman I Loved, and the Woman Who Loved Me; A Tuscan Wedding.* 1872.
       H:quote, Td©2: −, *5* cont, *6*−, *7* fly-title, *8*−, *9* 10-279 text, *280* C3. AB notice: 26Sep72. Copies wJun86:V, wMay92:C, z:B JWp M WB.
   *   NUC:6.

1258   **Ouida.** *Madame la Marquise and Other Novelettes.* 1872.
  a H:9, Td©2: −, *5* cont, *6*−, *7* 8-310 text, *311* C3. AB notice: 26Sep72. Copy z:V.
  b H:11. Copies z:WBp Xp.
  c H:21. Copy z:JW.

H half-title, T title, C colophon, − blank page. H:3 signifies half-title series in Arabic number with verso listing three titles. T symbols a anonymous, b 'By the Author of . . .', c author surname contrary to entry name, d author name as designated, f 'With the Portrait of the Author',

   d   H:30. Copies wMar93:C, z:B.
   *   NUC:4.

1259   **Hoey, Mrs. Cashel.** *A Golden Sorrow.* 1872.
       H:quote, Td©2: −, *5* ded, *6* −, *78*-312 text, C3. AB notice: 5Dec72. Co-
       pies wJun89:Cp, wMay09:BR, z:B M O S WBp.
   *   [Vol.2 = 1260]   NUC:1.

1260   [1259,vol.2]   1872.
       H: −, Td©2: −, *5* 6-312 text, C3. Copies wJun86:Cp, wAug94:BR, z:B
       M O S WBp Xp.

1261   **Thackeray, W. M.** *The Irish Sketch-Book.* 1872.
   a   H:12, Td©2: −, *5* ded, *6* −, *7* cont, *8* −, *9* 10-280 text, C3. AB notice:
       5Dec72. Copy z:M.
   b   H:13. Copies wJan91:C, z:B <LA WB.
   *   [Vol.2 = 1262]   In LA copy, first gathering, two outer-forme stereotype
       plates were imposed together so that pages now read *1* H, *4* −, *1* H, *4* −,
       5 ded, *8* −, *5* ded, *8* −, *9,* 12, *9,* 12, 13, 16, 13, 16.

1262   [1261,vol.2]   1872.
       H: −, Td©2: −, *5* cont, *6* −, *78*-296 text, C3. Copies wJan91:C(May93),
       z:B LAp M WB.

1263   **Harte, Bret.** *Prose and Poetry.* 1872.
   a   H: −, Td@2: −, *v* pref (licence), *vi* −, *vii*-viii cont, *1* fly-title, *2* −, *3* 4-310
       text, *311* C3. Compiled by the author at the request of Baron Tauchnitz.
       AB notice: 5Dec72. Copies z:LAp M.
   b   H:1. Copy z:Xp.
   c   H:9. Copies z:BP V X.
   d   H:24. Copies wNov93:C, [x9,y1]:cited in G09, z:B.
   e   H:38. Copy z:WB.
   f   H:39. Copies z:BR CM.
   *   [Vol.2 = 1264]   BAL 7265 (noting the new preface), NUC:12.

1264   [1263,vol.2]   1872.
       H: −, Td@2: −, *v* vi-viii cont, *1* fly-title, *2* −, *3* 4-319 *320* text, C3. Copies
       wMay90:C, wJul06:SM('21'), [x9,y1]:cited in G09, z:A B BP CM K M
       V WB X LA(Nov74).
   *   BAL 7265 (noting possible first book issue of 'Concepcion de Arguello').

1265   **Kingsley, Henry.** *Valentin. A French Boy's Story of Sedan.* 1872.
       H:5, Td©2: −, *5* 6-304 text, C3. T: Revised and Corrected Copyright Edi-
       tion. AB notice: 5Dec72. Copies wJul82:V, wFeb89:C, z:B H WB X
       M(Nov72).
   *   NUC:6.

1266   **Payn, James.** *A Woman's Vengeance. A Novel.* 1872.
       H:5, Tb©2: −, *5* cont, *6* −, *78*-318 text, *319* C3. AB notice: 5Dec72. Co-
       pies wOct84:C, wDec93:W, wMar25:BR, z:B H M S V WBp.
   *   [Vol.2 = 1267]   NUC:2.

1267   [1266,vol.2]   1872.
       H: −, Tb©2: −, *5*-6 cont, *78*-310 text, *311* C3. Copies wJun86:C(Mar94),
       wAug97:W(1Dec11), wJun29:BR, z:B H Mp S V WBp M(Aug72).

JW O S WB X.
* NUC:2.

3058   **Paston, George.** *A Study in Prejudices.* 1895.
H:quote, Td©2: −, *5* 6-272 text, C3. WV notice: 20Jun95. Copies wJun95:C
M O(Jun95), wSep95:BR, z:B WB.

3059   **Morrison, Arthur.** *Tales of Mean Streets.* 1895.
a   H: −, Td©2: −, *5* ded, *6* −, *7* 8-21 intro, *22* −, *23*-24 cont, *25* fly-title,
26 −, *27* 28-279 text, *280* C3. WV notice: 27Jun95. Copies wJun95:C
M, z:B JW K O WB.
b   H:3. Copies wDec22:CM, [x9,y1]:cited in G09, z:K.
* NUC:1.

3060   **Montgomery, Florence.** *Colonel Norton A Novel.* 1895.
H:8, Td©2: −, *5* ded, *6* −, *7*-8 cont, *9* 10-288 text, C3. WV notice: 4Jul95.
Copies wJun95:C M O, wAutumn20:CM, wJul23:BR, z:B CM S WB.
* [Vol.2 = 3061]   NUC:1.

3061   [3060,vol.2]   1895.
H: −, Td©2: −, *5*-6 cont, *7* 8-279 text, *280* C3. Copies wJun95:C M,
wAug95:O(Dec95), wAutumn20:CM, wJan24:BR, z:B CM S WB.

3062   **Pemberton, Sir Max.** *The Impregnable City A Romance.* 1895.
H: −, Td©2: −, *5* ded, *6* −, *7*-8 cont, *9* intro, *10* −, *11* 12-287 text, *288*
C3. WV notice: 11Jul95. Copies wJun95:BP C M, wOct07:<WB, z:B
JW X.
* NUC:1.

3063   **Marryat, Florence.** *The Beautiful Soul.* 1895.
a   H:46, Td©2: −, *5*-6 cont, *7* 8-279 text, *280* C3. WV notice: 18Jul95. Copies
wJul95:C M S, wAug95:CM(Jun95).
b   H:47. Copies wNov03:WB, wSep23:BR, z:B H(Dec95).
* Cited in 1939 General List.

3064   **Merrick, Leonard.** *The Man Who Was Good A Novel.* 1895.
a   H:quote, Td©2: −, *5* 6-268 text, *269-270* opinions of the press, *271* C3.
WV notice: 18Jul95. Copies wJul95:C M K(Oct95), wAug95:LA, z:JW
V WB.
b   H:3, Td©2:quote. Copies wOct03:HU, z:B.
c   H:12. Copy wFeb11:R(Mar12).
* NUC:1.

3065   **Hungerford, Mrs.** *The Three Graces A Novel.* 1895.
a   H:33, Td©2: −, *5* 6-287 text, *288* C3. WV notice: 25Jul95. Copies wJul95:
C M CM(Jul95).
b   H:35. Copies z:B X.
c   H:39. Copies wOct07:WB, x7d:A.
* NUC:3.

3066   **Maartens, Maarten.** *My Lady Nobody A Novel.* 1895.
H:4, Td©2: −, *5* ded, *6* −, *7*-8 cont, *9* 10-279 text, *280* C3. WV notice:
1Aug95. Copies wJul95:C M X('Aug95'), wAug95:R, wAug05:S, wOct11:
X, wApr18:BR, z:B CM H('96') T V W WB.
* [Vol.2 = 3067]   NUC:4.

H half-title, T title, C colophon, − blank page. H:3 signifies half-title series in Arabic number
with verso listing three titles. T symbols a anonymous, b 'By the Author of . . .', c author surname contrary to entry name, d author name as designated, f 'With the Portrait of the Author',

23e

3067 [3066,vol.2] 1895.
H: −, Td©2: −, *5-6* cont, *7* 8-279 text, *280* C3. Copies wJul95:C M
X('Aug95'), wAug95:R, wMar10:BR X, z:B CM H('Apr96') S T V W WB.

3068 **Moore, George.** *Celibates*. 1895.
a H: −, Td©2: −, *5* cont, *6* −, *7* fly-title, *8* −, *9* 10-336 text, C3. WV notice:
8Aug95. Copies wJul95:M, wMay96:V, z:BP H JW T X X(Mar97).
b H:1. Copies wJan03:G(1Jul02), z:B WB.
c H:6. Copies wJun18:T, z:LA.
* Acknowledging Colles's letter of 5 June 1895 Tauchnitz on the 8th
promised a quick decision on this book, which he had just received (AS).
Shortly thereafter, in an undated note received by Colles on 11 July,
Moore reported that he was sending 'a corrected copy of Celibates. Will
you send it on at once to the Baron and beg him to print from it' (Xms).
The possibility of revision is unnoted in Gilcher A21.3a.

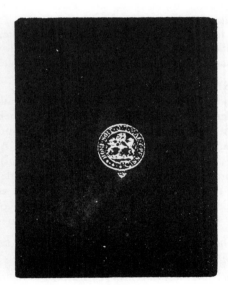

Tauchnitz Red 'Art Nouveau' Bindings
These earlier red-cloth bindings x7a and x7b were used from 1892 to 1903 and,
as indicated in Section Z6, over this period occur in at least eight definable variants.
Later bindings in this artistic mode are illustrated overleaf.

effervescent early years of the eighteenth century. The Journal de Trevoux, as it was familiarly known, was established by Louis Auguste de Bourbon, the sovereign prince of Dombes, a district in eastern France, and printed under the direction and editorship of the Jesuits there and at their College in Paris, Louis-le-Grand. A wide variety of book reviews, notices of new publications, essays and letters sprinkle the pages of this lively journal; historian Gustave Dumas in his 1936 study of this publication called it a literary monument.

Mr. Hoover undoubtedly enjoyed the folding map following the title page for the issue of May 1705: "A passage by land to California discovered by Father Eusebius-François Kino during the years 1698 to 1701." Kino was the founder of the mission San Xavier del Bac near present-day Tucson, Arizona. The text comments on the many new discoveries in California and adds that this new land, which had been regarded as an island, was actually "joined to the continent of America."

580. MENESTRIER, CLAUDE FRANÇOIS, 1631–1705.
La philosophie des images enigmatiques, ou il est traité des enigmes, hieroglyphiques, oracles, propheties, sorts, divinations, loteries, talismans, songes, Centuries de Nostradamus, de la baguette. Par le P. Cl. François Menestrier . . . Lyon, Chez Hilaire Baritel, 1694.

12 p. *l.,* 491 (*i. e.* 501), [1] p., 1 *l.* fold. plate, tables. 16 cm. Signatures: a¹² A-X¹². Title vignette. Ornamental initials and head- and tailpieces; marginal annotations. Binder's leaf embossed: Bibliotheque Occulte du Cᵗᵉ D'Ourches.

581. MERCATI, MICHELE, 1541–1593.
Michaelis Mercati . . . Metallotheca. Opus posthumum, auctoritate, & munificentiâ Clementis undecimi Pontificis Maximi è tenebris in lucem eductum; opera autem, & studio Joannis Mariæ Lancisii archiatri pontificii illustratum. Cui accessit appendix cum XIX. recens inventis iconibus. Romæ, Apud Jo. Mariam Salvioni, 1719.

5 p. *l.* (incl. front.), xiij-lxiv, 378, [17], 53, [1] p. illus., front., plates (part double) ports., table. 39 cm. Appendix has special title page and separate pagination. Titles in red and black; title vignettes; vignette above colophon. Colophon: Romæ MDCCXVII. Ex officina Jo. Mariæ Salvioni Romani. Initials on half-title: T. E. L. S. *Cf.* Geikie, p. 52, where 1574 is the date given for this work.

The beautiful copper engravings of this book by the director of the Vatican botanical gardens were discovered after his death and finally published in the early eighteenth century. Mercati catalogued the geological collections in the Vatican, was physician to Gregory XIII and Clement VIII, and a pupil of Caesalpinus. In this work he described the manufacture of alum and the use of manganese for coloring glazes.

582. LA METALLIQUE TRANSFORMATION.
La metallique transformation. Contenant trois anciens traictez en rithme françoise . . . Derniere edition. Lyon, Chez Pierre Rigaud, 1618.

Example 24

Claremont Colleges Libraries. *The Bibliotheca Herbert Clark Hoover de re Collection of Metallica, Mining & Metallurgy.* Annotated by David Kuhner; catalogued by Tania Rizza. Claremont, CA: Libraries of the Claremont Colleges, 1980. Courtesy Claremont College Libraries.

This bibliography is arranged alphabetically. New entries are marked by the blank space and by the entry number, which is flush left with the rest of the entry. After all bibliographical data, notes begin with one indented line. Further notes which comment on the volume are printed in italics and are separated from the rest of the entry by a line space.

The block style, the long line measure, and the small type used make locating elements in entries slightly difficult. But, in general, this is a readable and fairly attractive bibliography.

Example 25

Friedrich Blume. *Die Musik in Geschichte und Gegenwart Allgemeine Enzyklopädie der Musik.* Band 9. Basel: Bärenreite-Kassel, 1969. Courtesy International Felix Mendelssohn Gesellschaft.

While this volume, like the Tauchnitz bibliography (Example 23), contains a wealth of information, I cannot imagine why the designer of these columns decided upon this particular layout.

To begin with, the columns, not the pages, are numbered. I do not object to this, though it is unusual these days. But, much worse, just look at the page! This layout needs no further comment. It is practically illegible and so formidable that only the most dedicated or needy scholar would enter its labyrinth.

The learning and research displayed here are quite impressive, but . . . .

keit Mendelssohns im Auge zu behalten. Eine solche Betrachtungsweise wird auch die Ungleichheit seines Werks, bei aller Selbstkritik des Komp., nicht verkennen; darin wechseln vollkommene Kunstwerke mit schwachen Leistungen sonderbar ab. — Mendelssohns Hingabe an seine Mission, seine absolut menschliche und künstlerische Integrität wird immer seinen Namen verklären. Er hat wirklich nach seinem Wahlspruch gelebt: „*Res severa verum gaudium*", der später die Devise des Gewandhauses wurde. Ein ganz klares Bild von seinem Werk und seiner Person wird sich erst dann ergeben, wenn die vielen ungedr. Dok. und Kompos. des Meisters der Öffentlichkeit zugänglich sein werden.

Literatur. Vorbemerkung: Bedauerlicherweise sind die wichtigsten Quellen (Familienbriefe, Tagebücher, persönliche Dok. FMB's) noch immer nicht in wiss. Ausg. zugänglich. Völlig unzulänglich sind die populären Ausg. der „Briefe" (Reisebriefe und Briefe aus den Jahren 1829 bis 1847), die von Paul und Karl MB besorgt wurden (Lpz. 1861), sowie alle darauf fußenden späteren Ausg. Dass. gilt von dem bekannten Buch S. Hensels *Die Familie Mendelssohn* (Bln. 1879). Beide Quellenwerke unterdrücken, ändern, ja verstellen manche wichtigen Briefe. Diese Tatsache war schon George Grove bekannt (vgl. Ch. L. Graves, *The Life of Sir George Grove*, London 1903, 128 ff.), und auch E. Wolff hat in seiner Biogr. FMB's (Bln. 1906, 190, Note 70; s. auch Ph. Spitta in VfMw V, 1889, 221 f.) diesen Mangel beklagt. Noch schlimmer steht es mit R. Schumanns *Erinnerungen an FMB*. Hier hat W. Boetticher (*R. Schumann in seinen Schriften u. Büchern*, Bln. 1942) Schumanns Aufzeichnungen in weitgehendem Maße entstellt wiedergegeben; die von ihm hinzugefügte Interpretation entspricht nicht dem Sinn der Quelle, die inzwischen durch das Schumann-Arch. in Zwickau unter dem Titel *Erinnerungen an F. Mendelssohn-Bartholdy*, hrsg. v. G. Eismann, 1948, Städt. Museum Zwickau, als Facs.-Druck vorgelegt worden ist. Der übrige Briefwechsel des Meisters ist im allg. von diesen Unzuträglichkeiten verschont geblieben. Hunderte von Briefen liegen nur in Hs. vor. Außerhalb der Familie finden sich bedeutende Briefslgn. im Privatbesitz (London, Oxford, New York), in der Library of Congress, Washington, und der Internat. FMB-Ges., Basel. Tagebücher u. ä. persönliche Dok. befinden sich noch zum größten Tl. im Besitz der Familie. — Übersicht: A. Bibliographien, Quellenkunde, Ikonographie. ✧ B. Briefwechsel, Dokumente, Erinnerungen. 1. Briefe. — 2. Gespräche und Erinnerungen. ✧ C. Biographien, Studien, Würdigungen. 1. Biographien. — 2. Studien. — 3. Würdigungen. ✧ D. Mendelssohn und die Romantik. ✧ E. Kritiken, Analysen, Untersuchungen einzelner Werke. 1. Kirchenmusik. — 2. Oratorien. — 3. Weltliche Vokalmusik. — 4. Instrumentalmusik. — 5. Werke für Klavier und Orgel. — 6. Zu Mendelssohns Bearbeitungen. — A. Bibliographien, Quellenkunde, Ikonographie: Bibliogr. älterer Lit. in RiemannL, [11]/1929; E. Werner, *FMB als Kirchenmusiker*, Ffm. 1930/31; Ph. Radcliffe, *FMB* in Master Musicians, London 1947; E. Walker, *Concerning an Oxford Collection of Mendelssohniana* in M & L, 1938; M. F. Schneider, *Eine Mendelssohn-Slg. in Basel* in Amerbach Bote, Basel 1948; G. Grove, *FMB* (jetzt in Buchform, zusammen m. Essays über Beethoven u. Schubert, hrsg. v. E. Blom), London 1955/56; E. Werner, *Mendelssohn Sources* in Notes XII, März 1955, 201–204; M. F. Schneider, *FMB im Bildnis*, Basel 1953; ders., *Ein unbekanntes Mendelssohn-Bild v. J. P. Lyser*, Basel 1958. — B. Briefwechsel (nur gedr.), Dokumente, Erinnerungen der Zeitgenossen. 1. Briefe: *Briefwechsel Goethe-Zelter*, hrsg. v. M. Hecker, Lpz. 1913–1919 (1. Aufl. hrsg. v. F. W. Riemer, Bln. 1834); S. Hensel, *Die Familie Mendelssohn*, 3 Bde., Bln. 1879; P. u. K. Mendelssohn Bartholdy, *Briefe FMB's (1830–1847)*, Lpz. 1861; *FMB's Briefwechsel m. Karl Klingemann*, hrsg. v. K. Klingemann (Sohn), Essen 1909; K. Mendelssohn Bartholdy, *Goethe u. FMB*, Lpz. 1871 (die zweite engl. Ausg., London 1874, enthält 37 Briefe an verschiedene Personen); *Briefwechsel m. J. G. Droysen* in Deutsche Rundschau 1902; einige andere Briefe zwischen FMB u. Droysen in *J. G. Droysens gesammeltem Briefwechsel*, Lpz. 1929; C. Wehmer (Hrsg.), *Ein tief gegründet Herz. Briefwechsel Droysen-FMB*, Heidelberg 1959; F. Hiller, *FMB, Briefe u. Erinnerungen*, Köln [2]/1878; ders., *Aus Ferdinand Hillers Briefwechsel (1826–1831)*, hrsg. v. R. Sietz, Kongreß-Festgabe, Köln 1958; J. Schubring, *Briefwechsel m. FMB*, Lpz. 1892; E. Devrient, *Meine Erinnerungen an FMB*, Lpz. 1869 (m. 33 Briefen); E. Polko, *Erinnerungen an FMB*, Lpz. 1868 (m. 12 Brie-

fen); J. Moscheles, *Briefe v. FMB an Ignaz u. Charlotte Moscheles*, Lpz. 1888; H. Voigt, *8 Briefe v. FMB*, Lpz. 1871; E. Wolff, *6 unveröff. Briefe v. FMB an W. Taubert* in Mk VIII, 1908/09, 165–170; *Goethe-Jb.* XII, 1891 (9 Briefe v. FMB u. Goethe); H. F. Chorley, *Autobiography*, hrsg. v. H. G. Hewlett, London 1873 (m. einigen Briefen v. FMB); *FMB and his English Publisher* in MT 46, London 1905 (m. einigen Briefen); J. Eckardt, *Ferdinand David u. die Familie Mendelssohn*, Lpz. 1888 (m. 30 Briefen); H. Thompson, *Some Mendelssohn Letters* in MT 64, London 1923; E. Werner, *New Light on the Family Mendelssohn* in Hebrew Union College Annual 1955 (enthält einige unveröff. Briefe); E. Hanslick, *Briefe v. FMB an Aloys Fuchs* in Deutsche Rundschau, Okt. 1888; L. Nohl, *Musiker-Briefe*, Lpz. 1867 (enthält 30 Briefe, die sich z. T. in anderen Slgn. finden); G. Hogarth, *The Philharmonic Society of London*, London 1862 (enthält 10 Briefe); F. G. Edwards, *The History of Mendelssohn's „Elijah"*, London 1896 (enthält einige Briefe); A. Mendelssohn Bartholdy, *FMB* in Frankfurter Zeitung, 31. Jan. 1909, Nr. 31 (m. einigen Briefen); E. Wolff, *Meisterbriefe v. FMB*, Bln. 1907. — Außerdem einige Briefe in der folgenden Kategorie. — 2. Gespräche und Erinnerungen: A. B. Marx, *Erinnerungen*, Bln. 1865; Th. Marx, *A. B. Marx' Verhältnis zu FMB*, Lpz. 1869 (wichtig!); L. Rellstab, *Aus meinem Leben*, Bln. 1861; L. Schubring, *Erinnerungen an FMB* in Daheim, 1866; J. C. Lobe, *Erinnerungen an FMB* in Gartenlaube, 1866/67; H. Dorn, *Aus Moscheles' Leben, Briefe u. Tagebücher*, hrsg. v. seiner Frau, Lpz. 1872/73; H. Berlioz, *Mémoirs*, Paris 1870; ders., *Voyage musical en Allemagne et en Italie*, Paris 1844; ders., *Correspondance inédite (1819–1868)*, Paris 1879; L. v. Kretschmann, *FMB in Weimar* (Erinnerungen der Jenny v. Gustedt) in Deutsche Rundschau, Dez. 1891; Ph. Spitta, *Besprechung des Briefwechsels Mendelssohn-Schubring* in VfMw VIII, 1892, 419–422; H. v. Bülow, *Briefe u. Schriften* III, Lpz. 1896; W. J. v. Wasielewski, *Aus 70 Jahren*, Stg. 1897; H. Devrient, *Therese Devrients Jugenderinnerungen*, Stg. 1905; R. Schumann, *Erinnerungen an FMB*, hrsg. vom Schumann-Arch., Zwickau 1948; ders., *Gesammelte Schriften über Musik*, hrsg. v. M. Kreisig, Lpz. 1914; ders., *Memoirs of Mendelssohn*, hrsg. v. J. Galston, Rochester (N. Y.) 1951; W. Boetticher, *R. Schumann in seinen Schriften u. Büchern*, Bln. 1942 (unzuverlässig); F. Liszt, *Briefe an eine Freundin*, hrsg. v. La Mara, 1893–1904; L. Spohr, *Selbstbiogr.*, Kassel u. Göttingen 1860/61; M. Hauptmann-F. Hauser, *Briefwechsel*, hrsg. v. A. Schöne, Lpz. 1871; R. B. Gotch, *FMB and his Friends in Kensington*, London 1934; H. F. Chorley, *Modern German Music*, ebda. 1854; Ch. E. Horsley, *Reminiscences of Mendelssohn*, zuerst in Dwight's Journal of Music, Boston 1872, dann in The Choir, London 11., 25. Jan., 8., 15. Febr. 1873; B. Hake, *FMB als Lehrer* in Deutsche Rundschau 140, 1909, 453 ff.; A. Jullien, *Mendelssohn à Paris* in Airs variés, Paris 1877; H. F. Kling, *Mendelssohn en Suisse* in Revue internat. de musique, Paris 1899, Nr. 22; G. A. Sampson, *A Day with Mendelssohn*, London 1919, Hodden & Stoughton; J. Bulman, *Jenny Lind*, London 1956 (enth. einige Briefe FMB's u. interessantes Dok.-Material); E. Geibel, *Zu Mendelssohns Totenfeier* in Neue Musikzeitschrift, München 1947, Nov; R. Sterndale Bennett, *The Death of Mendelssohn* in ML, Okt. 1955; C. S. Holland-W. Rockstro, *Jenny Lind, the Artist*, London 1891 (einiges wichtige Material über FMB's letzte Jahre); R. Wagner, *Mein Leben*, München 1911; ders., *Besprechung v. E. Devrients Erinnerungen an Mendelssohn* in Gesammelte Schriften, Lpz. [4]/1907; J. Freiherr v. Bunsen, *Aus seinen Briefen, geschildert v. seiner Witwe*, 2 Bde., Lpz. 1869. — C. Biographien, biogr. Studien, krit. Würdigungen. 1. Biographien: W. A. Lampadius, *FMB, ein Denkmal*, Lpz. 1848, erw. in *ein Gesamtbild seines Lebens u. Schaffens*, Lpz. 1886; A. Reissmann, *FMB, Sein Leben u. seine Werke*, Bln. 1872; La Mara, *FMB*, Lpz. [10]/1911; G. Grove, *FMB*, zuerst in GroveD, 1879 bis 1889, dann separat hrsg. v. E. Blom, London 1951, 1955; J. C. Hadden, *FMB*, London 1909; S. Stratton, *Mendelssohn* in Master Musicians, London 1901; B. Schrader, *FMB*, Lpz. 1898; E. Wolff, *FMB*, Bln. 1906 (wichtig); C. Bellaigue, *Mendelssohn*, Paris 1920; H. Barbedette, *FMB, sa vie et ses œuvres*, Paris 1869; V. Magnien, *Étude biographique sur FMB*, Beauvais 1850; W. Dahms, *FMB*, Bln. 1922; F. Neumann, *FMB, eine Biogr.*, Kassel 1854; W. S. Rockstro, *Mendelssohn*, London 1884; C. Selden, *La musique en Allemagne (FMB)*, Paris 1867; P. de Stöcklin, *FMB*, Paris, 1. Aufl. in Les musiciens célèbres, 1907, 2. Aufl. Paris 1927; C. Winn, *Mendelssohn*, Oxford 1928; J. Petitpierre, *Le mariage de Mendelssohn*, Paris 1937, engl. Übs. London 1957; G.

Marietti, *Mendelssohn*, Rom 1937; B. B a r t e l s , *FMB, Mensch u. Werk*, Bremen 1947; J. E r s k i n e , *Song without Words. The Story of FMB*. New York 1941; W. R e i c h u. M. F. S c h n e i d e r , *FMB, Denkmal in Wort u. Bild*, Basel 1947; P. S u t e r m e i s t e r , *FMB, Lebensbild u. Briefe*, Zürich 1949; H. Ch. W o r b s , *FMB, Wesen u. Wirken im Spiegel v. Selbstzeugnissen*, Lpz. 1958; H. E. J a c o b , *FMB u. seine Zeit*, Ffm. 1959; F. H. F r a n k e n , *Das Leben großer Meister im Spiegel der Medizin. Schubert, Chopin, Mendelssohn*, Stuttgart 1959; E. W e r n e r , *FMB, eine biogr. u. krit. Neuwertung* (in Vorb.). — 2. Biogr. Studien: W. H. R i e h l , *FMB* in Mus. Charakterköpfe, Stg. 1879; C. H. M ü l l e r , *FMB, Frankfurt u. der Cäcilienver.*, Darmstadt 1925; M. B l u m n e r , *Geschichte der Singakad. zu Berlin*, Bln. 1891; G. S c h ü n e m a n n , *Die Singakad. zu Berlin 1791–1941*, Regensburg 1941; A. S e i d l , *FMB, der Gründer des Leipziger Kons.* (in Fs. zum 75. Jubiläum des Kons.), Lpz. 1918; Friedrich S c h m i d t , *Das Musikleben der bürgerl. Ges. Leipzigs im Vormärz*, Langensalza 1912; R. T r o n n i e r , *FMB* in Vom Schaffen großer Komp., Stg. 1927; A. D ö r f f e l , *Geschichte der Gewandhauskonz.*, Lpz. 1884; J. E s s e r , *Mendelssohn u. die Rheinlande*, Bonn 1923; J. A l f , *Die Niederrhein. Musikfeste in Düsseldorf* in der Stadt Düsseldorf, 1941, 1943; J. W e r n e r , *Felix and Fanny Mendelssohn* in ML, Okt. 1947; O. B o r m a n n , *J. N. Schelble*, Ffm. 1926; E. R y c h n o v s k y , *Aus FMB letzten Lebenstagen* in Mk Jg. VIII, Bd. XXX, 1908/09, 141–146. — 3. Würdigungen (nur die wichtigste Lit. seit etwa 1930 ist hier berücksichtigt, da eine umfassende Bibliogr. dieser Sparte viele S. füllen würde): H. B e r l , *Das Judentum in der Musik*, Bln. u. Lpz. 1926; P. C o l s o n , *Victorian Portraits*, London 1932; W. M e l l e r , *Music and Society*, London 1946; L. S t e i n , *The Racial Thinking of R. Wagner*, New York 1950; K. B l e s s i n g e r , *Judentum u. Musik*, Bln. 1944; R. C a p e l l , *Mendelssohn after 100 Years* in Hallé's Magazine, London Aug.-Sept. 1947; H. W e i s s , *FMB im Wandel der Zeit* in NZM, München Nov. 1947; W. F i s c h e r , *FMB in Österr. Musik-Zs.*, Wien Nov.-Dez. 1947; R. L. J a c o b s , *Mendelssohn. A Revaluation* in Penguin Music Magazine, London 1947, Nr. 3, 4; A. M o n t e l l i , *Il mondo poetico di Mendelssohn* in RaM, 1947; E. M e y e r s t e i n , *Some Remarks on the Genius of Mendelssohn* in Music Survey I, Nr. 2, London 1948; W. V e t t e r , *Res severa* in Fs. zum 175. Bestehen der Gewandhauskonz., Lpz. 1956; G. W h e a t l e y , *Famous Musical Controversies* in Musical Opinion, London Jan. u. Febr. 1948 (betr. die Kontroverse Mendelssohn-Wagner); K. W ö r n e r , *Mendelssohn u. wir* in Musica I, 1947, 245–250; A. P e l l e g r i n i , *Mendelssohn als deutscher Kulturträger* in NZM, Nov. 1947; H. E p p s t e i n , *Kring Mendelssohn och hans musik?* in Musikrevy, Stockholm 1951, Nr. 31; E. W a l k e r , *A History of Music in England*, hrsg. v. J. A. Westrup, Oxford ²/1952; E. W e r n e r , *Mendelssohn's Fame and Tragedy* in Reconstructionist 25, Nr. 1, New York 1959. — D. Mendelssohn und die Romantik: A. B. M a r x , *Die Musik des 19. Jh.*, Bln. u. Lpz. 1855; ders., *Über Tondichter u. Tonkunst*, hrsg. v. L. Hirschberg, Hildburghausen 1922; R. S c h u m a n n , *Gesammelte Schriften über Musik u. Musiker*, hrsg. v. M. Kreisig, Lpz. 1914; C. K r e t s c h m a n n , *Romantik in der Musik* in NZM XIV/XV, 1848; D. G. M a s o n , *The Romantic Composers*, London 1906; E. I s t e l , *Die Blütezeit der mus. Romantik*, Lpz. 1921; R. R o l l a n d , *L'école romantique* in LavignacE, Paris 1926; H. M a n d t , *Die Entwicklung des Romantischen in der Instr.-Musik FMB's*, Köln 1927; G. K i n s k y , *Was Mendelssohn Indebted to Weber?* in MQ XIX, 1933, 178 f.; E. B ü c k e n , *Musik des 19. Jh. bis zur Moderne*, Potsdam 1929; ders., *Musik der Nationen*, Lpz. 1937; A. S c h e r i n g , *Vom mus. Kunstwerk*, hrsg. v. F. Blume, Lpz. 1949; A. E i n s t e i n , *Music in the Romantic Era*, New York 1947; E. W e r n e r , *Instrumental Music outside the Pale of Classicism and Romanticism* in Instrumental Music, hrsg. v. D. Hughes, Cambridge, Mass. 1959. — E. Kritiken, Analysen, Untersuchungen einzelner Werke. 1. Kirchenmusik: S. K ü m m e r l e , *Enzyklopädie der ev. KM.*, Gütersloh 1886–1895; W. S t a h l , *Geschichtliche Entwicklung der ev. KM.*, Bln. 1926; H. J. M o s e r , *Die ev. KM. in volkstümlichem Überblick*, Stg. 1926; Ph. S p i t t a , *Die Wiederbelebung prot. KM.* in Zur Musik, Bln. 1892; A. S c h w e i t z e r , *Von Bachs Tod bis zur ersten Wiederauff. der Matthäuspassion* in Mk Jg. VII. Bd. 25, 1907/08, 76–88; J. M ü l l e r , *Die Choralbearb. v. Bach bis zur Choralfantasie Regers* in SMZ, 1922; R. W e r n e r , *FMB als Kirchenmusiker*, Ffm. 1930, Selbstverlag (wichtiges Quellenwerk); G. S c h ü n e m a n n , *Die Bachpflege der Berliner Singakad.* in Bach-Jb. 1928; R. H o h e n e m s e r , *Welche Einflüsse hatte die Wiederbelebung der älteren Musik im 19. Jh. auf die deutschen Komp.?*, Lpz. 1900; H. K r e t z s c h m a r , *Führer durch den Konzertsaal II, 1* (kirchl. Werke), Lpz. ²/1921; A. v a n d e r L i n d e n , *Un fragment inédit du „Lauda Sion" de Felix Mendelssohn* in AMl 26, 1954, 48–64.

487 – Bd. IX

— 2. Oratorien: J. Th. M o s e w i u s , *Zur Auff. des Or. „Paulus"*, Breslau 1836; R. W a g n e r , *Das Or. „Paulus"* in Gesammelte Schriften VIII (beigefügt einem Ber. an den Intendanten v. Lüttichau v. 27. Apr. 1843); O. J a h n , *Gesammelte Aufsätze über Musik*, Lpz. 1866/67; F. G. E d w a r d s , *The History of Mendelssohn's „Elijah"*, London 1896; A. S c h e r i n g , *Geschichte des Or.*, Lpz. 1911; H. K r e t z s c h m a r , *Führer durch den Konz.-Saal II* (Or.), Lpz. ³/1915; T. B a x t e r , *Mendelssohn's Elijah*, London 1880; D. F. T o v e y , *Essays in Music Analysis V*, London-New York 1949; Ph. R a d c l i f f e , *FMB*, London 1954; Th. A r m s t r o n g , *Mendelssohn's Elijah* in ML XIV, 1933, 396 f.; P. Y o u n g , *Introduction to the Music of Mendelssohn*, London 1949; J. W e r n e r , *Mendelssohn's Elijah, the 110th Anniversary* in MT, Apr. 1957. — 3. Weltliche Vokalmusik (einschl. Lieder u. Chöre): H. K r e t z s c h m a r , *Führer II u. III*. ²/1915; L. L e v e n , *Mendelssohn als Lyriker*, Ffm. 1926; P. Y o u n g , *Introduction to the Music of Mendelssohn*, London 1949; H. B e r l i o z , *Correspondance inédite*, Paris 1879; F. Z a n d e r , *Über FMBs Walpurgisnacht*, Königsberg 1862; W. K o c h ; M. L i t t l e , *Mendelssohn's Music to the Antigone*, London 1893; H. K r e t z s c h m a r , *Chorgsg., Sängerchöre u. Chorver.* in Mus. Vorträge, Lpz. 1879; J. B a n t z , *Geschichte des deutschen Männergsg.*, Ffm. 1890; Ph. S p i t t a , *Der deutsche Männergsg.* in Musical America, 1894, 297 f.; W. K. v. J o l i z z a , *Das Lied u. seine Geschichte*, Wien 1910; H. R i e m a n n , *Geschichte der Musik seit Beethoven*, Lpz. 1901; G. S c h ü n e m a n n , *Mendelssohns Jugendopern* in ZfMw V, 1923, 506–545. — 4. Instrumentalmusik (außer Kl. und Org.): D. M i n t z , *Melusina, A Musical Draft* in MQ 43, 1957, 480–499; A. H e u s s , *Das Dresdener Amen im 1. Satz der Reformationssymph.* in Signale 62, Lpz. 1904, 281 f., 305 f.; G. G r o v e , *Mendelssohn's Violin Concerto* in MT 47, London 1906, 611 f.; D. F. T o v e y , *Essays in Musical Analysis I* (Italian Symph.), II (Scherzo in *g*; aus dem Oktett), London 1935; ders., *The Main Stream of Music* (Ouv. zum Sommernachtstraum; Ouv. zu Ruy Blas; Trios op. 49, 66), London-New York 1949; H. K r e t z s c h m a r , *Führer*, I. Tl., Lpz. ⁵/1919; J. H o r t o n , *The Chamber Music of Mendelssohn*, Oxford 1946; G. A b r a h a m , *The Scores of Mendelssohn's „Hebrides"* in MMR, Sept. 1948; ders., *Die Verschiedenen Part. zu Mendelssohn „Hebriden"* im Almanach „Der Amerbacher Bote", Basel 1948; E. W a l k e r , *Mendelssohn's „Die einsame Insel"* in ML, Juli 1945; G. K i n s k y , *Die Part. der „Hebriden"-Ouv.* in Kat. des W. Heyer-Museums, Lpz. u. Köln 1916; E. W e r n e r , *Two Unpublished Mendelssohn Concertos* in ML, Apr. 1955; G. W i l k e , *Tonalität u. Modulation in den StrQu. Mendelssohns u. Schumanns*, Lpz. 1938; F. L i s z t , *Über FMB's Ouv. zum „Sommernachtstraum"* in Gesammelte Schriften III, hrsg. v. La Mara, Lpz. 1880–1883. — 5. Werke für Kl. und Org. (nur die neuere Lit. ist hier berücksichtigt): W. K a h l , *Zu Mendelssohns Lieder ohne Worte* in ZfM III, 1921; H. L e i c h t e n t r i t t , *Mus. Formenlehre*, 3. erw. Aufl., 2. Tl., Kap. 4, Lpz. 1927; H. u. L. T i s c h l e r , *Mendelssohn's Songs without Words* in MQ 1947, 1. H.; dies., *Mendelssohn's Style* in Music Review VIII, 1947; P. Y o u n g , *Introduction to the Music of Mendelssohn*, London 1947; K. D a l e , *Nineteenth Century Piano Music*, London-New York 1954; H. v. B ü l o w , *Vorw. zu Mendelssohns Rondo capriccioso op. 14*, München 1880, J. Aibl; D. F. T o v e y , *Essays in Musical Analysis IV* (Variations sérieuses), London 1935; M. F r i e d l a n d , *Zeitstil u. Persönlichkeitsstil in den Var.-Werken der rom. Romantik*, Lpz. 1930, B & H; P. E g e r t , *Die Kl.-Son. im Zeitalter der Romantik*, Bln. 1934; A. M. H e n d e r s o n , *Mendelssohn's Unpublished Organ Works* in MT, London 1947; F. G. E d w a r d s , *Mendelssohn's Organ Sonatas* in PRMA 21, London 1894; ders., *Mendelssohn's Organ Sonatas* in MT 42, London 1901; J. W. G. H a t h a w a y , *Analysis of Mendelssohn's Organ Works*, London 1898; Ch. W. P e a r c e , *Mendelssohn's Organ Sonatas* in ZIMG III, 1902, 337 f.; O. M a n s f i e l d , *Some Characteristics of Mendelssohn's Organ Sonatas* in MQ 1917, 3. H.; R. W e r n e r , *FMB als Kirchenmusiker II* (Orgelmusik), Ffm. 1930. — 6. Zu Mendelssohns Bearbeitungen: R. S t e r n d a l e B e n n e t t , *Mendelssohn as Editor of Handel* in MMR, London Mai-Juni 1956; H. Ch. W o l f f , *Mendelssohn and Handel* in MQ, Apr. 1959; F. C h r y s a n d e r , *Mendelssohns Orgelbegl. zu „Israel in Ägypten"* in Jb. f. Mw. II, 1867, 249 f.; W. A l t m a n n , *Mendelssohns Eintreten f. Händel* in Mk, Jg. XII, Bd. 46, 1913, 79–85; Ph. S p i t t a , *Die Wiederbelebung prot. KM. auf geschichtlicher Grundlage* in Zur Musik, Bln. 1892; A. S c h w e i t z e r , *J. S. Bach*, London ²/1945.

Eric Werner

Mendes, Manuel, * 1547? zu Lissabon, † 24. Sept. 1605 zu Evora. Mendes wurde am 24. Sept. 1575 zum

Example 26

A. S. Herbert. *Historical Catalogue of Printed Editions of the English Bible, 1525–1961*. London: British and Foreign Bible Society; New York: American Bible Society, 1968. Revised and expanded from the edition of T. H. Darlow and H. F. Moule, 1903. Courtesy British and Foreign Bible Society; American Bible Society.

At first glance, this page seems to have about ten entries listed, because the dates and the item numbers are at almost the same places on the page and because the numbers are all printed in the same size boldface type. Also, the use of spacing between entries and between parts of entries is confusing. In fact, there are only about five or six entries here.

Another little problem is that the size of the volume is given flush right (e.g., 'f° 374 × 218'), and it is not immediately apparent whether this information goes with the item just above, or if it refers to the entry whose number appears at the far left of the same line. The two bits of information (entry number and volume format and size) are separated too much on the line.

Furthermore, the presentation of data does not follow any current, familiar pattern. It goes: date, title, publisher, city (with the city in italics, the publisher in small caps, the title in regular roman type). This would take little time becoming accustomed to, but it is an unusual styling.

The actual volume is rather attractive; the pages themselves look, from a distance, well proportioned and legible. But actual use is slowed by the peculiar styling of the page.

Example 27a, b

d'Alté A. Welch. *A Bibliography of American Children's Books Printed Prior to 1821*. Worcester, MA: American Antiquarian Society and Barre Publishers, 1972. Courtesy American Antiquarian Society.

One of the problems with bibliographies that are filled with masses of information is that the more data there are, the more difficult it is to organize and present them. That is the case with this bibliography.

The use of caps and small caps to designate titles for *The Juvenile Magazine* (item 706.1) is inconsistent with the use of full caps for *The Prodigal Daughter* (item 1068.15). Perhaps there is some distinction in the original, but that is not clear here. And the use of a dash (at, for example, entries 706.3 and 707.2) is not perfectly clear.

The wealth of information that each entry gives is praiseworthy. But a full column of data run margin to margin (even if the column is narrow) is difficult to follow. Entry 1068.16 is a case in point. The designer has recognized this problem, and has tried to compensate for it by printing all entry numbers in boldface. But the information in 1068.16 is densely packed, and it is hard to see where one sentence ends and the next begins.

Furthermore, the long dashes within entries (e.g. 1068.15 and 1068.16) are obtrusive and not immediately understandable. They apparently are used as ellipses, denoting removed text.

Entries are separated from one another by boldface numbers, blank lines, and hanging indents. Citations are made to the standard bibliography (e.g., entry 706.1 cites Shaw 2476), and locations of copies in libraries are given using Library of Congress symbols (MWA; Ct; DLC; etc.). Full paginations are also offered; this is crucial in children's books to distinguish variants (of which there could be dozens for a single title).

This is a fine bibliography with the drawbacks almost necessitated by the subject matter and the mass of information it presents. I believe a single-column format with slightly larger type and more leading (and perhaps with some tabulation of data for entries such as 706.2) would have yielded greater legibility and access to the data, but probably at a slightly higher cost of production.

1169. (870)   12° 137 × 65   2 vols.

Doddridge (1702–1751), the celebrated Independent divine and hymn-writer, of Northampton, compiled a New Testament commentary with a paraphrase, published in six volumes between 1739 and 1756, under the title of 'The Family Expositor,' from which this translation was extracted.

Vol. 1 contains *The confession of a freethinker* (i.e. J. J. Rousseau), Preface, Introduction, and the text of the Four Gospels, ending on N 5 *a*. Vol. 2 contains the rest of the text, Acts–Revelation, ending on Q 2 *b*. Copy also in NNAB.

1766   The Universal Bible . . . Old and New Testaments. Illustrated with parallel Scriptures and notes . . . the whole intended and accommodated to the use and understanding of every Christian and the benefit of all families.

JOHN REID: *Edinburgh*

1170.   f°   374 × 218

OT ends on p. 1088; NT on p. 384. The OT is dated 1765. The title-page of the NT states that it is edited by John Guyse. Copy in NNAB.

1766   The Holy Bible . . .   M. BASKETT AND ASSIGNS OF R. BASKETT: *London*

1171. (871)   4°   224 × 175

NT ends on O 4 *a*, followed by Index and tables. Matt. xxiii. 24, *strain out*.

1766   The Grand Imperial Bible . . . By Wm. Luke Phillips . . .

FOR THE AUTHOR: *London*

1172.   4°   235 × 181

The general title is dated 1764 and the NT and Apocrypha are dated 1766. Text ends on 23 Y *b*. Copy in BM.

1766   The Pulpit and Family Bible, Containing the Sacred Text . . . large and the Psalms in Metre used by the Church of Scotland: with Annotations . . . and Marginal Notes of Mr. John Canne, the Parallel Scriptures of Mr. Samuel Clarke, and those of Wetsten's Greek New Testament . . .

J. ROBERTSON: *Edinburgh*

1173.   4°   238 × 179

The general title is dated 1766, the OT title 1764, and there is no title to the NT. The text ends on 8 U 4 *a*. No Apocrypha. Copy in BM.

1766   The Holy Bible . . .   M. BASKETT AND ASSIGNS OF R. BASKETT: *London*

1174. (872)   8°   160 × 94

Price Three Shillings Unbound.
Text ends on Sss 8 *a*. Apocrypha mentioned in list of books, but not required by signatures.
Matt. xxiii. 24, *strain out*. Wants Apocrypha?

1766   The Holy Bible . . .   M. BASKETT AND ASSIGNS OF R. BASKETT: *London*

1175.   8°   162 × 93

The general title is dated 1765; the NT title is dated 1766. The text ends on Sss 8 *a*. Copy in BM.

street. 1810. *See also* no. **817.1** for other separate editions.

4th title: The Young Robber; Or, Dishonesty Punished. New-York: Printed And Sold By John C. Totten, No. 155 Chatham-street. 1810. *See also* no. **1463** for the separate ed. of 1819. NjP°.

706.1 THE JUVENILE MAGAZINE, Or Miscellaneous Repository Of Useful Information. Vol. I. Philadelphia: Printed for Benjamin Johnson, & Jacob Johnson, High-Street. 1802.

vol. 1.: fr.[ii], t.[1], [2–3], 4–214, [215–216, index] p.; 3 pl.; 14.5 cm.; bound in leather; three numbers: No. 1.: [7], 8–72 p.; No. 2.: [pl. opp. p. [73]], [73], 74–144 p.; No. 3.: [pl. opp. p. 145, 145–214, [215–216] p. The three plates are: fr.[ii] signed *Tanner Sc*, pl. opp. p.[73] signed *Stothard del. Tanner Sc.*; pl. opp. p. 145 signed *J. Akin Sc.*

MWA°; PP (p. 5–8, 13–36, 49–60 & binding winting); PPiU (i. st. on t.[1], pl. opp. p. 145 wanting); Shaw 2476.

706.2 ——— Vol. II. [III.–IV.] Philadelphia [printed in a vignette] Printed for Benjamin Johnson, No. 31, High-Street. 1802.

vol. II.: fr.[ii], t.[1], [2–3], 4–214, [215–216, index] p.; 2 pl., 1 full page illus.; 14.5 cm.; bound in leather; three numbers: No. I.: [3], 4–72 p.; No. II. [73 bl.], [74, illus.], [75], 76–144 p.; No. III.: [pl. opp. p.[145]], [145], 146–214 p. The two plates, fr.[ii] signed: *Stothard del. Tanner sc.*; pl. opp. p.[145] signed *J. A.* [James Akin]; illus. p. [74] signed *A* [Alexander Anderson].

vol. III.: fr.[ii], t.[1], [2–3], 4–214, [215–216, index] p.; 3 pl.; 15 cm. bound in leather; three numbers: No. I.: [3], 4–72; No. II. [pl. opp. p.[73]], [73], 74–144 p.; No. III.: [pl. opp. p.[145]], [145], 146–214. The three plates, fr.[ii] & pl. opp. p.[145] signed *Stothard del, Tanner Sc.*; pl. opp. p. [73] signed *J. Akin sc.*

vol. IV.: fr.[ii], t.[1], [2–3], 4–214, [215–216, index] p. Three numbers: No. I. [3]–72 p.; No. II. [pl. opp. p.[73]], [73]–144 p.; No. III. [pl. opp. p.[145]], [145]–214, [215–216] p. Plates: fr.[ii], pl. opp. p.[73], and pl. opp. p.[145] signed *Stothard del Tanner Sc* or *Eng*. Pl. opp. p.[73] also has *Etched by G. Fox. N.Y.*; pl. opp. p.[145] has *Etched by Gilbert Fox.*

MWA° (vols. II.–IV.); DLC (II.–IV.); ICU

(IV.); MH (IV.); MWelC (IV.); NRU (vol. II.); OOxM (vol. IV.); PP (vol. 11. No. II. [pl. opp. p. [73]], p. [73]–74, 149–152 wanting; p.[75]–76 mut.; vol. III. p. 69 incorrectly numbered 67, p. 65–66 bound after p. 68); PPiU (vols. II.–IV. i. st. on each title page).

706.3 ——— Information. Philadelphia [not printed in a vignette]: Printed For Benjamin Johnson, No. 31, High Street. 1803.

vol. II.: t.[1], [2–3], 4–214, [215–216, index] p.; 2 pl., pl. opp. p. 59, 195 p.; 2 full page illus. p. [74], 130, both signed A [Alexander Anderson]; 3 numbers: No. I.: [3]–72 p.; No. II.: [75]–144 p.; No. III.: [145]–214 p.; vol. III.: t.[1], [2–3], 4–214, [215–216, index] p.; 3 pl., pl. opp. p. 61, 106, 196; 3 numbers: No. I.: [3]–72 p.; No. II.: [73]–144; No. III.: [145]–214 p.; vol. IV.: t.[1], [2–3], 4–214, [215–216, index] p.; 3 pl., pl. opp. p. 61, 136, 204; 3 numbers: No. I.: [3]–72 p.; No. II.: [73]–144 p. with pages 76, 81, 84–85, 88–89, 92–93, 96–97, 100, 103, 105, 108, 116 wrongly numbered 40, 45, 48–49, 52–53, 56–57, 60–61, 64, 10, 69, 72, 16 consecutively; No. III.: [145]–214 p.; 3 vols.; 14 cm.; bound in leather. The text of the three volumes is the same as no. **261.2** but with the plates opposite different pages.

CLU° (vols. II.–IV.); MWA (vols. III.–IV.); NB (vol. IV., i. st. on t.[1]; NN (vol. IV.); NRU (vols. II.–IV.); PPL (vol. IV.).

707.1 JUVENILE MISCELLANY, Including Some Natural History, For The Use Of Children. Ornamented with Eighteen Engravings. Philadelphia: Published By Jacob Johnson, No. 147, Market-Street. 1803.

t.[1], [2–72] p.; illus.; 10.5 cm.; bound in leather; colophon p.[72]: J. W. Scott, Printer. MWA-W.°; PP.

707.2 ——— Philadelphia: Published By Jacob Johnson, No. 147, Market-Street. 1808.

t.[1], [2–72] p.; illus.; 11 cm.; bound in marbled paper over bds., leather spine; colophon p.[72]: J. Rakestraw Printer. Adv. by Johnson & Warner, 1813 in **1449.2**.

MWA° (p. 61–62 mut.); CtHT; DLC; MSaE (emb. st. on t.[1]); Shaw 15343.

708 THE JUVENILE MISCELLANY, IN PROSE & VERSE. Selected From The Writings Of Eminent "vast estate"; "*Bristol*", line 6, is in large italics; with the exception of "*Gentleman*", line 6, "*How*", lines 10 and 11, the first letter of every word in the subtitle is printed in the lower case; there is a dash after "world.—", line 14. The caption p.[3] is in 4 lines, followed by 25 lines of verse. There is a comma after "attend,", line 5; "penn'd;" is spelled with two of the letter "n", which spelling is used in all following editions; "warning", line 7, "parents", line 8, "estate", line 10, and other words usually capitalized, have the first letter in the lower case. "Bristol", line 9, is in regular type; "clothed" line 13, is used instead of "cloathed"; "LORD", line 28, entirely in capitals. The book is printed in 83.6 (20 line measure) type. *See* note under no. **492.1.** Line 6, page 11 ends "sinner wild." The last 30 lines of the poem are on p. 12, and show variations. One of these is "crowns", line 30, instead of "crown".

MWA°; Ct; DLC; Evans 36166.

1068.15 THE / PRODIGAL / DAUGHTER, / OR A / STRANGE AND WONDERFUL/RELA-TION./*Shewing how a* ———— [same as **1068.14**] *in Bris-/tol, had* ———— *daughter,/who,* ———— *support/her* ———— *with/the Devil to poison them.—How an Angel in-/formed them of her design.—How she lay in a/trance four days: And when* ———— *and related/the wonderful things she saw in the other/world./*NEW-YORK:/ *Printed for the Traveling Booksellers./*1799.

t.[1], [2–3], 4–8+ p.; 16 cm. The type setting resembles that of no. **1068.14** in largely being printed in italics. The main title is in 6 lines instead of 5 and ends with "*Relation.*" The subtitle, in italics, follows the wording of no. **1068.14** and differs in not having a dash after "*word.*", line 16. The caption, p. [3], in 4 lines, has "*Prodigal Daughter,*", line 2, in large italics and followed by a comma. The verses below the caption and the text of the book closely resemble the type setting of no. **1068.14** and printed in the same size type. Only one type ornament is present. The modern form of the letter "*s*" is used.

RPJCB° (all after p. 8 wanting, probably p. 9–12).

1068.16 THE/PRODIGAL DAUGHTER:/Or, [same as **1068.10**] Relation: Shewing how a/ ———— in BRISTOL, in *England,* had ———— bar-

gained with the *Devil* to poison them.—How an Angel informed her Parents of her Design.—How ———— Trance four days, ———— life again ———— Things/she saw in the other World./ Printed and sold at the *Bible* & *Heart,* Cornhill, BOSTON./[ca. 1802].

t.[1], [2], 3–12+ p.; 4 illus.; 17 cm. The type setting and wording of the title page, which ends with the word "World" resembles no. **1068.10,** but the first three words are printed in two lines instead of one. This is the second Fleet edition with a comma after "Or," and a colon after "Relation:", line 3. "BRISTOL,", line 4, is printed in small capitals, followed by a comma. This edition is the first Fleet edition to add "in *England*", after "BRISTOL", line 4. The word "them.—", line 9 is followed by a period and a dash; "days", line 9, has a lower case "d"; the "l" of "life", line 10, is in the lower case. Page 3 has an entirely different type setting from **1068.10** and is closer to **1068.5.** The caption reads: The/*Prodigal Daughter:*/Or/ The Disobedient Lady Reclaimed, &c./[16 lines of verse, or lines 6–21]. The following words have the first letter in the lower case, where in no. **1068.5** it is capitalized: "child," line 6, "line", line 7, "parents-" followed by a dash, line 9; "estate", lines 11, "array", line 14; "child" and "truth", line 15; "heart" and "pride", line 16; "delight", "vanity", line 16. Line 7 has "penn'd" with two of the letter "n"; "Bristol", line 10, is printed in regular type. The type measured on p. 5 is 83.5 (20 line measure). *See* note under no. **492.1.** Line 29, p. 12, ends "a sinner vile". This is first edition in which "vile" is substituted for "wild", and appears only in later editions printed by Thomas Fleet, the son of John Fleet, **1068.17,** and by Nathaniel Coverly, **1068.21–25.** Pages 13–16 are missing from this edition. The type setting of the text is quite different from **1068.10,** because in the earlier book many portions are in italics, while in **1068.16** none of the text is in italics.

Three printer's ornaments are present. The illustrations are printed from the same blocks used in no. **1068.10,** but now characteristic breaks and differences appear. Cut 1, the Prodigal Daughter in her coffin, t.[1], no longer has the signature *P.F.* Cut 2, the devil dressed as a gentleman talking to the Prodigal Daughter, p. 6, has a very thin broken line for a basal rule. The wedge-shaped break in the lower

Example 28

Joseph Blumenthal, commentary. *The Spiral Press Through Four Decades: An Exhibition of Books and Ephemera*. New York: The Pierpont Morgan Library, 1966. Courtesy The Pierpont Morgan Library.

Like that in the bibliography in Blumenthal's *The Printed Book in America* (see Example 1), the line measure was quite long in this book. Therefore the designer chose to shorten it by having a shoulder note, 'Catalogue of the Exhibition', to use up part of the horizontal dimension. By shortening the line, the designer could use a smaller typeface, thus allowing a good deal of information to be imparted in a small space without sacrificing legibility or readability.

New entries are marked by the space and the entry number, which is indented in a fairly attractive way, though on some pages it might be difficult to determine if the number refers to the preceding or the following entry.

Data are given in the following order (for books): title; author (except when something else intervenes, as is the case with 'A monograph' for entry 27); publisher; date; pagination and illustration pages; typeface; number of copies; binding; and illustration types. Sometimes also the type of paper is mentioned (as in entry 29).

Since the bibliography covers the products of a press, a chronological presentation is logical. And since that order is established, there is no need to use authors' names first. In fact, titles make just as much sense. Titles are presented in full caps, clearly distinguishing them from the data which follow. As I have mentioned, it might have been better to use italics for the titles (italics were available, as is evident from entry 28) in order to reduce confusion about capitalization in the original titles.

The overall effect is efficient and pleasing, and the bibliography, though presenting the data in an idiosyncratic order, offers a good deal of information in a legible and fairly elegant style.

Example 29

Oak Knoll Books. *Recent Acquisitions of New Books*. Catalogue M522. New Castle, DE: Oak Knoll Books, [1990]. Courtesy Robert D. Fleck, Oak Knoll Books.

This catalogue uses full caps and boldface type for its filing entries, and full caps for book titles. The move from boldface to regular full caps to upper- and lower-case types is easy, and it clearly distinguishes elements in each entry. Having spaces between entries, prices at the right-hand margin, and the note portion of each entry indented also highlights important elements.

This is a good example of combined spatial and typographic coding which anticipates readers' needs. The simplicity of design can be a model for all bibliography compilers.

25

STEEPLE BUSH. By Robert Frost. Henry Holt and Company, New York, 1947. [x, 2]3-63[2] pp., 6 x 9¼ inches. Linotype Caledonia, with Bulmer and Blado Italic. 751 copies. Buckram spine, paper over boards, gold-stamped with a decoration by Loren MacIver. Slipcase. Line engraving from drawing on slate by Loren MacIver.

26

THE ROSE AND THE RING. By William Makepeace Thackeray. Reproduced in facsimile from the author's original illustrated manuscript in the Pierpont Morgan Library. With an introduction by Gordon N. Ray. The Pierpont Morgan Library, New York, 1947. [2, iv]v-xviii[2] pp. + 90 plates, 11 x 8⅜ inches. Linotype Fairfield, with Bulmer. 1000 copies. Bound in buckram, gold-stamped with rose and ring overall pattern. Slipcase with matching design. Collotype plates by the Meriden Gravure Company, hand-colored in *pochoir* by the Martha Berrien Studio, New York.

27

STEUBEN GLASS. A monograph. By James S. Plaut. H. Bittner and Company, New York, (1948). [x, 2]3-30[4] pp. (including 11 illustrations in gravure) + 61 halftone plates, 9¼ x 12¼ inches. Linotype Janson, with Bulmer and Bodoni Titling. 1500 copies. Bound in buckram, with gold-stamped decoration. Slipcase. Illustrations in text reproduced by gravure. Halftone plates printed at The Spiral Press.

28

CH'ING MING SHANG HO. SPRING FESTIVAL ON THE RIVER. A scroll painting (*Ex Coll. A. W. Bahr*) of the Ming dynasty after a Sung dynasty subject. Reproduced in its entirety and in its original size in a portfolio of twenty-three collotype plates and twelve enlarged details. With an introduction and notes by Alan Priest. The Metropolitan Museum of Art, New York, 1948. [ii, 12, 2] pp. + 30 plates, 12¼ x 18 inches. Linotype Janson, with Bulmer and Bodoni Titling. Archer paper. 500 copies. Portfolio, buckram spine, paper over boards. Collotype plates by the Meriden Gravure Company.

29

ITALIAN MANUSCRIPTS IN THE PIERPONT MORGAN LIBRARY. Descriptive survey of the principal illuminated manuscripts of the sixth to sixteenth centuries, with a selection of important letters and documents. Catalogue compiled by Meta Harrsen and George K. Boyce. With an introduction by Bernard Berenson. The Pierpont Morgan Library, New York, 1953. [vi]vii-xii[2]3-79[4] + 72 collotype plates + 6 color plates, 9 x 12 inches. Linotype Baskerville, with Bulmer and Perpetua. Curtis Rag

59

68. (TYPE SPECIMENS) FRY. SPECIMEN OF MODERN PRINTING TYPES BY EDMUND FRY, 1828. A Facsimile with an introduction and notes by David Chambers. London: Printing Historical Society, 1986, 8vo., cloth. 18 pages followed by the facsimile. $40.00

> Limited to 1500 numbered copies of which 500 are for sale. This specimen book was the last to be prepared by Fry before the sale of his foundry to William Thorowgood and is known in only one copy. Includes some foldout sheets.

A Selection of Books on Book-Collecting and Bookselling

69. ADELMAN, SEYMOUR. HELP FROM HEAVEN. New Castle: Oak Knoll Books, 1984, long scroll inserted in plastic container with specially printed label. $25.00

> Autobiographical sketches of some of the most interesting book collecting "miracles" experienced by this well known collector. Limited to 325 copies and printed by the Bird & Bull Press.

70. AHEARN, ALLEN. BOOK COLLECTING, A COMPREHENSIVE GUIDE. New York: G. P. Putnam's Sons, (1989), 8vo., two tone paper over boards, dust jacket. 320 pages. $24.95

> First edition. The successor to the classic work THE BOOK COLLECTOR'S HANDBOOK OF VALUES by Van Allen Bradley. A good guide which will prove of value to the novice and professional alike. Covers what to collect, sources for books, pricing variances, authors most often requested, first books, etc..

71. (ALEMBIC PRESS) LOW, DAVID AND GRAHAM GREENE. DEAR DAVID, DEAR GRAHAM, A BIBLIOPHILIC CORRESPONDENCE. Oxford: The Alembic Press with The Amate Press, 1989, 8vo., cloth. 91 pages. $90.00

> First edition. Limited to 250 copies, of which this is one of the 200 trade copies bound thus. Set in Spectrum and printed by letterpress at The Alembic Press on Zerkall paper. David Low was one of the leading antiquarian booksellers of his day and established a friendship with the novelist Graham Greene in the 1930s. This collection of letters mainly covers news and reminiscencies of books and booksellers.

72. (ALEMBIC PRESS) LOW, DAVID AND GRAHAM GREENE. DEAR DAVID, DEAR GRAHAM, A BIBLIOPHILIC CORRESPONDENCE. Oxford: The Alembic Press with The Amate Press, 1989, 8vo., quarter leather with marbled paper over boards, slipcase. 91 pages. $180.00

> First edition. Limited to 250 copies, of which this is one of the 50 special copies bound thus.

73. BARKER, NICOLAS. TREASURES OF THE BRITISH LIBRARY. With a foreword by Lord Quinton. New York: Harry N. Abrahams, (1989), 4to., cloth, dust jacket. 272 pages. $49.50

> First edition. A magnificent production which will be a delight to any bibliophile, being filled with illustrations of rare and interesting items. The British Library's fifteen-million item collection includes many of the world's most famous books—the Gutenberg Bible, a First Folio of Shakespeare, the earliest dated printed book, first editions of Chaucer, etc.. This work traces the history of the Library from its foundation with Sir Hans Sloane right up to the twentieth century.

12

29

74. BELANGER, TERRY. LUNACY AND THE ARRANGEMENT OF BOOKS.
New Castle: Oak Knoll Books, 1985, 8vo., stiff paper wrappers. (ii), 24 pages. $10.00
> Second printing of the third Oak Knoll publication issued at Christmas time.
> Belanger, the well known Columbia library authority, gives a humorous discussion of the arrangement of books.

75. BETTMANN, OTTO L. THE DELIGHTS OF READING, QUOTES,
NOTES & ANECDOTES. With a Foreword by Daniel J. Boorstin. Boston: David R.
Godine, (1987), small 4to., cloth, dust jacket. xvi, 139, (2) pages. $14.95
> First edition. A delightful selection of quotes from the famous and infamous on
> such subjects as Rapid Readers, Book Burners, The Book that roused the Nation,
> Three pioneer American Bookman, etc.. Well illustrated.

76. (BIRD & BULL PRESS) MORRIS, HENRY. THE PRIVATE PRESS-MAN'S
TALE. With illustrations by Lili Wronker. Newtown, PA: Bird & Bull Press, 1990, 4to.,
paste paper over cloth-backed boards, leather spine label. 61, (2) pages. $200.00
> First edition, limited to 230 numbered copies. Letterpress printed with Van
> Dijck types on Arches mouldmade paper and bound by Barbara Blumenthal. A
> humorous collection of satire and prose, inspired by Chaucer's CANTERBURY
> TALES. All the text is related to the book arts - book-collecting, bookselling,
> printing, papermaking, etc. It includes an imaginary interview with William
> Morris, a great poem about the attitude of FINE PRINT magazine, Henry's
> explanation of the HANDMADE PAPER TODAY incident and a review of the
> antics in FINE PRINT's book reviews. There are also two excellent articles by
> Sidney Berger on Book Fair's and Book Scouts. The illustrations have been very
> well executed and express all the humour of the text. An essential for anybody
> who is known in the books about books field, because they are bound to have
> been mentioned! With prospectus loosely inserted.

77. (BIRD & BULL PRESS) MORRIS, HENRY. TRADE TOKENS OF BRITISH
AND AMERICAN BOOKSELLERS & BOOKMAKERS, WITH SPECIMENS OF
ELEVEN ORIGINAL TOKENS STRUCK ESPECIALLY FOR THIS BOOK. Newtown,
PA: Bird & Bull Press, 1989, 8vo., quarter morocco leather with paper covered
sides and leather spine label. 83, (3) pages. Accompanied by a heavy die-cut board folder
containing 11 different copper tokens minted by individual booksellers & bookmakers
especially for this book, all enclosed in a slipcase. $260.00
> First edition, limited to 300 numbered copies of which 250 are for sale. Morris has
> provided a history of these tokens and given a bibliography of all known British
> and American examples and included many illustrations of tokens reproduced
> from original examples. The participants include seven booksellers including
> Oak Knoll Books, the Bird & Bull Press, one marbler, one bookbinder and one
> papermaker. A fascinating book textually as well as a fine example of private
> press printing.

78. (BOOKS ABOUT BOOKS) THE ALIDA ROOCHVARG COLLECTION OF
BOOKS ABOUT BOOKS; SIX CATALOGUES AND INDEX, WITH AN INTRO-
DUCTION BY ALIDA ROOCHVARG, AND AN ENVOI BY LAWRENCE
CLARK POWELL. New Castle: Oak Knoll Books, 1981, 8vo., cloth. (viii), 63, 65, 63,
55, 55, 59, 58, (2) pages. $45.00
> Limited to 350 numbered copies. Consists of 2690 catalogued items comprising
> one of the finest collections of books about books ever assembled. Thoroughly
> cross-referenced in the large index.

13

Georg Kurt Schauer: Hermann Zapf, calligrapher und book designer, Frankfurt/Main (Germany). In: *Book Design and Production*. Vol. 2, No. 4. Printing News Ltd., London 1959. S. 25–32. Mit 18 Abb.

Joh. van Eikeren: Geschriften van Hermann Zapf. In: *Drukkersweekblad*. 47. Jahrg. Nr. 39. Amsterdam 26. September 1959. S. 926–927. Mit 2 Abb.

Alexander Lawson: Hermann Zapf. Major contemporary type designer. In: *Inland Printer/American Lithographer*. Chicago July 1960. S. 82–83. Mit 2 Abb.

Noel Martin: Hermann Zapf, calligrapher – type designer – typographer. In: *Carnegie Magazine*. Carnegie Institute of Technology, Pittsburgh/Pennsylvania Oktober 1960. S. 277–279.

Leo H. Joachim: Zapf will contact seminar. His work shown in exhibit. In: *Printing News*. Vol. 65, No. 10. New York 3. September 1960. S. 9.

Noel Martin: Hermann Zapf, Calligrapher, type-designer and typographer. An exhibition arranged and circulated by The Contemporary Arts Center, Cincinnati Museum 1960–1961. *(Ausstellungskatalog)*. Mit 25 Abb.

Seán McBrinn: Hermann Zapf, calligrapher – book designer. In: *Modern Irish Printer*. Vol. 2, No. 3. Graphic, Dublin. Winter 1960/61. S. 21–28. Mit 16 Abb.

Paul Standard und Sigfred Taubert: Hermann Zapf in Amerika. Betrachtungen zu einer Ausstellungsfolge. In: *Börsenblatt für den Deutschen Buchhandel*. Nr. 4. Frankfurt am Main 13. Januar 1961. S. 49–51.

Martin K. Speckter: The versatile Mr. Zapf. In: *Type Talks*. No. 116. New York March/April 1961. S. 10–12. Mit 3 Abb.

Ernst A. Ihle: Hermann Zapf. Weg und Werk des Frankfurter Schriftgestalters. In: *Frankfurt. Lebendige Stadt*. Heft 2, 1961. S. 54–57.

Nanci Lyman: Hermann Zapf, type designer und calligrapher. In: *Print*. Vol. XV, No. 2. CR Publications, Inc., New York March/April 1961. S. 44–49. Mit 15 Abb.

Karl Vöhringer: Über Alphabete. In: *Form und Technik*. 12. Jahrg. Nr. 4. Stuttgart April 1961. S. 200.

Wim Bloem: Hermann Zapf. In: *Mahez News*. Nr. 7. Amsterdam Mai 1961. 4 Seiten. Mit 14 Abb.

Kalligraphische
Titelseite
für eine Veröffentlichung
über das Herstellen
von handgeschöpftem
Büttenpapier

Example 30

Hermann Zapf: Ein Arbeitsbericht, Herausgegeben von der Lehrdruckerei der Technischen Hochschule Darmstadt. Hamburg: Maximilian-Gesellschaft, 1984. Courtesy Maximilian-Gesellschaft.

While the individual entries are clearly delineated by a large space in this bibliography, there is practically no typographic coding except for some book or periodical titles. Entries, listed chronologically, offer authors' first names first, followed by a colon (quite unusual for readers in English-speaking countries), followed by titles in the same type as the authors' names. Sometimes this is followed by a book or periodical title in italics, but by this time we have already been confused by the use of roman type for titles. Another peculiarity is the mention of a city followed immediately by a date (with no punctuation intervening). This is not easy to decipher.

Running 'heads' appear at the foot of each page – not quite where one is likely to look for them. And the ragged-right margin, while not distracting in itself, seems to have been foreshortened too much in some entries (as in the works by McBrinn and Lyman, which exhibit quite short lines). The shoulder note works well to keep the lines on the page short.

This is an 'artsy' format, perhaps suited to the innovative yet classical work of Zapf. But it takes some getting used to.

Example 31a, b

Jeff Weber Rare Books. *The History of Science & Technology* . . . . Catalogue Twelve. Glendale, CA: Jeff Weber Rare Books, Winter 1990. Courtesy Jeff Weber.

Book catalogues are bibliographies of part (or all) of the stock of dealers. This one uses typographic and spatial coding fairly well. The bold face and full caps, while somewhat redundant in helping a reader to find the first elements in entries, nonetheless stand out clearly. The marginal numbers, balanced by the opposite-marginal prices, help one find crucial information quickly.

As is common in such catalogues, dealers wish to highlight particular features of their books; hence the internal, full-caps, headline-like line about the book on electromagnetism (item 84). By inserting such a line, the dealer announces to the reader that this book deserves special attention, and therefore justifies whatever price is asked.

This carefully researched catalogue also contains extensive notes, some on the physical appearance of the book (essential data for the buyer), and some on the edition, the author, the text, and other citations of the item in published sources.

A drawback of using full caps for the authors' names is that names like *MACKENZIE* (item 95) are ambiguous. Also, the use of very small type in the bibliographic part of the entry makes these lines difficult to read. See, for example, the book description for entry 84. This is too small a type size for such a long line length.

75   **HUMBOLT, Alexander von.** *Ideen zu einer Physiognomik der Gewächse.* Tübingen: J. G. Cotta'schen, 1806. Sm. 8vo. 28pp. Old green wrappers, ink title. Rubbed. Front cover detached with manuscript title, else very good. RARE. $ 400.00

76   **KENNEY, Louis A.** *Catalogue of the Rare Astronomical Books in the San Diego State University Library. Introduction by Owen Gingerich.* San Diego: The Friends of the Malcolm A. Love Library, San Diego State University, 1988. Folio. 210 titles. With 309 illustrations, 18 color illustrations Slipcase.

    $ 125.00

FIRST EDITION, LIMITED to 1,000 copies. This heavily annotated catalogue is embellished with many illustrations.

77   **KEPLER, Johannes.** *Kosmische Harmonie. Herausgegeben und übertragen von W. Harburger.* Leipzig, Insel, 1925. 8vo. 315pp. Large folding table at rear. Vellum backed orange boards. Back top creased relative to the folding table, otherwise very good. Scarce. $ 100.00

78   **[KEPLER] JARDINE, N.** *The birth of history and philosophy of science. Kepler's A DEFENCE OF TYCHO AGAINST URSUS with essays on its provenance and significance.* Cambridge: University Press, (1984). 8vo. ix, 301pp. Text figures, index. Blue cloth, dust-jacket. Fine.

    $ 50.00

FIRST ENGLISH EDITION, of Kepler's work with added relative essays.

79   **[KEPLER] LINZ, STADTMUSEUMS.** *Johannes Kepler Werk und Leistung. Ausstellung im Steinernen Saal des Linzer Landhauses, June 19 - August 29, 1971.* Katalog. 1971. 8vo. 177pp. Illus., bibliog. Wrappers. Scarce.

    $ 75.00

Essays by Adolf Adam, Heinz Balmer, Volker Bialas, Michael Dickreiter, Wilhelm Freh, Owen Gingerich (pp.109-114), Rudolf Haase, Jürgen Hübner, Ulrich Klein, Martha List, Jiri Marek, Konradin Ferrari d'Occhieppo, Edward Rosen (pp.137-158), Georg Wacha, with a bibliographic supplement of Kepler's work.

80   **KERL, Bruno.** *Grundriss der Allgemeinen Hüttenkunde.* Leipzig: Arthur Felix, 1872. 8vo. xvi, 284pp. 163 engraved illus., index. Cloth-backed boards. Bookplate. $ 100.00

81   **KERL, Bruno.** *Grundriss der Metallhüttenkunde.* Leipzig: Arthur Felix, 1873. 8vo. xx, 445pp. 246 engraved illus., index. Cloth-backed boards. Bookplate. $ 125.00

82   **KESSLER, Thomas.** *Vierhundert ausserlesne Chymische Process und Stücklen theils zur innelichen.* Nurnberg, 1641. 2 parts in 1. Fourth edition. 12mo. [12], 188, [10], [2 blank]; [6], [2 blank], 160, [4]; [4], 96, [4]pp. Woodcuts. Old vellum. Early ownership manuscript on title-page; title light soiled, edges a bit roughed; covers darkened, otherwise a very good copy of this rare work.

    $ 400.00

An early treatise of the Iatrochemist variety, treating illness with chemical recipes for medicinal application.

31a

83   **KIRBY, William & William SPENCE.** *An Introduction to Entomology: Or elements of the Natural History of Insects: Fourth edition.* London: Longman, Hurst, Rees, Orme, and Brown, 1822-6. 4 volumes. 8vo. Plates. Original boards, rebacked. Very good. $ 400.00

THE FIRST USE OF THE TERM "ELECTROMAGNETISM"

84   **KIRCHER, Athanasius.** *Magnes Sive de Arte Magnetica Opus Tripartitum, quo Praeterquam quod Universa Magnetis Natura ... Editio secunda post Romanam multo correctior.* Coloniæ, Apud Idocum Kalcoven, Anno MDCXLIII. [1643]. 4to. [30], 797, [39]pp. With an added engraved title showing Austrian arms and view of Cologne, title-page vignette of two magnets, 29 engraved copperplates and many woodcuts in the text (including 1 volvelle plate at page 254), dedicatory epistle to Emperor Ferdinand III of Austria, dated from Rome, 4 May 1641, the privilege from Superior General Mutius Vitelleschi is dated from Rome, 30 November 1639, printed music. Modern full antique style calf, blind rules, gilt corner fillets, preserving original endleaves, brown morocco spine label with gilt title. Bookplate of "Christianus Schoettgenjus", lengthy nineteenth-century inscription, "Lynmmn Doctor Becker ... Carl Zinikensen, 12 May 1845"; ink stamp of "J.C.M.," title-page recto: title-page inscribed, "Donùm mei memoris Amiej, ... soldi Fridricbsen Donnse possideo M. Albertius Line, mannùs Malbem: Profes: D. 10 Maÿ 1646. ex Belgio missian"; verso: "Dr. G. Fenner, Flüls L. Krefeld, Alechemist ... 1930"; back inscribed "Feril Frider ..." Some spotting, occasional small waterstains, though a very good copy. SCARCE.

$ 1,750.00

SECOND EDITION, corrected. One of the most interesting works of Father Kircher's wonderful and all-embracing scientific genius (or at least industry), and most valuable as a storehouse of all the most famous authors of his time, including Gilbert, Cabeo, Descartes, etc. Moreover, it contains several original observations, i.e., the influence of volcanic eruptions on the magnetic needle, numerous experiments, including one ascertaining the carrying power of magnets (now used for lifting the heaviest castings), the first use of the term "electro-magnetism", and a table of places with their declination. "... He sought to define the strength of a magnet by means of the balance ... Much of Kircher's book is taken up by his schemes for healing diseases and wounds with the aid of magnetism ... Kircher attributes many phenomena of the animal world, such as the flight of birds, to magnetic agency ..." -- Wolf.

The work is also of importance in connection with the early history of electro-telegraphy, Father Kircher asserting that persons could communicate with each other by means of magnetic needles although many miles distant. -- Zeitlinger.

Kircher (1602-1680), member of the order of Jesuits, believed in the magnetism of all things. He was greatly influenced by Gilbert, whose work on the magnet was published in 1600, and of Kepler. His *Magnes* is filled with curiosities, dealing not only with physical magnetism, but also with magnetism in geometry, medicines, metals, heavenly bodies, the attraction and repulsion in animals and plants, magnetic attraction in music and love. Some constructions of scientific instruments and toys are given.

Brigham Young catalogue, No. 5; Brunet: III, 667; Caillet, *Manuel bibliographique des sciences psychiques ou occultes,* II, 362.5779; Clendening, *Athanasius Kircher, 1602-1680: An Exhibition,* 5.3; De Backer, *Bibliothèque des écrivains ...* I, 422-23.5; Græsse IV, 21; Mottelay, *Bibliographical History of Electricity & Magnetism,* p.120; Poggendorff: I, 1259; Ronalds, *Catalogue of books ... relating to electricity, magnetism ...* (1880), p.267; Sommervogel IV, 1048-49.6; *Wheeler Gift Catalogue*: 116a (note); Wolf, *History of Science,* p.298.

95   MACKENZIE, Colin. *Memorial pratique du Chimiste-Manufacturier, ou recueil de procedes d'arts et de manufactures, traduit de l'Anglais sur la Troisieme Edition ...* Paris: Chez Barrois L'Aine, 1824-1825. 3 volumes. 8vo. xxiv, 456; [4], 468; [4], 492pp. Paper covers soiled, chipped, spines darkened, corners curled. Lacks 3 plates in volume I mentioned in Cole, but contains 1 folding plate in volume II not mentioned in Cole. Very rare. Uncut and partly unopened.

$ 125.00

FIRST FRENCH TRANSLATION of the work. The unknown translator used the London, 1823 edition. The Cole copy lacked volume three as well as the folding engraved plate in volume two. Cole, 1988: 859 (no locations). Not in *NUC* or the supplement; not in Duveen or Ferguson.

96   MATHIEU, Émile. *Théorie de l'Élasticité des Corps Solides.* Paris: Gauthier-Villars et Fils, 1890. Series: Traité de Physique Mathématique. 2 volumes. 4to. viii, 219, ads. (32); 184pp. Original blue printed wrappers. Very good set. SCARCE.

$ 500.00

FIRST EDITION. Mathieu (1835-1890), French mathematician and phyical theorist, and professor of science at the University of Nancy and at Besançon, was interested in the theory of first and second potential and the mathematical theory of elasticity. This led to "generalized solutions for partial differential equations and to solutions for problems of the elsticity of three-dimensional bodies, especially those of anisotropic elasticity or subject tp noninfintesimal deformations." -- *DSB*, vol. IX, pp.174-175; Cajori, *History of Mathematics*, p.473.

97   MIDDLETON, W. E. Knowles. *A History of the Thermometer and its Use in Meteorology.* Baltimore: Johns Hopkins Press, (1966). 8vo. xiii, 249pp. Text illustrations, index. Cloth, dust-jacket. $ 75.00

CONTAINING REFERENCES TO GALILEO

98   NELLI, Giovambatista Clemente. *Saggio De Storia Letteraria Fiorentina del secolo XVII. Scritta in varie lettere ...* Lucca: Vincenzo Giuntini, 1759. 4to. [iv], 144pp. With large folding engraved plate showing hygrometers [?] and diagrams. Title vignette, some manuscript notations in margin within text and on front endpaper, 8 woodcut seals reproduced towards the rear. Old flexible paste-paper boards, library paper label on lower spine. Some worming in gutter, otherwise very good.

$ 200.00

Carli & Favaro, *Bibliografia Galileiana* #513.

WITH THE IMPORTANT ADDITIONAL QUERRIES

99   NEWTON, Sir Isaac. *Optice: sive de Reflexionibus, Refractionibus, Inflexionibus & Coloribus Lucis libri tres. Latine reddidit Samuel Clarke. Reverendo admodum Patri ac Dno. Joanni Moore Episcopo Norvicensi a Sacris Domesticis. Accedunt Tractatus duo ejusdem Authoris de Speciebus & Magnitudine Figurarum Curvilinearum, Latine scripti.* Londini: Impensis Sam. Smith & Benj. Walford, Regiæ Societatis ... MDCCVI. [1706]. 4to. [14], 348, [2], 24, [2], 1-24, 21-43, [1 blank]pp. 19 folding engraved plates, with the errata, corrigenda and addenda. Original full dark antique calf, rebacked with corners neatly renewed. A beautiful copy with ownership inscriptions on title-page, including an early manuscript hand dated 1734, stamp of the Library of Haverford College and the Bibliotheque du Tribunal. A clean copy.

$ 3,500.00

FIRST LATIN EDITION. The Latin edition is the first with Newton's name appearing on the title. A classic of English writing in its 1704 original, Newton's *Opticks* actually presented some of its most challenging ides in its 1706 Latin and 1717 second English editions.

The *Opticks* as initially published summarized Newton's main discoveries and theories concerning light and color - the spectrum of sunlight; the degrees of refraction associated with the different colors; the color circle (where red and violet at the extreme ends of the straight spectrum are linked and twisted into a circle, the first in the history of color theory, illustrated in the *Opticks*); the invention of the reflecting telescope; the first workable theory of the rainbow; and experiments on what would later be called interference effects (e.g. "Newton's rings,") which supplied Thomas Young in the 19th century with "extraordinarily accurate measurements - so much so that when [he] devised an explanation of Newton's rings based on the revived wave theory of light and the new principle of interference, he used Newton's own data to compute the wavelengths and wave numbers of the principle colors in the visible spectrum and attained results that are in close agreement with those generally accepted today." (*DSB*).

Newton's discovery of periodicity in "Newton's rings" was one of the strongest arguments for a wave theory of light. Unlike his contemporaries Hooke or Huygens who is usually considered the founder of the wave theory. Newton postulated periodicity as a fundamental property either of waves of light of waves associated with light and suggested that a particular wavelength characterizes the light producing each color. (He also suggested that vision might be the result of propagation of waves in the optic nerves.) Nevertheless he preferred the corpuscular theory, with which he is usually associated, because of its explanatory value for certain optical phenomena, and because it allowed him to link the action of gross bodies with the action of light.

It is in the 1706 Latin *Optice* that Newton takes the strong position in favor of the corpuscular theory, in the section of "Queries" at the end of his text. There were sixteen queries in the English *Opticks*; seven more are added in the Latin, and seven m,ore in the second English edition of 1717. The queries were the most important element of the *Opticks* to future generations, as they sketched out the lines of future research.

In connection with the discussion of double refraction in the queries added to the Latin edition, Newton brought out the difficulties posed by a theory of waves in an ethereal medium, and argued for rays of light being composed of very small bodies. He also brought up the "convertibility" of gross bodies and light, discussed the forces holding matter together, the causes of motion, fermentation, the circulation of the blood and animal heat, putrefaction, the force of inertia and occult qualities.

In his first series of queries, he had treated vision in four of them, discussing the vibrations excited by rays of light on the optic nerves, the wavelengths associated with different colors, binocular vision, the persistence of vision. The concept of semi-decussation of the optic nerves originated with him, as an explanation of single vision with two eyes in these queries.

The *Optice* closes, as did the 1704 *Opticks*, with the two papers in which Newton wanted to assert his priority over Leibniz in the invention of the calculus. Hirschberg, trans. Blodi IV 264-71; Gorin 56-57; Schmitz I 403-11; Birren, *History of color in painting*, (1965) 20-23, reproducing the title page of the *Optice* with caption: "This Latin edition of Newton's work revolutionized scientific thought and made him recognized as one of the greatest geniuses of all time." See Dibner 148; Andrade; Babson 137; Not in Becker or *BOA*; Blake 323; Horblit 79b; Norman 18: 438; Waller 11413.

Example 32

Christopher Gould and Richard Parker Morgan. *South Carolina Imprints, 1731–1800: A Descriptive Bibliography*. Santa Barbara, California; Denver, Colorado; and Oxford, England: ABC-Clio Information Services, 1985. Courtesy ABC-Clio.

The two-column format on this page is good, considering the size of the type chosen for the text. The beginnings of entries are marked by the marginal numbers as well as the use of all caps in the authors' (or corporate authors') names. A quasi-facsimile presentation for the title pages is given, using caps and lower case type, as the original had them. One criticism of this method is that all words in caps are given in the same size capital letters, not distinguishing the type size. Hence, a word set in six-point all caps and one in 24-point caps will look the same in the quasi-facsimile.

Full title-page transcriptions are given, which takes up space, but which could be quite useful in distinguishing one printing from another.

Each 'paragraph' of each entry holds a separate field of information: author, title, pagination, size/contents, collation, references, holding libraries, and notes. This is a tremendous resource of information, laid out with line breaks so that one can easily locate any field of information quickly.

The volume is arranged chronologically, with a sub-arrangement: alphabetical by author. The year 1764 has an additional entry (see item number 220) which is a 'Dubious Imprint'; so it appears at the end of the year's list. Then '1765' is centered in the column with small decorative plusses around it to catch the eye. The headline of the page tells us that 1765 begins on that page, another device to help the searcher.

Despite my personal reluctance to use all caps, I find them not at all obtrusive in this book. In general, these pages are well thought out and easy to use.

FOR ESTABLISHING / OTHER REGULA-TIONS / IN THE SAID TOWN. [rule. Royal seal, double rule] SOUTH-CAROLINA: / CHARLES-TOWN, Printed by PETER TIMOTHY, Printer / to the Honourable the *Commons-House* of *Assembly*, 1764.

[1–2], 3–4+

29 cm; tp, blank verso, 3–4+ text

[A]²+

Ref: Evans 9843

NN* (impf)

Notes: Unique copy lacks all after p. 4.

Act reprinted, complete, pp. 3–15, entry 215.

218. SOUTH CAROLINA (Colony). Laws.

ANNO REGNI / GEORGII III. / *REGIS* / *Magnae Britanniae, Franciae, & Hiberniae*, / QUARTO. / At a GENERAL ASSEMBLY, begun and holden at CHARLES- / TOWN on *Monday* the *Twenty-fifth* Day of *October*, in the *Third* / Year of the Reign of our Sovereign Lord *GEORGE* the *Third* / by the Grace of God, of GREAT-BRITAIN, FRANCE, and IRE- / LAND, KING, Defender of the Faith, and so forth, and in the / Year of our Lord 1762: And from thence continued, by a Pro- / rogation and divers Adjournments, to the 6th Day of *October*, in / the Year of our Lord 1764. [rule, Royal seal, double rule] *SOUTH-CAROLINA*: / CHARLES-TOWN, Printed by *Peter Timothy*, 1764.

[1–2], 3–36

30 cm; tp, blank verso, 3–16 text, 17–36 Schedule

[A] – I²

Ref: Evans 41489

DLC*

Notes: See entry 229.

219. SOUTHERN CONGRESS.

JOURNAL / OF THE / CONGRESS / OF THE FOUR / SOUTHERN GOVERNORS, / AND THE / SUPERINTENDENT OF THAT DIS-TRICT, / WITH THE / FIVE NATIONS OF IN-DIANS, / AT AUGUSTA, 1763. / SOUTH=CAR-OLINA. / CHARLES-TOWN: PRINTED BY PE-TER TIMOTHY, M.DCC.LXIV.

[2], [1–2], 3–45

36 cm; half-title, blank verso, tp, blank verso, 3–45 text, blank verso

[A]⁴ B – L² (A₃ mislabeled A₂ and K mis-labeled I)

Ref: Evans 9706 Turnbull p. 156

MiU-C GU-De *NN**

Notes: Turnbull: "Fifty copies ordered to be printed 'Chicasahs, Upper and Lower Creeks, Choctahs, Cherokees, and Catawbas.' "

Reprinted in *State Records of North Carolina*, XI, 156–207.

† Dubious Imprint †

220. GARDEN, Alexander.

[An Account of the medical properties of the Virginia pink-root.]

Ref: Evans 9675

Notes: No copy located; title from Evans, who, according to the Early American Imprint File, took it from Haven.

† 1765 †

221. SMITH, Josiah.

THE / *Character, Preaching, &c.* / OF THE REV-EREND / Mr. GEORGE WHITEFIELD, / *Impartially* / Represented and Supported, / IN A / *SERMON*, / Preach'd in CHARLESTOWN, SOUTH CAROLINA, / *March* 26th. *Anno Domini* 1740. [rule] By JOSIAH SMITH, V. D. M. [rule] With a *PREFACE* by the REVEREND, / Dr. *Colman* and Mr. *Cooper*, / Of BOSTON, *New-England*. [rule, nine lines of Biblical quota-tion, rule] BOSTON printed: / CHARLESTOWN Re-printed, by PETER / TIMOTHY, *in* BROAD-STREET, 1765.

[4], [i], ii–vi, [1], 2–22

15.5 cm; half-title, blank verso, tp, blank verso, [i] – vi To the Reader, [1] – 20 text, 21–22 postscript

[A] – D⁴

Ref: Evans 10165 Sabin 83433

CtY* NcMHi ScU

Notes: Advertised in SCG, 30 Mar. 1765 ("Just Published, Price Seven Shillings and Six Pence").

Sabin:

The above is the Brinley copy (no. 6299), bought by Yale. Collation supplied by Miss Ann S. Pratt. Another copy was sold at Charles F. Heartmann's auction rooms, Oc-tober 2nd, 1925. Reprinted also in the vari-ous editions of George Whitefield's "Twelve Sermons," "Fifteen Sermons," and "Sermons

2578 **Conservative Party** (Saskatchewan)
Cleared? ... What have the royal commissions revealed? ... Bradshaw has been
vindicated. [n.p., 1917] cover-title, 8p. 22cm.

Quotations on title-page.   Sask. Arch.

2579 **Conservative Party** (Saskatchewan)
Conservative platforms. 'No compromise with wrong.' The Conservative Party of
Saskatchewan hereby pledges itself to support the following policies and to put
them into effect when returned to power. [n.p., 1917] caption-title, 4p.
22cm.   Sask. Arch.

2580 **Conservative Party** (Saskatchewan)
Handbook, campaign, 1917. Regina, Provincial Conservative Association
[1917] 32p. 22cm.   Sask. Arch.

2581 **Conservative Party** (Saskatchewan)
How Liberal members of the Saskatchewan Legislature were bought. Shameless
representatives of people sold themselves for a few hundred dollars to thwart
the popular will. The old gang still controls. [n.p., 1917] cover-title, 16p.
22cm.   Sask. Arch.

2582 **Conservative Party** (Saskatchewan)
Kindersley Dam. Hon. W.R. Motherwell 'deals the cards.' [n.p., 1917]
cover-title, [3]p. 22cm.   Sask. Arch.

2583 **Conservative Party** (Saskatchewan)
The liquor traffic and the Saskatchewan government ... [n.p., 1917]
cover-title, 16p. 22cm.   Sask. Arch.

2584 **Conservative Party** (Saskatchewan)
The patriotic tax; money collected by the assessment of one mill on the dollar
goes to pay fat salaries to favored civil servants who have enlisted and the wages
of special watchmen on public buildings while the Patriotic Fund suffered ...
[n.p., 1917] cover-title, 7, [1]p. 22cm.   Sask. Arch.

2585 **Conservative Party** (Saskatchewan)
Phantom roads, fake contracts, false pay rolls. Some facts in the story of the
looting of the public treasury through the Highways Department ... [n.p. 1917]
cover-title, 22p. 19cm.

Six-line poem on back cover.   Sask. Arch.

2586 **Conservative Party** (Saskatchewan)
Weed Lake bridge. Government contracts and political methods. [n.p., 1917]
cover-title, [3]p. 22cm.   Sask. Arch.

2587 **Feilberg**, H[enning] F[rederik]
Hjemliv pa praerien. De derovre en raekke breve fra Canada. Kobenhavn and
Kristiana, 1917. 298p. 19cm.

A continuation of a Danish family's experiences in Saskatchewan, covering the period May
1912 to October 1917.
    Other printings appeared in 1918 and in 1927.   Denmark

33   295

Example 33

Bruce Braden Peel, comp. *A Bibliography of the Prairie Provinces to 1953, with Biographical Index*. 2nd ed. Toronto: University of Toronto Press, 1973. Courtesy University of Toronto Press.

This page offers a fairly legible text with some slight peculiarities. The entries are clearly delineated from one another in three ways: with a line break between entries; with a marginal number at the beginning of each entry; and with bold face type used for the filing entry (which will either be the last name of the author or the corporate author). All three means of designating the new entry were not necessary, but they do not hinder the reader, nor are they unsightly in any way.

For some entries (not shown in the sample page), there is neither an author nor a corporate author (as with entry 857, *Winnipeg War Sketches*). In such cases, the title begins the 'text' for the entry. It is peculiar to have only the last names of authors in bold face, while first names and initials are in regular roman type. Since such a coding was really not necessary to help a reader find the filing element for the entry (the line space and entry number were already in place for that purpose), it would have been useful to use the bold face (or italics) for titles. Because titles are in the same roman type as that which follows, it is not instantly apparent where a title ends and the publication data begin. (See, for example, entry 2587 in the sample page.)

While the ragged right setting is reasonable, it does yield some fairly short lines (like the one in entry 2583). With notes in smaller type (see entry 2587), the secondary line break is no problem. However, all page numbers appear at the lower left corner of the page, on rectos and versos alike. This makes all odd page numbers difficult to locate.

In all, this is a fairly legible page, with the standard information efficiently presented and only a minimum of inconvenience in finding elements within entries.

Example 34a, b

John J. Walsdorf. *William Morris in Private Press and Limited Editions: A Descriptive Bibliography of Books by and about William Morris 1891.–1981*. Phoenix, Arizona: Oryx Press, 1983. Courtesy Oryx Press.

This is a sumptuously produced bibliography, offering one entry per page (though some entries go on to two or more pages). Since this is the case, it is never a problem to see the beginning of successive entries.

Nonetheless, the items are distinguished by large numbers, followed in the same line by the name of the press responsible for the item. This is followed by more large type, in all caps, giving the full title. The letter spacing and word spacing are well printed (not always the case when all caps are used).

Following this are four information fields: Pagination/ Size; Colophon/Limitation; Binding; and Notes – and all of these fields are marked with large boldface type. Finding any piece of information is a snap in this bibliography.

The design reminds one of some of William Morris's pages – generous margins, clear printing, good paper. While the large sizes of the type are somewhat overwhelming at first, the overall impression is in keeping with the bibliography's subject matter, and the information is presented in good order.

176. The Tunnel Road Press

THE FOLLOWING HITHERTO UNRECORDED ANECDOTE WAS TOLD TO D. G. BRIDSON SOME TWENTY YEARS AGO BY THE DRAMATIST, CLIFFORD BAX, WHOSE FATHER, E. BELFORT BAX, THE NOTED SOCIALIST COLLEAGUE OF AND CO-AUTHOR WITH WILLIAM MORRIS, WAS PRESENT AT THE TIME.

Pagination/Size: 1972,[1] p., 1 ill., 288 x 125 mm.

Colophon/Limitation: "200 copies printed at The Tunnel Road Press to commemorate the visit on September 10, 1972 by the joint bodies of the Zamorano and Roxburghe Clubs to the premises of the Press,—and 35 copies for the private circulation of D. G. Bridson, Esq."

Binding: 1 page broadside, unbound.

Notes: The Tunnel Road Press is the private press of Sanford L. Berger of Carmel, California. Mr. Berger is the owner of what is probably the finest private collection of William Morris materials in the world. It was his collection which made up the vast majority of items on display and catalogued in the publication, *Morris & Co.*, published by the Stanford Art Gallery in 1975. (See No. 188) The exhibition contained stained glass windows, painted tiles, and ceramics. Also included were printed papers and chintzes, as well as woven fabrics and tapestries, carpets, and embroideries from the Berger collection. The Stanford and Helen Berger collection is truly incomparable, containing much primary research materials on William Morris and the firm.

200. Scenic Road Press

MY DEAR SMITH.

Pagination/Size: 1980, [1] pp., 179 x 118 mm.

Colophon/Limitation: "200 copies of a letter from The Sanford & Helen Berger Collection printed at The Scenic Road Press 1980 ROXBURGHE ZAMORANO S.F."

Binding: Single sheet, unbound.

Notes: The Scenic Road Press, successor to The Tunnel Road Press, is the private press of Sanford Berger.

This item is a reprint of a Morris letter dated Feb. 24 [1887] to "My dear Smith." In the letter Morris complains about a woman whom Smith had sent to see Morris, a woman who wanted Morris to see some of her own designs. Morris then proposes that a visit charge be made of all but known and useful customers; £5.5.0 in London and £21 in the country.

322	Thurstone LL	1954	The measurement of values	Psychological Review 61, pp.47-58
323	Tinker MA	1926	Reading reactions for mathematical formulae	Journal of Experimental Psychology 9 (December), pp.444-67
324	Tinker MA	1927	Legibility and eye movements in reading	Psychological Bulletin 24 (November), pp.621-39
325	Tinker MA	1928	A photographic study of eye movements in reading formulae	Genetic Psychology Monographs 3 (February), pp.95-136
326	Tinker MA	1928	Numerals versus words for efficiency in reading	Journal of Applied Psychology 12 (April), pp.190-9
327	Tinker MA	1928	How formulae are read	American Journal of Psychology 40 (July), pp.476-83
328	Tinker MA	1928	The relative legibility of the letters, the digits, and of certain mathematical signs	Journal of General Psychology 1 (July-October), pp.472-96
329	Tinker MA	1928	Eye-movement duration, pause duration and reading time	Psychological Review 35, pp.385-97
330	Tinker MA	1929	Visual apprehension and perception in reading	Psychological Bulletin 26 (April), pp.223-40
331	Tinker MA	1929	Photographic measures of reading ability	Journal of Educational Psychology 20, pp.184-91
332	Tinker MA	1930	The relative legibility of modern and old style numerals	Journal of Experimental Psychology 13 (October), pp.453-61
333	Tinker MA	1931	Apparatus for recording eye movements	American Journal of Psychology 43 (January), pp.115-8
334	Tinker MA	1931	Physiological psychology of reading	Psychological Bulletin 28 (February), pp.81-97
335	Tinker MA	1932	The effect of color on visual apprehension and perception	Genetic Psychology Monographs 11 (February), pp.61-136
336	Tinker MA	1932	The influence of form of type on the perception of words	Journal of Applied Psychology 16 (April), pp.167-74
337	Tinker MA	1932	Studies in scientific typography	Psychological Bulletin 29 (November), pp.670-1
338	Tinker MA	1932	The relation of speed to comprehension in reading	School and Society 36, pp.158-60
339	Tinker MA	1933	Use and limitations of eye movements measures of reading	Psychological Bulletin 30, p.583 (abstract)
340	Tinker MA	1934	Experimental study of reading	Psychological Bulletin 31 (February), pp.98-110
341	Tinker MA	1934	Illumination and the hygiene of reading	Journal of Educational Psychology 25 (December), pp.669-80
342	Tinker MA	1934	The reliability and validity of eye movement measures of reading	Psychological Bulletin 31, p.741 (abstract)

Example 35
Herbert Spencer. *The Visible Word.* New York: Hastings House, 1969. 2nd ed. Courtesy Herbert Spencer.

For someone who has written on the design of bibliographies, and who has offered 18 samples of usable page designs (see entries 219 and 220 in bibliography of present volume), Spencer seems to be trying to be quite innovative in his design of this page. It is the only bibliography I have seen designed this way.

This is a five-column page, with each column a different length, and containing a different data field. Column one contains entry numbers. Column two gives authors' names (repeating names in full for subsequent works by the same author). The bibliography is arranged alphabetically by author. The third column is a chronological subarrangement for each author. The fourth column is an alphabetical sub-subarrangement, listing titles alphabetically for each year. The fifth column contains publication data.

Books and journal titles are all printed in the same sans serif type used throughout. But with such distinct spatial coding (the five columns and the spaces between entries), typographic coding such as italics or underlining is rendered unnecessary. (This is true, as well, of the lack of quotation marks for journal titles.) The only typographic coding on the page is the use of boldface type for authors' names.

The columnar setup is extremely effective. No line on the page is so long that one cannot easily move on to the next. The data fields are small enough to be perfectly legible; and they are distinct and easily located. This is a cleverly and sensitively designed bibliography. (Incidentally, items 323 to 418 in *The Visible Word* are by Miles A. Tinker, the most prolific writer on legibility. He would have appreciated having his name in such a legible format.)

APPENDIX II

A P P E N D I X I I
LEGIBILITY

Donald G. Paterson and Miles A. Tinker. *How to Make Type Readable: A Manual for Typographers, Printers and Advertisers.* New York and London: Harper & Brothers, 1940.

The following four pages summarize Paterson and Tinker's findings after a dozen years of research into the legibility of printed matter. As they note, however, and as I say many times in this book, no single way is always right. These recommendations are flexible to such an extent that if designers do not follow a single one, they could still produce a perfectly legible and accessible text.

Tabular Summary of Typography Recommendations

Typographical Factors	Satisfactory Printing Arrangements	Undesirable Printing Arrangements
1. Style of type face	Any commonly used modern or ultra modern type face.	American Typewriter, Old English.
2. Type form	Caps and lower case. Bold face for emphasis and for reading at a distance. Italics for emphasis only.	All capitals.
3. Size of type	9, 10, 11, or 12 point leaded and in optimal line widths.	6 and 7 point; larger than 12 point.
4. Width of line	Moderate line widths (in neighborhood of 19 picas).	Excessively short line widths (less than 14 picas). Excessively long line widths (more than 28 picas).
5. Leading in relation to type size and line width:		
6 point type	2 point leading, 14 to 28 pica line width.	Set solid in short line widths (less than 14 picas), or in long line widths (more than 28 picas).
8 point type	2 point leading, 14 to 28 pica line width.	Set solid in short line widths (less than 14 picas) or in long line widths (28 picas or more).
10 point type	2 point leading, 14 to 28 pica line width.	Set solid and leaded one point in all line widths.
11 point type	2 point leading, 16 to 28 pica line width.	Set solid in short line widths (16 picas and shorter) and in long line widths (more than 28 picas).
12 point type	Set solid or leaded one or 2 points in moderate line widths (in neighborhood of 25 picas).	Set solid or leaded in short line widths (9 picas or less) and in long line widths (more than 33 picas).

TABULAR SUMMARY OF TYPOGRAPHY RECOMMENDATIONS

(*Continued*)

Typographical Factors	Satisfactory Printing Arrangements	Undesirable Printing Arrangements
6. Margins	One-quarter inch for top, outer, and bottom margins, three-quarters inch for inner margin.	Wide margins unnecessary from standpoint of legibility.
7. Columnar arrangement	Single column or double column.	Readers dislike single-column composition in comparison with double-column.
8. Space between columns	One-half pica space with no rule.	Inter-columnar rule or more than one-half pica space unnecessary on basis of legibility.
9. Color of print and background	Black print on white background, or dark colored print on light colored background.	White on black, or dark print on dark background, or light print on light background.
10. Paper surface	Dull finish opaque paper stock.	Glazed paper unsatisfactory because of poorly distributed artificial light; thin semi-transparent paper stock.

PRINTING SPECIFICATIONS FOR AN IDEAL PRINTED PAGE
USING DOUBLE-COLUMN COMPOSITION

Style of type face: Cheltenham or Antique.

Size of type for text: 11 point.

Line width: 19 picas.

Leading: 2 points.

Paper surface: dull finish opaque paper stock.

Width of inside margin: ¾ inch.

Width of top, outside and bottom margins: ¼ to ¾ inch.

Columnar arrangement: double-column composition.

Inter-columnar space: ½ pica (no rule).

Total page size: 7⅜ x 9½ inches.

Running heads: caps and lower case.

Section headings: caps and lower case.

Paragraph headings (if used): caps and lower case in bold face.

Color of ink: jobbing black.

Color of paper: white.

Footnotes: 8 point, leaded one point, 19 pica line width.

Page numbers: Cheltenham or Antique, 11 point.

Chapter numbers: Cheltenham or Antique Arabic, 14 point, bold face.

Chapter headings: Cheltenham or Antique, 14 point, bold face, caps and lower case centered on page.

Specifications for tables: Cheltenham or Antique type face, Arabic numerals, 9 point lower case type for headings and numerals, rules in headings but not between columns of data, caps and lower case bold face for table titles, 9 point with 2 point leading in lower case for notes below titles.

PRINTING SPECIFICATIONS FOR AN IDEAL PRINTED PAGE USING SINGLE-COLUMN COMPOSITION

Style of type face : Cheltenham or Antique.

Size of type for text : 11 point.*

Line width : 22 picas.*

Leading : 2 points.

Paper stock : dull finish, opaque paper stock.

Width of inside margin : ¾ inch.

Width of top, outside and bottom margins : ¼ to ¾ inch.

Columnar arrangement : single-column composition.

Total page size : 4⅝ x 7 inches.*

Running heads : caps and lower case.

Section headings : caps and lower case.

Paragraph headings (if used) : caps and lower case in bold face.

Color of ink : jobbing black.

Color of paper : white.

Footnotes : 8 point, leaded one point, 22 pica line width.*

Page numbers : Cheltenham or Antique, 11 point.*

Chapter numbers : Cheltenham or Antique Arabic, 14 point, bold face.*

Chapter headings : Cheltenham or Antique, 14 point, bold face, caps and lower case centered on page.*

Specifications for tables : Cheltenham or Antique type face, Arabic numerals, 9 point lower case type for headings and numerals, rules in headings but not between columns of data, caps and lower case bold face for table titles, 9 point with 2 point leading in lower case for notes below titles.*

*The above specifications are for books of short or moderate length. Since the results cited earlier show that considerable variation in type size and line width is possible without loss of legibility, these items would probably be changed in longer books.

INDEX

The index lists all of the issues considered in the main text (page numbers printed in lightface roman type); the same issues discussed in items in the annotated bibliography (entry numbers printed in boldface type); and the issues as they are represented in the sample pages from bibliographies (example numbers given in square brackets). These fields are separated by semi-colons. Readers are urged not to rely solely on the bibliography annotations, but to go to the original sources for a more thorough treatment than was possible in the present volume.